TRIUMPH
AND TRAGEDY

To my parents, who first opened my eyes
to the wonders of ancient Rome.

TRIUMPH AND TRAGEDY

The rise and fall of Rome's immortal emperors

ALEXANDER CANDUCI

PIER 9

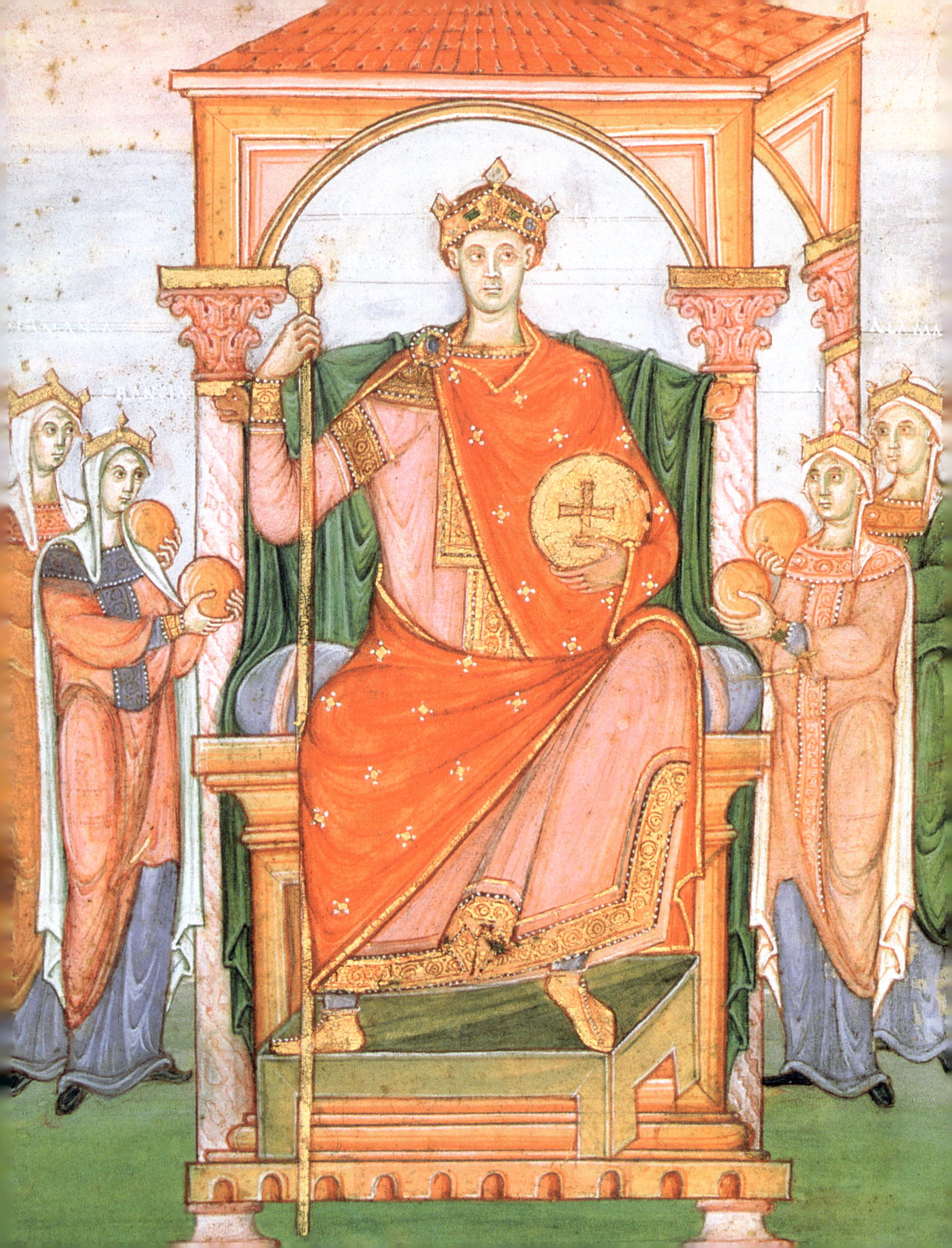

CONTENTS

PREFACE **6**

PROLOGUE **12**

THE HIGH EMPIRE (27 BC – AD 180) **15**

THE CRISIS OF THE THIRD CENTURY (180–260) **45**

THE AGE OF THE USURPERS (260–285) **77**

ROMAN REFORM AND RECONSTRUCTION (285–392) **107**

DIVISION AND DECAY (392–491) **141**

THE PRICE OF UNITY (491–802) **177**

RESTORATION AND RENEWAL (802–1028) **211**

THE CRUSADES (1028–1204) **253**

FALL OF THE EASTERN EMPIRE (1204–1453) **291**

THE END OF IMPERIAL DREAMS (1453–1806) **329**

BIBLIOGRAPHY **356**

ACKNOWLEDGEMENTS **360**

IMAGE CREDITS **360**

INDEX **361**

PREFACE

THE ROMAN EMPIRE—in Latin, *imperium romanum*—means, literally, the extent of Roman authority. Straddling three continents, from the bitterly cold, snow-capped Scottish mountains in the north to the endless Saharan furnace in the south, from the windswept Atlantic shoreline in the west to the steaming boundaries of far distant India in the east, its existence and wavering fortunes shaped the destiny of Western civilisation. Few names conjure images that stir the imagination so vividly—visions of disciplined legions maintaining the frontiers against hordes of barbarians, of senators in their purple-bordered robes walking past cool, flowing fountains and of emperors riding in their triumphs through the marble arches of Rome.

> **Lend me your ear, Queen of the world, over which you rule! Rome, whose rightful place is amongst the stars! O lend me your ear, mother of men and mother of gods! Through your temples are we brought to the very heavens! To you do we sing, and truly while the Fates give us life, to you shall we always sing, for who can forget thee?**
>
> RUTILIUS NUMANTIUS

There are the Romans who strode like giants across the pages of history—men like Augustus, who engineered the perilous transition from republic to empire; Trajan, the warrior emperor who pushed the boundaries of the empire to their farthest limits; Constantine, who began the momentous transformation of the pagan empire into a Christian one; and Justinian, who managed to achieve the impossible, returning Rome to the empire. Then there are the monsters—Caligula, Nero, Commodus, Phocas and Andronicus Comnenus. All these and many more graced the stage in one of the greatest ruling lines that the world has ever produced, each emperor unique in style, temperament and achievements. Ruling for more than 1800 years, they are the immortal emperors who carried their ancient legacy through to the birth of the modern world.

Over the centuries, historians have written countless books about the empire, its leaders, politics, social structures, coinage and even its sewer systems. So why write add to the many and write yet another book? Previous works about the emperors have tended to focus on the period from the first emperor in 27 BC, through to the reign of the last western usurper, Romulus Augustulus, in AD 476. Books written about the Eastern Roman emperors have usually considered them separately from the Western emperors, extending from the founding of Constantinople in 330 through to the final fall of the empire in 1453, a period historians invariably term the Byzantine Empire to distinguish it from the unified Roman Empire. Finally, no modern treatments have included the history of the empire after its restoration in the west by the emperor Charlemagne in 800; again, he and his successors have books dedicated to them alone.

This book will provide a brief summary of all of the men and women who were crowned or declared 'Emperor of the Romans', from Augustus in 27 BC, all the way through to Constantine Palaeologus, who was ruling when the Eastern Roman Empire fell in 1453, and to Napoleon's extinction of the only other entity that could legitimately be called the Roman Empire, the Holy Roman Empire, in 1806.

Yet if the Roman Empire did last until the nineteenth century, why do works on the emperors generally focus on the earliest period? The reason is that the eighteenth century Enlightenment scholars were keen to chop up history into manageable chunks, and they considered the Roman Empire an empire of antiquity, not one that stretched into their own age. The eastern and western entities that existed after the so-called 'Fall of Rome' gave them some difficulty, and so they deemed these empires different from the original, indeed unworthy to bear the name 'Roman'.

In their eyes, there were four reasons why these were no longer Roman. Firstly, in 285 Rome had ceased to be the capital, which was relocated at various times to Nicomedia, Milan and Ravenna. Secondly, after the division power was based in the eastern Mediterranean or Germany, not in the western Mediterranean. Thirdly, Latin language and culture no longer dominated the empire; they were replaced by Greek culture and eastern perspectives, or by German and Teutonic ones. Finally, there was Christianity's integration into the social and political fabric of the empire. For the Enlightenment scholars, this was enough to cause a demarcation between the various manifestations of the empire.

Yet the inhabitants of Europe did not recognise such divisions at the time, nor throughout the centuries. The empire was single, indivisible, unified. It did not matter if one emperor or four ruled it. Consequently, the administrative division of the empire in 395 into eastern and western portions did not sever the empire. When the Germanic king Odoacer deposed the usurper Romulus Augustulus in 476, Odoacer did not declare that the empire was dead and that he was the sovereign of the west—he asked the eastern emperor, Zeno, to recognise him as his personal representative in Italy and he ruled under the emperor's name. The eastern emperors never abandoned their claims to the western provinces, nor indeed did the western provinces consider themselves anything other than still part of the Roman Empire. When Justinian reclaimed territory in the west in 553, the result was the reunification of Rome with the east, and Rome would continue to be a part of it until 751. It was only then, with the fall of the Roman Exarchate in Ravenna, that the western provinces began to look for a more permanent solution to their problems, since the empire obviously could not hold the Italian provinces any longer, nor was the empire in a position to move beyond Italy. Thus, in 800 the popes declared that the Frankish king, Charles, after he had conquered all the former provinces of Germania, Gaul, Italy and parts of Spain, was the emperor of the Romans in the west. In this Charlemagne, as he later became, was no different from any of the other emperors who ruled during the empire's earlier years of greatness, such as Vespasian, Septimius Severus and Diocletian. Even the eastern emperors, though contemptuous of the west, did occasionally, albeit very reluctantly, acknowledge Charlemagne and his successors as western emperors. The western provinces recognised Charlemagne's realm as being the legitimate continuation of the empire in the centuries that followed.

Yes, the western empire under Charlemagne and his successors did become something very different by the sixteenth century. This does not detract from the fact that, at its birth, the Carolingian (and later, Holy Roman) Empire was the legitimate continuation of the Roman Empire, in nearly the same way that the Byzantine Empire was the same entity that had arisen out of the genius of Augustus. It did not matter that by 900 no one spoke Latin, the Senate was virtually disbanded and Rome was no longer a part of its dominion. Indeed, the Roman Empire of about 300 had very little in common with the principate from which it had sprung, and so any argument seeking to separate the empire's earlier manifestations from its later incarnations because of differences in scope or polity is fundamentally flawed. Each part, with all its glories and failures, belonged to the one entity.

Therefore, this book covers the Roman emperors of:

- the unified Roman Empire (27 BC to AD 395)
- the Western Roman Empire (395 to 751)
- the Eastern Roman Empire (395 to 1453)
- the restored 'Carolingian' and 'Holy' Roman Empires (800 to 1806).

It covers not only the legitimate emperors, but also any usurpers who were elevated by the armies or the Senate and claimed the title 'emperor'. It does not include rulers who did not claim that title. This includes the Gothic kings of Italy after 476 and the rulers of Trebizond after the reign of John II—although claiming descent from the Comnenus family, they abandoned the imperial title for a lesser one.

Several other entities have claimed to be successors of the Roman Empire but were not recognised as such by the true successor states. They are not included in this book. They include the Russian czars, who claimed to be legitimate successors of the emperors after the fall of Constantinople in 1453, and that Moscow was the 'Third Rome'. No one outside the Russian state recognised this fiction. In this category also fall the Ottoman sultans. After conquering Constantinople, Sultan Mehmet II declared that his was the successor state to Rome and Constantinople. Again, the provinces of the former empire rejected this, as did the Roman emperors ruling in Germany. It also excludes the short-lived Latin Empire (1204 to 1261), which was born when the Fourth Crusade overthrew Constantinople. Though these rulers styled themselves as emperors, they were not Roman emperors.

A NOTE ON ORDINALS

The numbering convention used to identify a specific emperor in this work reflects the traditional method of numbering, which tended not to recognise usurpers (and occasionally co-emperors) as being valid rulers in the Roman succession.

There are also some inconsistencies in this traditional numbering. Occasionally an ordinal is reused, such as is the case for Constantine III and Constans II. For these emperors, historians have followed the approach that the empire formally divided after AD 395 and, therefore, each was the third of that name in his respective portion of the empire—Constantine III in the west in 407, and Constantine III in the east in 641. For the purposes of this work, the ordinals for these western emperors have been placed in brackets, so that the western Constantine is referred to as Constantine (III). This convention also applies for Alexius (I), Emperor of Trebizond.

The numbering of the later Germanic Roman emperors has traditionally followed a sequence that leads back to the Carolingian empire and the East Frankish kingdom that emerged from it. Emperor Lothair III (1133–1137), although the second Lothair to be crowned Emperor of the Romans, is so called because tradition sees him as the successor of King Lothair II of Lotharingia (855–869), most of whose kingdom was eventually absorbed into Germany even though Lothair II was never crowned emperor.

An additional complication for the Germanic emperors was the fact that their title of King of the Romans did not automatically mean they were crowned Roman Emperor. For example, Conrad II (1027–1039) was the first Conrad to be crowned emperor but was the second Conrad to be crowned King of the Romans. Thus, historians have traditionally referred to him as Conrad II.

One difficulty inherent in the span of this work, encompassing all the Roman emperors, was how to present it in a form that allows for an understanding of the links between the various rulers. A traditional listing of the unified emperors, followed by the Byzantine emperors and finally the Holy Roman emperors would only reinforce the artificial divisions of the empire made by later historians and force the reader to travel from 1453, when the Byzantine empire fell, back to 800 to start the list of emperors of the restored western empire. It would further obscure the connectivity between the various portions of the empire and force the reader to readjust from a medieval back to a 'Dark Age' perspective.

From the empire's earliest days there was a tendency for rulers to manage it from either the east or the west. This happened during the Second Triumvirate, when the Roman world was split between Octavian in the west and Marc Antony in the east. In the period of the empire's greatness, there was no need for a co-ruler to manage half the empire (nor did usurpers take control in the distant provinces). However, the crisis of the third century resulted in the empire's division, sometimes willingly on the part of the emperor and sometimes not, into eastern and western spheres, with only the occasional emperor managing to unite the empire for short periods. Inevitably, however, the empire's problems were too great for one ruler to handle.

During this time and afterwards, especially after the formal division of the empire, the various emperors did indeed have much communication and interaction with each other, and a separate listing of the western and eastern emperors would obscure such relationships. However, a strict chronological listing of emperors that alternated between eastern and western emperors would also cause the reader to lose track of the continuity of rulers in each of the dominions. To navigate through these problems, the author has developed a third solution for the reader.

Each of the chapters that deals with emperors after the division of the empire is divided into sections corresponding to one half of the empire, covering a period whose parameters coincide with either a change in dynasty or a momentous event. For example, half of Chapter 8 deals with the eastern emperors from Romanus Argyrus (1028) to Alexius Murtzuphlus (1204)—the period of the Crusades. The other half deals with the western emperors from roughly the same period—Conrad II (1027) to Henry VI (1197). This will highlight the frequent interaction between the two halves of the empire during the specified period but ensure that the reader will not be overwhelmed with details of one empire at the expense of the other.

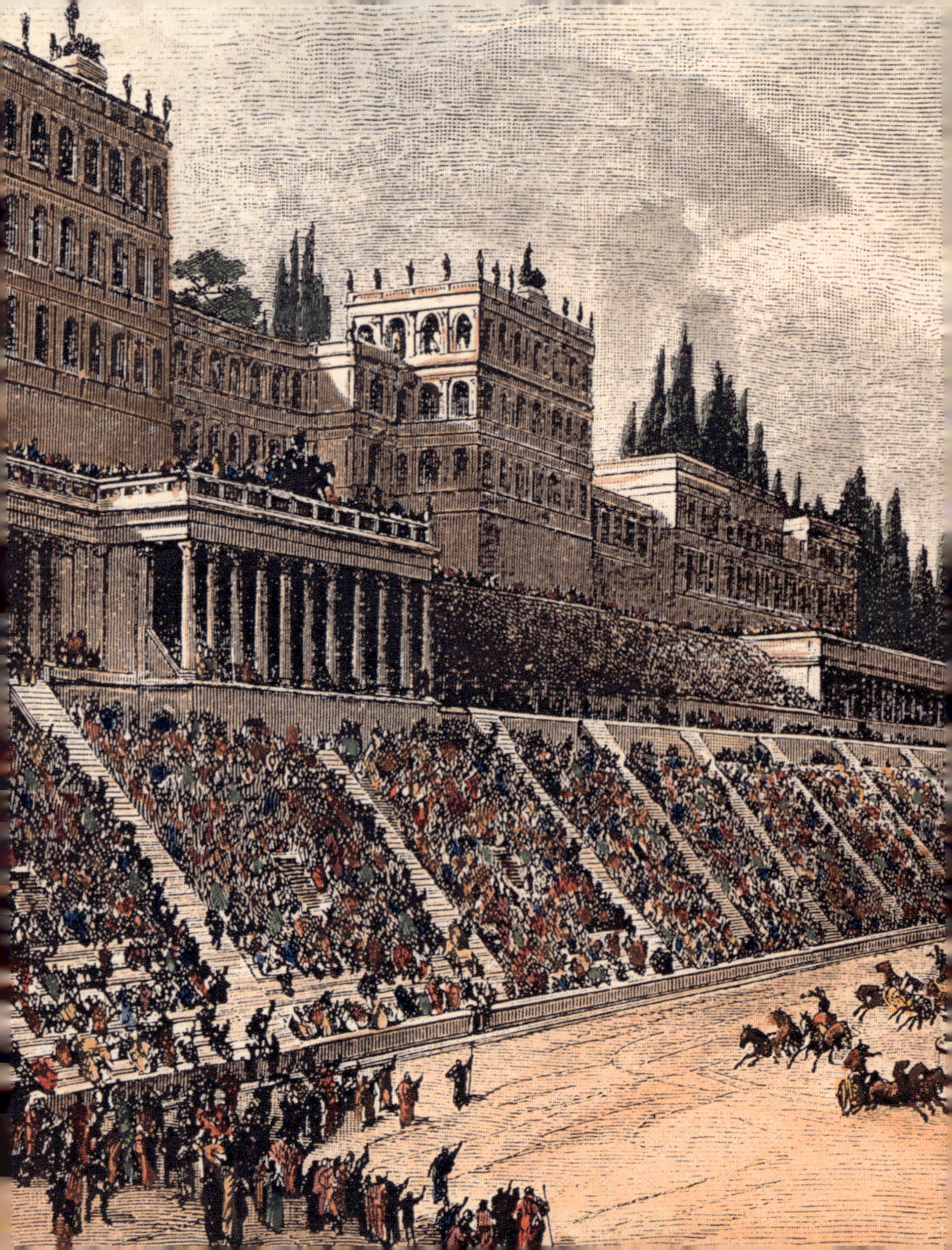

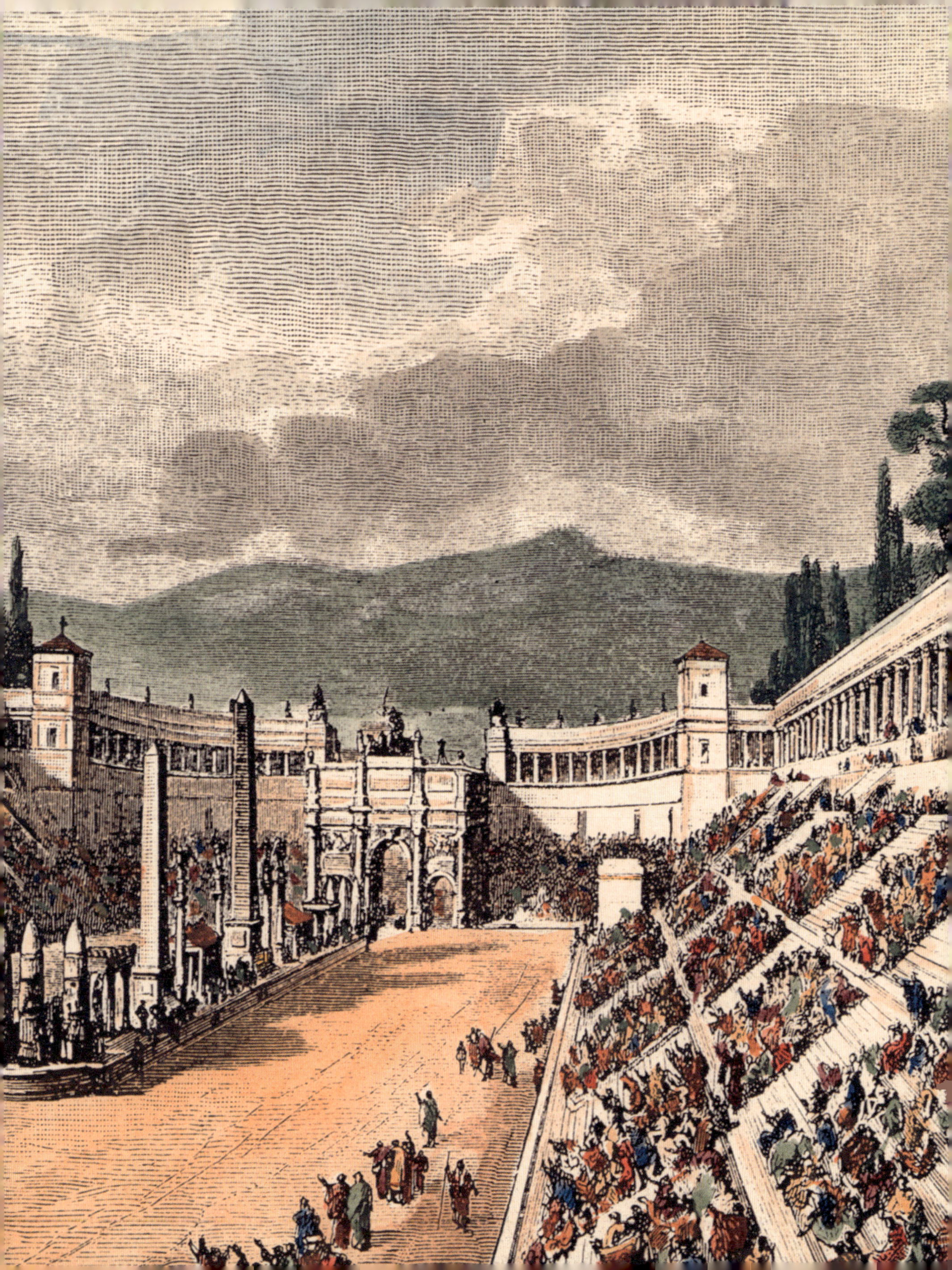

PROLOGUE

DAWN OF AN EMPIRE

ROME WAS NOT ALWAYS an empire, nor did it spring fully formed into the ancient world. By the time of Augustus, its first emperor, the city had been in existence for some seven hundred years, marching along to its manifest destiny. Located halfway up the Italian peninsula, on the Tiber River, it was founded, according to legend, in 753 BC by the twins Romulus and Remus, who had been orphaned as babies and suckled by a she-wolf. Originally Rome was a minor city-state ruled by a king, but the people rose up in 509 BC to overthrow the monarchy and establish a republic—in Latin, the *res publica*. In place of a king, they installed two consuls, elected magistrates who governed for a year before new elections installed another set of consuls. Legislative and consultative bodies were established to manage the affairs of government, with other officials created as time went on to fulfil various needs that political circumstances forced on the state, usually the result of conflict between the aristocratic patrician and common plebeian classes.

For the first two centuries of its existence, the Roman Republic slowly extended its power and influence throughout Italy south of the Po River. At first, the Romans defeated their Latin and Etruscan neighbours, before proceeding south and encountering the warlike Samnites and the patchwork of Greek city-states in the far south of Italy. By 275 BC, Roman domination of the peninsula was complete, and the Romans were soon involved in their first conflict with an overseas power for control of an overseas possession.

The First Punic War began in 264 BC and pitted the land-based might of Rome against the maritime strength of the North African city of Carthage, the major power in the western Mediterranean. Fought for control of Sicily, the war raged for over twenty years before Roman perseverance and ingenuity won through. With this victory, the Roman Republic won its first overseas possession, setting it on an irrevocable course towards acquiring an empire. The Second Punic War, beginning in 218 BC, would be the fire that forged the strength of Rome, as the Carthaginian general Hannibal invaded Italy, forcing Rome into a titanic life-or-death struggle. The Roman victory in 201 BC gave Rome additional territory in Spain, Sardinia and North Africa, and confirmed its position as a regional power.

As a regional power, Rome soon found itself asked to intervene in foreign affairs, principally in the east. Initially asked to help the Greek states against the Macedonians, over the following century Rome managed to subdue Macedonia, Greece and Illyria, and even to extend its influence into Asia Minor through the establishment of client states subservient to Rome. By 100 BC, the Roman Republic was the ruler of the Mediterranean.

Unfortunately, the republic's rise as a world power only brought conflict back home. The Roman Republic was constructed to run a small city-state, not to administer a world empire, and very soon cracks began to emerge within the body politic. Reformers emerged, eager to rectify the abuses that were now commonplace within the governing classes, whether by land reform to protect the Italian farmers against wealthy senators, or by gubernatorial reform to protect the provinces from the ravages of greedy senatorial governors. They met a solid wall of resistance from the Senate, the pre-eminent body in the republic and the bastion of aristocratic conservatism.

THE CURSUS HONORUM

The *cursus honorum* (literally, the 'way of honour') was the traditional method by which a man would climb the political ladder in ancient Rome. Its origins lie in the Roman Republic, but it survived intact during the years of the principate, although some offices fell out of use after the third century. The *cursus* comprised four positions that a Roman citizen had to fill in sequence, with most offices generally lasting for a year.

MILITARY TRIBUNE This was the first office that a man had to occupy to begin a political career. Tribunes were elected by the people to serve and command the legions under the consuls. During the empire these duties were taken over by the legates.

QUAESTOR This was the first position a man had to fill to become a senator. The quaestor was the chief financial officer in the state, working in the treasury, collecting custom duties or managing the finances of a province. The quaestorship was gradually superseded by the imperial bureaucracy.

PRAETOR The praetor was the officer responsible for the administration of justice and the law courts in Rome and the provinces. He was the officer who decided whether litigants should proceed to a formal hearing in court. By the later empire, this role had changed to managing the expenditure of money for the games or on public works, duties that had originally been the role of the aediles.

CONSUL Under the republic, the consuls were the head of the executive in the Roman state, responsible for carrying into effect all decisions made by the Senate and the assemblies. The consuls were the ones who commanded the legions in time of war. Again, the emperors gradually eroded the consuls' roles, though they continued to be appointed into the sixth century.

There were other magisterial positions outside the *cursus* that were vital for the running of the state. These included:

PLEBEIAN TRIBUNE Elected by the plebeians, the plebeian tribunes were meant to protect the interests of the common people. They were able to veto almost all aspects of government, including the passage of laws, the holding of elections and even decisions about war, and it was forbidden to harm them. The position became obsolete under the emperors.

AEDILE These officers were responsible for caring for Rome's streets, public buildings, temples, water supply, drains, traffic, markets, the public grain supply and, most importantly, the games. The office had disappeared by the third century when aediles were replaced by urban prefects.

CENSOR This role was limited to ex-consuls of great standing (*auctoritas*). The censor ensured appropriate standards for members of the Senate and conducted a regular census of citizens. It was virtually abandoned as an office of the state by the time of Nerva.

PROVINCIAL GOVERNOR This position could be held only by an ex-praetor (non-military province) or an ex-consul (military province). By the middle of the third century, career military officers generally filled these positions.

INTERREX AND DICTATOR These were extraordinary positions filled only in times of crisis. They were made obsolete by the emperor.

The position of emperor was foreign to the republic. It overrode all other magistrates in the empire, as the holder possessed a tribune's veto and the rights of an ex-consular governor, as well as unique magisterial rights in Rome, which no other governor had.

The most obvious sign of the problems besetting the Roman Republic was the steady increase in the use of mob violence to influence elections and to prevent the passage of laws. Both the reformers and the conservatives used these methods to promote their agendas or stifle their opponents, and as political murder began to be ever more commonplace, the republic began to collapse. The arrival of powerful individuals, eager to become the pre-eminent Roman citizen and prepared to break every law to do so, only hastened the republic's end. Marius was first, becoming the first man elected consul for five consecutive years, in breach of the unwritten Roman constitution. His reforms politicised the Roman army and transferred the army's loyalty from the state to its commanding officer. Next up was Sulla, the first man to lead an army into Rome, and the first to institute proscriptions, the judicial murder of his opponents. His passing saw the rise of Pompey the Great, who annexed Asia Minor and Palestine to Rome without senatorial approval. To cement his power in Rome, in 60 BC he entered into an arrangement with two other powerful Romans, the rich Crassus and the up-and-coming Julius Caesar, to share power between them in what was known as the First Triumvirate. By the time it ended in 50 BC, the situation in the republic had changed markedly.

The arrival of Julius Caesar would be the catalyst that would send the republic into its death throes and hasten the arrival of the emperors. Julius Caesar was an avid reformer and had earned the enmity of many members of the Senate. He was an aristocrat of impeccable lineage, but his enemies saw him as a traitor and were determined to bring him down, no matter the cost to themselves or the republic. After a spell as consul, as per the triumvirate's agreement, Caesar was posted to Gaul, where he spent the next ten years annexing that huge territory to Rome, again without senatorial approval.

By the time he had finished in 49 BC, his enemies were preparing to bring charges against him in the courts, hoping to ruin him forever. When he reached the Rubicon River, which was the limit of his jurisdiction as governor of Gaul, he was supposed to leave his army behind and proceed to Rome to present himself after the closure of his term. Believing that his enemies would convict and banish him from Rome for life, he took a gamble and crossed into Italy with his army at his back. The result was civil war.

Over the next three years Julius Caesar fought a bloody civil war against his enemies in the Senate, and by 46 BC he had managed to win. During that time, he obtained a number of powers that would become the basis of the power of the emperors. He was granted the powers of a tribune for life, meaning he could veto any law and that his person was sacrosanct. He was given the position of dictator, an office that overrode all other offices in the republic, initially for a year, then for ten years, and by 44 BC for life. By this stage, large numbers in the Senate believed that Julius Caesar was going to make himself king of Rome. To prevent this outcome, a plot was orchestrated to assassinate the dictator as he entered the Senate House on 15 March 44 BC. As he strode in, he was greeted with a flurry of dagger thrusts that left his bloodied corpse huddled on the floor of the Senate. These insular and tradition-bound senators had no idea that they had inflicted a similar wound on their beloved republic. With Caesar's death, the Roman Republic lurched into a new round of civil wars, and into this confusion stepped a new man, young, confident and determined to take advantage of the times to achieve power for himself. His name was Gaius Octavius, and with him the story of the emperors begins …

THE HIGH EMPIRE

(27 BC – AD 180)

In the second century of the Christian era, the Empire of Rome comprehended the fairest part of the earth, and the most civilized portion of mankind. The frontiers of that extensive monarchy were guarded by ancient renown and disciplined valour.

EDWARD GIBBON
The Decline and Fall of the Roman Empire, 1880

FOLLOWING PAGE: Maecenas presenting the liberal arts to Augustus

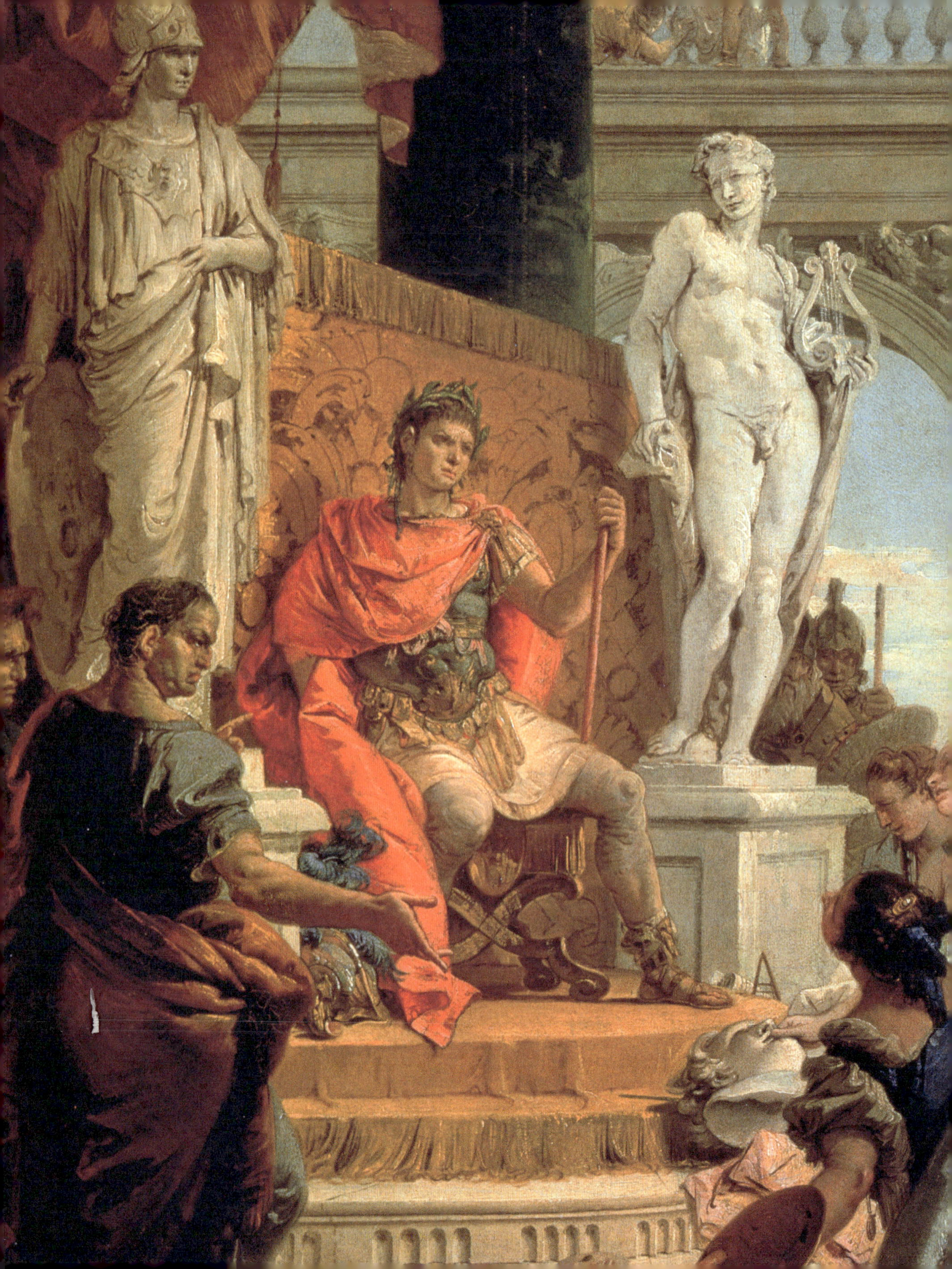

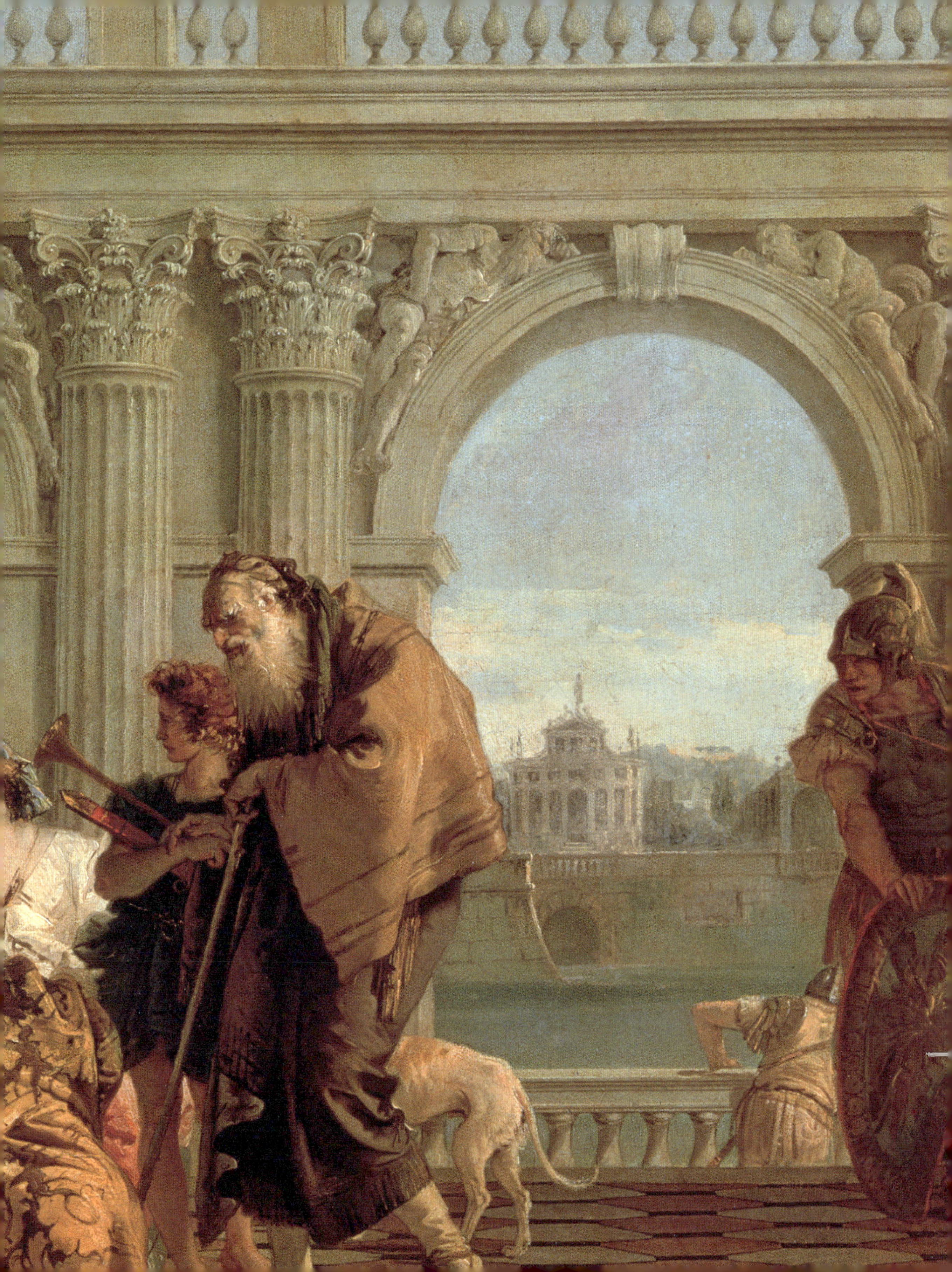

AUGUSTUS

THE CRAFTY TYRANT

NAME: Gaius Julius Caesar Octavianus
BIRTH NAME: Gaius Octavius Thurinus
BORN: Rome, 63 BC
RULED: Emperor, 27 BC – AD 14
DIED: Of natural causes, Nola, Italy, AD 14

ANY MAN WHO SET HIMSELF the task of navigating the Roman state from a disintegrating republic into a stable monarchy needed immense ability, robust vigour and colossal ambition. The dictator Julius Caesar, who believed that someone needed to rescue the republic from its own contradictions, observed these latent characteristics in his grandnephew, Gaius Octavius. With an almost prophetic insight, he nominated this teenager as his adopted son, judging him the most capable within the Julian family to accomplish the grand task that he suspected he might not have the time to finish. That boy in time would become Augustus, first of the Roman emperors.

Being thrust as a nineteen-year-old from obscurity onto a national stage full of intrigue and danger was quite a step up for a young man from a relatively undistinguished plebeian family on his father's side—the Octavii. It was 44 BC and the republic was collapsing in on itself. Marcus Antonius (Marc Antony), Julius Caesar's cousin and right-hand man, was engaged in a battle for supremacy with members of the Senate who had assassinated the great dictator.

Sensing an opportunity in the chaos to advance his own agenda and calling himself Gaius Julius Caesar Octavianus (traditionally he is referred to as Octavian until his formal acceptance as emperor), the future Augustus used his adoption as Caesar's heir to gain the loyalty of the legions that Caesar had gathered in preparation for a great campaign against the Parthians in the east. To help in his quest, Octavian began to imitate Caesar's mannerisms and gestures, and he commenced wearing high heels to give himself an approximation of Caesar's height. Forcing Antony to come to terms with him as an equal, he then played a dangerous game of cat and mouse with Antony and the Senate, shifting sides whenever it suited him, helped by his own natural cunning and his opponents' underestimation of his abilities and ruthlessness.

By the age of twenty Octavian had been made a senator and given formal command of the armies of the republic to take on Antony. Having beaten Antony, he then turned on the Senate, which he coerced into electing him consul, head magistrate of the Roman Republic. From this position of strength, in 43 BC he entered into a formal partnership with Antony and Marcus Aemilius Lepidus, known as the Second Triumvirate. Their first act was to order the judicial execution of all their enemies, resulting in the decimation of many of the old senatorial families. Octavian and Antony then divided the Roman world between them, with Octavian ruling the western provinces and Antony the eastern. This partnership would last, with the occasional flare-up, for ten years, until their final showdown in 31 BC at the battle of Actium, which saw Octavian defeat Antony and finally achieve sole command of the entire Roman Empire.

> **Since I have played my part well, could you all clap your hands, and under your applause I shall depart from the stage.**
>
> AUGUSTUS

Octavian then confirmed just why Julius Caesar had placed such faith in his abilities. Whereas most men in his position would consolidate their position and crush every potential rival, Octavian went out of his way to hide his actual power. In 27 BC he constructed the careful power-sharing arrangement known as the 'principate', which would be the basis of the Roman imperial system for centuries to come. Octavian set himself up as the *princeps*, or 'first citizen', a position he

ROMAN SOCIETY: CLASSES, ORDERS AND NAMES

By the time the empire was erected on the crumbling ruins of the republic, Roman society had already developed its most recognisable forms.

SLAVES AND CITIZENS All the people living within the empire belonged to a particular class. At the lowest level were the slaves. Considered a type of property, they had very limited rights, though they could be freed. Above them were the native peoples who lived in territories conquered by Rome, the citizens of Roman client states and Roman allies. These had certain rights granted to them, such as the right to make legal contracts and to hold property as a Roman citizen, as well as the right to retain a limited form of citizenship. At the top were the *cives romani*, Roman citizens, who enjoyed full legal protection under Roman law. They were subdivided into two classes: the *non optimo jure*, who held rights of property and marriage, and the *optimo jure*, who held these and were also able to vote and to hold office. At the time of Augustus, only the people of Italy had been extended the right of Roman citizenship. By the 220s, it would be made available to every free person within the empire.

PATRICIANS, PLEBEIANS AND EQUESTRIANS Roman citizens were also categorised into orders, according to the families they were born into—the patricians and the plebeians. Patricians were the elite families of the old Roman Republic, and originally only they were allowed to sit in the Senate. Plebeians formed the majority of the citizens in Rome, the common people, and they had their own assembly that could enact legislation recommended by the *princeps*. The distinction between patrician and plebeian was made purely on birth, not wealth. There were many rich plebeians and also quite destitute patrician families. The emperors had the right to raise plebeians to the rank of patrician, and by the time of Augustus, though patrician families still existed, their order had been supplanted by the senatorial order. There was also a third order: the equestrian order. It was a lower aristocratic order and was based not on family relationships but on meeting a wealth threshold—400,000 sesterces by the reign of Augustus.

ROMAN NAMES A name for a male citizen consisted of three parts, with the family name second: *praenomen* (the given name, chosen by the parents), *nomen* (the name of the gens or clan) and *cognomen* (the name of a family line within the gens). Sometimes a second or third *cognomen*, called *agnomen*, was added. The *nomen* and *cognomen* were virtually always hereditary. Therefore, in Augustus's name—Gaius Julius Caesar Augustus—Gaius is the given name, Julius is the family or clan name, Caesar is the name used to distinguish a family within the Julian clan, and Augustus is the nickname given in gratitude for his accomplishments. The *gens* Julii signified an esteemed patrician family, while the *gens* Octavii possessed a much lower social standing, which is why Augustus discarded that name when he was adopted by Julius Caesar.

Adoption was a common feature of Roman life and was not considered shameful, since the one adopted nearly always ended up in a family higher up the social ladder. With their adoption, they gained the same rights as a blood descendent of the adopted family and were considered to be a true member of that *gens*. So with Augustus's adoption by Julius Caesar, he became in the eyes of the Roman world a fully fledged member of the Julian clan.

would hold for ten years at a time, to be reconfirmed by the Senate as needed. He relinquished the consulship and returned to the Senate much of its traditional role. It helped that he had a Senate populated with new blood, families who owed their position to Octavian, so that it was a more subservient body than its counterpart during the civil war. He developed a system whereby he appeared to act in partnership with the Senate but was, in fact, in control of all the important military and legal powers of the state. The empire was divided between the provinces that were under the command of the Senate and those controlled directly by him, but all

Battle of Actium, 31 BC, which established the dominance of Octavian

the legions were within the provinces controlled by the *princeps*. He established a personal guard, the Praetorian Guard, within the city of Rome itself and had the power of veto over any law. His gift was that he never flaunted those powers, and he always maintained that he had re-invigorated the republic after the chaos of the civil wars and that his position was simply one of a magistrate within the Roman system. In gratitude, the Senate named him 'Augustus'—the revered one.

After the establishment of the principate, the major topic of conversation was the unique nature of the position held by Augustus, and the question of what would happen should he pass away. Technically, his appointment was at the behest of the Senate, but should the Senate enforce its power, the possibility of a new civil war would emerge. Therefore, he turned to members of his family to provide a solution to this problem.

During the years of the Second Triumvirate, Augustus had fallen in love with a woman called Livia. Both she and Octavian were married at the time, but he obtained a divorce and Livia's husband agreed to the separation on Octavian's orders. Each had children—Julia, Augustus's daughter, was born on the day Augustus divorced her mother, and Livia had two sons, Tiberius and Drusus. After their rapid divorces Octavian and Livia married and, according to all accounts, were happily married for the next fifty years. However, their union produced no children, and so the succession question was one that dominated their thinking until Augustus's death. Initially, Augustus placed all his hopes on the children of the Julian line—Julia's first husband was his sister's son, Marcellus, who became the first of his designated heirs. After Marcellus's death, Julia was married to Marcus Agrippa, and they had five children. Of the three males, Augustus adopted the first two—Gaius and Lucius—but they both died before Augustus's reign ended.

By this stage, Augustus had lost hope of a succession through the Julian line. After the death of Agrippa, Julia was married to Livia's son Tiberius, but the marriage was a failure. Julia's banishment in 2 BC for repeated adultery and treason, and her son Agrippa Postumus's banishment in AD 7, saw Augustus become increasingly embittered. Both Julia and her son would die within a few months of Augustus's death, on the orders of Tiberius, who had been adopted by Augustus and succeeded him.

The failure of the Julian line was always a cause of deep sadness for Augustus, one that he blamed principally on himself and his failure as a father. Though adoption was always a well-respected and common feature of Roman family life, the fact that his own bloodline had failed did darken his days, though not to the extent that similar misfortune would blacken those of his stepson Tiberius.

One forgotten aspect of Augustus's rule was the fact that the empire expanded in all directions. Served as he was by very able generals, his armies pushed deeply into Germany and established the northern frontiers at the Rhine and Danube rivers. This reflected Augustus's unrelenting desire to equal in every possible sense the achievements of the great Julius Caesar. It was also a pragmatic policy—it exposed future emperors to military discipline and command, it kept the armies focused on foreign, not domestic, affairs and it siphoned off the excess population who would normally have come to the major cities to live off the free bread provided by the Roman state. Augustus's successors would not possess the foresight to continue this policy, and the state would pay a very dear price.

By the time of his death, most Romans had known no other system apart from the principate, allowing Augustus's political solution to endure. Had he died within the first ten years of his reign, it is certain that the Roman state would have descended into chaos once again. As it was, the Senate and the people of Rome gratefully deified the *princeps*, and meekly asked his choice of successor if he would consent to take up the principal magistracy of the Roman people. Tiberius taciturnly agreed and so the line of emperors was born.

TIBERIUS I

HEART OF DARKNESS

NAME: Tiberius Julius Caesar
BIRTH NAME: Tiberius Claudius Nero
BORN: Rome, 42 BC
RULED: Emperor, AD 14–37
DIED: Of natural causes, Misenum (Capo Miseno, Naples), Italy, AD 37

WHERE AUGUSTUS WAS able to deal with personal tragedies with a calm and pragmatic acceptance, this was not true of his successor, Tiberius. Misfortune and personal heartbreak haunted his life and turned a dark, introspective boy into a debauched tyrant.

Catapulted at the age of three into the imperial family by his mother's marriage to the future Augustus, he was inevitably overshadowed by Augustus's grandchildren, their Julian descent flaunted before his Claudian ancestry. This would have serious ramifications later in his life. Once these heirs died prematurely, however, Tiberius became Augustus's likely successor.

The next act that shaped his life was being forcibly divorced from his beloved wife so that he could marry Julia to secure the succession, something that he never forgave and that embittered him further with regard to the Julians. Nevertheless, he tried to be a dutiful son by campaigning, quite successfully, against the Germans. Augustus, however, did not seem to appreciate the efforts of his stepson; indeed, he seemed to take quite a dislike to him. So the fame of the victories tended to go to his brother, Drusus, and once again someone overshadowed him. Ironically, it was not only Tiberius's brother who earned the praise, but eventually his gifted and more popular nephew, Germanicus.

However, after the deaths of the principal Julian heirs, it was Tiberius, by virtue of being the last man standing, who became Augustus's adopted son and successor. After taking the reins of power in AD 14, he was initially quite a successful and stable ruler. However, as the years progressed he endured unfavourable comparisons with his adopted father, the deified Augustus, especially in regard to his tactless dealings with the Senate. This comparison to a man he admired and loathed in equal measure only clouded his mind and poisoned his relationship with his so-called partners in the Senate. He soon began to distance himself from Rome and place his faith in a trusted lieutenant—Sejanus, head of the Praetorian Guard.

Sejanus had Tiberius so convinced that the Senate was plotting against him that he agreed to move from Rome and establish himself in a villa on the island of Capri, in the Bay of Naples. A contributing factor was the death of Tiberius's only son, whom Tiberius later discovered had been murdered by Sejanus so that he could have an affair with the murdered man's wife. The loss of his son seemed to be the point at which Tiberius turned from being a devoted, if flawed, Roman *princeps* into a tyrant. At Capri, Tiberius abandoned himself to his pleasures, mostly involving young girls and boys who took his fancy, while Sejanus was all-powerful in Rome. Over the next five years, he had Tiberius order the deaths of his senatorial enemies as well as rivals from the imperial family itself, most notably members of Germanicus's family.

> **Let them hate me, provided they respect my actions.**
>
> TIBERIUS

Eventually Tiberius's paranoid gaze became fixed on his over-mighty 'first minister' and he instigated a plot to overthrow Sejanus. He ordered the death of Sejanus and dozens of his supporters, mostly from the ranks of the Julians, whom Sejanus courted in his rise to power. Thus Tiberius finally gave vent to all those years of resentment towards that most esteemed of patrician families. The terror created by his paranoia continued until Tiberius died, a crazed old man, at the age of seventy-eight.

During Tiberius's reign the empire, outside Rome, was generally at peace, as he did not attempt to expand the frontiers and was a conscientious and economical administrator. The people were contented, well fed and protected against overzealous imperial officials, and thus they were inclined to view his reign favourably. Not so the Roman aristocracy: they were on the receiving end of Tiberius's fury and, as they were the ones who passed down the traditions about his reign, it was inevitable that his legacy would be framed by their fear and hatred.

GAIUS CALIGULA

CORRUPTED YOUTH

NAME: Gaius Julius Caesar Germanicus
BORN: Antium, Italy, 12
RULED: Emperor, 37–41
DIED: Murdered, Rome, 41

REGARDLESS OF WHAT strain Tiberius's final years had placed on the shrewdly constructed framework established by Augustus, Gaius brought it near to breaking point. Where Tiberius came to the principate after serving his apprenticeship for years as a commander of the Roman armies and had shared imperial power in Augustus's final years, Gaius was a youth who had served only in a minor post prior to his accession.

He was the son of the revered Germanicus, Tiberius's nephew, who had married Augustus's granddaughter. Germanicus was beloved by the people and the legions, and this affection was transferred to little Gaius, who travelled with his parents on military campaigns in the north. He was frequently shown to the troops wearing a miniature soldier's outfit, and so the soldiers called him 'Caligula', meaning 'Little Boot'.

Gaius's childhood was a deeply unhappy one. His father was probably murdered when he was seven and he was forced to live with his grandmothers for twelve years. Then he was summoned to Tiberius's residence at Capri and was to remain there until Tiberius died. It was during this period that his mother and two brothers were killed, making him one of the few members of his family to survive the purges of Tiberius and Sejanus. Exposure to Tiberius's dark and debauched side at Capri may help to explain his subsequent behaviour as emperor.

The traditional image is of the insane Caligula, the man who attempted to elevate his horse to the consulship, who had incestuous relations with his sister and who ordered his solders to gather seashells from the English Channel as tribute from Neptune. This reflects the judgement of his senatorial enemies, who were able to tell the story and so write history to their satisfaction. The reality is quite different.

In all likelihood Gaius was simply an inexperienced young man elevated into a position of unlimited power and not caring for the niceties established by Augustus. Feeling his way slowly at first, he saw fairly soon that the *princeps* was in reality the ruler of the Roman world, and he began to act accordingly. His youth and his difficult childhood all played their part in his contempt of the senatorial elite, and the recent example of Tiberius pointed the way to the future. So, while it is unlikely that Gaius declared it a capital offence for anyone to look down on him as he passed or to mention goats in any context, it is quite probable that he indulged his sexual passions in ways the Romans considered deviant, and that his whims did see some prominent Romans killed for trivial reasons.

What brought him undone was not an organised senatorial conspiracy, but a personal grudge by members of the Praetorian Guard. Gaius took to mocking members of the imperial guard by giving out obscene watchwords for the night. In early 41, after watching some performances at the theatre, he returned to the palace for lunch. Having dismissed his cronies, he was isolated in a remote part of the palace and cut down by his disgruntled troops. His murder by the military set a dangerous precedent, one that would be re-enacted with nightmarish regularity in the years to come.

CLAUDIUS I

THE STUTTERER

NAME: Tiberius Claudius Nero Germanicus
BIRTH NAME: Tiberius Claudius Drusus
BORN: Lugdunum (Lyon), Gaul, 10 BC
RULED: Emperor, 41–54
DIED: Poisoned, Rome, 54

OF ALL THE MEMBERS of the Julio-Claudian dynasty, Claudius appeared the least likely to inherit the throne. The son of Tiberius's brother, Drusus, and brother to Germanicus, he too should have been groomed for the principate and thus fallen foul of both Tiberius and Gaius Caligula. What saved him was the fact that he was born with a deformity that resulted in a limp, he drooled, and he had a pronounced stutter—a stunning contrast to the heroic Germanicus. The result was that his family considered him an idiot and kept him as far as possible from the public eye. His outward appearance concealed an inquisitive mind, but the ridicule he endured and the humiliations of his childhood would have a profound impact on him when he finally found himself ruler of the Roman world.

Where Augustus and Tiberius generally ignored him, Gaius was more than happy to torment his poor, idiotic uncle. Claudius, who had seen the devastation wrought on the remnants of his family, wisely played the fool to avoid suffering a similar fate. He expected to see the remainder of his life out in this manner, but fate intervened.

In the aftermath of the assassination of Gaius, the Praetorian Guard began looting the imperial palace. One soldier noticed a pair of feet protruding from behind a curtain and, pulling it aside, he discovered Claudius hiding for his life. Instead of the death he was expecting, the troops surprised him by offering him the throne—at the age of fifty-one. The Senate was supposed to confer the position of *princeps* on the most deserving individual but Claudius's elevation showed that authority actually rested with the military. It was a lesson the Senate never forgot.

Once on the throne, Claudius was determined to make his mark. Having been in the shadow of Germanicus all his life, he decided to eclipse his brother's military record to prove that the deformed and rejected boy was more capable than those who had been favoured ahead of him. The target he chose was Britannia. Within two years, he had organised the successful invasion of the island, managing to achieve something that even the great Julius Caesar could not, and his was a permanent conquest instead of Germanicus's transient victories in Germany.

This overwhelming desire to prove to the world what sort of man he was had one unwanted consequence for Claudius personally. Given his unpopularity throughout his life, he was unprepared for the effect that his sudden elevation had on others. Starved for affection, he assumed that women were now interested in him because they saw him now as a Roman man instead of the bumbling idiot they had all assumed him to be. He did not comprehend that they were interested in him only because of his position as emperor.

> **A monster of a man, who was started but not finished by Mother Nature.**
>
> ANTONIA THE YOUNGER (mother of Claudius)

Though Claudius had been married previously, his first post-accession marriage was to Valeria Messalina. A young and frivolous aristocrat eager to exercise power through him, she seduced the much older emperor, who then turned a blind eye to her numerous lovers and decadent orgies, to the point where everyone said that he was the only person in Rome who did not know about his wife's infidelities. The marriage lasted ten years and she gave him a son (Britannicus) and a daughter (Octavia), but he finally executed her when he discovered that she had undergone a marriage ceremony with an incoming consul.

Claudius, emperor and conqueror of Britain

THE HIGH EMPIRE 25

Failing to learn his lesson, he soon married his niece Agrippina the Younger, who brought to the marriage her sexual expertise, her boundless ambition and a son—Nero. Agrippina so dominated her husband that he began to favour Nero over Britannicus. In the year of his death, after six years of marriage to Agrippina, he marked his stepson as his heir, even marrying him to his daughter Octavia. Fearing that further delays would endanger her plans, Agrippina had Claudius poisoned in 54 to ensure Nero's accession.

Given his family's dismissal of his abilities, it is ironic that, after Augustus, Claudius was the most able and successful of the Julio-Claudians. Though he could be vindictive and cruel to his enemies, he ensured stable government across the empire, instituted much-needed public works and took very seriously what was the emperor's principal responsibility—his role as the chief judicial magistrate of the state. Though he was never especially liked by the Senate, it speaks volumes that upon his death they deified him for his services, a recognition not afforded to either Tiberius or Gaius.

SCRIBONIANUS

SECRET REPUBLICAN

NAME: Furius Camillus Scribonianus
BIRTH NAME: Lucius Arruntius Scribonianus
BORN: Unknown
RULED: Usurper, 41
DIED: Suicide, island of Issa (modern Vis), Dalmatia, 41

WITH THE FALL OF GAIUS CALIGULA, a number of men were considered for the position of emperor. One of these was the imperial legate of Dalmatia, Scribonianus, who was approached by an influential senator, Annius Vinicianus, with a plot to overthrow the newly installed Claudius. Scribonianus had been consul in 32 and had been quite close to Claudius in the past, as his sister had been engaged to Claudius for a time. This did not stop him making an attempt on the throne, and initially it went quite successfully, with many senators and equestrians in Rome flocking to Annius while they waited for Scribonianus, whose troops had proclaimed him *imperator*, to arrive. Claudius was so concerned that he contemplated abdicating in favour of Scribonianus.

> **I shall restore the republic and give you back your ancient freedoms!**
>
> SCRIBONIANUS (addressing the troops)

He need not have worried. Scribonianus attempted to motivate his troops by declaring his intent to restore the republic, and to give them back their freedom. This was not what they wanted to hear, and they refused to march against Claudius. Scribonianus grew fearful at this point and decided to flee to the island of Issa, just off the Dalmatian coast, where he committed suicide. His rebellion had lasted five days. Imperial propaganda later declared that the reason it failed was divine intervention: the standards of the legions could not be pulled from the ground, and so the soldiers refused to march and killed Scribonianus.

NERO

THE POET

NAME: Nero Claudius Caesar Drusus Germanicus
BIRTH NAME: Lucius Domitius Ahenobarbus
BORN: Antium, Italy, 37
RULED: Emperor, 54–68
DIED: Suicide, just outside Rome, 68

THE AHENOBARBI WERE a family with a long and distinguished history during the republic. Young Lucius Domitius Ahenobarbus had the added advantage of being a member of the imperial family through his mother, Agrippina, who was the daughter of Germanicus as well as the husband of the emperor Claudius. When the ageing emperor adopted him, he subsequently changed his name to the more suitable Nero Claudius Caesar Drusus Germanicus. Unfortunately, upon attaining the throne it soon became clear that his name was the only suitable attribute he brought to the principate.

Nero was seventeen when Agrippina achieved her goal, and for the next five years he worked with a group of able advisors appointed by his mother and by Claudius. During this period he showed himself more than capable of ruling effectively, but it was not to last. His fickle and suspicious nature was on display within a year, when he arranged the poisoning of Britannicus, and Agrippina's desire to rule through her son proved to be her undoing, for Nero's feelings of gratitude were not enough to prevent him having her murdered in 59. He grabbed this opportunity to take the reins of power into his own hands by removing his old advisors, replacing them with younger favourites, and divorcing Octavia, whom he later banished and executed. His mistress, Poppaea Sabina, was the key instigator in all these events, and he married her shortly afterwards.

What an artist the world is losing!

NERO

Spending the remainder of his reign in an endless cycle of parties, games and debauched celebrations, Nero emptied the treasury faster than he could gather imperial taxes. What he required was money to fund his ever more outrageous lifestyle, and he hit upon a plan of using treason charges to confiscate the property of popular or critical senators. The resulting insecurity inevitably led to a real conspiracy against his life in 65. Once it was uncovered, Nero acted with characteristic brutality—high-ranking individuals were tortured, others were forced to commit suicide, and there were numerous executions. It was soon evident that no one was truly safe from Nero's paranoia and greed, and thus in 68 the provinces of the empire rose up in revolt. As various armies moved ever closer to Rome, Nero's supporters and flatterers mostly abandoned him. He fled to a small villa outside Rome, where he committed suicide on 9 June 68. With him perished the Julio-Claudian dynasty.

Nero was a conundrum. His creative and artistic side sat uneasily next to his bloodthirsty paranoia and indiscriminate disregard for others. He loved to write poetry, compose music and perform in the theatre, but his subsequent overthrow meant that all critiques of

THE FIRST REBELLIONS

The first uprisings against Nero began in early 68 when Gaius Julius Vindex raised the standard of revolt in the province of Lugdunensis in Gaul. A number of others quickly joined him, including Sulpicius Galba, the future emperor. The commander of Upper Germany, Lucius Verginius Rufus, remained loyal to Nero and the two armies met, resulting in the defeat and death of Vindex. In the aftermath, the troops of Rufus declared him emperor, but he refused the honour and gave the Senate the opportunity to name the next *princeps*. Meanwhile, in Africa the legate of the Third Legion, Lucius Clodius Macer, cut off Rome's grain supply and refused to recognise any emperor. Galba eventually had him killed.

These were not Roman emperors. Vindex did not declare himself emperor at any point during his revolt. Rufus, though declared emperor, actively refused to accept the position. Finally, Macer, though he issued his own coinage and raised a new legion, did not call himself emperor, but rather *propraetor*. The usurpers who were to follow would not be so backward in coming forward.

his ability displayed an inevitable bias against him. Lazy and capricious, he was still more than capable of acting responsibly when the situation demanded it, such as during the Great Fire of Rome in 64. When he was made aware of the fire, he returned from his holiday house at Antium and organised extensive relief programs for the people of Rome, even going so far as to open up his palaces for the frightened and desperate populace. He then poured massive funds into the rebuilding of Rome, and the images of Rome that we are familiar with today stem from his restoration of the capital.

However, even such actions had their darker side. In the aftermath of the fire, rumours spread that Nero was the culprit who had started it. In order to throw suspicion

Great Fire of Rome, with Nero depicted singing while Rome burns

28 TRIUMPH AND TRAGEDY

off himself he needed a scapegoat. His wife, Poppaea, suggested that the perfect target would be the Christians; in this, her Jewish friends, who were antagonistic towards this breakaway Jewish sect, influenced her. Nero took her advice and began a campaign against the Christians, first blaming them for the fire because of their apocalyptic belief that Rome and the world would end by fire. He then actively persecuted them, feeding them to the beasts at the great games, crucifying them and setting them alight. The fire and the persecutions became the defining images of his reign.

NYMPHIDIUS

PETTY OPPORTUNIST

NAME: Gaius Nymphidius Sabinus
BORN: Rome, 35
RULED: Usurper, 68
DIED: Murdered, Rome, 68

THE SON OF A GLADIATOR, Nymphidius had, by the year 68, become the Praetorian Guard's unofficial commander, and he was eagerly pushing Galba to become emperor in the wake of Nero's death. When Galba nominated a different man as the head of the praetorians, Nymphidius decided that it was better to be king than kingmaker and so declared himself the legitimate successor to Nero because of his bloodline. It seems that Martianus the gladiator was not Nymphidius's father after all; improbably, that honour went to the former emperor Gaius Caligula.

Nymphidius enjoyed the position for a short period. With the approach of Galba, the praetorians decided that they would live a lot longer if they accepted the inevitable, killing this presumptuous usurper before their new emperor had even arrived at the gates of the capital.

GALBA

UNEQUAL TO THE IMPERIAL OFFICE

NAME: Lucius Livius Ocella Sulpicius Galba
BIRTH NAME: Servius Sulpicius Galba
BORN: Tarracina, Italy, 3 BC
RULED: Emperor, 68–69
DIED: Murdered, Rome, AD 69

WHILE A NUMBER OF MEN believed they could be Nero's successor as *princeps*, few had the pedigree of Galba. Hailing from the Sulpicii and adopted by the Servii, he was almost the equal of the Julian and Claudian families. He served with distinction throughout the early years of the empire and by 68 was the governor of Tarraconensis in Spain.

The reason for Galba's rebellion was quite simple—Nero had ordered his death. Throwing his lot in with the rebels, he watched as Vindex died in battle and Rufus rejected the imperial crown. Galba then gathered his troops, declared himself emperor, and marched on Rome in the company of Otho, imperial legate of Lusitania.

> It is my habit to levy troops,
> not to buy them.
>
> GALBA (shortly before his troops killed him)

Showing arrogance and stupidity in equal measure, Galba imposed severe military discipline on the pampered Praetorian Guard at the same time as he withheld the promised payment for their loyalty. When he nominated an inexperienced successor, he alienated Otho, who believed the position should have been his. In revenge, Otho won over the disgruntled praetorians, who slew Galba in the Roman Forum.

OTHO

THE BETTER MAN LOST

NAME: Marcus Salvius Otho
BORN: Ferentium, Italy, 32
RULED: Emperor, 69
DIED: Suicide, Cremona, Italy, 69

YOU WOULD THINK THAT OTHO would have been used to slights and insults. Bow-legged and wearing a wig to cover his baldness, he had been married to Poppaea Sabina before Nero took her as a mistress, married her and banished Otho to be the legate of Lusitania in Spain. However, the childless Galba's decision to snub him over the succession was one slight too many.

After Galba's murder, the Senate, in what was becoming a regular display of meekness, accepted Otho's elevation by the Praetorian Guard. This was in sharp contrast to the legions of Vitellius, imperial legate of Lower Germany. Crossing the Alps, they halted just north of the Po River. Without waiting for reinforcements, Otho ordered an attack on Vitellius's forces at Cremona. Defeated and with his troops scattering after the battle, he behaved like the Romans of old and took his own life with a sword thrust, ending a fifty-nine day reign.

VITELLIUS

THE GLUTTON

NAME: Aulus Vitellius Germanicus
BORN: Italy, 15
RULED: Emperor, 69
DIED: Assassinated, Rome, 69

VITELLIUS WAS A MAN WHO had climbed the ladder of success not by his own merits, but through his family's influence. Galba, worried about the potential for rebellion in Germany, had sent Vitellius to be imperial legate of Lower Germany, hoping that he would not be the focus of imperial ambitions. It was a vain hope.

Loyal and talented officers served Vitellius, and they marched south to defeat Otho. In a sign of things to come, when Vitellius was finally given the all clear he travelled to Rome, partying all the way, while his soldiers plundered the Italian countryside. The Senate again fulfilled its now familiar role in this process by accepting the army's choice of emperor. Vitellius thanked them for their wisdom and foresight and promptly devoted himself to the pleasures of the banqueting table. His victory was short lived as another legate—Vespasian, the imperial legate of Syria—decided that, actually, he would make a better emperor.

Vespasian sent loyal lieutenants to Italy to secure the prize, but Vitellius's troops stood firm and fought those in favour of Vespasian at Cremona. This time Vitellius was not so fortunate, and his army was defeated. Back in Rome, he decided that it was time to negotiate and offered to abdicate the throne in favour of Vespasian. His soldiers prevented this sensible course of action, resulting in Vespasian's men storming and sacking the capital. The conquering troops found Vitellius trying to hide and carted him off semi-naked to the Forum, where the Roman mob tortured and killed him, and threw his mangled remains into the Tiber.

VESPASIAN

THE ECONOMICAL EMPEROR

NAME: Titus Flavius Vespasianus
BORN: Falacrinum, Italy, 9
RULED: Emperor, 69–79
DIED: Of extreme diarrhoea, Rome, 79

VESPASIAN OF THE FLAVIANS was the first emperor not to have been born into a noble or ancient family. Consequently, he rose through the military and political offices on merit and ability, not on powerful family ties. By the final years of Nero's reign he found himself stationed in Judaea, charged with putting down the Jewish rebellion, a collision of Hellenic anti-Semitism and Jewish zealotry, resulting in the massacre of Jews at Caesarea and the butchering of Greeks and Romans in Jerusalem. Vespasian very quickly subdued most of the province, but Jerusalem was still holding out when he decided to make his bid for the principate.

Vespasian had initially supported Galba, then Otho and finally Vitellius, but eventually the prize was too great a temptation to resist, especially when he discovered a prophecy that the ruler of the world would emerge from Judaea. Armed with this divine recommendation and a forged letter from Otho asking Vespasian to avenge him, Vespasian's supporters overthrew Vitellius, and Vespasian was installed at Rome by the army's authority and the Senate's resigned acclamation.

Oh crap! I think I am becoming a god!

VESPASIAN

Vespasian inherited a government in total disarray, with rebellions and uprisings throughout the empire. With his demonstrated common sense and eye for detail, he spent the next ten years reorganising the administration of the state and strengthening the frontier provinces bordering Germany and Parthia. He boosted Senate numbers and always treated that esteemed body with the utmost respect. Coming from the lower levels of society, he appreciated his good fortune and was one of the few emperors who truly understood that the principate was a privilege, not a right, and that with it came responsibility.

The state was also on the brink of bankruptcy due to recent civil wars and the extravagances of his predecessors. He imposed new taxes (including a urinal tax) and avoided all but the most needed expenses, leading to the observation that he was even more miserly than Tiberius. Yet this was how he repaired the wounds inflicted on the Roman state since Nero's death, and he is justifiably recognised as the ablest emperor since Augustus.

TITUS

DEARLY BELOVED

NAME: Titus Flavius Vespasianus
BORN: Rome, 39
RULED: Emperor, 79–81
DIED: Fever, Rome, 81

TITUS, NAMED AFTER HIS FATHER (and so rightfully he should be known as Vespasian II), was a man in a hurry. Before and after his accession, he worked diligently at the tasks he set himself, reproaching himself harshly if he were indolent at any time. He may have felt this way because it seemed he was forever finishing someone else's job. When his father became emperor, he left Titus behind in Judaea to end the Judaean War, which he successfully concluded, storming Jerusalem in 70. Then, after Vespasian died, he had to finish off the new amphitheatre, the Colosseum, which he opened in the usual stupendous Roman way in 80, with one hundred days of spectacles involving the deaths of beasts and men.

Titus was trusted implicitly by his father, to the point where Vespasian installed him as head of the Praetorian Guard, the position from which so many of the empire's recent troubles had stemmed. He was quite deserving of that trust, doing much of his father's dirty work while praetorian prefect.

His time in the east affected Titus in two ways. Firstly, he began an affair with a Jewish queen, Berenice, who ruled parts of modern-day Syria as a client state of Rome. She visited Rome in the years 75 and 79, but both times Titus sent her away—the Romans had a deep suspicion of

TRIUMPH AND TRAGEDY

dalliances with eastern queens, stemming from Antony's infamous love affair with Cleopatra. Secondly, there is a story related in the Hebrew Talmud that during the Judaean War an insect flew into Titus's nose and gnawed at his brain for seven years, during which time he was in constant pain, though the sound of a blacksmith hammering did help ease the pain. The story goes that when he died, they opened his skull and found the insect had grown to the size of a small bird.

Universally admired as an emperor, Titus was deeply mourned when he passed away so young—one suspects his reputation was enhanced by the near universal loathing of his brother and successor, Domitian.

DOMITIAN

DEARLY DESPISED

NAME: Titus Flavius Domitianus
BORN: Rome, 51
RULED: Emperor, 81–96
DIED: Assassinated, Rome, 96

EVERYONE LOVED TITUS—everyone, that is, except his brother, Domitian. Insecure and ambitious, Domitian was kept away from important positions of authority by his father and brother, thus indicating the level of trust they had in him. He was convinced he had greater ability than Titus and resented his father's preference for his elder brother, doing everything he could to undermine Titus. During his brother's brief reign, he was involved in numerous plots against the emperor, stirring up disaffection among the praetorians whenever possible. In the end, he did not have to wait long to acquire supreme authority throughout the empire.

Titus's triumphal procession through Rome after the capture and plunder of Jerusalem

Yet against all expectations, his reign was not a disaster, at least not initially. Domitian was by instinct an autocrat, and his administration was characterised by enormous energy and ability. He focused his attention on the needs of the provinces, making sure his officials did not abuse their authority. He desired military success in order to bolster his position and show he was just as gifted as his father and brother. His officers pushed forwards into Scotland, and he himself led an army into Germany to annex new territories. His long-term plans included the conquest of Scotland and Ireland, but his pursuit of the Dacian and Pannonian wars along the Danube were his first priority. His rash decision to widen the front in Dacia, though initially successful, ended in defeat and a hastily made peace with the Dacians. However, this did not stop him celebrating a triumph and receiving an ovation for his deeds.

> **Your Master and your God bids that this be done.**
>
> DOMITIAN

Domitian's descent into paranoia and tyranny originated with his relationship with the Senate. The members of that august body were the elite of the Roman nobility, with some senatorial families stretching back to the foundation of the republic. By contrast, the Flavians were upstart nobodies who through luck had managed to secure the imperial crown. While the senators were prepared to tolerate Vespasian and Titus, since they worked co-operatively with the Senate, they were unwilling to endure the autocratic approach of Domitian, who lorded it over his social betters. Knowing what discontent his reign was generating, Domitian began to crack down on enemies, both real and imagined. His reign again saw the rise of spies, informers and treason trials, with the inevitable execution of senators.

By the end of his reign, Domitian believed that all of Rome was plotting to overthrow him, and so he had the walls of the rooms and columns in the imperial palace covered with reflective materials so that he could see if assassins were lurking nearby. He also refused to eat mushrooms, but it did him no good. He was by all accounts a difficult man to live with, and so it should come as no surprise that when there actually was a conspiracy, his wife, Domitia, was at the centre of it. Theirs had been a long and difficult marriage, with a divorce and reconciliation along the way, as well as Domitian's affair with his own niece. It was typical that it was Domitia who was charged with adultery, accused of having an affair with an actor by the name of Paris. By 96 she had had enough, as had a number of court officials. Domitian died at his desk, killed by a group of men who approached with news that there was a conspiracy against him.

While the deaths of Vespasian and Titus saw them deified, the Senate cursed Domitian's memory and his name was erased from public monuments. His soldiers mourned him, however, grateful that he had increased their pay by a third.

SATURNINUS

OVERLY SENSITIVE

NAME: Lucius Antonius Saturninus
BORN: Unknown
RULED: Usurper, 89
DIED: Assumed killed in battle, Moguntiacum (Mainz), Germania, 89

SOME PEOPLE JUST DID not get Domitian's sense of humour. One of these was the legate of Upper Germany, Antonius Saturninus. He was the typical military man of the first century, born most likely somewhere in the western provinces, and he probably held various posts under the favour of Vespasian. Annoyed by Domitian's reference to him as a male prostitute, not to mention

Domitian's humiliating efforts against the Pannonian and Dacian tribes, this former Roman consul declared himself emperor at Mainz, backed by the two legions stationed at the garrison.

The rebellion did not last long. Saturninus had asked the Chatti, a German tribe to the north, to bring aid, but the sudden thawing of the Rhine River prevented their joining him. Isolated, Saturninus was in no position to overcome the forces arrayed against him and was defeated in battle by the legate of Lower Germany. His reign was over in just twenty-four days, with his name subsequently erased from all official records.

NERVA

THE GREAT SURVIVOR

NAME: Marcus Cocceius Nerva
BORN: Narnia, Italy, 30
RULED: Emperor, 96–98
DIED: Of natural causes, Rome, 98

WITH NERVA'S ACCESSION, we once again find an emperor with highborn ancestry and impeccable breeding. Spending his whole life in close proximity to the imperial court, he developed the skills to survive a number of regime changes with his head still attached to his body. Initially, he came to Nero's attention by uncovering a plot to murder the emperor in 65, but after Nero's fall he managed to convince the Flavians that he was their man through and through. Having luck on his side, Nerva alerted Domitian to the revolt of Saturninus, for which he was made consul for a second time. Yet by Domitian's final years, even Nerva was falling out of favour and he was only saved by the emperor's unexpected death.

Though Nerva was not mentioned as part of the conspiracy against Domitian, the fact that he became emperor on the same day as Domitian's assassination does raise suspicions. It certainly did in the minds of the Praetorian Guard, who were very angry about the death of Domitian. The praetorians confronted the new emperor, held a sword to his neck and demanded that he hand over the murderers to them as a gesture of good faith. The sixty-six-year-old had no choice but to agree to their demands and he was forced to give thanks publicly for their patriotic actions. Nothing demonstrated the weakness of the emperor more clearly than this.

Yet Nerva was nothing if not a survivor. The wily old fox turned the tables on the praetorians by declaring as his successor the legate of Upper Germany, the military man Trajan. By this act, he secured the loyalty of the troops and ensured that the praetorians would not again attack him and risk incurring the wrath of the legions. With the empire and the succession thus stabilised, Nerva was enjoying a private audience when he suffered a stroke on 1 January 98. Shortly afterwards he passed away, happy in the knowledge he had steadied the ship of state after the terror of Domitian's final years and passed it on to a worthy successor.

TRAJAN

THE ROMAN ALEXANDER

NAME: Marcus Ulpius Traianus
BORN: Italica, Baetica (modern-day Spain), 53
RULED: Emperor, 98–117
DIED: Of oedema, Selinus, Cilicia (Asia Minor), 117

TO HIS CONTEMPORARIES Trajan was the embodiment of what being a Roman was all about. In him, they saw the spirit of Scipio Africanus, Pompey the Great and Julius Caesar made flesh again, as his policy of conquest looked back to the glory days of the Roman Republic. It was quite ironic, therefore, that the man who extended the empire to its largest size was about as 'Roman' as Hannibal from Carthage or Herod from Judaea. Trajan was a native of Spain and, though he possessed Italian ancestors, was the first born outside Italy to attain the principate. His rise demonstrates quite clearly how effective the Romanisation of the provinces was, as well as giving the first concrete sign of the decline of the old Italian and Roman families, and the loss of the vigour that had maintained the ideals of Roman society. Very soon, Italy would become a backwater and the fate of the empire would rest in the hands of provincials and barbarians. But that is in the future.

Trajan was career military and had worked his way up the military and political ladder since his twenties. He was one of the army commanders summoned by Domitian to crush the rebellion of Saturninus. Trajan lived and breathed military life, and his unexpected elevation as Nerva's successor did nothing to change that. He did not rush to Rome on hearing the news, but assumed the imperial office at Colonia Agrippinensis in Germany.

After settling the affairs of Nerva and establishing a cordial relationship with the Senate, Trajan began the conquest of Dacia in the third year of his reign. He, like many others, was appalled by Domitian's ignominious treaty with the Dacian king and was determined to

Roman legion, led by the 2nd Pannonian cavalry, crosses the Danube River on a pontoon bridge

recover Roman pride. That king, Decebalus, mocked the Romans for their inability to conquer his lands and demanded that they keep paying the annual tribute he had extracted from Domitian. Trajan had long admired Julius Caesar and his brilliant Gallic campaigns, and he wished to surpass the great Roman general. It took him two years to subdue the fierce Dacians, but their king finally sued for peace when the legions approached his capital. Trajan returned to Rome to celebrate a triumph, but the Dacians again attacked, forcing the emperor to return and finish the job. This time Trajan was determined to ensure that the Dacians would not rise again. Building a mammoth stone bridge across the Danube River, he launched a massive co-ordinated attack against the Dacians. By the time it was over in 106, Dacia was the newest province of the empire, and the head of King Decebalus was on display in the Roman Forum.

> **I would definitely have crossed over to India, if I were still a young man.**
>
> TRAJAN

Trajan's other idol was Alexander the Great, but it was not until the final years of his reign that an opportunity arose for him to emulate Alexander's achievements. The Parthians, a people whose 300-year-old empire was centred in present-day Iran, coveted Rome's eastern provinces, which lay adjacent to their lands. They had been at peace with Rome for over fifty years but had recently toppled Armenia, a client state of Rome. Trajan took the opportunity to invade Armenia in 114, and the Parthians sued for peace. Wanting a permanent solution to this problem, however, Trajan decided to complete the conquest of Parthia. He invaded upper Mesopotamia (modern-day Iraq) and Assyria, and finally captured Ctesiphon, the Parthian capital, in 116. His desire to emulate the great Alexander was overpowering; having been the first Roman emperor to set foot in Babylon, he asked to go to the mouth of the Tigris River to see the ocean. Once there, spying a boat in the distance, he declared that he too would have liked to march to India. He may well have achieved his aim, but events soon turned against him. First, there was a revolt in Mesopotamia—during which the Parthians recaptured their capital—and he only managed to put it down with great cost and effort. Then more dire news arrived—an uprising in Judaea, revolts in Africa and Britain, and new troubles on the Danube. Trajan, now in his sixties, felt old age creeping up on him. Wearily, he turned towards Rome, but he died while still in the east, his dream unfinished.

Yet it was not all about military conquests with Trajan. He undertook a large building program in Rome and the provinces (funded by enormous quantities of Dacian gold), and hosted many imperial games, including a four-month festival at the Colosseum in honour of his Dacian victories. During the course of these games, some eleven thousand animals were slaughtered for entertainment, and over ten thousand gladiators fought to the death. Millions attended and Trajan's popularity increased in leaps and bounds. While he was mostly disciplined in his personal life, he was a heavy drinker when not on campaign and he had a fondness for young boys that he indulged regularly. Yet everyone forgave him because of his obvious talents. Many would claim his heritage—even the Catholic Church in the Middle Ages had a belief that Pope Gregory I, through divine intercession, had resurrected Trajan from the dead and baptised him into the Christian faith.

With the reign of Trajan, the Roman Empire reached a turning point. Never again would it command the same territorial reach. Rarely would an emperor strike out to conquer new lands for the empire, for Trajan's successors were happy to maintain the existing borders or perhaps reconquer territory that had been lost. Though the empire would prove unable to hold its conquests and in time would lose many of its provinces, it would always look back to the reign of Trajan in its endless attempts to once again rule over all it surveyed.

HADRIAN

MICRO-MANAGER

NAME: Publius Aelius Hadrianus
BORN: Italica, Baetica, 76
RULED: Emperor, 117–138
DIED: Of natural causes, Baiae, Italy, 138

WHERE TRAJAN REPRESENTED the Roman military ideal, Hadrian epitomised the other side of the Roman mind—a love of order and good government. For the new emperor, though, this aptitude for efficient administration manifested itself in an irritating micro-managerial approach that made him very hard to work for or live with. It also gave him a very pragmatic approach to the demands of government, and in one of his first imperial decrees he abandoned Trajan's recent conquests of Mesopotamia and Assyria, deeming them too expensive in men and gold to maintain.

From this, many have deduced that Hadrian did not esteem Trajan, or that he was not militarily inclined. Neither was true. He was Trajan's cousin and at the age of ten he had been adopted by Trajan when his natural father died. He later married Trajan's grandniece Sabina, before Trajan, on his deathbed, made him his heir,

THE EMPIRE IN THE FIRST CENTURY

The Roman Empire was a complex state, consisting of a number of territories, both provinces and client states, across Europe, Asia and Africa. Under the principate, the empire was nominally governed by both the emperor and the Senate, each with specific responsibilities and jurisdictions. The provinces were classified as either senatorial or imperial.

ITALY As the heartland of the empire, Italy was managed directly by the Senate. There were no troops garrisoned in Italy apart from the Praetorian Guard, which was under the authority of the emperor.

SENATORIAL PROVINCES The governor (*proconsul*) was appointed by the Senate and the post was granted to senators who were ex-consuls or ex-praetors, depending on the particular province. Legions were stationed in these provinces.

IMPERIAL PROVINCES These were governed in the emperor's name by either legates or procurators (except Egypt, which was governed by a prefect). The legates generally managed the provinces where legions were stationed. In provinces with one legion, the legate was responsible for the provincial administration and was also the chief judicial officer and commander-in-chief of the military forces based in the province. In provinces with more than one legion, each legion was commanded by its own legate with praetorian *imperium*, while the province as a whole was commanded by a legate with consular *imperium*, who had general command over the entire army stationed there, as well as administering the province as a proconsul. These men were generally of senatorial rank. The procurators, on the other hand, managed the smaller imperial provinces where few or no troops were stationed, and they were sourced from the equestrian order.

CLIENT STATES These managed their own affairs under their own kings but had treaties with the Romans and were protected by the legions. They were those regions associated with the empire that Rome did not want to manage directly. This was the favoured position during the republic, but they were gradually absorbed into the empire as provinces.

highlighting his intimate connections with the imperial family. Hadrian also had a distinguished military career and in 117 was the commander of the army in Syria. However, he acted always from a position of prudence, and his approach to government was to be as risk averse as possible. He was also moderate in his private life, never overindulging—though one of his favourite foods was *tetrafarmacum*, made up of pheasant, a cow's udder, ham and pastry.

His prudence also had a darker side. Four of Trajan's most senior and able generals met mysterious deaths in the first few weeks of Hadrian's reign. It was later circulated that these men had been involved in a plot against his life, but many had doubts—not least the Senate. It was clear that Hadrian did not tolerate rivals, and this included the Senate, which found its traditional oversight of Italy removed and given to the imperial bureaucracy. The senators never forgave this slight.

Hadrian was the first emperor to undertake an extended tour of the empire, to get first-hand experience of the true condition of the provinces. Consequently, he was the first emperor since Augustus who had a firm grasp of the needs of the empire as a whole, and not merely those of Italy. He undertook extensive judicial and administrative reforms, codifying Roman civil law and beginning to move responsibilities away from military officers and governors to a centralised bureaucracy.

Hadrian was married to Sabina for nearly forty years, but they had no children. Possibly this had something to do with Hadrian's relationship with a young man called Antonius. The emperor was on a tour of Egypt together with his wife and a large entourage that included the young and beautiful Antonius when, during the trip up the Nile, Antonius fell into the river and drowned. Rumours abounded that the young man had committed suicide after a lovers' quarrel. Hadrian's visceral grief and subsequent actions seemed to confirm this interpretation. He had the boy deified before founding and naming a city after him, and statues of Rome's newest god began to appear throughout the empire. This was not an unusual event for the Greek east of the empire, but in Rome it caused a scandal and was further evidence, or so the old-style Romans declared, of the corrupting influence of the soft, effeminate Greeks and the unhealthy impact they were having on the empire, and on Hadrian in particular. It was not for nothing that they gave him the nickname 'the little Greek'.

By the final years of his reign, Hadrian was slowly dying and everyone knew it, yet he had not nominated a successor. Therefore, in 136, his eye turned to young Lucius Ceionius Commodus, who had nothing to recommend him apart from his good looks and political connections. Frivolous and decadent, his accession would have been disastrous for the empire but, luckily, his health was poorer than the emperor's and he died at the beginning of 138. This left Hadrian in a quandary, and in haste he turned to an elderly senator, Antoninus. The price of his nomination was to be his adoption of both Commodus's young son, Lucius Ceionius Commodus, and the nephew of Antoninus's wife, Marcus Aurelius, thereby securing the succession. By July, Hadrian, one of the best of Roman emperors, was dead.

ANTONINUS PIUS

THE DUTIFUL ONE

NAME: Titus Aurelius Fulvius
Boionius Arrius Antoninus
BORN: Lanuvium, Italy, 86
RULED: Emperor, 138–161
DIED: Of fever, Lorium, Italy, 161

NOT EVERYONE WAS UNHAPPY that Hadrian was dead. The Senate, in particular, had felt the ageing emperor's moodiness and suspicion and wanted to condemn his memory. It the end it was his successor, Antoninus, who ensured that Hadrian was honoured. In return, it granted Antoninus the name of 'Pius' for his filial devotion.

The new emperor had had a long and distinguished career, serving as quaestor, praetor, consul and proconsul, and had dutifully performed his obligations in both his public and private lives. A polished speaker, dignified and very learned, he restored a harmonious relationship with the Senate and continued Hadrian's peaceful foreign policy.

> **I must not begin my career as your leader with such deeds.**
>
> ANTONINUS PIUS

Where Hadrian had a vast amount of military experience that he chose not to exercise during his principate, Antoninus was the first emperor since Nero not to have significant military training. He was fortunate, then, that his reign was the most peaceful that the empire was ever to know, to the point where he did not leave Italy once during his twenty-three-year reign, unlike the restless Hadrian. His governors and legates smoothly dealt with any minor problems arising at the frontiers, with his only input coming in the form of imperial correspondence. Without foreign wars to finance, the people avoided heavy taxation, and there was no need for excessive recruitment of men. He was a fair emperor and did not punish wrongdoers severely but was moderate in his approach. Nor did he indulge in egotistical and mammoth building projects or spend the empire's wealth on a decadent lifestyle—what little building he did was to complete those projects begun by his predecessors.

By the time Antoninus died quietly in 161, he left an empire at peace and a full treasury. Loved by the people and the Senate, his reign was soon regarded as a golden age and he as the model Roman emperor, especially during the troubles that were shortly to descend on the empire.

MARCUS AURELIUS
THE PHILOSOPHER EMPEROR

NAME: Marcus Aelius Aurelius Verus
BIRTH NAME: Marcus Annius Verus
BORN: Rome, 121
RULED: Emperor, 161–180
DIED: Of natural causes, Vindobona (Vienna), Pannonia, 180

WHAT MARCUS AURELIUS wanted more than anything was a reign like that of his predecessor's. Growing up as Antoninus's heir, he was trained as a kind and benevolent administrator, living and ruling by the principles of the Stoic philosophy that he so admired. What he got was unceasing warfare raging across the whole empire, but he accepted stoically the role that the gods had selected for him and, strapping on his armour, rode to the empire's defence.

Nominated as Antoninus's eventual successor ever since the final year of Hadrian's reign, Marcus Aurelius served his apprenticeship under the firm yet kindly hand of Antoninus and was ready to take up his burden in 161. Almost immediately, troubles broke out in Britain, on the Danube and in the east, as a result of pressures that had been growing during Antoninus's peaceful reign.

The Parthian War was the most serious, and Marcus Aurelius sent his colleague Lucius Verus, Antoninus's other adopted son, to deal with the situation. After a conflict lasting five years, Verus was to return to Rome triumphant, but in so doing his army brought with it a plague that devastated the empire. The year was 166 and a weakened empire was unable to contain the Germanic tribes that smashed through the Danubian defences. It was not until 169 that the emperor was able to gather enough resources to deal with the invaders, who managed to penetrate Italy. Barring the brief occasional return, he was to spend the next eleven years at the war front.

For a man who had never undertaken any serious military service, Marcus Aurelius soon demonstrated that he had a keen military mind with sound tactical planning.

Marcus Aurelius granting clemency to captured prisoners during his German Wars

THE HIGH EMPIRE

So well did he take to his new role that when he died the legions grieved deeply, mourning the loss of such a warrior. He quickly forced the German tribes out of Italy, pushing them back to the Danube, where he hammered them mercilessly, grinding away at them year after year. He had hit upon a plan to annex two new provinces in the northeast, Marcomannia and Sarmatia, which correspond to the Hungarian plain and the area to the west of the Black Sea, but two events derailed his plans. The first was an uprising in 175 by one of his generals, Avidius Cassius, an event that forced him to make peace with some of the tribes. After neutralising this threat, he returned to the front and came within a whisker of achieving his aims, but he soon became ill and died in 180, trying desperately

RUINS FROM THE HIGH EMPIRE

THE MAUSOLEUM OF AUGUSTUS, ROME (Augustus) This large tomb on the northern side of the Tiber was built by Augustus after the battle of Actium in 31 BC. Circular in design, it housed the remains of Augustus and many of his immediate family, as well as those of the emperors Tiberius, Claudius and Nerva. It was sacked in 410 by the Goths, who stole the urns.

VILLA JOVIS, CAPRI (Tiberius) The villa from which Tiberius ruled during the later part of his reign, the Villa Jovis is situated at the top of Mount Tiberius on the island of Capri. Rumours persisted that people were thrown from its height after they incurred Tiberius's wrath. Fair amounts of the building's lower levels remain.

THE COLOSSEUM, ROME (Vespasian) The Colosseum, the common name for what the Romans called the Flavian Amphitheatre, was the largest amphitheatre built during the Roman Empire. Originally capable of seating around eighty thousand spectators, it became famous for gladiatorial contests and other public spectacles, such as mock sea battles, animal hunts, executions and re-enactments of famous battles. It survived various reuses in the Middle Ages, including a time as a castle.

THE ARCH OF TITUS, ROME (Titus) Commemorating Titus's successful siege and capture of Jerusalem during the Judaean War, the arch bears reliefs depicting scenes of Titus's numerous achievements during his reign. Standing next to the Colosseum, at the southeastern entrance to the Roman Forum on the old Via Sacra, it survives intact. At one point during the Middle Ages it was incorporated into defensive fortifications.

THE COLUMN OF TRAJAN, ROME (Trajan) Built to celebrate Trajan's victories in the Dacian Wars, the column is covered with carvings depicting scenes of his two campaigns. Located in Trajan's Forum, for centuries it had a statue of Trajan atop it, but this disappeared in the Middle Ages and was replaced by a statue of St Peter.

THE MAUSOLEUM OF HADRIAN, ROME (Hadrian) Known today as the Castel Sant'Angelo, this was originally the tomb of the emperor Hadrian. Erected on the right-hand side of the Tiber River, it contained the ashes of Hadrian and all subsequent emperors up to Caracalla. Eventually converted into a fortress and incorporated into the city's defensive walls, it was used by the popes as a castle during the Middle Ages, before becoming their residence and finally a prison. Legend has it that in 590 the Archangel Michael appeared on top of the castle sheathing his sword, signalling that the plague had ended.

to convince his son, Lucius Aurelius Commodus, to stay for the one additional year needed to complete the subjugation of the tribes. However, it was not to be, and Rome's enemies survived to fight another day.

Yet not a day went by during those eleven long years that he did not dwell upon his one true love—philosophy. Spending every spare moment he had on the front writing, he produced the *Meditations*, a personal work in Greek, part diary and part manual on Stoic philosophy. It is a deeply influential work on how to live one's life through practical activities and the importance of public duty. With its understanding of human nature, it has been revered by thinkers and philosophers throughout the centuries. This approach to life and belief meant that Marcus Aurelius was a tolerant individual, who acknowledged the legitimacy of other people's beliefs, including those of the Christians, to such an extent that the Christian writer Tertullian called him a friend of Christianity.

> **Waste no more time arguing about what a good man should be. Be one.**
>
> MARCUS AURELIUS

Then what is to be made of his greatest failure—his decision not to continue the practice of adopting a worthy Roman to wear the purple but to invest all his hopes in a worthless and indolent son? It is inconceivable that this man, whose belief in Stoicism led him to sacrifice all personal gain for the good of the state, would abandon the state for that most evolutionary of emotions—paternal pride. It was probably the first decision he had ever made that took into account his own desire; it was a choice that future generations would rue. It revealed, finally, that behind the cold facade of the philosopher was a father, as human as everyone else.

LUCIUS VERUS

THE PLAYBOY PRINCE

NAME: Lucius Aurelius Verus
BIRTH NAME: Lucius Ceionius Commodus
BORN: Unknown, 130
RULED: Co-emperor, 161–169
DIED: Of a stroke, Altinum, Italy, 169

LIKE FATHER, LIKE SON. Antoninus Pius had adopted Lucius Verus (along with Marcus Aurelius) as part of the deal with Hadrian that secured his path to the throne. Lucius was the biological son of Hadrian's first choice of successor, Lucius Ceionius Commodus, who died before Hadrian. This man had had little military experience and lived a flamboyant and luxurious lifestyle focused on fulfilling his own pleasures. His son inherited these traits in abundance.

When Marcus Aurelius inherited the throne, against all expectations he nominated Lucius Verus as co-emperor, an event that had no precedent in the principate. To cement their working relationship, Marcus Aurelius married his daughter Lucilla to the handsome and vain Verus.

By now Verus had quite a reputation as a playboy, with a string of lovers, married and unmarried, and a love of partying. Marcus Aurelius soon put a stop to that, as one of Verus's first duties was to oversee the Parthian campaign in the east. On his way to the front, he paid visits to Corinth and Athens, where he continued his enjoyable lifestyle. Concerned that he might not take his command seriously, Marcus Aurelius appointed Avidius Cassius to command the forces in Syria. Though he continued to indulge himself, Verus surprised everyone by showing some efficiency in selecting the correct generals to run the war. Within five years, the Romans had won, mostly because of Cassius, and Verus returned to Rome loaded with spoils and titles from his victories.

This was not the only thing he returned from the east with. A plague came back with the victorious troops and crippled the empire for a number of years. Verus also took his lifestyle to a completely new level after exposure to the decadent eastern provinces, and he continued this lavish lifestyle in Rome under the nose of his co-emperor. What Marcus Aurelius needed was an excuse to get him out of the capital, and this came with the German wars of 167. He took Verus with him to the warfront, where Verus died in 169, worn out by the toughness of the remote frontier life.

AVIDIUS CASSIUS

COMMITTED TO THE PATH

NAME: Gaius Avidius Cassius
BORN: Unknown, 130
RULED: Usurper, 175
DIED: Murdered, Syria, 175

AVIDIUS CASSIUS, LEGATE OF SYRIA, was the first usurper in nearly a hundred years, and a harbinger of things to come. He was one of Marcus Aurelius's most trusted lieutenants, showing great courage and leadership during the Parthian War and capturing some of the most important cities in Mesopotamia. He was also renowned for the strictness and discipline that he enforced on his troops. Rumour had it that he was related to Cassius, an assassin of Julius Caesar, on his mother's side.

Hearing the premature news that Marcus Aurelius had died while on campaign on the Danubian frontier, Cassius's troops declared him emperor in 175. When Cassius discovered his error, it was too late and he was firmly committed to the very end, no matter the cost.

The Senate formally declared Cassius an enemy of the Senate and the people of Rome, as Marcus Aurelius quickly negotiated a peace with the Sarmatian people and began his march on Syria. Cassius quickly discovered that he had no support among his neighbouring legates and governors, and so his troops murdered him after a reign of three months. As a gesture of apology, they sent Cassius's head to Marcus Aurelius, but Cassius's brief reign pointed the way to the future. The next century would see the empire brought to its knees by the legions and almost destroyed by barbarians and usurpers, before the rise of a new breed of emperors who would once again wear the title of *imperator* with pride.

THE CRISIS OF THE THIRD CENTURY

(180–260)

The limits of the Roman empire still extended from the Western Ocean to the Tigris, and from Mount Atlas to the Rhine and the Danube. To the undiscerning eye [the emperors appeared] no less powerful than Hadrian or Augustus had formerly been. The form was still the same, but the animating health and vigour were fled. The discipline of the legions, which alone, after the extinction of every other virtue, had propped the greatness of the state, was corrupted by the ambition, or relaxed by the weakness, of the emperors. The strength of the frontiers, which had always consisted in arms rather than in fortifications, was insensibly undermined; and the fairest provinces were left exposed to the barbarians, who soon discovered the decline of the Roman empire.

EDWARD GIBBON
The Decline and Fall of the Roman Empire, 1880

FOLLOWING PAGE: Crowd with thumbs downwards signifying death for defeated gladiator

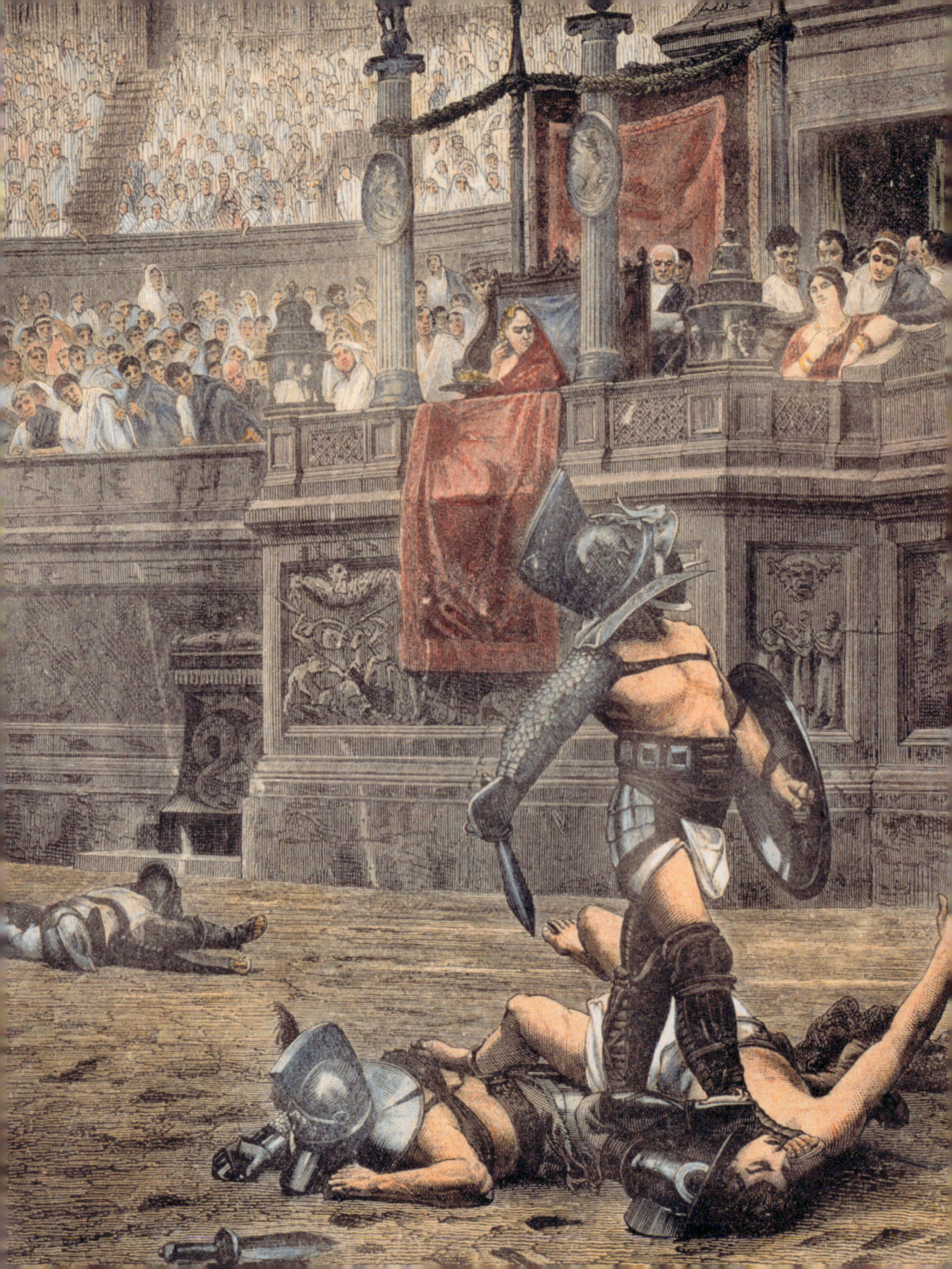

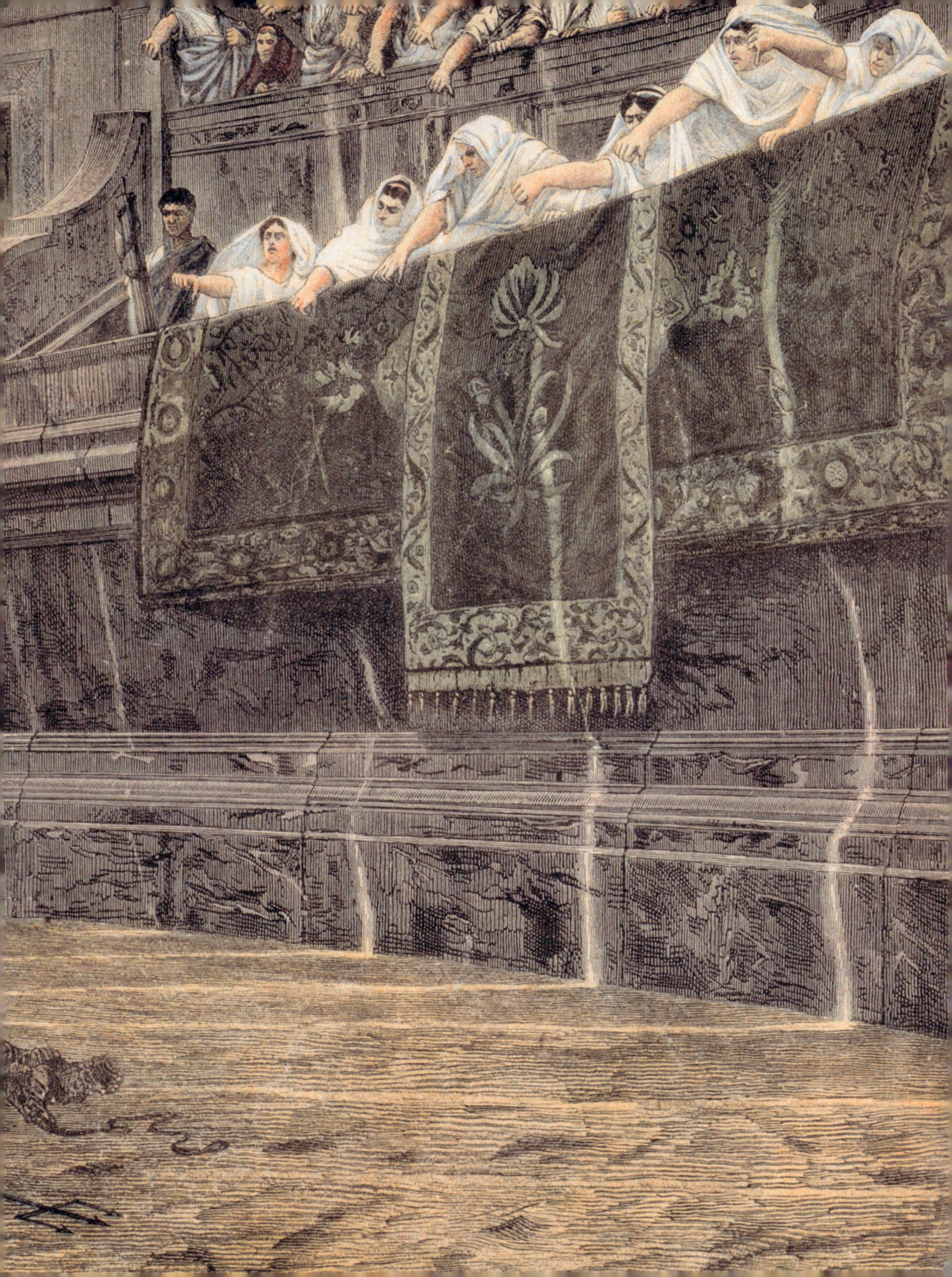

COMMODUS

THE GLADIATOR

NAME: Marcus Aurelius Commodus
Antoninus Augustus
BIRTH NAME: Lucius Aurelius Commodus Antoninus
BORN: Lanuvium, Italy, 161
RULED: Co-emperor, 176–180; sole emperor, 180–192
DIED: Assassinated, Rome, 192

SONS OFTEN REBEL against everything their fathers stood for, and this was certainly true for Commodus, son of Marcus Aurelius. How does one live up to the expectations of a father who was considered the model Roman emperor? Commodus discovered soon enough that he could not, spending his youth enduring comparisons to his father. Inevitably, he abandoned his father's policies and instituted his own, regardless of the wisdom of this course. It speaks volumes that by the end of his reign he had dropped 'Antoninus' from the official name he had adopted on his accession to the throne, becoming Caesar Lucius Aelius Aurelius Commodus Augustus.

One of his first acts was to end his father's German wars as quickly as possible, on the most lenient terms imaginable. No matter that his brother-in-law begged him to fight for one more year to finish the job, or that the advisors whom Marcus Aurelius had provided for his son also counselled otherwise. A new reign inevitably attracted new companions, hopeful of promotion at the imperial court, and they all wondered why he—and by extension they—were enduring the hardships of the frontier when the pleasures of Rome awaited them.

> **Fortune has given the empire not to an adopted successor but to me.**
>
> COMMODUS

Upon his triumphant return to the capital, Commodus did try to rule like his father, but one fateful day brought everything undone. His sister Lucilla had not recovered from her displacement as the 'First Lady' when he had married. In 182 she planned to kill him and rule through a lover, but Commodus was saved by the assailant's pre-emptive shout, 'The Senate sends you this!' These fateful words turned an indolent young man into a cowardly and cruel tyrant, and the Senate would bear the brunt of his hatred and paranoia. His first victims were his sister and his wife, banished to Capri and eventually executed.

Abandoning any pretence to be a model ruler, Commodus gave himself up to a life of pleasures, indulging his fantasies with young boys and girls, with

Commodus, in the guise of Hercules

IMPERIAL TITLES

Throughout the empire's existence, various titles were used to identify the emperor. The earliest one, and the one that lasted in the west until Latin was supplanted as Europe's universal language, was the term *imperator*, from which the English word *emperor* is derived. It was originally an honorific title given to a military commander by his troops on the field after an especially great victory. This was one of the titles conferred on Augustus by the Senate, but he converted it into a permanent title and restricted it almost exclusively to the *princeps*.

Soon, two additional titles were added—*Caesar* and *Augustus*. Originally these were names given to the first emperors when they were adopted into the imperial family, stemming as they do from Julius Caesar and the emperor Augustus. Within a century, however, they became titles the emperor was entitled to use and they were added to the names of many of the emperors upon their accession to the throne, usually as an *agnomen* but sometimes as a *praenomen* (*Caesar* Marcus Ulpius Nerva Traianus Augustus) or a *cognomen* (Titus Flavius *Caesar* Vespasianus Augustus).

Over time, however, *Caesar* ceased to be a title for the ruling emperor and instead became a title held by the heir to the imperial throne; when he became emperor he then used the title *Augustus*. During the period of the tetrarchy, *Caesar* was the title bestowed on the two junior emperors, while the two senior emperors were called *Augusti*.

In the Greek east, the emperors at Constantinople had their own variations on these titles that were used once Latin fell into disuse. *Imperator* was translated as *Autokrator*, *Augustus* became *Sebastos*, and *Caesar* turned into *Kaisar*. By the eighth century, however, these terms for the emperor were supplanted by a new term—*Basileus*, a Greek word for king. Over time, *Caesar* was translated into other languages to signify an emperor or king, originally because these rulers—the Russian *Czars*, the Bulgarian *Tsars*—claimed that they were successors of the Romans. Later it simply became the accepted term for an emperor. The Ottoman use of *Kayser*, the German word *Kaiser*, old English *Cāsere*, Slovene *Cesar* and Icelandic *Keisari* are all derived from Caesar.

---

all real power exercised through the praetorian prefect. In the final years of his reign, Commodus's sense of reality began to fracture. Beginning to dress like the god Hercules, wearing a lion skin and carrying a club, he claimed to be the new founder of the capital, renaming Rome as Colonia Lucia Annia Commodiana as well as renaming the months of the year after his names. However, his chief ambition was to win fame as a gladiator, and he frequently appeared in the arena, riding in chariot races and fighting wild beasts. To fund these festivities, Commodus charged senators with treason and confiscated their property.

For his crowning achievement, he planned to assume the consulate on 1 January 193, wearing a gladiator's costume. The night before this event, his mistress and the praetorian prefect, believing that Commodus was planning to have them killed, had him assassinated by an athlete, Narcissus, who strangled Commodus in his bath. The Senate cursed Commodus's memory, but the soldiers, who quickly forgot his tyranny and remembered only his financial liberality and the reduction in military discipline during his reign, soon mourned his passing.

PERTINAX
STRICT DISCIPLINARIAN

NAME: Publius Helvius Pertinax
BORN: Alba Pompeia, Italy, 126
RULED: Emperor, 193
DIED: Murdered, Rome, 193

WHAT THE PRAETORIAN GUARD wanted was an easily dominated, gentle old man; what they got was a cranky and severe disciplinarian. Pertinax's origins were lowly. The son of a freedman, he became a teacher of grammar and joined the army after a midlife crisis in his thirties. He showed a great deal of talent during Marcus Aurelius's Parthian and German wars and he put down a revolt in Britain against the emperor Commodus, during which one legion rebelled and attacked him, leaving him for dead. When he recovered, he dealt with the mutineers ruthlessly, gaining a reputation as a fierce disciplinarian. In 192 Pertinax was serving as urban prefect in Rome and is assumed to have been involved in the conspiracy that removed Commodus from power. After the murder, he was brought to the Praetorian Camp and proclaimed emperor the following morning.

Pertinax would have made an excellent emperor but for one flaw—he could not adjust to the circumstances through which he found himself *princeps*. His instinct was to enforce discipline within the Praetorian Guard: this had been his preferred approach in the provinces. Labouring under the unaccustomed rigour of military discipline, the praetorians had their patience pushed to the limit when Pertinax discovered there was not enough gold in the treasury to pay them the accustomed gift upon the accession of an emperor. Within three months, they mutinied. Pertinax confronted them and was managing to overawe them when one soldier leapt forward and struck him. He fell under a host of sword thrusts and had his head stuck on a spear for good measure.

DIDIUS JULIANUS
MORE MONEY THAN SENSE

NAME: Marcus Didius Severus Julianus
BORN: Mediolanum (Milan), Italy, 137
RULED: Emperor, 193
DIED: Murdered, Rome, 193

THE PRAETORIANS NOW FOUND themselves in a most unusual situation, holding in their hands the most valuable commodity in the Roman world—the throne. They were conducting unenthusiastic negotiations with Pertinax's father-in-law, Sulpicianus, whom Pertinax had previously sent to quell the riot, when an elderly and wealthy senator, Didius Julianus, approached and proceeded to make a bid for their support. The praetorians decided the fairest way to choose who would be worthy of the throne was to have an auction. Backwards and forwards the bidding went, with Julianus the eventual winner, promising twenty-five thousand sesterces per soldier. The praetorians opened their camp, saluted him with the name 'Commodus', and proclaimed him emperor.

> But what evil have I done?
> Whom have I killed?
>
> DIDIUS JULIANUS'S FINAL WORDS

Didius Julianus was not without talent or skill. He had risen through various administrative positions, including the governorship of various provinces, and distinguished himself in some small military encounters with the German tribes. Yet his prestige among his fellow senators was poor—*miserly* and *overindulgent* were words frequently used to describe him.

Though his wife and daughter encouraged his bid for the principate, Julianus began to rue it almost immediately. The praetorians accompanied him to the

Senate House, where the senators met him in silence. The threat of military violence was enough to encourage the Senate to confirm the praetorians' choice, but the Roman people were not so obliging, pelting him with stones in public, and the praetorians, after spending their large reward, soon repented of their actions. The armies on the frontiers, wondering on whose behalf they were fighting, asserted their claim to appoint the *princeps* and three men were saluted as *imperator*: Pescennius Niger in Syria, Clodius Albinus in Britain, and Septimius Severus in Upper Pannonia. Severus was the first to reach Italy, and Julianus responded by issuing threats that no one took seriously. Severus demanded the praetorians stand down, and the Senate proclaimed him emperor and passed a death sentence on Julianus. Unloved and unmourned, Julianus was executed on 1 June 193.

not a man of keen and penetrating intelligence and his elevation as emperor only served to increase his pride and ambition. Moreover, he soon acquired a retinue of flatterers, who began comparing him to Alexander the Great. While his overall position was excellent, as he commanded at least five legions and controlled Egypt, there was one problem—Rome was in the hands of Septimius Severus.

Severus gathered his forces and crossed into the eastern provinces where Niger proceeded to lose the next four battles. After his first loss, he refused Severus's offer of exile, and by the final battle he had lost all support from the eastern provinces. That battle ended in disaster, forcing him to flee to his Parthian allies, but Severus's troops cut him down before he reached them. For Niger, speed had been essential: had he reached Rome ahead of his rival, or had he been a little faster to get to Parthia, his end might not have been so bloody.

PESCENNIUS NIGER

NOT FAST ENOUGH

NAME: Gaius Pescennius Niger
BORN: Aquinum, Italy, c. 140
RULED: Usurper, 193–194
DIED: Killed, Antiochia ad Orontem
(Antioch), Syria, 194

THE ROMAN WORLD, for centuries ruled from Italy, could easily support a rival ruler in the rich provinces of the east, if one chose to set himself up there. Marc Antony had shown this in the days of Augustus's youth, and Pescennius Niger, almost two centuries later, was to demonstrate it again. The legate of Syria, he was surprised to discover that not only was the capital in chaos, but the crowds in Rome were calling for him to return and overthrow Didius Julianus.

Encouraged by his apparent popularity, Niger had himself proclaimed emperor in Antioch—not bad for the son of a minor Italian equestrian family. Niger was

CLODIUS ALBINUS

NOT DETERMINED ENOUGH

NAME: Decimus Clodius Albinus
BORN: Hadrumetum, North Africa, c. 150
RULED: Usurper, 193–197
DIED: Suicide, Lugdunum (Lyon), Lugdunensis, 197

THE MOST ILLUSTRIOUS of the imperial contenders after Pertinax's assassination was Clodius Albinus, of a wealthy senatorial family. After efficient service on the Danubian frontier, he had been rewarded with the position of proconsular legate in Britain and was proclaimed emperor by his army, which consisted of three legions. Albinus quickly contacted the Senate and managed to obtain some support. However, the recognition of Severus quickly changed the political landscape.

Albinus was considering his options when a letter arrived from Severus, offering him the title of Caesar, and thus making him his heir. Not being in Rome and commanding fewer legions than Severus, he was overly cautious and agreed, perhaps naively believing that Severus would keep his word. For two years, Albinus remained in Britain while Severus tackled his other rival, Niger. Though Albinus was later accused of conspiring against Severus, the fact that he made no move from the remote province to secure power in Rome during this time disproves the accusation.

By the time Albinus realised his mistake, it was too late. Severus returned from the east much stronger, having made his own son, Caracalla, Caesar. Goaded, Albinus declared himself emperor again in 196, crossing the channel into Gaul with his troops and gaining the support of the governors in Gaul and Spain. The next two years saw perpetual warfare, with Albinus successful at first, but a series of indecisive battles hindered his drive towards Rome. Two battles in early 197 determined the fate of the civil war, the second, at Lyon, being one of the bloodiest in Roman history. Albinus's forces almost won the day, but a late surge crushed his hopes and his forces fled the battlefield. Trapped in a house by the Rhone River, rather than fall into enemy hands he took the traditional Roman solution—suicide.

SEPTIMIUS SEVERUS

THE MILITARY EMPEROR

NAME: Lucius Septimius Severus
BORN: Leptis Magna, North Africa, 145
RULED: Emperor, 193–211
DIED: Of natural causes, Eboricum (York), Britain, 211

THE ARRIVAL OF SEPTIMIUS Severus foreshadows a new epoch in the history of the Roman Empire: the arrival of the military monarchy. The son of a wealthy North African family, he gained a place in the Senate through his family connections and a rapid career path through the *cursus honorum*. However, he was not without ability, as the year 193 would show.

Maintaining the frontiers in Upper Pannonia (modern Austria and Hungary) where he was imperial legate, he took advantage of the political chaos in Rome. His troops declared him emperor and he quickly marched to the capital, where the praetorians, unwilling to defend the emperor they had created, quickly declared their loyalty to him. Outmanoeuvring his two other rivals for the throne, by 197 this North African was the undisputed Roman emperor.

Look after the soldiers; and disregard everyone else.

SEPTIMIUS SEVERUS

Given his rise to power, Severus needed to legitimise his rule quickly. Emperors normally ensured the succession by adopting their candidate into the imperial family, as had happened with Trajan and Hadrian. To achieve legitimacy, Severus engineered his posthumous adoption as the son of Marcus Aurelius and renamed his own son, Bassianus, as Marcus Aurelius Antoninus. He then undertook a campaign against the Parthians to demonstrate his worthiness to be Roman emperor, and in two short years he crushed them, sacking the two Parthian capitals (Seleucia and Ctesiphon) and returning northern Mesopotamia to Roman hands some eighty years after Trajan had originally conquered it. To honour his victory, the Senate granted him the title *Parthicus Maximus*.

Severus also required security, and in this he was far less agreeable. His first action was a sensible one— he disbanded the Praetorian Guard. The praetorians, created by Augustus to intimidate the Senate, had caused mayhem during times of crisis, their sale of the empire to Julianus being the last straw. Severus created a larger Praetorian Guard out of provincial soldiers from the legions, the theory being that active, hardened soldiers would not interfere in politics as the pampered and bored Italian court guards had. His next act, after Albinus's defeat, was a murderous purge of all his opponents in the Senate. This act set the tenor for all his dealings with the Senate over the course of his reign. Finally, he sought to placate another source of instability throughout the empire—the military.

To Severus, the military was all. The principate's source of power was its control of the legions and Severus made no move to disguise the fact that all power rested with the legions. He removed what little authority remained with the Senate, to the point where their only remaining function was to register approval of his measures. More and more posts traditionally filled by senators were now going to the rich equestrian class, and Rome began to fall under the direct control of the *princeps*.

To keep the support of the legions, Severus raised the pay of the troops, relaxed discipline by allowing soldiers to marry while they were on military service, and provided

Septimius Severus besieging Byzantium in 197

for centurions to advance into the officer ranks and the civil service. He turned Italy into a garrisoned province, no different from any other province within the empire. Finally, he increased the power of the praetorian prefect but formally divided the office into two posts, one with military functions and the other with civil ones. The civil office was filled by the most prestigious and eminent jurists, and the emperor came to rely on it to fulfil his traditional role of principal magistrate.

As his reign progressed, Severus still hungered for military glory. In response to an invasion of Roman Britain by the Caledonians in 208, he hit upon a plan to subjugate the whole of the island. By the time he died at York in 211, his task was still incomplete, and it was to his sons that he bequeathed the challenge.

In the same way that Augustus developed the template for the principate of the first two centuries, Severus created the conditions that dominated the empire in the coming century. The system of the principate effectively died during Severus's reign. In its place arose a military dictatorship; inherently unstable, it was to bring about the dissolution of the empire some fifty years later, during the reign of Gallienus.

Severus's reign was the longest and most stable for the next seventy years, as his military reforms, though successful in raising morale in the short term, proved disastrous in the longer term. The empire could not afford the increased military expenditure, and the relaxation of discipline was disastrous when the barbarians discovered it. Even Severus's annexation of Parthia destabilised the empire as the cost of maintaining the remote province added to the financial burden of the state. Additionally, the Parthian kingdom did not long survive its humiliation at Roman hands, and in its place a far more dangerous threat emerged—the Persian Sassanids. For all these reasons, the reign of Severus is a watershed in the history of the Roman emperors. The empire that would arise from the ashes of the third century crisis would be a very different beast from the one that gave it birth.

ANTONINUS CARACALLA

A MAN WITH AN INFERIORITY COMPLEX

NAME: Marcus Aurelius Antoninus
BIRTH NAME: Lucius Septimius Bassianus
BORN: Lugdunum (Lyon), Lugdunensis, 188
RULED: Co-emperor, 198–211;
sole emperor, 211–217
DIED: Murdered, Carrhae,
northern Mesopotamia, 217

CARACALLA MIGHT HAVE BEEN a much happier person if he had been an only child. Sharing the stage with the younger and more popular Geta embittered him and caused him to act irrationally throughout his young life, especially towards anyone who looked like they were taking his brother's side.

What began as sibling rivalry took an ominous turn with the elevation of Severus's impetuous and hot-blooded sons as joint emperors at York. Their first, and last, agreement was to end their father's campaign in Britain and return to their power bases in Rome as quickly as possible. Their relationship was so acrimonious that they even contemplated dividing the empire between them, but Caracalla's murder of Geta ended the squabble. This triggered a two-week orgy of bloodshed and destruction, with the murder of twenty thousand of Geta's supporters and sympathisers in the streets and palaces of the capital. It was also claimed that he murdered many others due to their pre-eminence or ability.

Caracalla did not take ridicule well. The only city that dared to mock him openly was Alexandria, during his visit in 215: the Alexandrians laughed at his claims that he had killed his brother in self-defence. Any mention of Geta was bound to set Caracalla off, and this was no exception. He had the prefect of Egypt and Alexandria's leading citizens executed, before allowing his soldiers to butcher as many of the city's residents as they could find. From then on, people kept their criticism to themselves, and their use of the emperor's nickname 'Caracalla'—a term of derision, referring to a cloak that the emperor liked to wear. No one dared call him that to his face—on all official correspondence his name was Antoninus.

Like his father, he was very fond of the military and he granted them another pay rise. To fund it he passed the Antoninian Constitution, which extended Roman citizenship to virtually all residents of the empire, thus increasing the numbers of people eligible to pay certain taxes. He also began the last of Rome's great imperial architectural achievements, the enormous Baths of Caracalla, putting further strain on the treasury.

> **Since you ask nothing of me,
> I don't have your confidence;
> if I haven't your confidence, you must be
> suspicious of me; if you're suspicious,
> you fear me; and if you're afraid of me,
> you must hate me.**
>
> CARACALLA

Caracalla was not without military ability, and when he was not expunging any mention of his brother's existence, he campaigned with the legions. After gaining victories against the German tribes, he transferred his attention to the Parthians. However, just before setting out for the war, he stopped off to perform some religious observances at the temple of the moon god at Carrhae. On his way back from the temple, and unfortunately while defecating during a toilet stop, he was killed by a disgruntled soldier, in a plot probably orchestrated by the praetorian prefect Macrinus. It was an ignoble end for a man who, though cruel and flawed, may well have stopped the rot that would consume the empire shortly after his death.

GETA
WOLF IN SHEEP'S CLOTHING

NAME: Publius Septimius Geta
BORN: Rome, 189
RULED: Co-emperor, 209–211
DIED: Murdered, Rome, 211

SENATORIAL PROPAGANDA after Caracalla's death painted Geta as a noble prince who was no match for the fierce beast that was Caracalla. The reality was very different. Where Caracalla was wild and tempestuous, Geta was subtle and insidious. Both were determined to be the victor in this contest of wills, and their increasingly violent confrontations required the constant intervention of their mother, Julia Domna.

For his part, Geta resented Caracalla gaining honours and advancement before him and did all he could to ensure that he would share in the imperial honours. He courted favour more successfully than his brother, so that when Caracalla tried to have himself crowned sole emperor after Severus died in 211, the legions insisted Geta become co-emperor, as he reminded them of his father. Caracalla was under no illusion who was the more popular prince.

Upon arrival in Rome, they tried to make the arrangement work, but mutual suspicion ground government activity to a halt. Caracalla then took the ultimate step of having his brother killed. He arranged a meeting of himself, Geta and their mother, and when the unsuspecting Geta arrived soldiers loyal to Caracalla attacked him. Suffering numerous wounds, Geta dragged himself to his mother and died in her arms. His name was then damned throughout the empire, as Caracalla wiped all trace of his existence from official records.

His personality may not have merited it, but death transformed Geta into a noble Roman youth cut down in the prime of life.

ROMAN EMPIRE AD 200

THE CRISIS OF THE THIRD CENTURY

MACRINUS

THE ACCOUNTANT

NAME: Marcus Opellius Macrinus
BORN: Caesarea, North Africa, c. 165
RULED: Emperor, 217–218
DIED: Executed, Cappadocia, Asia Minor, 218

MACRINUS WAS AMBITIOUS. A Moor from North Africa, he was not a senator nor did he come from a senatorial family—as emperor, this was a first. Nor was he a military man, having achieved the post of praetorian prefect through his work as a lawyer. Had he overthrown Caracalla in Rome, he may have succeeded in cementing his rule. Out in the distant provinces, trying to prosecute a war with unreliable troops, he lasted barely a year.

Macrinus lacked military ability and political acumen, and the Parthians took advantage of his inexperience by attacking the Romans at Nisibis, in modern-day Turkey, forcing Macrinus to pay two hundred million sesterces to secure a temporary peace. The soldiers were disgusted, but they had not heard the rest of Macrinus's plan. Needing to find this enormous amount of cash, this former accountant decided to save money by enlisting new soldiers on less pay and poorer conditions than those enjoyed by the currently serving soldiers. Morale plummeted, and when the legions heard that Caracalla's cousin was claiming the throne, they deserted to him during a battle against his forces at Antioch. Macrinus decided to flee to Rome to prop up his fading authority. He never made it, executed while travelling across Asia Minor disguised as a courier.

> **Many are more eager to see an emperor killed than they are to live themselves.**
>
> MACRINUS

DIADUMENIANUS

VERY UNLUCKY

NAME: Marcus Opellius Diadumenianus
BORN: Place unknown, 208
RULED: Co-emperor, 218
DIED: Executed, Antiochia ad Orontem (Antioch), Syria, 218

DIADUMENIANUS WAS ANOTHER emperor who really could have done with better timing. Macrinus's son, he became co-emperor at a tender age and in the final months of his father's reign, in a pitiful attempt to shore up Macrinus's fast-diminishing authority. Elagabalus was winning over the army by his youth and his supposed relationship with Caracalla, and this was Macrinus's way to neutralise that threat. It failed miserably. After Macrinus's defeat at Antioch, Diadumenianus was sent off with an ambassador to seek sanctuary at the court of the Parthian king. En route, a Roman centurion captured him and sent him back to Antioch, where the nine-year-old co-emperor was killed. He remained unburied until Elagabalus had time to arrive and gloat over his body.

ELAGABALUS

REALLY, REALLY CONFUSED

NAME: Marcus Aurelius Antoninus
BIRTH NAME: Varius Avitus Bassianus
BORN: Possibly Emesa (Homs), Syria, c. 203
RULED: Emperor, 218–222
DIED: Murdered, Rome, 222

THROUGHOUT THE CENTURIES, very few of those exposed to imperial power were unaffected by it. Elagabalus ended up totally unhinged by the experience.

Named Bassianus, this grandson of Severus's sister-in-law spent years in well-deserved obscurity in the town of Emesa, in Syria, before becoming the high priest of the sun god El-Gabal, known as Sol Invictus in Rome. This was a hereditary position held by the members of Severus's wife's family and no one expected great things from such a minor player in the imperial household.

Circumstances changed with Caracalla's death and the arrival of Macrinus. The Severan male line perished with the death of Caracalla, and Macrinus banished Severus's wife and family to Emesa. Julia Maesa, Severus's sister-in-law, hatched a plot to overthrow the new emperor and decided that Bassianus would be the perfect vehicle for her ambitions. She and the boy's mother, Julia Soaemias, spread rumours that he was Caracalla's illegitimate son. The legions, having grown weary of Macrinus, flocked to them, and in a very short time Bassianus was the new emperor.

He was fourteen on his accession and power went straight to his head. The Romans, for all their love of decadence and amusements, were an intensely conservative people when it came to religion and politics. The name chosen for him as emperor was the very Roman Marcus Aurelius Antoninus, which he quickly

THE SEVERAN USURPERS

The historian Cassius Dio mentions that during Elagabalus's reign there were numerous insurrections, of which we know little. He names two individuals declared emperor, and another secondary source, the fifth-century historian Polemius Silvius, mentions two others. Severus Alexander also suppressed two individuals who reportedly attempted to usurp the throne.

SELEUCUS This usurper was possibly either Julius Antonius Seleucus, the legate in Moesia, or M. Flavius Vitellius Seleucus, the consul in 221. Given that the rebellions tended to arise in the provinces during this period, it is most likely to have been Julius Antonius Seleucus.

GELLIUS MAXIMUS (219) This ambitious senator, whose father was a humble doctor, not as prestigious a career as it is be today, became an officer of the Fourth Legion in Syria. He took advantage of the soldiers' discontent to declare himself emperor. The revolt's suppression by troops loyal to Elagabalus saw Maximus put to death.

VERUS (219) Verus began his career as a centurion before attaining the rank of senator. By 219 he was the commander of the Third Legion, which revolted against the rule of Elagabalus. Again, the revolt was suppressed, the legion dispersed and the leader executed.

URANIUS Evidence from coinage suggests that this usurper, supposedly the final claimant during Elagabalus's reign, was Uranius Antoninus, the usurper in 253.

SALLUSTIUS (227) Severus Alexander's father-in-law was accused of seeking to overthrow the emperor. This is very unlikely, since he was quite fond of Alexander; most likely he tried to get the praetorians to overthrow the emperor's dominating mother.

TAURINUS (232) While Severus Alexander was preparing to cross the Tigris and Euphrates rivers during his Persian campaign, his troops broke out into open rebellion. The Syrian legion proclaimed one of their own, Taurinus, as the new emperor of the Romans. This mutiny, quickly discovered and suppressed, saw the unfortunate usurper flee to the Euphrates River, where he drowned.

changed to Elagabalus. Continuing his role of high priest of El-Gabal, he began a religious revolution that would cause his downfall. He declared El-Gabal to be the supreme deity in the Roman pantheon and created a temple for the god in Rome. In it he housed a black rock that was supposed to have fallen from the skies in the distant past. He also underwent circumcision, a practice that the Romans considered barbaric and un-Roman. But the ultimate sacrilege was his marriage to a Vestal Virgin, thereby desecrating someone who was dedicated to the goddess Vesta, whose protection ensured Rome's good fortune—this act should have seen him whipped in the Forum, thrown into prison and then put to death. He declared that the children of this union of the high priest and high priestess of Rome would be god-like, but the union was childless. He also made his mother and grandmother senators, the first women ever to set foot in that august chamber.

Having become used to seeing a military emperor on the throne, the legions looked on in disgust at behaviour they considered effeminate and beneath the dignity of the emperor. Stories circulated that Elagabalus was married to a number of young men, including Hierocles, a blond slave who was his chariot driver—Elagabalus forced senators to acknowledge his 'husband's' presence and insisted he himself be called the mistress and wife of Hierocles. Imitating an eastern despot, Elagabalus would paint his eyelids, plait his hair and don a wig before prostituting himself in inns and brothels, while within the imperial palace he would solicit passersby by standing naked behind a curtain. Rumour had it that he even planned to have his genitalia removed and replaced with an opening in order to mimic a vagina.

Julia Maesa, the power behind the throne, saw he was losing favour with the troops, especially the praetorians. She unearthed another grandson, Alexander, whom the troops insisted Elagabalus make Caesar and his heir. Unwilling to have his earthly power restricted, Elagabalus tried to kill his cousin but botched the attempt, infuriating the already exasperated praetorians. They turned on him and his mother, butchering them and cutting off their heads, before stripping them naked, dragging their corpses all over the city and casting them into the Tiber.

Elagabalus's reign was a disaster from start to finish, and historians still debate whether he was merely a sexually confused teenager, or if his inability to father children despite multiple wives was a sign of some chromosomal defect that left him with both male and female attributes.

SEVERUS ALEXANDER
MUMMY'S BOY

NAME: Marcus Aurelius Severus Alexander
BIRTH NAME: Marcus Julius Gessius Bassianus Alexianus
BORN: Arca Caesarea, Syria, c. 208
RULED: Emperor, 222–235
DIED: Murdered, Moguntiacum (Mainz), Germania, 235

FOR JULIA MAESA, one grandson was a disappointment. She had more luck with another, Severus Alexander. After the excesses of Elagabalus, this fourteen-year-old quickly showed he was level headed, well meaning and conscientious, but he soon exposed one clear flaw: he was completely in the clutches of his mother, Julia Mamaea. Since his grandmother died soon

Emperor Elagabalus

after his accession, his mother acted as his regent and dominated his early years.

Greedy and miserly, Julia Mamaea's domination was clear from the start. She chose his wife but two years later, when the girl's father dared to complain to the praetorians about Julia Mamaea's insolence towards his daughter, she had him executed on treason charges and banished the girl to Libya. Then, during Alexander's campaigns against the Persians, she banned him from taking part in battle as was expected of a Roman emperor, something that cost him the respect of the legions.

In another place and time, he may have been a great *princeps*. He revived the Senate's influence on imperial policy by establishing two separate councils of senators to act as an imperial cabinet and an advisory legislative council, and he promoted the employment of noted jurists to oversee the administration of justice. However, such an emperor was not capable of maintaining the discipline of the troops, in particular the praetorians. When the praetorian prefect Ulpian, Alexander's trusted counsellor, fled to the emperor for protection from rebellious troops, the soldiers chased him down and ignored Alexander's pleas as they plunged their swords into the prefect's body. No one feared this emperor.

> **At first I sent letters and tried to persuade him to restrain his mad greed and his desire for the property of others.**
>
> SEVERUS ALEXANDER

Alexander was also required to take action against Rome's increasingly aggressive neighbours. The new Sassanid Empire, determined to reclaim any Persian territory currently held by Rome, drove the Romans out of Mesopotamia in 231, but after a messy campaign in which the discipline of the legions was already starting to buckle, the Romans recaptured Mesopotamia in 233. Then, in 234, German tribes attacked the defences on the Rhine, forcing Alexander and his mother to undertake a new offensive to subdue the barbarians. Upon their arrival the situation had settled, so Julia Mamaea convinced her son that securing peace by paying off the Germans was a more sensible course of action than risking his life.

Angry at this stain on Roman military honour, the troops, led by one of their commanders, Maximinus, mutinied. On Maximinus's orders, Alexander and his mother were killed, bringing to an end the Severan dynasty and, with it, whatever life remained in the principate. On Maximinus's accession, we begin a story of confusion, anarchy and despair—the crisis of the third century.

MAXIMINUS

THE THRACIAN

NAME: Gaius Julius Verus Maximinus
BORN: Thrace (modern Bulgaria), c. 173
RULED: Emperor, 235–238
DIED: Aquileia, Italy, 238

AND SO IT HAD COME TO THIS—a semi-literate peasant from the backwaters of the empire sat on the throne of the Caesars. Maximinus cut an imposing figure: according to some accounts, he was just over 2.4 metres (8 feet) in height, with great, piercing eyes and milky white skin. He was the perfect candidate for the military life, coming quickly to imperial notice. According to one story, a mounted Septimius Severus had him run alongside his horse for a lengthy spell, before commanding him to wrestle a group of rested Roman soldiers, whom he defeated easily.

It was during Severus Alexander's campaigns that Maximinus gained new responsibilities. By the time the emperor moved to the German frontier Maximinus was responsible for training recruits for the army of the Rhine. Their loyalty to Maximinus was absolute, and when they mutinied against Alexander, Maximinus became emperor by their acclamation. It was the first time the legions had dethroned an emperor while he was on campaign, and Maximinus was the first emperor who not only was not a senator, but also had no experience other than being a soldier.

For the next three years Maximinus was constantly on campaign and never reached Rome. He reversed the humiliating peace imposed by Alexander, launching a devastating campaign against the German tribes. A straightforward man, he believed the empire would accept his elevation to the throne by murder and military muscle. However, many rejected his legitimacy, and within a year coups were springing up everywhere, including one led by an ex-consul named Magnus, who planned to seize power by destroying the bridge over the Rhine, leaving the emperor to the mercy of the Germans. The plot was uncovered and the conspirators put to death without trial.

Maximinus's training taught him that the only people he could count on were his fellow soldiers; everyone else was a potential enemy. He therefore treated anyone who would not support him in the same way he dealt with any enemy of Rome—brutally. The more people turned against him, the more savage he became. Possessing a peasant's distrust of the elite, his suspicion focused on the Senate, which had never really accepted the murder of the legitimate emperor and resented the heavy taxation of their estates to fund his wars. When a rebellion broke out in North Africa and the locals elevated the proconsul Gordian to the throne, the Senate backed Gordian and declared Maximinus an enemy of the state. When news of this treachery reached Maximinus, he reacted with animal fury, throwing himself against the walls and on the ground, ranting and raving against the rebels, grabbing his sword and beating his slaves. Vowing revenge, he began his march on Rome.

On reaching Italy, Maximinus laid siege to Aquileia but, to his great surprise, it held out. He spent a month trying to storm the city; he took his failure to conquer it out on his soldiers, who soon resented him, especially as they were running out of food and clean water. Before long, a group of soldiers burst into his tent during a lull in the fighting and killed him and his son. They were decapitated, and their heads were taken to Rome while their bodies became food for the dogs and birds.

In the end, Maximinus was the first casualty of a war between the military and the Senate, which branded him with the mocking nickname 'Thrax', or 'the Thracian'.

QUARTINUS

UNWILLING OCCUPANT

NAME: Quartinus
BORN: Unknown
RULED: Usurper, 235
DIED: Murdered, Germania, 235

SOMETIMES HIGH-RANKING officials ended up in the imperial position against their will. Quartinus was one such person. Not a great deal is known about him, aside from the fact that he was a former consul, a confidant of Severus Alexander, and that he had been dismissed from Maximinus's army.

While he was serving with another legion, Quartinus was recognised by a company of archers who were not happy with Alexander's assassination and they made him their general, before placing upon him a purple toga, symbolising his accession as emperor. He protested vigorously, but they would not retract their fatal claim, and they barred all access to him as if they were the personal soldiers of the emperor.

Quartinus was not to enjoy his unwelcome elevation for long. He was killed while sleeping in his tent by Macedo, a supposed friend and one of those pushing him to accept the purple. Macedo decapitated him and sent the head to Maximinus in order to win the emperor's gratitude. All Macedo earned for his trouble was a quick death.

GORDIAN I

AN OLD-STYLE ROMAN

NAME: Marcus Antonius Gordianus
Sempronianus Romanus Africanus
BORN: Possibly Phrygia, Asia Minor, c. 159
RULED: Emperor, 238
DIED: Suicide, Carthage, North Africa, 238

MANY STORIES CIRCULATED about Gordian I, principally that he was descended from some of the noblest Roman families from the glorious days of the Roman Republic. It was not true, of course, but such was the conduct of Gordian that many believed it. His was a wealthy equestrian family, but his lack of political connections showed itself in his rather late appointment to high political office, when he was well into his fifties.

The fateful year of 238 found him serving as proconsul of Africa. This was a comfortable position and no doubt as he approached eighty he was looking forward to a quiet retirement. Yet discontent with Maximinus's reign was increasing, and the emperor's need for cash meant that his personal representatives were being pressured to find the money, or else. The procurator in Africa was especially devious, falsifying charges against the local aristocracy so that they lost much of their wealth. A riot followed, resulting in the procurator's death, after which the locals begged and then ordered Gordian to assume the purple. He protested in vain, saying he was too old, too frail, but they threatened to take his life should he refuse. He was probably scared witless, and rightly so.

A message was sent to the Senate asking for their approval. The old aristocracy had never accepted the imperial pretensions of the military upstart Maximinus, and so they enthusiastically supported Gordian's claim. Yet by the time they decided in his favour, it was all over. Gordian had moved into the capital of the province, Carthage, but the legate of neighbouring Numidia supported Maximinus as emperor and possessed something Gordian lacked—an army. After a battle in which his hastily gathered militia was defeated and his son died, Gordian took the traditional Roman option of suicide, hanging himself with his belt after a three-week reign.

GORDIAN II

SWEPT UP IN THE MAELSTROM

NAME: Marcus Antonius Gordianus
Sempronianus Romanus Africanus
BORN: Place unknown, c. 192
RULED: Co-emperor, 238
DIED: In battle, Carthage,
North Africa, 238

HISTORY RECORDS LITTLE of the younger Gordian. At the time of his elevation as emperor, he was serving as legate to his father and became co-emperor because of his father's advanced age. There was talk that he was only interested in books and women. If this was so, then it was a poor preparation for what fate had in store for him.

Victory!

GORDIAN II (as written on his coins)

He was given no time to enjoy the imperial privileges. Almost immediately on his accession, his father ordered him to take command of the local militia at Carthage and get them ready to take on a trained Roman legion that was marching on the city. There was never any hope. In a pitched battle outside Carthage, Gordian II died; his forces were slaughtered; and his body remained unrecovered.

BALBINUS

HALF OF THE 'DYNAMIC DUO'

NAME: Decimus Caelius Calvinus
Balbinus Pius
BORN: Place unknown, c. 178
RULED: Emperor, 238
DIED: Murdered, Rome, 238

ONE CAN IMAGINE the Senate's horror when news arrived of the defeat and deaths of the Gordians. Believing reconciliation with Maximinus to be out of the question, they nominated two of their own as joint emperors.

Balbinus was one of those selected. A Roman patrician of wealth and family connections, he had held a second consulship with the emperor Caracalla, suggesting he was a very important man during the Severan dynasty. Having held several governorships in the non-military provinces and being held in high esteem by the Senate, he was the perfect example of the 'born to rule' elite in Rome who resented their subservience to a Thracian barbarian. The Senate had high expectations of Balbinus and gave him the task of running the civil administration in Rome.

It was a disaster. Almost immediately fighting broke out between the praetorians and the Roman mob, and they ignored calls from Balbinus for calm. For days, the fighting raged before the praetorians started a fire that devastated a large portion of the city.

Reports now began filtering back of Maximinus's death, proven when his head arrived at the Senate on the end of a spear. There was great rejoicing when Balbinus's co-emperor, Pupienus, returned from leading the army to Aquileia (although Maximinus had been killed before he arrived), but it was soon evident that with the threat of their impending deaths removed, the two emperors could not get along. Balbinus, believing he was the more worthy to be emperor because of his noble birth, refused to work with his colleague. When Pupienus came to him with news of a plot to kill them both, Balbinus believed Pupienus was trying to murder him. They were still arguing when the praetorians burst into the throne room, took them both, and beat and tortured them, before ending their lives in a shower of sword thrusts. Balbinus probably felt that such a death was beneath him. He had reigned for ninety-nine days.

PUPIENUS

THE OTHER HALF OF THE 'DYNAMIC DUO'

NAME: Marcus Clodius Pupienus Maximus
BORN: Possibly Volterra, Italy, c. 178
RULED: Emperor, 238
DIED: Murdered, Rome, 238

WITH BALBINUS MINDING Rome's civil affairs, the Senate needed someone to command the armies that would fight Maximinus. They selected Pupienus, another Roman who had made his mark through the military and had held the usual accumulation of posts, including a consulship in 234. He had achieved outstanding victories against the barbarians, and his only drawback was a reputation for severity, which made him feared and hated in certain quarters. Nevertheless, it was with the cocksure attitude of a hardened general that he promised victory as he marched out of Rome.

Basing himself at Ravenna, he took a few weeks to gather troops, especially from his old German command. In the end they were unnecessary, as word came through of the difficulty Maximinus was having breaking through at Aquileia. As Pupienus marched out of Ravenna, he received the even better news that Maximinus had died at the hands of his soldiers, and so he entered Aquileia in triumph, without ever having engaged the enemy in battle.

Things were looking great for Pupienus, but upon his return to Rome he immediately began having difficulties with Balbinus. He was used to giving orders in true military style and, as emperor, this felt right and natural. Having a colleague went against this inclination. He also felt that he deserved to be sole emperor because he had served as prefect of Rome and had built up a good reputation with his administrative efforts. Unsurprisingly, Balbinus disagreed.

It was then that the Praetorian Guard struck. Fearful that Pupienus was going to replace them with his faithful German troops, they stormed the palace and made for the emperors, who were busy squabbling about who was plotting to kill whom. Their lack of trust and mutual ambition saw them both killed as the military again crushed the Senate's choice of emperor.

GORDIAN III

THIRD TIME LUCKY

NAME: Marcus Antonius Gordianus Pius
BORN: Rome, 225
RULED: Emperor, 238–244
DIED: Murdered, Circesium, Mesopotamia (Iraq), 244

LIKE HIS GRANDFATHER and uncle, Gordian III found himself in a situation beyond his control. In 238 he was staying with his mother in Rome when news arrived of the revolt against Maximinus in Africa, but the main supporters of the emperor were killed before they could

Murder of Emperor Balbinus

THE CRISIS OF THE THIRD CENTURY

target the boy. Many Romans were unhappy about the elevation of Balbinus and Pupienus and the memory of the Gordians was still fresh in their minds. Therefore, the Roman mob, stirred to violence, demanded that young Gordian become co-emperor. The two emperors sent the Praetorian Guard to disperse the rioters, but the praetorians could not overcome the sheer weight of numbers against them. The Senate named Gordian as Caesar, and the mob returned to their homes, pleased by the turn of events.

Normally, the Caesar would have quite a wait before becoming emperor, if he managed to make it at all. Three months was all it took for Gordian to become sole emperor after the experiment of the joint emperors ended in acrimony, recrimination and death. The murderous praetorians and a cowed Senate acclaimed the young man, and he ruled quite well by all accounts, helped by an outstanding praetorian prefect of proven ability. All he wanted was a quiet reign, but it was not to be.

By 240 Rome was again at war with the newly reborn Persian Empire and at first the Romans were quite successful, recapturing a number of cities. By 243 Gordian had joined the armies in the east and was planning a major campaign into the heart of Persia. In early 244, the two armies met at Misiche (modern Fallujah, in Iraq), and the Romans were crushed. At this point in Roman history, emperors did not long survive such defeats, and this was no exception. There are three differing accounts as to what happened next. According to the Persians, Gordian died during the battle and his successor, Philip, bought peace for the price of 500,000 dinars. According to the few remaining Roman sources, Gordian did not die in the battle but the new praetorian prefect, Philip, fomented discontent within the legions, leading to Gordian's death and Philip's acclamation by the army. Philip's own account was that the young man died of an illness. The modern reader can take their pick.

SABINIANUS

JUST ANOTHER FACELESS USURPER

NAME: Cornelius Valerius Gratus Sabinianus
BORN: Unknown
RULED: Usurper, 240
DIED: Unknown

BY THIS STAGE, it was clear that men of sufficient ambition and a little luck could become emperor of the Roman world. The events of 238 did not deter Sabinianus, a former consul, who tried his luck against Gordian III in 240.

This man obviously had not been paying attention. Like Gordian I, he was the proconsular governor of Africa; like Gordian I, he soon found himself in desperate trouble, as he had no legions within the province. Finally, again like Gordian I, he was soon suppressed by one of the neighbouring imperial legates who did possess an army and who was loyal to the emperor. Receiving no support in the Senate, his supporters quickly handed him over to Gordian, all the while apologising and asking for forgiveness.

PHILIP I

THE ARAB

NAME: Marcus Julius Philippus
BORN: Shaba, Syria, c. 204
RULED: Emperor, 244–249
DIED: Killed in battle, Verona, Italy, 249

FIRST 'THE THRACIAN', now 'the Arab'—these were racist epithets from an aristocracy still coming to grips with a power shift from the Latin heartland to the provinces. Although Philip was born in Syria and was the son of a Roman citizen, his family originally hailed from the Arabian Peninsula, and the Roman elite never forgot such things.

Philip came to prominence as Gordian III's final praetorian prefect. During the eastern campaign, he either killed the emperor outright, or was the senior governmental figure present in the aftermath of Gordian's death in battle or by disease. With a massive payment, he was able to arrange a truce with the Persians.

Upon returning to Rome, he consolidated his regime, claiming victory over the Persians with the titles *Parthicus Adiabenicus*, *Persicus Maximus* and *Parthicus Maximus*. However, another war was taking place against the Carpi and other German tribes, and so he rushed to the Danube to oversee the campaign. Though it was successful, the legions were not wholly satisfied with the result, leading to unfortunate consequences for Philip later.

Given Philip's 'alien' status, it is ironic that he became the emperor who celebrated Rome's millennial foundation in 248. Using the animals collected for Gordian's abandoned Persian triumph, Philip hosted numerous games during which elephants, elk, tigers, lions, leopards, hyenas, hippopotamuses, rhinoceroses, giraffes, wild asses, wild horses, and countless other animals were slaughtered, and one thousand pairs of gladiators fought. Yet throughout the celebrations, the empire was beginning to fall apart. Out on the frontiers, the legions resented Rome's apparent indifference. They were unhappy, and a string of usurpers took advantage of their discontent. Even the emperor's personal representative on the Danube, Decius, accepted the purple from the very troops he was supposed to bring under control. Crossing into Italy, he and Philip met at Verona. Philip's army was crushed, and he died in battle.

Though Philip had a bad press, one group liked him. The Christians believed that Philip was the first Christian emperor and was once ordered by the bishop of Antioch to confess his sins before attending Easter service. However, since he made no improvements in Christians' legal status, this 'conversion' is doubtful.

PHILIP II
BAGGAGE

NAME: Marcus Julius Philippus Severus
BORN: Unknown, c. 238
RULED: Co-emperor, 247–249
DIED: Murdered, Rome, 249

IT WAS COMMON TO DEMONSTRATE a regime's stability and future prospects by having the son of the emperor made Caesar and then co-emperor. Of course, if the regime fell, the future rapidly became the past, with the son sharing the fate of the father.

This is precisely what happened to Philip Junior. Made co-emperor at the age of nine and Roman consul at the age of ten, he was dead at the age of eleven. The young co-emperor was holding the fort in Rome when news arrived of the defeat and death of his father, and he was soon killed by the Praetorian Guard, who had decided to curry favour with the new regime. After all, there was always another emperor somewhere.

IOTAPIANUS
NO MORE TAXES!

NAME: Marcus Fulvius Rufus Iotapianus
BORN: Unknown
RULED: Usurper, 248–249
DIED: Killed, possibly Antiochia ad Orontem (Antioch), Syria, 249

PRIOR TO THE ARRIVAL of the Romans, the east was awash with royalty. Greek royal houses, a legacy of the break-up of Alexander the Great's empire, had sprouted everywhere before being slowly supplanted as the Romans extended their power. Though the Romans brought much technological advancement, they also brought excessive taxation, which the eastern provinces resented most of all.

One man who certainly resented it was Iotapianus, a member of the royal family of Commagene, which claimed descent from the great Alexander himself. He raised the standard of revolt over the issue of excessive taxation levied on Syria and Cappadocia by the emperor's brother, Priscus, who was arch-governor of the eastern provinces. Iotapianus made Antioch his capital and began minting his own coinage, but was eventually defeated during the final months of Philip's reign, before dying at the hands of his troops.

PACATIANUS

TROUBLE ON THE DANUBE

NAME: Tiberius Claudius Marinus Pacatianus
BORN: Unknown
RULED: Usurper, 248
DIED: Killed, Moesia, 249

THERE ARE FEW RECORDS for this period, but it is believed that he was a member of a senatorial family and that his father was the imperial legate of the Roman province of Arabia. A well-connected man, Pacatianus attracted people who hoped to further their own careers.

Death of Emperor Decius fighting the Goths at the battle of Abrittus, 251

Stationed on the Danube in 248, he commanded one of the numerous armies that were protecting the provinces from the Goths. These armies seemed to attract unrest, with reports describing recurring disciplinary problems. The legions in Moesia (modern-day Serbia and Bulgaria) raised Pacatianus to the purple. This rebellion was considered serious enough by Emperor Philip that it was discussed at length with the Senate, and Philip sent the senator Decius to the Danube to put down the rebellion and restore discipline. By the time Decius got there, Pacatianus was dead, killed by his own soldiers, and the Goths were preparing to pour into Moesia.

DECIUS

AT LEAST HE TRIED

NAME: Gaius Messius Quintus Decius
BORN: Budalia (Martinci), Pannonia, c. 195
RULED: Emperor, 249–251
DIED: Killed in battle, Abrittus (Razgrad), Moesia, 251

THERE WERE USURPERS who, upon becoming emperor, protested that they did not want this honour bestowed upon them. One should be sceptical about such claims, yet in the case of Decius they do seem sincere. A long-serving senator from a noble provincial family, he had been the imperial legate of some important military provinces before finding himself in Rome serving as urban prefect during Philip's reign.

As a well-respected member of the Senate, Decius received orders to bring the rebellious legions in Moesia and Pannonia under control. He advised Philip that sending him was a bad idea, but Philip insisted he was the right man for the job, especially as he had governed there previously without abusing his position. He soon had the situation well in hand but then, to his horror, the troops declared him their emperor. To ensure his acceptance, they told him they would kill him unless he agreed. Knowing that intent was meaningless when the troops forced his hand, he quickly prepared for a showdown before Philip could gather his forces. Striking at Verona, Decius emerged victorious.

Rome finally had an emperor who thought he understood the causes of the empire's deterioration and was determined to rectify them. He instituted two measures to reinforce the old virtues of the empire. Firstly, he revived the office of censor, an old republican position that was responsible for reviewing the Senate and maintaining public morals. For this task, he chose Valerian, the *princeps* (leading member) of the Senate. Secondly, believing the failure of the armies and the lack of virtue in the citizenry was due to the abandonment of the old traditions, in particular the correct worship of the old Roman gods who had granted Rome its victories over the centuries, he ordered everyone in the empire to declare their adherence to the rituals required by the Roman gods for the wellbeing of the state, and they were to perform these rituals in the presence of an official. One group who felt the effects this decree more than any other was the Christians—though they were not Decius's specific target—as they refused to perform these pagan rituals and were, therefore, subjected to their first systematic persecution.

> **Now we have them trapped.**
>
> DECIUS (just before engaging the Goths at the battle of Abrittus)

The new measures did not help. In 250 the Danube froze, and seventy thousand barbarians poured into the provinces of the empire, as the legions that were supposed to be manning the frontiers were sitting around Verona having a grand old time. Decius put on his armour and rushed to the rescue, leaving Rome in the hands of Valerian. Successful against the Carpi in Dacia, he turned in pursuit of the Goths, who were approaching the city of Philippopolis in Thrace, but they defeated him in a surprise attack. Decius became the first emperor to flee in confusion before a half-armed barbarian horde, although he eventually managed to join up with the imperial legate of Moesia, Gallus. Humiliated, Decius hungered to strike back and got his opportunity near the town of Abrittus. The Goths, tired and depleted, offered to give up their prisoners and treasure for safe passage, but Decius wanted total victory. His stubbornness killed him—in swampy ground the legions were no match for the Goths, and the emperor's body was never recovered. In better times, Decius would have made a fine emperor; these were not such times. He became the first emperor to die in battle against a foreign foe, as Gallus saved what remained of the army.

HERENNIUS ETRUSCUS

NO FUTURE

NAME: Quintus Herennius Etruscus Messius Decius
BORN: Sirmium (Sremska), Pannonia, c. 227
RULED: Co-emperor, 251
DIED: Killed in battle, Abrittus, Moesia, 251

HAVING A SOLID ROMAN SENATOR like Decius for a father meant that Herennius Etruscus did not get to enjoy his elevation to Caesar. Having already accompanied Decius in 248 as a military tribune to deal with Pacatianus, he was entrusted with important affairs almost immediately, and was carted off to the provinces by his father to secure the legions against possible insurrection. He was quickly made co-emperor in an attempt to stabilise the succession as well as to show the people that he was the new hope for the future.

The luckless young man joined Decius's ill-fated campaign against the Goths and became a very early casualty in the battle of Abrittus, when an enemy arrow hit its target and struck him down. The troops considered this a bad omen, but his father declared that the loss of one soldier was no big thing and that they should fight on. He should have listened.

PRISCUS

FIRST PUPPET EMPEROR

NAME: Titus Lucius Priscus
BORN: Unknown
RULED: Usurper, 251
DIED: Philippopolis (Plovdiv), Thrace, 251

IN THE AFTERMATH of Decius's initial defeat by the Goths, the man who felt the pressure most keenly was the governor of Macedonia, Priscus. He was holed up in the city of Philippopolis, which was now the Goths' principal target. The siege was a long and difficult one, but Priscus was a man of considerable talents, and he employed his ample abilities to repeatedly rally the defenders. Much of the Goth army perished beneath the walls of the city.

However, the protracted defence was to no avail—the Goths eventually stormed the city, and in the ensuing sack nearly 100,000 people died. Though the Goths spared Priscus, they decided to raise him to the purple and declared him emperor of the Romans. This gave him the dubious honour of being the first Roman to become a puppet emperor of the barbarians—he would not be the last. Goodness knows what he thought his long-term prospects were, but once the Goths departed to the Danube, he found himself alone and a declared enemy of the state, by order of the Senate. He was dead shortly afterwards.

LICINIANUS

TREASON DOESN'T PAY

NAME: Julius Valens Licinianus
BORN: Unknown
RULED: Usurper, 251
DIED: Executed, Rome, 251

PRISCUS WAS NOT THE ONLY man to take advantage of Decius's failure in the north. In Rome, a certain senator decided that his time had come. Licinianus had secured the support of a good number of his senatorial colleagues before beginning his grab for power. During the revolt, he named himself emperor, promising what every politician pledges at such times—victories and a happy, prosperous future.

Luckily Decius had chosen wisely, leaving the faithful Valerian in charge. Valerian was efficient in rounding up the principal players in the revolt, preventing its gaining any momentum and ensuring its suppression, as well as Licinianus's arrest and quick death.

HOSTILIAN

THE FORGOTTEN SON

NAME: Gaius Valens Hostilianus Messius Quintus
BORN: Sirmium (Sremska), Pannonia, c. 230
RULED: Emperor, 251
DIED: Of plague, Rome, 251

HOSTILIAN WAS FATED to remain in his older brother's shadow. Decius obviously favoured Herennius Etruscus, giving him special titles such as *princeps iuventutis* and then co-Augustus but, given Decius's death in battle, this may not have been a good thing.

As it was, Hostilian was in Rome with his mother when word came back of his father's and brother's deaths. The Senate supported Hostilian's claim to the throne and, since the humiliation of the legions at the hands of the Goths had humbled them, the army agreed to the accession of Decius's younger son to the throne, with one proviso—that Gallus, the man who had managed to extricate the soldiers from the disaster at the battle of Abrittus, become co-emperor.

Hostilian may have hoped for a long life, but the empire was about to be hit with a perfect storm—the mutiny of the army, fierce barbarian invasions and a plague that would ravage the empire for the next twenty years. Dying of the plague was the fate of the young Hostilian, his death leaving the door open for the peaceful transfer of power to his nominal co-emperor, Gallus.

TREBONIANUS GALLUS

OVERWHELMED BY THE CHAOS

NAME: Gaius Vibius Trebonianus Gallus
BORN: Perusia (Perugia), Italy, 206
RULED: Emperor, 251–253
DIED: Murdered, Interamna (Terni), Italy, 253

TREBONIANUS GALLUS, though a career politician like so many senators, did not simply rely on his respected family background for career advancement. During this time of crisis, he clearly showed why Decius had placed so much faith in him when making him imperial legate of Upper Moesia by successfully defending the town of Novae against the Goths. The soldiers appreciated his decisive action in saving much of the army in the aftermath of Abrittus, and they declared him worthy of being Decius's successor. Word reached Gallus of the Senate's decision to make Hostilian emperor, to which he submitted, adopting Hostilian as his own son, to which the Senate subsequently agreed.

THE CRISIS OF THE THIRD CENTURY

FACES OF IMPERIAL POWER

For the emperors, propaganda played an important part in establishing and maintaining their rule, and one of the most successful ways of getting a message across in the ancient world was to control coinage or, more specifically, what was printed on the coins. Coins not only demonstrated that the person who minted them controlled the mint and thus was able to support the financial needs of the state, but they also served to remind the people of their shared collective greatness, linking the diverse peoples of the empire together as a cohesive whole.

The two faces of the Roman coins portrayed the hopes, dreams and aspirations of the imperial ruler, and conveyed to the people just what they could expect from their emperor. On one side was the face of the emperor, majestic and potent, and circling the outside border of the coin was their imperial name. On the reverse was some sort of symbol, expressing either actual achievements or plans for reinvigoration of the state. Images used included personifications of *Virtus*, virtue and bravery, used to convey the supposed virtues of the emperor and his family; *Pax*, the promise of peace; *Roma*, implying the support of the capital for the emperor; or, most importantly, *Victoria*, claiming the emperor brought victories over the enemies of the state. By the fifth century, it was the Christian God who brought peace, harmony and good fortune to the state, and images of Christ and the Cross dominate from that time onwards.

But coins were not just important for the time when they were minted. They are durable and survive the vicissitudes of history far better than written records. For certain periods in Roman history there is such a lack of sources that the only evidence that points to the existence of an emperor or usurper may be the coins they minted. Such is the case with the usurper Silbannacus, only one of whose coins exists, and with little else known of him, guesses about who he was are based on that one coin. Scholars believe he was of Gallic origin and that he was the commander of auxiliary troops who rebelled in either Gaul or Germany. The troops declared him emperor during Philip's reign, and his rebellion continued into the reign of Decius.

Then we have a coin of the usurper Sponsianus, his elevation originally believed to have occurred during the reign of either Gordian III or Philip I. However, many scholars have grave reservations about this coin: it has a reverse that is identical to that of a coin from the second century BC. From this, many people believe the coin to be a forgery and, therefore, that Sponsianus never existed.

Gallus's talents promised so much, yet it all went horribly wrong. His first act was to buy off the victorious Goths with an annual tribute. Though a practical solution for a man with a decimated and demoralised army, it gained him the contempt of Rome and the legions in other areas, all of whom saw it as selling Roman dignity. The Goths returned to their homes, and Gallus rushed to Rome to secure his accession. Confronted on his arrival by an epidemic (it appears to have been smallpox) that was killing thousands, he spent most of his time and energy dealing with this crisis, as was expected of Rome's chief magistrate. Galleus's problem was that he was needed everywhere.

The Persians took this opportunity to invade Syria, defeating the Roman armies and capturing Antioch as Gallus looked on helplessly, overwhelmed by the management of the plague. Then, to cap it off, the humiliating peace with the Goths, so dearly bought, did not last even a year. They again crossed the Danube and began looting the plague-wracked provinces. With Gallus stuck in Rome, his replacement as legate in Upper Moesia, Aemilianus, marshalled the legions and defeated the Goths, who fled back across the border. In honour of this victory, Aemilianus's troops declared him emperor and he quickly marched towards Rome. Gallus, fearful of taking on this new rival with the few troops available to him, requested help from Decius's old comrade, Valerian. Valerian began his march, but Gallus was soon dead—his troops, deciding it was useless to lay down their lives in a battle they could not win, murdered him in cold blood.

VOLUSIANUS

SILENT PARTNER

NAME: Gaius Vibius Volusianus
BORN: Unknown
RULED: Co-emperor, 251–253
DIED: Murdered, Interamna (modern Terni), Italy, 253

AFTER THE PLAGUE killed Hostilian, Gallus decided that his next co-emperor should be his natural son, Volusianus. He was already Caesar, and so becoming emperor was only a small step up the ladder. It is a measure of Gallus's unpopularity that accusations were made that he had had Hostilian poisoned in order to ensure Volusianus's succession.

Few records exist about Volusianus, as his reign coincided with that of his father. Official propaganda through his coins promised harmony, but he too perished at Interamna at the hands of the army.

URANIUS ANTONINUS

MYSTERIOUS USURPER

NAME: Lucius Julius Aurelius Sulpicius Severus Uranius Antoninus
BORN: Unknown
RULED: Usurper, 253–254
DIED: Syria, 254

GALLUS'S LACK OF ENTHUSIASM for the affairs of the provinces caused locals to take matters into their own hands. During the invasion of Syria in 252 by the Persian king Shapur I, a usurper named Uranius Antoninus accepted the purple, becoming the principal figure in the Roman defence of Syria. History records nothing more about him, not even his fate. His coins display a youthful man, possibly in his twenties. The sources are so poor for this period that he has even at times been identified with usurpers during the reigns of Elagabalus and Severus Alexander.

AEMILIANUS

DÉJÀ VU

NAME: Marcus Aemilius Aemilianus
BORN: Island of Girba (modern Djerba), North Africa, 207
RULED: Emperor, 253
DIED: Murdered, Spoletium, Italy, 253

JUST AS URANIUS took matters into his own hands in Syria, Gallus's inaction forced Aemilianus to go his own way. The troubled times opened unparalleled opportunities for this native of North Africa. He came from an insignificant family but the usual career path found him promoted as Gallus's replacement in Upper Moesia. The Goths, announcing that tribute was not forthcoming, invaded the empire, only to retreat before the legions of Aemilianus. As was becoming the norm, his troops declared him emperor, and his rival, Gallus, was killed before battle. The Senate opposed Aemilianus's elevation, but that body was now so ineffectual that he managed to overcome all opposition within a few days.

He did not enjoy his victory for long, as Valerian, marching to the aid of Gallus, was, in his turn, made emperor by the army. In a repeat performance, Aemilianus gathered his troops, but before the armies could meet he was murdered by his soldiers, after a reign of three months. Aemilianus, like so many before him, was not without ability. But when every general believed that he had a chance of becoming emperor, each reign was a short, stormy and bloody affair.

VALERIAN

THE NOBLEST OF INTENTIONS

NAME: Publius Licinius Valerianus
BORN: Unknown, c. 200
RULED: Emperor, 253–260
DIED: Flayed alive, Persia, c. 262

FATE OR PROVIDENCE now decreed that at this troubled time the imperial power should fall into the hands of the greatest living Roman of his generation. Valerian was descended from some of the noblest families in Rome, and his pedigree was impeccable. He had come to prominence as Gordian I's representative when negotiating with the Senate, and his nobility and stern embracing of Roman traditions saw him rewarded with the most prestigious title that a senator could obtain—*princeps senatus*, the leader of the Senate. Further recognition for his commitment to the Roman ideal saw him elected censor under the emperor Decius. This position, largely neglected since the early days of the empire, was nearly always occupied by the emperor. Such was the trust that the emperor and his fellow Romans had in Valerian and, until he became emperor, he did not let them down.

> **Therefore I ask to be excused from this office, to which my life is unequal, my courage unequal, and the times so unfavourable that human nature does not desire the office of censor.**
>
> VALERIAN

In the year 253 he was the imperial legate in the German provinces when he received an urgent summons from the emperor Gallus, whom he knew and admired, and who was about to encounter the army of Aemilianus. Valerian was not able to get to Italy in time to prevent Gallus's murder, but he decided to avenge the emperor's death and, having been proclaimed emperor, continued on his journey to Italy. The troops of Aemilianus, comparing their choice as emperor with the fame and superior status of Valerian, decided that this was no contest at all and threw in their lot with the noble Valerian, killing Aemilianus before offering battle.

For the first time in years, the armies, the Senate and the people of Rome were in one voice in acclaiming Valerian as being the Roman most worthy to don the purple robes. His first act as emperor was to choose a co-emperor—he was near sixty and his age meant that he needed the services of a younger associate to wield the sword while he managed the civil affairs of the empire. His decision was sensible but his choice was not. What was required was a Trajan or a Marcus Aurelius; instead, he selected his eldest son, Gallienus, for the honour, and under the joint reign of father and son the provinces endured continuous barbarian invasions and usurpations as the empire dissolved all around them.

No measures were effective to stem the chaos; nothing in Valerian's long years had prepared him for a disaster on such an unprecedented scale. No part of the empire was unaffected, and the whole Roman world seemed to be ending. Under such circumstances, Valerian took the brave and crucial step of dividing the empire between himself and his son. To Gallienus went the western provinces and the problems of the Germanic hordes, while Valerian took on the eastern half of the empire and the seemingly less dangerous Persians. It was a sign of things to come, and what was originally an emergency measure soon became a permanent feature of the empire, leading to the existence of two separate and increasingly different states for the majority of its history.

Valerian did have some success. By 257 he had recaptured Antioch and pushed the invading Persians out of Syria. However, a new Gothic incursion gave the Persians some breathing space, and by 259 Valerian was forced to return to defend Antioch once again. When he moved forward to defend the city of Edessa, the plague struck down his troops, their morale plummeted and they blamed their misfortunes on him. Under such circumstances it was inevitable that, when forced to fight, the legions were no match for the Persians, and in the aftermath of the battle Valerian became the first Roman emperor taken prisoner by the enemy.

Emperor Valerian is captured by the Persian King Shapur I

Valerian never saw Rome again. Kept in chains at the court of Shapur I and robed in the imperial purple, he was mocked by the Persians at their leisure. Whenever the king mounted his horse, he used the neck of the Roman emperor as a footstool. Finally, when Shapur had tired of this game, he skinned poor Valerian alive and had his skin stuffed with straw and put on display at a Persian temple.

History's judgement of Valerian's reign has been harsh, for it is doubtful that even a man with Trajan's skills could have steadied the ship of state in such circumstances. Valerian's reputation also endured a savage blow from the accounts of the Christians who suffered under his reign. Like Decius, he believed the abandonment of age-old rituals had cursed the empire with plague and war. Decius did not focus on the Christians but Valerian did, for while Christians were few and relatively unimportant in Italy, they were in greater numbers in the eastern provinces. Decius's decrees for sacrificing to the gods had made no specific mention of the Christians, and nor had those of Valerian while he was in Rome, but his edicts in 257 and 258 were directed specifically against them, most likely in response to his contact with the underground faith in Antioch and the Christians' obstinate refusal to conform to the required rituals of the Roman state.

With Valerian's death the empire was about to enter its darkest time and its most difficult test. During its first 180 years of existence, it had seen twenty emperors, while the following eighty years had witnessed a further thirty-nine. Now, over the course of the next twenty-five years, thirty-four emperors attempted to command the loyalties of the legions, stem the barbarian tide and resurrect the Roman state from the crisis into which it had descended. The time of the *princeps* was over; the age of the usurpers had begun.

THE AGE OF THE USURPERS

(260–285)

At a time when the reins of government were held with so loose a hand,
it is not surprising, that a crowd of usurpers should start up in every province
of the empire. [They] reduced the empire to the lowest pitch of disgrace and ruin,
from whence it seemed impossible that it should ever emerge.

EDWARD GIBBON
The Decline and Fall of the Roman Empire, 1880

FOLLOWING PAGE: *Queen Zenobia Before Emperor Aurelian* by Giovanni Battista Tiepolo, 1717

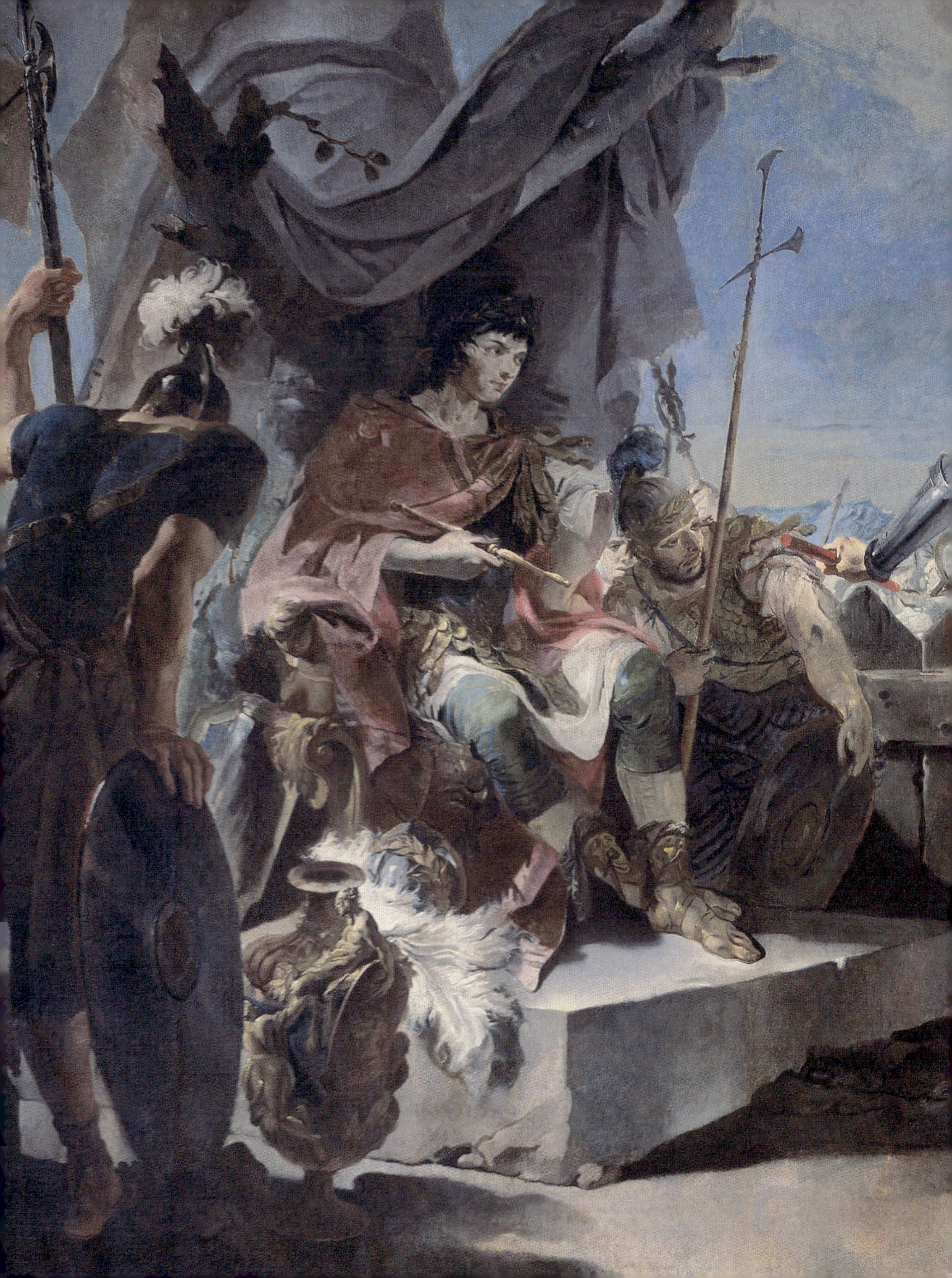

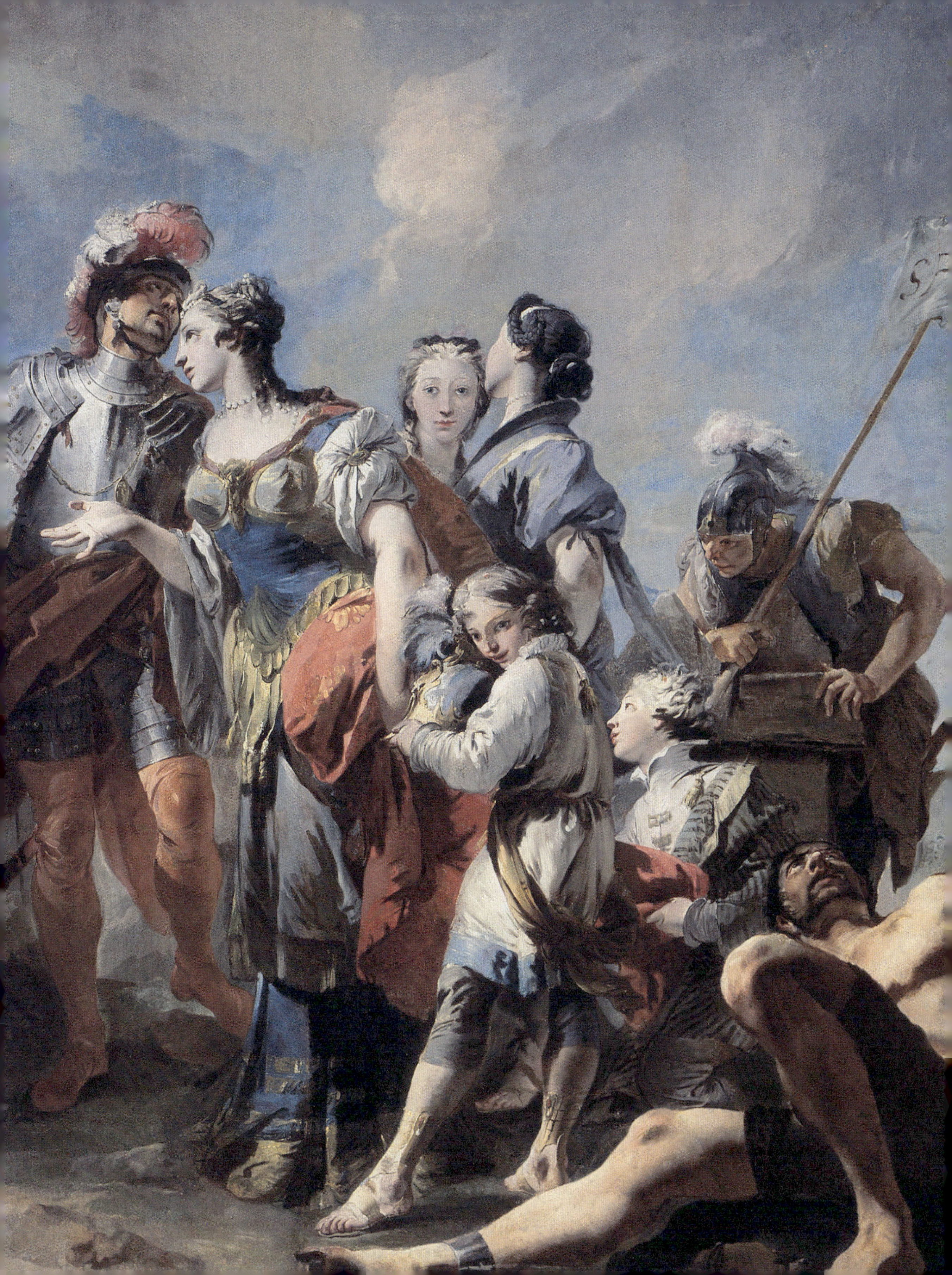

GALLIENUS

UNJUSTLY VILIFIED

NAME: Publius Licinius Egnatius Gallienus
BORN: Unknown, c. 218
RULED: Co-emperor, 253–260;
sole emperor, 260–268
DIED: Murdered, Mediolanum (Milan), Italy, 268

> Let everyone die who has dropped an expression, who has entertained a thought against me, against *me*, the son of Valerian.
>
> GALLIENUS

IF THE OPENING QUOTATION is anything to go by, the character of Gallienus must be one of the most vindictive and callous in history. However, these words did not come from the mouth of Gallienus; his senatorial enemies attributed them to him decades later. Since Roman history is inevitably told from the senatorial viewpoint—the authors came from the senatorial class—they painted Gallienus in the worst possible light imaginable. The truth is that he was a diligent emperor, but he was confronted by a situation that was impossible to manage—the collapse of the Roman Empire into anarchy and independent provinces.

It is safe to assume that Gallienus, prior to his elevation, had had very little experience of public life. Given that he was the son of a very distinguished senator, he must surely have started his climb up the *cursus honorum*; however, his accession as co-emperor at the age of thirty-five meant that, at best, he would have filled only minor offices. Nevertheless, Valerian had soon realised that one man could not manage the situation confronting the empire, and so he made Gallienus co-emperor and almost immediately sent him to the Danube frontier to deal with the invasions pouring into the weakened empire. From then on, Gallienus's reign would be characterised by constant movement across the western provinces of the empire.

Until his father's capture in 260, Gallienus's numerous victories had kept the barbarian tribes out of Germany and Gaul, and he had dealt successfully with the Goths within the province of Dacia. He might have actually been able to deal with all the barbarian incursions had it not been for the simultaneous revolts by usurpers throughout the provinces. The events around the year 260 are a case in point. The year began with Gallienus handling an uprising by the imperial legate in Pannonia with great speed and efficiency, but the troops needed to quell the revolt left the Rhine frontier exposed, allowing the Franks and Alamanni to descend upon Gaul and Italy. The emperor wheeled around, dealt with the Franks in Gaul, and then headed straight for Rome, where the Alamanni battled an army raised by the Senate. Returning with great plunder, the Alamanni were at Milan when the emperor descended upon them and crushed them utterly. He then sent his most able general to deal with the Persians and the usurpers in the east while he dealt with a new usurper in Gaul. This pretty much sums up the whole of his reign.

This ongoing warfare was not without personal cost to the emperor. Fifteen years of constant campaigning hardened him, to the point where he felt it was not so important to observe the civil niceties of the Roman capital and its elite. The usurper Ingenuus may have killed Gallienus's eldest son, and another usurper, Postumus, murdered his second son, so that it is no wonder he took the rebellions against his reign very personally. Yet he persevered throughout his whole reign, never giving in to what seemed to be a hopeless cause. Given his overall successes against the barbarians and usurpers, you would think his reputation would be far greater than it is. After all, he was on campaign for virtually all of his fifteen years as emperor, and according to all available information did not actually lose many battles; when he did, he generally regained the upper hand eventually.

There are three reasons why his reputation suffered. First, the majority of his subjects considered his response to his father's capture shameful. Roman tradition held that the place of a father in the family was sacrosanct and that the child owed all honour to the father. For Gallienus not to even try to purchase his father's release from captivity left a sour taste in most people's mouth, especially given Valerian's reputation. It is not coincidental that most of the usurpations began after Valerian's capture.

Second, Gallienus accepted the eastern usurpers in order to stabilise the empire while he dealt with the problems in the west. He made the strategic decision that the most important province in the empire was Italy, meaning that he focused on the barbarians and usurpers in the west as they threatened the capital of the empire. Consequently, he allowed various usurpers to reign unchallenged in the east, counting on them to hold the eastern provinces together and repel the Persians until he had secured the west, at which point he would deal with them. He took action against them only if they crossed over to Europe to challenge him.

Murder of Gallienus outside Milan

THE AGE OF THE URSURPERS

He followed a similar policy towards the German nations, forging treaties with Germanic kings and using their troops to defend the provinces from other tribes. However, such actions were not what was expected of an emperor: his duty was to defeat his enemies, not come to terms with them.

Third, he decided to remove all senators from military commands after the Senate's successful defence of Rome. The invasion of Italy by the Alamanni found Gallienus hundreds of kilometres away. With nothing standing in the way of the barbarians, the Senate roused itself and organised a force comprising the Praetorian Guard and volunteers from all available able-bodied men within the capital. To their great surprise, they repulsed the invaders, who were then defeated at Milan when the emperor returned. So imagine their disappointment and anger when the emperor, instead of rewarding them with a greater share of responsibility, took away one of their few remaining privileges by declaring that henceforth no senator would obtain a military command. From now on, military appointments would be made only from within the army.

The Senate, left with no other way of expressing its displeasure, defamed Gallienus's memory in the chronicles of the time. The *Historia Augusta* describes a man who was devoted to luxury and debauchery. He responded to the calamities of the empire with indifference: if a province was overrun, he wondered

THE *HISTORIA AUGUSTA*

Our only detailed source for the activities, or even the existence, of a great many of the third century emperors is the remarkable *Historia Augusta*. Detailing the reigns of all the emperors, co-emperors and usurpers from the reign of Hadrian to that of Carinus, it was supposedly written by six authors during the reigns of Diocletian and Constantine.

However, because of anachronistic terms and variant Latin usage, consensus is that it is the work of a single author, writing at least fifty years later. This in and of itself would not be an issue, but the real problem with the *Historia* is its use of fake information, either to pad out the lives of the major emperors or to invent a life history for some of the minor figures. For the major emperors up to the reign of Severus Alexander, the *Historia* is reasonably useful; from that point onwards it descends into almost complete fiction.

To beef up its credibility, the work cites over 130 fake supporting documents, including Senate proceedings and letters supposedly written by the emperors, and lists numerous invented authors. It even goes to the extreme of having the invented authors disagree with each other about aspects of the emperors' lives.

A good example of the unreliability of the *Historia* is its account of the supposed usurper Cyriades. Some late sources speak of a certain Mareades (or Mariades) who, during the reign of Valerian, betrayed the city of Antioch to the Persians, after which the Persian king had him killed. The *Historia* turns Mareades into the tyrant Cyriades and says the Persian king created him emperor. He supposedly led his armies on campaigns in the east, before his own troops killed him. It appears that the author has taken the Aramaic name *Maryad'a*, which means 'My lord knows', and translated 'lord' into the Greek *kyri* (in Latin the 'k' becomes 'c', making *cyri*). Since *kyri* in Greek could designate a Caesar or an Augustus, the author of the *Historia* invented a whole story around this minor individual.

where his favourite cloth would come from. When questioned about what he planned to do about his captured father, he asked about the amusements planned for his lunch. His skills were limited to cooking, gardening and poetry, and he roused himself to action only in the direst emergency. Few men in history have had their name so successfully blackened.

The circumstances of Gallienus's death suited the times. In 268 the Goths had broken through the Danube fortifications and were ravaging Greece. Gallienus quickly intervened and defeated the invaders in battle. Before he could pursue them, however, he had to contend with a revolt by the commander of his elite cavalry force. He turned around, defeated the usurper and proceeded to lay siege to him in Milan. Things were looking desperate for the usurper when he bribed the members of Gallienus's inner council to have the emperor murdered. A conspiracy took shape and one of the commanders killed Gallienus. He deserved better.

Though every effort was made to devalue Gallienus's reign, there was one matter in which his legacy was so profound it could not be denied—changes to the structure of the Roman army. For centuries the legions had been the foundation of Roman might, each consisting of five thousand foot soldiers, supported by an equal number of auxiliary troops and a little light cavalry. Yet by the third century they were no longer as effective at maintaining the frontiers, especially with barbarian incursions occurring at multiple points throughout the empire. Gallienus introduced a mobile, heavily armoured cavalry unit that could be easily dispatched to any trouble spot as needed. This innovation revolutionised Roman military tactics and was to be the basis for the reorganisation of the armies of the late empire. Within two hundred years, the traditional legions would be gone; in their place were squads of heavy cavalry, which became the cornerstone of all European armies for the next thousand years, until the introduction of gunpowder.

INGENUUS

FIRST CAB OFF THE RANK

NAME: Ingenuus
BORN: Unknown
RULED: Usurper, 260
DIED: Suicide, Mursa Major (Osijek), Illyricum, 260

THOUGH VALERIAN'S CAPTURE afforded a number of talented individuals the chance to shoot for imperial glory, it is possible that some had been planning for this moment for some time. Ingenuus may well have been one of those.

The imperial legate in the Pannonian provinces, his orders were to give military instruction to Gallienus's eldest son, the Caesar Cornelius Licinius Valerianus. He was a good choice as he had successfully repulsed a Sarmatian invasion and secured peace in the area for a time. Then, in 258, the young Valerianus died in mysterious circumstances while under Ingenuus's care. After Ingenuus's revolt there were whispers that he had killed the boy; if that was indeed the case, it would strengthen the probability that Ingenuus had been planning his revolt for some time.

As it was, the troops of Moesia and Pannonia declared him emperor upon hearing news of Valerian's capture. They needed no encouragement from Ingenuus, who from all reports was a well-liked and admired commander. His popularity, however, did him no good. Gallienus was in Germania on the Rhine frontier when he summoned his troops and marched swiftly to meet the usurper at Mursa. The battle featured Gallienus's new heavy cavalry units, and this gave him the edge over Ingenuus, whose traditional forces were routed. Defeated, the intrepid legate decided that death was better than falling into the emperor's hands, and he drowned himself in a nearby river.

1. Roman commander, 2. Soldier with fasces, 3. Roman cavalier, 4. Numidian cavalier, 5. Cavalier with scaled harness, 6. Dacian cavalier

REGALIANUS

PICKED UP WHERE INGENUUS LEFT OFF

NAME: Cornelius Publius Cassius Regalianus
BORN: Unknown
RULED: Usurper, 260
DIED: Killed, possibly at Carnuntum, Pannonia, 260

MANY OF THE USURPERS who rose to prominence during the 260s were military men, appointees of Valerian, and it was to him that they owed their loyalty and devotion. Regalianus was no exception: a senator who was married to a highborn Roman noblewoman, he held a military command in Illyricum during the revolt of Ingenuus.

In the aftermath of Ingenuus's death, the local legions and provincials hoped that Gallienus would stay and put their affairs in order. However, the invasion of Italy by the Alamanni forced the emperor to move immediately, leaving the province unprotected. A Sarmatian invasion forced the Illyrians to declare Regalianus as their emperor. Moving swiftly, he first gathered all the troops who had supported Ingenuus, and then turned to face and comprehensively defeat the invaders.

Once the immediate threat had passed, the provincials began to think about what Gallienus would do now, knowing that this was the second time in a year they had raised a usurper. In fear, they captured the hero of the hour, and the very people Regalianus had saved butchered him.

MACRIANUS

LEFT IT ALL TO DAD

NAME: Titus Fulvius Iunius Macrianus
BORN: Unknown
RULED: Usurper, 260–261
DIED: Killed, Thrace, 261

MOST TIMES a man became emperor via inheritance, military exploits or personal bravery. Not so Macrianus, who became emperor because of his father and remained under his control throughout his reign. Theirs was not a noble or, indeed, a senatorial family. Macrianus Senior was an equestrian who had served in the military under Valerian. By 260 he was the minister responsible for maintaining the imperial accounts and expenditures of the treasury and had followed Valerian to the east to support his Persian expedition.

> **And so give us your sons Macrianus and Quietus, most valiant young men.**
>
> BALLISTA (the praetorian prefect)

In the aftermath of Valerian's capture, the legions of the east demanded a new emperor. Since Gallienus was far away in the west, there needed to be someone in Syria to deal with the Persian crisis. The praetorian prefect Ballista recommended Macrianus Senior for the role, but he declined, declaring that old age, ill health and a deformity precluded him from assuming the purple. Instead, he nominated his two sons as emperors—Macrianus Junior and Quietus.

Macrianus Junior, though emperor in name, was merely the figurehead through which his father operated. The young man had not achieved much by the time of his accession; however, the eastern provinces accepted his rule for two reasons. Firstly, his father controlled the enormous funds that Valerian had raised to finance his eastern campaigns. Secondly, Ballista scored a resounding victory against the Persians, thereby temporarily securing the eastern provinces and solidifying the power of the usurpers.

Once the immediate Persian threat had receded, Macrianus Senior concluded that in order to secure his son's rule, he needed to defeat and kill Gallienus. Therefore, in 261, father and son gathered what legions they could without leaving the east totally undefended and marched into Europe. They got to Thrace before the army of Gallienus, commanded by one of his generals, the future usurper Aureolus, met them. The legions of the west were too good on this occasion, and it quickly became evident to the Macriani that they would soon become prisoners. Given the father had made every decision about this reign so far, it seems fitting that he also chose the manner in which his imperial son would die: before the battle had ended he asked their troops to kill them both.

QUIETUS
LEFT HOLDING THE FORT

NAME: Titus Fulvius Iunius Quietus
BORN: Unknown
RULED: Co-usurper, 260–261
DIED: Killed, Emesa (Homs), Syria, 261

WHILE HISTORY SAYS very little about Macrianus Junior, it says even less about his younger brother, Quietus. Though he is said to have been a military tribune under Valerian, most historians dismiss this as a fiction. When Macrianus Senior decided to take on Gallienus, he left Quietus in the east under the care of Ballista. Together, they kept an eye on the Persians while they waited anxiously for news from the west. When word arrived, it was not good: both father and brother had perished in battle. This destabilised the situation in the east, and another minor power emerged to take advantage of the situation.

The rich caravan town of Palmyra, located between the Roman province of Syria and the Persian Empire, was ruled by a local family whose leader at this time was a man named Septimius Odaenathus. Though classified as a Roman colony, Palmyra was technically independent of the Roman Empire. Odaenathus had been a loyal client king of the Romans and had, in fact, aided the Romans in pushing the Persians out of the eastern provinces in 260 and recovering Roman Mesopotamia. When Odaenathus heard that Macrianus had fallen in 261, he moved against Quietus, who fled for safety to the city of Emesa. There, Odaenathus besieged the usurper and, during the course of that siege, with supplies running low, the people starting murmuring against the Roman upstarts. Ballista, in an effort to save himself, handed Quietus over to the local populace, who then killed him. Ballista fled, and the city opened its gates to Odaenathus.

VALENS THESSALONICUS
LOYAL TO A POINT

NAME: Valens Thessalonicus
BORN: Unknown
RULED: Usurper, 261
DIED: Killed, place unknown, 261

FOR MACRIANUS, marching towards his date with destiny in the west, one of his many problems was those legates and governors loyal to Gallienus who stood in his way. Valens, the proconsular governor of the province of Achaea (southern Greece), was one such individual. He had been appointed by Gallienus and was apparently quite devoted to the emperor's cause. Macrianus had initially sounded him out, seeking his support, but was firmly rebuffed by the loyal Valens. Renowned as both a warrior and a just administrator, he was one potential threat that Macrianus was keen to neutralise. Therefore, he sent a force under the command of Piso to deal with him.

Valens was preparing to handle this situation, but his life suddenly took an unexpected turn when his soldiers declared him Augustus and raised him to the purple. His loyalty to the emperor did not stretch so far as to refuse this dangerous but attractive offer. He took the initiative and sent soldiers to kill his would-be nemesis, Piso, and then, thinking that he was safe, at least for a time, he let down his guard, only to die at the hands of his own soldiers.

PISO

AN HONOURABLE ROMAN

NAME: Lucius Calpurnius Piso Frugi
BORN: Unknown
RULED: Usurper, 261
DIED: Murdered, Thessaly, Macedonia, 261

BY THIS STAGE in the empire's history, nearly all the great families of the republic had vanished. Piso represented the exception, being a member of the Calpurnian family, whose lineage stretched back to the old kings of Rome.

A man with such an ancestry would be conscious of his own reputation. Many said that Piso lived a life of great virtue, and in acknowledgement of his attachment to the old Roman ideals, they gave him the name 'Frugi'. According to the *Historia Augusta*, he had been a consul, and by 260 he was serving in the east—probably one of the officers selected by Valerian for his grand expedition. In the confusion following Valerian's capture, Piso supported the imperial dreams of Macrianus. On their way to the west, Macrianus selected Piso for a very special task—to eliminate the threat of Valens. Going ahead of the main armies, Piso crossed the Bosphorus into Thessaly, but at this point he decided to go one step further and declared himself emperor: after all, his family were of nobler Roman stock than the common Macriani.

His gamble did not last long. Valens sent troops to prevent Piso establishing himself, and the great Calpurnian died at their hands. He was mourned both by the Senate and by the man who arranged his death: Valens was reputed to have said that no explanation would suffice in his defence for having given the order to put Piso to death, for there was no one like him left within the Roman Empire.

MUSSIUS AEMILIANUS

CHOSE THE WRONG SIDE

NAME: Lucius Mussius Aemilianus
BORN: Unknown
RULED: Usurper, 261–262
DIED: Murdered, Egypt, 262

IN THE ANARCHY that followed Valerian's defeat, Egypt was one of the provinces that supported the claims of Macrianus, and his chief adherent was the prefect of Egypt, Aemilianus. Aemilianus seems to have been one of the many equestrians who had gained appointments in the army during the previous twenty years, and he had served effectively in Gaul and Alexandria before this posting. He was of Italian heritage, and the emperor obviously considered him reliable, since Egypt was Rome's breadbasket and any troubles in Egypt would have led very quickly to strife in the capital.

In the eyes of Gallienus, however, Aemilianus was now a rebel. With the death of Macrianus, Aemilianus felt he had no choice but to take the next step and declare himself emperor in Egypt. Gallienus sent one of his trusted generals, Aurelius Theodotus, to the rebel province to deal with the situation quickly and decisively. Theodotus acquitted himself admirably, defeating the unlucky usurper in battle and capturing him into the bargain. Since Aemilianus was a rebel and a traitor, he was strangled in a prison cell as tradition demanded, considered too unworthy of an honourable Roman death.

POSTUMUS

SAVIOUR OF GAUL

NAME: Marcus Cassianius Latinius Postumus
BORN: Probably Gaul, date unknown
RULED: Usurper, 260–269
DIED: Murdered, Moguntiacum (Mainz), Germania, 269

IT WAS UNUSUAL FOR A USURPER to last out a year; Postumus survived almost nine. Yet nothing about the young Postumus singled him out for such an exalted climb: he was born of a lowly family and owed his career to above average competency in the military sphere.

By 260 the situation in the western provinces was dire. Usurpers had risen up on the Danube frontier, while the Franks had pushed the Romans back across the Rhine. All Roman possessions on the eastern bank of the Rhine were lost at this time, and the Roman Empire would be a very different beast when it eventually reclaimed them some six hundred years later.

Gallienus had his hands full dealing with these problems, and so he left his younger son, Saloninus, in Gaul in the hands of the praetorian prefect Silvanus. At the time, Postumus was one of the commanders in Germany. He was distributing the booty from a victory over the Franks when Silvanus ordered him to send the spoils to Cologne. The legions, infuriated, declared Postumus emperor; he promptly marched to Cologne, laid siege to the city and, upon its capture, executed both Silvanus and the emperor's son Saloninus.

By the time Gallienus was able to turn his attention to the situation in Gaul, Postumus had firmly entrenched himself. He had campaigned against the Franks and expelled them from Gaul, so that by 261 he was acknowledged as emperor in Gaul, Spain, Germania and Britain. In 263 Gallienus sent his most trusted commander, Aureolus, to bring Postumus to heel. Aureolus managed a number of victories against the usurper, but when Postumus was within his grasp, Aureolus mysteriously allowed him to escape. The emperor recalled Aureolus, and it was not until 265 that Gallienus, freed from other military crises, could gather enough troops to attack Postumus himself. Gallienus had the upper hand but, as he was besieging the usurper in a Gallic town, he was struck by an arrow and had to abandon his revenge on the man who had killed his son.

Gold aureus with facing portrait of Postumus

Postumus was unique among the usurpers in this period in that he did not want to overthrow Gallienus and make himself sole emperor. He made no effort to extend his dominion into Italy or any other province, focusing solely on defending Gaul and Germania from continuous barbarian inroads. He probably saw himself as Gallienus's co-emperor and equal, especially since Valerian had divided the empire to allow two emperors to deal with simultaneous crises. Of course, Gallienus and the Senate never recognised his claim to the throne. Nevertheless, Postumus fixed his capital at Cologne and organised a Senate and other institutions on the Roman model, including consuls. Even his coins bear this out, declaring his link to Roma Aeterna—Eternal Rome.

> **He is a man at whom I marvel above all others and well deserving of the office of prince.**
>
> VALERIAN (supposedly writing about Postumus)

This attachment to peaceful imperial cohabitation would soon be the death of Postumus. His troops did not understand his policy, believing he was not interested in rewarding their loyalty by becoming the sole emperor. Financial difficulties only worsened the situation, and by 269 Postumus was himself fending off usurpers. It was in crushing the rebellion of Laelianus that he gave the fateful order to his troops not to sack the city of Moguntiacum, which they had just taken. Their patience stretched beyond endurance, his troops mutinied and murdered him before the walls of the city. He had outlived Gallienus by a few months.

Postumus did much to stabilise the Rhine frontier in a time of grave crisis, and the ability of Rome to reclaim the former provinces virtually intact in the years to come was due to his steady hand and disciplined spirit. Had he not been involved in the murder of Saloninus, Gallineus may well have come to an accommodation with him.

AUREOLUS

A MAN SPURNED

NAME: Marcus Acilius Aureolus
BORN: Possibly Dacia, c. 230
RULED: Usurper, 268
DIED: Murdered, Mediolanum (Milan), Italy, 268

AS HE WAS MINDING HIS SHEEP and cattle, young Aureolus probably looked around and decided he did not want to do this for the rest of his life. Believing shepherding was not his true calling, he left home to join the military, eventually coming to the attention of Gallienus, who made him Master of the Imperial Horse. He showed great ability and the emperor soon put him in charge of the new elite cavalry force he had developed. For his base he selected Milan, since it allowed him easy access to the various provinces in the empire that might need his intervention.

For a while, it seemed that Aureolus could do no wrong. In defeating the usurper Ingenuus and challenging the rebellious eastern legions under Macrianus, he showed superior tactical skill in defeating an enemy with greater numbers than his own. Impressed, the emperor turned to his commander to take on a task of great personal interest to himself—the defeat of the usurper Postumus in Gaul. It was make or break time for Aureolus, and he stuffed it up superbly. After winning a number of battles against Postumus and trapping the usurper, he allowed him to slip away to fight another day.

Gallienus was not impressed, demoting Aureolus from his top position and posting him to a small command in the province of Raetia (roughly, modern Switzerland), which Aureolus had recovered in his campaign against Postumus. By 268 the emperor was battling the Goths, who had invaded the eastern European provinces, and Aureolus had to deal with the humiliation of having his cavalry forces (now under the command of Claudius) achieve some stunning victories against the barbarian invaders. Unable to cope with the change in fortune, he took advantage of the emperor's absence to march from Raetia and capture his old power base of Milan. He sent messages to Postumus in Gaul, asking him to march down and claim the empire for himself. Postumus was not interested in the offer, and so Aureolus declared himself emperor.

Gallienus was now doubly furious, as he was forced to deal with yet another usurper just as he was about to finish off the Goths for good. Reaching Italy, he defeated Aureolus at the River Adda, where the bridge over the river was renamed Aureolus's Bridge, before besieging him in Milan. A desperate Aureolus bribed members of Gallienus's military command, including his replacement as commander, Claudius, to take the emperor's life. The conspiracy against Gallienus was successful, and the troops elected Claudius to be the next emperor. Surrendering to Claudius, Aureolus believed he would be rewarded for his role in Claudius's accession. He was sorely mistaken—the Praetorian Guard killed him, most likely on Claudius's orders to ensure that no one could implicate him in the former emperor's death.

CLAUDIUS II GOTHICUS

NEMESIS OF THE GOTHS

NAME: Marcus Aurelius Claudius
BORN: Sirmium (Sremska), Pannonia, 213
RULED: Emperor, 268–270
DIED: Of plague, Sirmium, Pannonia, 270

THE *HISTORIA AUGUSTA* CLAIMS that Claudius Gothicus was descended from a Trojan king and even the god Zeus. In fact, he was a dirty peasant from the backwaters of Illyricum who had risen through the ranks of the military like so many before him. But where others had failed, he succeeded: he became the first in a line of emperors who would rejuvenate the empire.

Claudius was a very tall man with a full, broad face and flashing eyes, who had demonstrated his superior military skills to the point of being assigned the plum job of commander of Gallienus's elite cavalry force. His success pushed his predecessor to the point of rebellion, and Claudius found himself assigned as a military tribune with the emperor at the siege of Milan in 268. The pretender, Aureolus, made contact with the army commanders to overthrow Gallienus, which they did, before electing Claudius as the next emperor. The troops of Gallienus, quite attached to the old emperor, were initially furious—after all, he had been their constant companion for the past fifteen years—but a quick payment saw them settle down and accept the new situation.

After killing Aureolus, Claudius's next act was to re-assign some underperforming officers and allot a new commander to the elite cavalry unit—for this he chose the promising officer Aurelian. Then, perhaps sensing he might not have a lot of time to get the job done, he went on campaign and did not stop.

His major problem was the Goths. These foes had become a major nuisance for the empire ever since they had gained access to the Black Sea and were able to sail south and attack any settlement they chose. So almost immediately Claudius went to Macedonia and Greece to hunt the Goths, who had been pillaging with abandon ever since Gallienus had been called away to deal with Aureolus. Facing a foe of some 320,000 able-bodied men, Claudius defeated them in battle after battle; where he left off, bad weather, hunger and plague did the work for him. By the end of 269 only a tiny remnant of that host returned to their forested homelands. It was such a tremendous victory that the Senate awarded Claudius the title 'Gothicus', and the provinces in Spain, which had previously followed the usurper Postumus, decided to return to the fold, voluntarily swearing allegiance to the mighty Claudius.

Claudius might have accomplished more had the plague that had finished off the Goths not also taken an imperial victim, and so Claudius died in his fifty-sixth year, mourned by both army and Senate.

Claudius Gothicus

CENSORINUS

TOO STRICT FOR HIS OWN GOOD

NAME: Censorinus
BORN: Unknown
RULED: Usurper, 269
DIED: Murdered, Bononia (Bologna), Italy, 269

EVEN THOUGH THINGS were beginning to improve for the empire, usurpers were still appearing in record numbers. Censorinus had an illustrious consular and military career prior to his being wounded and honourably discharged from the Persian wars. He supposedly decided to become emperor because someone made fun of his injuries while comparing him to the peasant Claudius.

What little is recorded of his revolt states that his soldiers acclaimed him emperor, most likely while Claudius was off fighting the Goths. Because he was an old-style disciplinarian, they turned around and murdered him before burying him in Bologna, where the revolt is assumed to have taken place.

LAELIANUS

UNGRATEFUL SUBORDINATE

NAME: Gaius Ulpius Cornelius Laelianus
BORN: Unknown
RULED: Usurper, 269
DIED: Moguntiacum (Mainz), Germania, 269

USURPERS WERE NOT ONLY overthrowing legitimate Roman emperors—they even began targeting other usurpers. In Gaul, Postumus had the misfortune of experiencing this phenomenon, courtesy of Laelianus. On the basis of his name and coins, he was possibly of Spanish descent and by 269 was the legate of Upper Germania. By now many of Postumus's troops were starting to show definite signs of disloyalty, and this gave Laelianus an idea. After successfully repulsing a Germanic invasion, his troops raised him to the purple. Listening to their grievances, he believed he had a chance of toppling Postumus, but his major problem was that such seditious talk was mainly confined to the legions on the Rhine.

Postumus quickly gathered his forces and marched on the city of Mainz, where Laelianus had his capital. After a siege of two months, the city surrendered, and Laelianus was executed by order of Postumus.

MARIUS

THE BLACKSMITH

NAME: Marcus Aurelius Marius
BORN: Unknown
RULED: Usurper, 269
DIED: Murdered, possibly Augusta Treverorum (Trier), Germania, 269

SOMETIMES PEOPLE in a hurry make the wrong choices. Sometimes in a fit of pique you end up killing your emperor, and in the confusion you end up electing—a blacksmith. Given Marius's background, he had great strength and massive forearms; unfortunately, neither of these things qualified him for the imperial office. Nevertheless, finding himself in this situation, he tried to make the most of it, probably allowing the troops finally to pillage Mainz. However, the soldiers resented taking orders from him and soon Victorinus, a man with much higher military qualifications and prestige, decided that a lowly blacksmith would not do as emperor. Within a few weeks, Marius was murdered. Tradition holds that his killer greeted him with the following words: 'This is a sword which you yourself have forged.'

VICTORINUS
THE GREAT SEDUCER

NAME: Marcus Piavonius Victorinus
BORN: Unknown
RULED: Usurper, 269–271
DIED: Murdered, Colonia Agrippina (Cologne), Germania, 271

BY THE TIME VICTORINUS took possession of the Gallic provinces, many areas were thinking of rejoining the empire, given Claudius's heroic exploits. Consequently, most of Victorinus's reign saw him trying to keep his subject provinces from fleeing the sinking ship of state.

This was a shame, as Victorinus was a man of great wealth and some ability. Achieving prominence under the rule of Postumus as co-consul, he was the current tribune of the praetorians at Cologne when the army declared him emperor at Trier. The majority of his reign was then spent in the siege of Augustodunum Haeduorum (modern Autun), which had switched allegiance to Claudius. Victorinus captured it, and his troops plundered and then destroyed the city.

Such acts of liberality to his troops were not enough to save him. He was a notorious womaniser and had recently seduced the wife of his quartermaster, Attitianus. When the aggrieved husband found out, he was enraged and murdered his commanding officer.

QUINTILLUS
THE SENATE'S CHOICE

NAME: Marcus Aurelius Claudius Quintillus
BORN: Sirmium (Sremska), Pannonia, c. 220
RULED: Emperor, 270
DIED: Suicide, Aquileia, Italy, 270

NOTHING IN QUINTILLUS'S past would have marked him out as a future emperor. A plain man, he is ignored in the historical records until his brother Claudius was made emperor. Claudius then took care of his younger brother, possibly making him procurator of Sardinia in 268. He was fortunate to be in Italy in 270 when Claudius died of the plague in distant Sirmium, and the Senate decided to invest him with the purple.

It seems that he felt the responsibility was beyond his abilities, especially when Claudius's legions rejected the Senate's choice, electing Aurelian as the next emperor. Seeing he had no military support, Quintillus took the old Roman route of suicide to end the uneven contest, opening his veins and bleeding to death after reigning for just a few weeks.

AURELIAN
RESTORER OF THE WORLD

NAME: Lucius Domitius Aurelianus
BORN: Sirmium (Sremska), Pannonia, 214
RULED: Emperor, 270–275
DIED: Murdered, Caenophrurium (Çorlu), Thrace, 275

THE PROVINCE OF ILLYRICUM bred some of the toughest soldiers in the empire—fearless men who dominated the upper echelons of the army to become the natural rulers of a system that was virtually a military dictatorship. None was more imposing or more celebrated than the emperor Aurelian. Building upon the foundations created by the sweat and toil of Gallienus and Claudius II, he reunified the fractured empire.

Aurelian's origins were humble. His father was the tenant of a Roman senator, and Aurelian took the first opportunity to join the military and begin his climb through the ranks. His big break came with the assassination of Gallienus: he was one of the officers who supported Claudius's decision to overthrow the emperor

TRIUMPHS AND OVATIONS

In a culture that prized an individual's accomplishments as a reflection of the greatness of society, there was nothing greater that could be bestowed on a Roman citizen than a triumph. Originating in the early years of the Roman Republic, it was an honour paid to a successful general who had won a major land or sea battle, killing at least five thousand of the enemy, and who had been hailed on the field as *imperator* by his men. He also needed to be an elected magistrate with the requisite *imperium* (authority) to hold command, such as a consul or a praetor.

When such an honour was granted by the Senate, the victorious general was allowed to ride in triumph through the streets of Rome with his army before the procession terminated at the steps of the temple of Jupiter Optimus Maximus. In the procession, riding behind the senators, musicians, sacrificial animals, spoils of war and captured prisoners, was the victorious general, wearing a royal purple and gold tunic and toga, holding a laurel branch in his right hand and an ivory sceptre in his left. A slave held a golden crown over the general's head while reminding him that he was just a mortal man. At the end, the general went into the temple and offered Jupiter the laurels of victory, after which a feast was held.

With the establishment of the principate, the granting of triumphs became rare, as they became the prerogative of the emperor and his immediate family before eventually being restricted to the emperor himself, although there was the odd exception, such as Belisarius's triumph in 534. The reason for this was twofold. Firstly, the imperial generals commanded under the emperor's auspices as lieutenants, and therefore the glory belonged to the emperor, and, secondly, the acclamation of the victorious general as *imperator* soon meant he was making a claim to become the next Roman emperor. Instead, the victorious general was granted an *ornamenta triumphalia*, having the dress and privileges traditionally granted to a *triumphator*, but without the elaborate triumphal procession through the streets of Rome.

Where a general was not awarded a triumph, he may have been given an ovation. During the republic, an ovation was awarded when war had not been declared against an enemy state (such as when fighting against pirates), when an enemy was considered basely inferior (such as slaves) or when the general resolved the conflict with little or no bloodshed. In this case, the general walked along the route, wearing the purple-bordered toga of an ordinary magistrate and a wreath of myrtle. Again, during the principate, ovations were restricted to the imperial family before the honour eventually faded away.

and, for his support, Claudius gave him the coveted job of commander of the empire's heavy cavalry units. He soon was on campaign with Claudius and was with him when the emperor succumbed to the plague. The legions in Pannonia proclaimed Aurelian to be the most worthy of imperial honours, and so he quickly marched into Italy to confirm the prize, eliminating Quintillus in the process.

From then on, Aurelian's record is of one victory after another. He first had to deal with the Alamanni, who had taken advantage of Aureolus's rebellion in 268 by plundering Raetia and Italy. Aurelian quickly crushed them, but he recognised that he could no longer guarantee the security of Italy's cities, and so he ordered the building of a series of massive fortifications,

TRIUMPH AND TRAGEDY

including a new set of walls for Rome. Then he forced back a Vandal invasion and pounded the Goths into submission, before demonstrating his practical side by abandoning the province of Dacia, making the Danube the frontier of Roman *imperium*. These actions finally put a halt to the repeated Germanic invasions, and the northern frontiers were to be relatively stable for the next seventy-five years.

By late 272 Aurelian was ready to turn his attention to the divided empire. He first dealt with a rash of usurpers who sought to test their mettle against the new emperor, before heading east to battle the successors of Odaenathus of Palmyra, who had gone from being just supporters of Roman power to exercising imperial power through the usurper Vaballathus and his mother Zenobia.

> **It is clear that the immortal gods have granted me no victory without some hardship.**
>
> AURELIAN

Aurelian extended his winning streak by defeating the Palmyrenes, before crossing the desert and laying siege to Palmyra. Zenobia attempted to escape but his soldiers captured her at the Euphrates River, returning her in chains. A second rebellion in the city saw Aurelian return and completely obliterate the once great trading city. By the end of 273 the east was resting once again within the bosom of the empire.

That left Gaul. The usurper Tetricus did not put up much of a fight, so that by the middle of 274 the empire that had broken apart in 260 was once again whole. It was a remarkable achievement—one that the Senate duly recognised by giving Aurelian the title *restitutor orbis*—Restorer of the World. In his well-deserved triumph, Aurelian marched his captive prisoners in

General view of Rome at the time of Emperor Aurelian with the circus of Alexander Severus in the foreground

THE AGE OF THE URSURPERS

chains before the adoring Roman populace, who once again believed that they were the pre-eminent power in the world.

Aurelian was a typical peasant with a no-nonsense approach to all matters, be they military, religious or civil. Used to giving unquestioned commands in the field, he had no time for the traditional, collegiate approach of the principate. Consolidating the process of centralisation that had been transforming Roman political life for the past half century, he assumed the titles *dominus et dues natus*—he who was born as Lord and God—not too bad for a peasant from the backwaters of the empire. Three hundred years before, the Romans had killed Julius Caesar because they thought he wanted to be king. Now they joyfully accepted his spiritual descendant as the absolute monarch of Rome. To ensure that there would be little resistance to the change, he reintroduced the official cult of Sol Invictus—the unconquered sun god that Elagabalus had failed so spectacularly to introduce fifty years before. Sol Invictus would be the chief of the Roman deities, and the emperor, the incarnation of the divine spirit. Thus was born the notion of One God, One Emperor, One Empire—the catchphrase of the Roman Empire from now until its death 1500 years later, although it would be transfigured by the acceptance of a different god—the Christian God.

Aurelian's popularity could not prevent him meeting the classic death of this period—murder. He was preparing for a new campaign against the Persians when his secretary, fearing punishment on impending corruption charges, approached the praetorians and told them that the emperor had marked a number of their senior officers for execution. Deciding to strike first, they murdered him while he was waiting to cross over from Thrace into Asia Minor. Aurelian achieved much during his five years as emperor, and his reforms became the basis of the reorganisation of the empire that would occur under another emperor from Illyricum—Diocletian.

DOMITIAN PIUS
IF YOU HANG AROUND LONG ENOUGH...

NAME: Domitianus Pius
BORN: Unknown
RULED: Usurper, 271
DIED: Unknown, c. 271

THE ACCESSION OF a new emperor was problematic, and the elevation of Aurelian was no exception, especially in the troubled provinces of Gaul. Domitian's only known claim to fame was as a subordinate of Aureolus in 261, when he was instrumental in the defeat of the usurper Macrianus. The year 271 found him somewhere in Gaul or Germania, where he was declared emperor, possibly during the confusion resulting from the fall of the usurper Victorinus. Domitian's reign was to be short, maybe a couple of weeks at best. Only two coins attest to his existence.

URBANUS
REMEMBERED BY SOMEBODY

NAME: Urbanus
BORN: Unknown
RULED: Usurper, 271
DIED: Killed, place unknown, c. 271

THERE IS AT LEAST SOME coinage to verify the reign of Domitian Pius. We lack even that for the usurper Urbanus: there is merely a single reference to him by the Byzantine historian Zosimus, who stated that he rebelled against Aurelian but was soon defeated and killed. From the context of the passage, it is possible that Urbanus's revolt happened somewhere in Italy, but his existence has been questioned by some scholars.

SEPTIMIUS

OUTLIVED HIS USEFULNESS

NAME: Septimius
BORN: Unknown
RULED: Usurper, 271
DIED: Unknown, c. 271

THE INVASIONS OF THE GOTHS had everyone concerned for their own safety. In the provinces the presence of the emperor was about the only security blanket there was, so when the real emperor was busy elsewhere, the troops regularly raised a local pretender to deal with the crisis at hand. The problem with this approach was that once the crisis was over, the need for the usurper disappeared, leaving the once glorious emperor vulnerable. Certainly, this is what happened to Septimius.

A commander in the province of Dalmatia (modern Croatia), he was turned to by the people when the Goths were running amok. Whether he actually did anything about it is a good question; what is certain is that once the threat had receded, his own troops very quickly killed him. Gratitude was a luxury few could afford in the third century.

VABALLATHUS

MOTHER'S PRIDE AND JOY

NAME: Lucius Julius Aurelius Septimius
Vaballathus Athenodorus
BORN: Palmyra, Syria, c. 260
RULED: Usurper, 267–273
DIED: On his way to Rome, 273

THE SITUATION IN THE eastern provinces had stabilised remarkably since Odaenathus of Palmyra had toppled the usurper Quietus. Recognising that he could do nothing about the situation, the emperor Gallienus declared that Odaenathus was to be his personal representative in the east; in recognition of this, the emperor awarded him the titles *dux Romanorum* (Roman Duke) and *corrector totius orientis* (Corrector of the Whole East). Content with this, Odaenathus ensured that the Persians did not take advantage of Roman infighting to expand their empire.

After Odaenathus's assassination in 267, the role of eastern defender passed to his young son, Vaballathus. Though only a child, possibly eight years of age, he inherited his father's titles; however, all power in Palmyra was concentrated in the hands of his mother, Queen Zenobia, who claimed descent from the famous Cleopatra. She directed all policy decisions in the kingdom, and her subsequent actions came from a desire to see Vaballathus recognised as co-emperor—and if that were not forthcoming, then sole emperor it would be.

I am just a simple woman.

ZENOBIA (mother of Vaballathus)

History has not recorded many details about the young Vaballathus. Zenobia, on the other hand, was described as eye-catching, gifted, with a dark, beautiful face and black, luminous eyes that contrasted with her pearly white teeth. Her voice was powerful, yet sweetly melodic; she was incredibly charming and well educated, and reportedly spoke Latin, Greek, Egyptian and Aramaic. Most unusually for an eastern monarch, she adopted the Roman model of personally leading her troops into battle.

Upon Vaballathus's accession, Claudius II was more than happy to see the situation continue in the east as it had under Odaenathus, and so Rome accepted his claim as inheritor of his father's protective role against the Persian Sassanids and any usurpers. However, by 270, with the Persians momentarily pacified, Zenobia decided it was time to enlarge her son's kingdom.

Her target was not Persia; rather, it was the eastern provinces of the Roman Empire. If her son were indeed to be co-emperor, he should be ruling the eastern provinces directly.

Zenobia's campaign began in Syria but soon stretched into Asia Minor in the north, and into Palestine and Egypt in the south. While she was in the north, the new emperor Aurelian was not too concerned. However, when she interfered in the important province of Egypt, expelling and beheading the Roman prefect, Aurelian was forced to bring the rebellious provinces to heel. By 272 he was in Asia Minor, where some brilliant and devastating campaigns pushed Zenobia from Antioch to Emesa and finally to Palmyra itself.

It was here that the boy emperor Vaballathus was kept, and soon mother and son beheld Aurelian's victorious legions encamped before the walls. Not trusting their fate to the outcome of the siege, they fled Palmyra by stealth on camelback. They planned to cross the Euphrates River and seek refuge at the court of the Sassanids, but they never made it past the river. Captured, they were returned to Aurelian. Aurelian proceeded to take Palmyra but refused to sack it, until further rebellions forced him to turn around and finally destroy the city.

Mother and son were sent to Rome in anticipation of Aurelian's triumph, since it was customary to parade conquered enemies before the people of Rome, but Vaballathus died on the trip. However, Zenobia survived, to be marched before the conquering emperor wearing golden chains. Though tradition demanded she be strangled as soon as the triumph was over, Aurelian decided to let her live, granting her an estate at Tibur in Italy. Zenobia became quite a celebrity; eventually marrying a senator, she turned into the quintessential Roman matron before dying of old age. It may have been quite a letdown for a woman who gambled all to make her son emperor, but there were worse fates for a usurper's mother.

TETRICUS I

PRAGMATIC COWARD

NAME: Gaius Pius Esuvius Tetricus
BORN: Unknown
RULED: Usurper, 271–274
DIED: Of natural causes, Italy, date unknown

VICTORINUS'S MURDER IN GAUL made it possible for a new usurper to emerge. This time the key player in selecting the new emperor was Victorinus's wealthy mother, Victoria. She had set her sights on the imperial legate in Gallia Aquitania, Tetricus, and so she bribed the troops at Cologne, who heartily endorsed the new candidate. Tetricus was not present at these proceedings; he assumed the purple in the city of Burdigalia (modern Bordeaux).

> **Save me, O hero unconquered, from these my misfortunes.**
>
> TETRICUS I

A senator descended from a noble family, Tetricus had given distinguished service in the rebellious provinces for many years. If anyone had doubts about his suitability for the position of emperor, he dispelled them with swift action in defeating a new series of Germanic invasions, as the Germans tried to take advantage of Victorinus's death. Tetricus quickly established his seat at Trier and got down to governing the provinces with firmness and ability.

His greatest test came when Aurelian finally turned his eye to Gaul. Tetricus gathered his troops and met Aurelian near Châlons-sur-Marne, where the two armies eventually clashed. Tradition holds that Tetricus was unwilling to risk a battle and surrendered himself to the emperor, although his soldiers had already begun the defence of their homeland. In

Zenobia, Queen of Palmyra

THE AGE OF THE URSURPERS

disgust, his soldiers kept fighting, but the cause was lost before it even began.

Whether or not Tetricus did surrender, Aurelian recognised a useful servant when he saw one. Therefore, after parading the defeated usurper in the requisite triumph, Aurelian released him and gave him a new career, which included serving as *corrector Lucaniae*. This position involved observing, on behalf of the emperor, lower level bureaucrats against whom grave charges were pending and, if necessary, replacing them. Tetricus lived the rest of his life very quietly, before dying of old age somewhere in Italy.

TETRICUS II
USURPER'S SON

NAME: Gaius Pius Esuvius Tetricus
BORN: Unknown
RULED: Co-usurper, 273–274
DIED: Unknown

THE USURPER TETRICUS, like so many before him, obviously planned to start a new dynasty that would take Rome to previously unattained heights of greatness. Therefore, after initially giving him the title of *princeps iuventutis*, or first youth, during 273 he nominated his son, also named Tetricus, as his co-emperor. The son would not enjoy the honour long. Just after he began his first consulship with his father, Tetricus Senior marched south to do battle with Aurelian, and the son's fate was set the moment his father surrendered to the emperor. Like his father, he was permitted to keep his head after the triumph, and he was then rehabilitated into Roman society and allowed to keep his senatorial status. His talents ensured that the emperors utilised him in various suitable offices.

FAUSTINUS
LAST ROLL OF THE DICE

NAME: Faustinus
BORN: Unknown
RULED: Usurper, 274
DIED: Unknown, c. 274

WITH TETRICUS BUSY PREPARING for Aurelian's expected invasion, it was inevitable that some in the Gallic provinces would take advantage of the situation to make their own bid for power. This appears to have been the case with the usurper Faustinus, imperial legate in Gallia Belgica, who raised the standard of revolt at the provincial capital, Trier.

With Tetricus marching south, Faustinus had a free hand during the first few months of 274, and he might have thought that his road to imperial stardom was open when Tetricus surrendered. If that was so, he misjudged Aurelian's temperament. The emperor crushed the last of the Gallic usurpers so effectively that no one recorded how or when Faustinus died.

TACITUS
PULLED OUT OF RETIREMENT

NAME: Marcus Claudius Tacitus
BORN: Unknown, c. 200
RULED: Emperor, 275–276
DIED: Of fever, Antoniana Colonia Tyana, Cappadocia, 276

SEVENTY-FIVE-YEAR-OLD TACITUS was probably looking forward to a quiet retirement in his villa in Campania. He had served the empire with distinction and had capped a successful career with a consulship in 273 while Aurelian was off campaigning against Zenobia.

It was, therefore, quite a shock when word arrived from the Senate that, after Aurelian's murder, his armies in Thrace had elevated Tacitus to the purple. Given his subsequent actions, it is likely that Tacitus was ex-military, and that the command staff who accompanied Aurelian to the east knew of his exploits and abilities.

Tacitus quickly gathered his belongings and rushed to Rome, where he accepted the nomination. His first action was to deify Aurelian, before arresting and executing the murderers. Unlike his military predecessors, he made moves to re-involve the Senate in some consultative capacity, but such arrangements were short-lived as the emperor was soon marching at the head of his legions. This time the barbarian tribes gathered by Aurelian had begun rampaging through Asia Minor. Donning his military gear, Tacitus headed east, quickly engaging the enemy, who were resoundingly defeated, for which the Senate awarded him the title *Gothicus Maximus*.

He had no time to savour his victory, as word had already reached him of a new barbarian threat, a Frankish and Alamannic invasion of Gaul. He set off for the west but began acting strangely, declaring that he would change the names of the months to honour himself and giving other signs of megalomania. It was the first evidence of the fevered delirium that within days would take his life, at Tyana in the province of Cappadocia.

FLORIAN

OUTFOXED

NAME: Marcus Annius Florianus
BORN: Unknown
RULED: Emperor, 276
DIED: Murdered, Tarsus, Cilicia, c. 276

FLORIAN WAS ANOTHER EMPEROR who owed his accession to a family member. Tacitus needed someone he could trust as his right-hand man for the post of praetorian prefect, and no one was better qualified than his half-brother Florian. He was with Tacitus when the emperor passed away.

Where Tacitus was hesitant, Florian was eager. Not bothering to wait for the army's acclamation or the Senate's approval, he swiftly declared himself the next Roman emperor. It was a rash decision that would prove to be his undoing, for though he continued to fight the barbarians who were still running amok in Asia Minor, the loyalty of his troops began to waver. The eastern armies rejected his elevation, instead nominating their own commander, Probus, and thus forcing Florian to turn around and engage his rival in battle.

The armies skirmished near the city of Tarsus. Though Florian looked like he had the advantage with a much larger force, Probus was a wily fox, who avoided a direct confrontation. Florian's Danubian legions were not used to the eastern summer heat and, as the weather began to take its toll, support for Florian, never strong to begin with, collapsed further. Hearing good things about Probus, Florian's soldiers mutinied and proceeded to kill the unfortunate emperor. His rule had lasted eighty-eight days.

PROBUS

OLD-SCHOOL DISCIPLINARIAN

NAME: Marcus Aurelius Equitius Probus
BORN: Sirmium (Sremska), Pannonia, 232
RULED: Emperor, 276–282
DIED: Murdered, Sirmium, Pannonia, 282

PROBUS WAS THE LATEST in a long line of warrior emperors who hailed from the province of Pannonia—perhaps it was the drinking water. His father was a soldier and so a military career seemed to be his destiny. He became a military tribune in Valerian's reign and was awarded many prizes in recognition of his bravery and exploits in battle. Recognising his talents, Aurelian soon

Assassination of Probus

acknowledged Probus as the most able of his commanders. Tacitus gave him a high command in one of the eastern provinces, and it was from this base that he challenged Florian for the imperial crown, falsely claiming that Tacitus had named him as the rightful successor.

Soon we shall have no need of soldiers.

PROBUS

After his victory over Florian in 276, Probus began a non-stop rolling campaign against barbarians and usurpers in all parts of the empire. On his way to Rome, he punished the Goths, who had again crossed the Danube, and after his formal ratification as emperor by the Senate, he proceeded north to the Rhine, where the Franks and Alamanni were still causing havoc. His victory there was so complete that sixteen German chiefs knelt and did homage at his feet. By the end of 279 he had subdued the Burgundians and the Vandals as well, but before long he was dealing with a new batch of usurpers, including one from Britain whose name history has not recorded.

Therefore, it was not until 281 that Probus, exhausted, managed to return to Rome to celebrate his triumph. For his great processional march, he lined up companies of fifty men from each nation he had defeated. Trees were uprooted and replanted in the Circus Maximus so that it resembled a giant forest in the middle of the city, and into it were released one thousand different types of creatures, including ostriches, stags, wild boars, deer, ibexes, wild sheep, and other grass-eating beasts. The citizens of Rome could then enter and take whatever they wanted, and afterwards there were tournaments where lions, leopards, bears and gladiators died for their amusement.

Satisfied, the emperor then began his campaign against the Persians. Setting out in 282, he was encamped near his birthplace of Sirmium, in Pannonia, when trouble began. Over time, the Roman commanders had abandoned a custom whereby the legions had to perform various public services, laborious tasks such as draining marshes and clearing land, when they were not on campaign, and so the legionaries became resentful when Probus put them to work. He had them drain land, erect buildings and defensive fortifications, construct bridges and even plant vineyards. After five years of this, the men had had enough. When a new usurper, Carus, rose up to challenge the emperor, Probus's troops decided that he was too strict and killed him in the camp.

Probus's reign, while generally successful, saw the widespread introduction of a custom that would cause problems in the future—it was during this time that the policy of settling defeated barbarians in the provinces was generally adopted. Though useful for repopulating devastated areas of the empire, the process soon introduced a host of peoples who had no loyalty to Rome or its sovereign.

BONOSUS

ONE CARELESS MISTAKE

NAME: Quintus Bonosus
BORN: Spain, date unknown
RULED: Usurper, 280
DIED: Suicide, Colonia Agrippina (Cologne), Germania, 280

BONOSUS WAS BY ALL ACCOUNTS an excellent soldier with a very distinguished career. A true native of the empire, he was born in Spain, though his father was from Britain and his mother from Gaul. In 280 he had recently been assigned to the Rhine and was in charge of the fleet stationed there. Because of what one source described as a fondness for wine, he allowed the Germans to cross the frontier and burn the fleet to cinders. This was not a good career move.

Fearful of what Probus was going to do to him, he fled to the town of Cologne, shut himself in and declared himself emperor. The real emperor was quickly on the scene, but it was a very difficult campaign, with Bonosus making Probus fight all the way. It took weeks, and it may have taken even longer had Bonosus not succumbed to despair and hanged himself. It is possible that this was a negotiated settlement with Probus, who may have agreed to spare the life of his wife and sons if Bonosus took the honourable way out.

PROCULUS

DON'T TRUST THE FRANKS

NAME: Proculus
BORN: Albingaunum (Albenga), Italy, date unknown
RULED: Usurper, 280–281
DIED: Murdered, Gaul, 281

THERE ARE MANY STORIES told of Proculus, mostly about the great wealth that he had inherited from relatives who were thieves and murderers. It seems he considered himself the big man around town, and he liked to flash his wealth and connections around. This may be what got him into trouble.

Proculus had had a minor career in the military when he found himself trapped in the chaos of a rebellion in the city of Lugdunum (modern Lyon). The locals were unhappy with Probus and during the uprising they chose as their own emperor the unfortunate Proculus. He may have promised much; he certainly delivered very little. As Probus marched towards him, Proculus retreated steadily northwards, and it is uncertain whether he even offered battle with the emperor. He eventually reached the Franks, whom he claimed he could summon to help with the rebellion. They did no such thing. They captured the hapless Proculus and handed him over to a very grateful Probus, who promptly had him killed. Some sources say that both Proculus and Bonosus rebelled together as co-emperors. If so, it did not help.

SATURNINUS

WITH FRIENDS LIKE THESE …

NAME: Sextus Julius Saturninus
BORN: North Africa, date unknown
RULED: Usurper, 281
DIED: Murdered, Palestine, 281

SOMETIMES ALL YOU NEED to send you down the wrong path is a small, tantalising suggestion. That seems to be what happened to the next usurper, Saturninus. Hailing from Gaul, Saturninus was a colleague of Probus, and a close friend to boot, and the emperor felt quite confident leaving him as the imperial legate in Syria while he went to deal with threats elsewhere in the empire. During 280 Saturninus made his way south to Egypt, possibly to deal with some unrest there. While he was there, the people and the local Roman garrison decided that he would be their perfect candidate for emperor. He refused the dangerous honour, and promptly left for his home province.

> **My friends, you do not know what an evil thing it is to rule.**
>
> SATURNINUS

While he was travelling north through Palestine, the thought that he had been so close to becoming emperor of the Roman world gnawed away at him. Should he take the opportunity or not? Would he regret the decision to refuse such a privileged honour? Eventually, temptation got the better of him and he claimed the imperial purple for himself. Alas, like most usurpers, he did not enjoy the experience, which proved short-lived. Even before Probus could lay his hands on him, his own troops murdered him for some unspecified reason.

CARUS

PUNISHED BY THE GODS

NAME: Marcus Aurelius Numerius Carus
BORN: Narbo (Narbonne), Gallia Narbonensis, 224
RULED: Emperor, 282–283
DIED: Of illness, Tigris River, Mesopotamia, 283

CARUS WAS ANOTHER MILITARY MAN, but the first emperor not to hail from Illyricum in a very long time. Yet he too possessed great military ability. A senator as well as a career military man, he was finally rewarded for his efforts with the post of praetorian prefect in 282. While he was inspecting troops in Raetia and Noricum, they acclaimed him emperor, revolting against the harsh discipline of Probus. He may not have wanted the honour, but when Probus was murdered, Carus easily slipped into the role.

Although Carus did not bother going to Rome for confirmation, he sent a letter to the Senate advising them of his elevation, a fact the Senate grudgingly accepted. As he saw it, he had too many other pressing chores to do. After a quick and vicious campaign against the Quadi and Sarmatians on the Danube, he was off to complete the great Persian campaign that Probus had organised. He was fortunate that the Persians were dealing with internal problems. The Roman legions carved a path of destruction through the western parts of the Persian kingdom, sacking their two principal cities, Seleucia and Ctesiphon, and Carus had the distinction of becoming the first emperor since Trajan to take the Roman eagles beyond the Tigris. Not satisfied with reclaiming the province of Mesopotamia, he was keen to add more territory to the empire, but it was not to be. Struck down by a mystery illness, he died near the Tigris River; rumour had it that the gods had struck him with lightning as punishment for travelling so far east.

NUMERIAN

DEATH ON THE ROAD

NAME: Marcus Aurelius Numerius Numerianus
BORN: Unknown, c. 253
RULED: Co-emperor, 283–284
DIED: Of an eye infection, Emesa (Homs), Syria, 284

AFTER HIS DECLARATION as emperor, Carus swiftly moved to stabilise the succession. He named his elder son, Carinus, as co-emperor, and his younger, Numerian, as Caesar. He then took the younger son with him to Persia, and Numerian was with his father on the Tigris when Carus passed away.

The army elected Numerian *imperator* immediately, but it seems his talents were more suited to giving speeches than wielding a sword. His first hesitant steps in continuing the campaign were not promising, and so he quietly organised a withdrawal back to Roman Syria, where he spent the winter. He continued his trip westwards in 284 but was struck down by a serious eye infection somewhere near Emesa. His father-in-law, the praetorian prefect Aper, ordered that Numerian travel in a closed litter for his health. Over the next few days, whenever anyone enquired, Aper reported that the emperor was in good health. Unfortunately, by the time the army reached Bithynia, in Asia Minor, the soldiers noticed a familiar smell coming from the litter. Thrusting open the curtains, they discovered Numerian's rotting corpse.

In a hastily set up tribunal, the commander of the emperor's bodyguard, Valerius Diocles, accused Aper of having Numerian killed. He promptly picked up his sword and plunged it into the praetorian prefect, vindicating his claim. The army then proclaimed Diocles emperor, and he prepared to march on Carus's surviving son, Carinus.

CARINUS

A POOR REPUTATION

NAME: Marcus Aurelius Carinus
BORN: Unknown, c. 250
RULED: Co-emperor, 283–285
DIED: Murdered, Margus River, Moesia, 285

CARINUS WAS RAISED from the depths of obscurity to the imperial heights because of his father's elevation. Of the two sons, Carinus seems to have been the one with the greater drive and military talent, and so he was the obvious choice to remain in the west while his father went off to fight the Persians. Carus's judgement seemed to be confirmed by a successful continuation of the war against the Quadi in 283, followed by an unspecified victory in Britain during 284. Yet there were darker undercurrents to Carinus's reign.

Accounts suggest that Carinus, though gifted, was a man who bore grudges, and he had his enemies indicted on false charges and then killed. The more extreme stories about his rampant sexual appetites, pleasing of mediocre favourites and general unfitness to rule were exaggerations put about by his successor. There may have been some truth to the accounts, however, as towards the end of his reign a usurper rose against him and the Senate condemned Carinus's memory after his death.

He was also very unlucky. Engaging the army of Diocles at the Margus River in Moesia, Carinus was on the verge of defeating his rival when a military tribune, whose wife the emperor had seduced, murdered him. Thus perished the son of Carus, opening the door for the man who would go on to shape the destiny of the empire for the next thousand years—Diocles or, as he became known as emperor, Diocletian.

SABINUS JULIANUS

WHEN THE CAT'S AWAY ...

NAME: Marcus Aurelius Sabinus Julianus
BORN: Unknown
RULED: Usurper, 285
DIED: Killed, Verona, Italy, 285

AN EMPEROR WAS always in need of trusted lieutenants to manage affairs while he was on campaign. Carinus believed this was exactly what he had when he left Julianus as the *corrector* of northern Italy while he was campaigning in Britain. Sadly, his trust in Julianus was misplaced, probably because Carinus was by this stage deeply unpopular because of his tyrannical actions.

Julianus declared himself emperor in early 285, with the help of the Pannonian legions stationed on the Danube. He was quickly challenged by Carinus, who marched south from Britain to confront his betrayer. The armies met near Verona, in northern Italy, where it was soon evident that Carinus was the superior military tactician. His army beaten, the usurper Julianus did not survive the encounter.

ROMAN REFORM AND RECONSTRUCTION
(285–392)

In their civil government, the emperors were supposed to exercise the undivided power of the monarch, and their edicts, inscribed with their joint names, were received in all the provinces, as promulgated by their mutual councils and authority. Notwithstanding these precautions, the political union of the Roman world was gradually dissolved, and a principle of division was introduced, which, in the course of a few years, occasioned the perpetual separation of the Eastern and Western Empires.

EDWARD GIBBON
The Decline and Fall of the Roman Empire, 1880

FOLLOWING PAGE: Julian the Apostate presiding at a conference of sectarians

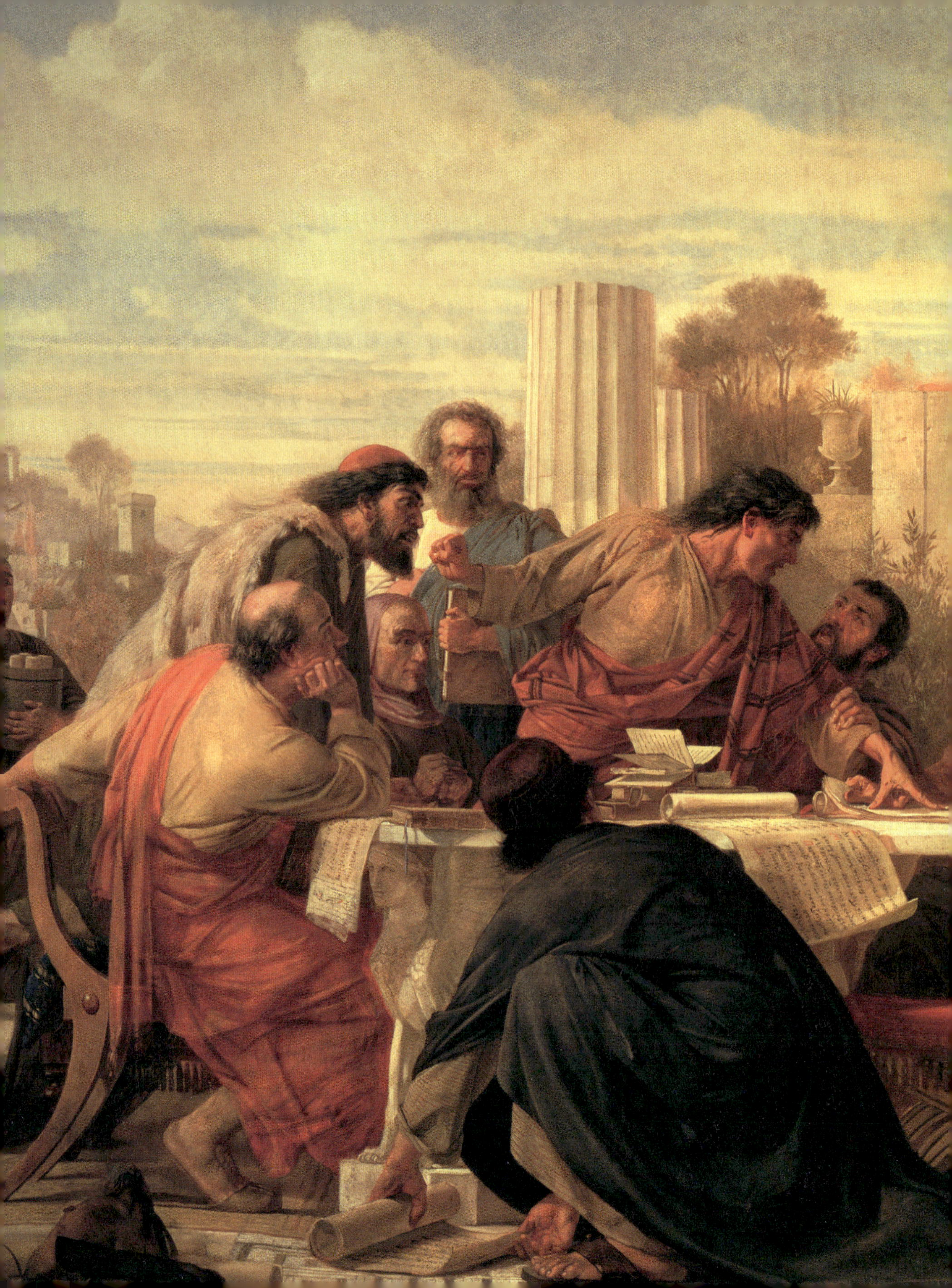

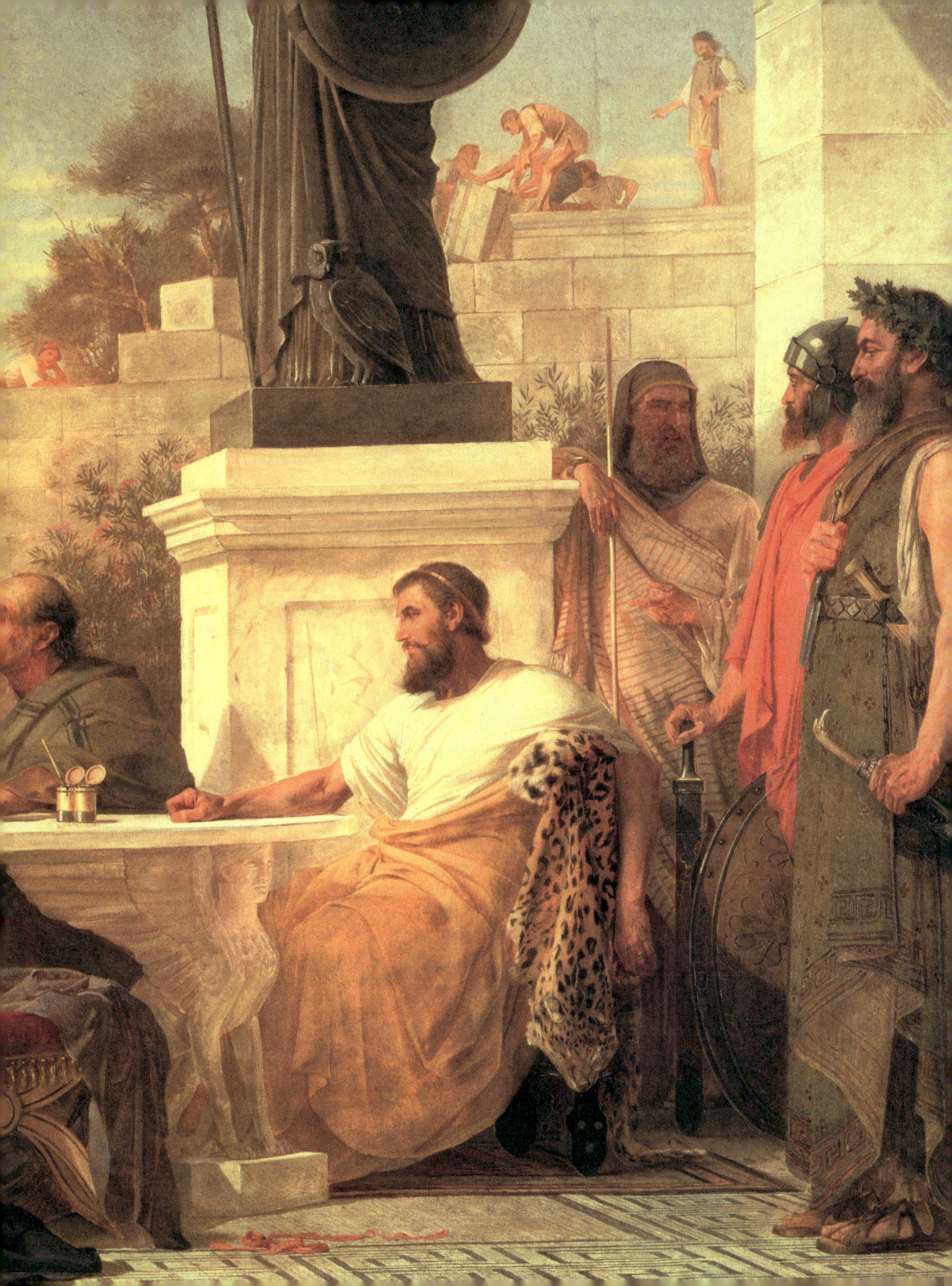

DIOCLETIAN
THE NEW AUGUSTUS

NAME: Gaius Aurelius Valerius Diocles
BORN: Salonae (Solin), Dalmatia, c. 244
RULED: Sole emperor 284–286;
eastern emperor 286–305
DIED: Of natural causes, Spalatum (Split),
Dalmatia, c. 313

THE CRISES OF THE PREVIOUS fifty years had brought the empire to its knees. It needed radical reorganisation if it were to survive, but neither the ossified aristocracy nor the self-absorbed army could provide the necessary vision or authority. It would not be until the son of a former slave sat on the throne of the Caesars that the empire found a man capable of saving it.

Diocletian had risen through the army's ranks from the lowliest social standing imaginable through sheer ability and force of character, and his reward was promotion to commander of the imperial bodyguard under Carus and Numerian. That both emperors died under his watch in somewhat suspicious circumstances speaks less of incompetence than of ambition. The troops elevated Diocletian to the position of emperor after blaming Numerian's death on the praetorian prefect, and Diocletian then marched against Carus's surviving son, Carinus. His victory saw him become sole emperor of a Roman world ready to accept any solution to stop the rot.

Given Diocletian's background, it is unsurprising that he embraced a radicalism that paid scant respect to old imperial traditions, focusing instead on the master–slave relationship that was familiar to his family. Supremely confident in his abilities, he pressed forward with the most complete reorganisation that the Roman state had ever experienced, expanding what had been present in primitive form for some time. Like the earlier emperor Valerian, he was convinced that one individual could not rule the empire. Therefore, his first step was to elevate a colleague as co-Augustus, in order to share the burden of running the state. For this role, he selected Maximianus, a tough soldier like himself, freeing himself to focus on the Danube and the east while Maximianus minded the western provinces. This division was formalised in an attempt to correct a major weakness of the Augustan system: the succession.

Diocletian introduced two measures to deal with the civil wars that had drained the military might of the empire and devastated the provinces. Firstly, he doubled the number of provinces in the empire, while at the same time reducing the actual power of the governors by splitting the civil and military branches of provincial government to avoid concentration of power in the hands of one individual. Provinces were grouped together in dioceses, under the control of a *vicarius*, and the dioceses were organised into prefectures, controlled by a praetorian prefect. By prohibiting senators from seeking high-level military or civil positions, he made it difficult for regional commanders to accumulate the resources needed to challenge for the imperial throne.

> **If you could only see the cabbages which I have planted with my two hands, you would no longer desire the heavy burden of service to the State.**
>
> **DIOCLETIAN**

Secondly, he created a subordinate position under each emperor. Known as Caesars, these junior partners of the emperors were men of great military and administrative ability. They would manage the more difficult areas of the empire while remaining under the authority of the relevant emperor, eventually succeeding the emperor in their half of the empire. Not only did this formalise the succession, but potential challengers would have to battle all four imperial rulers before usurping the throne. Under this system, known as the 'tetrarchy', they divided the empire. Diocletian, overall emperor of

St Catherine of Alexandria, martyred during the Diocletian persecutions

the east, took Thrace, Egypt and the Asiatic provinces, and Galerius, as his Caesar, handled the Danubian and Balkan provinces. Maximianus, as overall emperor of the west, claimed Italy, Raetia, Spain and Africa, while Constantius, his Caesar, held Gaul and Britain.

One change was felt immediately: no longer was Rome the capital of the empire. Each ruler had his own capital, with Diocletian residing in Nicomedia (modern Izmit, in Turkey) and Maximianus ruling from Milan. Rome, though it remained part of the Roman Empire in one form or another for much of the next 1500 years, would no longer be the centre of power and influence, a change that greatly affected the empire's future shape.

With the administration thus secured, Diocletian turned his attention to the position of the emperor, turning it into a blatant oriental monarchy. Access to the emperor was restricted; people prostrated themselves on the ground before his august majesty and kissed the hem of his robes. Seeing how orderly and effectively a Roman household was run when a master controlled his slaves, the emperor became master and lord of the Roman world.

Oriental monarchies considered their kings to be gods or related to the gods, and Diocletian declared himself the son of Jupiter, chief of the gods, while Maximianus was the son of Hercules. Though it had been common practice for deceased emperors to become Roman gods, no previous emperor, apart from Caligula and Elagabalus, had declared himself a living god, and both of them were considered deranged. Not all Romans appreciated this change and Diocletian hated going to Rome for this very reason, believing the citizens of the city were not respectful of his exalted position. He was also on a collision course with the Christians, who completely rejected emperor worship. Under Diocletian such refutation of religious orthodoxy was for the first time considered high treason, since it rejected an aspect of the imperial persona, and so began the Great Persecution. (This expansion of imperial power into the spiritual was to change Christianity forever once it became the official religion of the empire, as the eastern emperors became the personal representatives of Christ on earth, with absolute power over life and death.)

Diocletian did not stop there. He expanded and reorganised the military, dividing the army into border troops stationed on the frontiers of the empire and highly mobile troops capable of reaching trouble spots as needed. He created a huge bureaucracy to manage the affairs of the empire, where every aspect of life was tightly regulated and monitored. Certain occupations—including soldiers, farmers, bakers and, of course, bureaucrats—became compulsory, and individuals were forced into them as needed. Once you were selected, this occupation would be yours for life and your children would inherit it. This was almost as unpopular as the Edict of Prices in 301, which set a uniform price for every commodity and all forms of labour or professional service. Tied into a new and complex taxation system designed to curb inflation and stabilise economic conditions, the edict

The Tetrarchs—Diocletian, Maximianus, Galerius and Constantius—at St Mark's Basilica, Venice also prescribed the death penalty for all breaches of the price code, so that selling a pound of pork for more than twelve denarii or a lion for more than 150,000 denarii would find you facing a public executioner.

Yet for all this, Diocletian was not simply a megalomaniac bureaucrat. He was also a soldier, investing a great deal of time strengthening border defences and enhancing the fleet. Vigorously defending the empire from barbarian invasions, he advanced the Roman frontier in Mesopotamia to the upper Tigris. His military and administrative successes stabilised the empire, giving it some respite from decades of civil and military unrest.

There were failures, however. The military and administrative expansion cost a fortune, with 500,000 men perpetually under arms, while the tax burden crippled the economy. The coinage was so debased as to be worthless, leading to the introduction of a new monetary system; when this failed, he resorted to allowing payment in kind. The Edict of Prices saw a flourishing black market and the disappearance of unprofitable goods.

Although in 303 Diocletian celebrated his twentieth anniversary with magnificent games, a serious illness in 304 gave him second thoughts about his future. He had always ruled with an impartial and calculating eye, never wedded to the trappings of power—even the oriental theatrics were an illusion, overawing the impressionable with the authority and majesty of his position. Concerned that his rules on the imperial succession might not survive his death, he and Maximianus abdicated on 1 May 305, passing the imperial crowns smoothly to their nominated successors, Galerius and Constantius. Diocletian, believing the future of the state was secure, retired to his fortified palace at Split and tended his garden until his death some seven years later, by which time his successors were tearing the empire apart. Asked to take up the imperial purple again, he refused, becoming the first emperor to retire voluntarily from public life; there would not be another for over 1200 years.

MAXIMIANUS

IF AT FIRST YOU DON'T SUCCEED ...

NAME: Marcus Aurelius Valerius Maximianus
BORN: Sirmium (Sremska), Pannonia, 250
RULED: Western emperor 286–305, 307–308 and 310
DIED: Suicide, Massilia (Marseilles), Viennensis, 310

WHILE DIOCLETIAN'S NATURE was such that he could walk away from absolute power, his colleague was made of different stuff. Maximianus was brave but also quite stupid, and so he was perfectly cast for the role Diocletian had planned for him as co-Augustus. The son of a small-town shopkeeper, he was a dedicated soldier and his task was to supply the military muscle while Diocletian reorganised the empire. Always in awe of his senior partner, he did not have that measure of contempt required to launch a rebellion, making him a safe pair of hands.

> **But more important than simple gratitude were those services you undertook when the imperium was conferred upon you: to place the well-being of such a great commonwealth into your heart, and to bear upon your shoulders the destiny of the whole world.**
>
> *THE PANEGYRIC OF MAXIMIANUS*

His temperament suited the role and he applied himself immediately, easily crushing a peasant rebellion in Gaul, though he found it more difficult to halt a German invasion. However, by 288 he and Diocletian were advancing into Germany, punishing the German tribes and extending the boundaries of the empire. For the remainder of his early reign he dealt with a British usurper, who managed to keep the emperor at bay for a number of years. When the tetrarchy was established in 293, Maximianus received a Caesar, Constantius. Though he undertook further campaigns, such as his successful 297 campaign against the Berbers in North Africa, the arrival of the Caesar meant he could spend the last years of his reign in comfort in his court at Milan. He generally ignored Rome and treated the Senate with contempt, which did not endear him to the Roman elite—of course, the uncouth Maximianus did not care one bit about this.

When Diocletian informed Maximianus in 305 that he was going to resign, it did not bother Maximianus. What did bother him was that Diocletian expected him to resign as well and hand his power to Constantius. Unsurprisingly, he was won over only with great difficulty and, unlike Diocletian's, Maximianus's retirement would not last very long.

Maximianus had a son, Maxentius, who missed becoming Caesar when the new emperors took their turn. In 306 Maxentius rebelled in Rome, and when Galerius sent troops to deal with the upstart, Maxentius asked his father to join him as co-emperor. Maximianus eliminated the threat of Galerius before travelling to Gaul to seek the aid of the son of Constantius, Constantine. He secured it by marrying his daughter to the young man.

Returning to Rome with the good news, he quickly fell out with Maxentius. Before an assembly of soldiers in Rome, Maximianus ripped the imperial toga off his son, but he could not win over the army. Humiliated, he fled to the court of Constantine where, after Diocletian forced the contenders to come to terms, he again abdicated in 308. Staying at the court of his son-in-law, Maximianus took advantage of Constantine's preoccupation with the Franks to declare himself emperor for the third time, in 310. Unable to turn any of Constantine's legions, he retreated to Massilia and, after a brief siege, surrendered to Constantine. He perished soon afterwards, probably after being pressured to commit suicide.

AMANDUS

LED THE FIRST FRENCH REVOLUTION

NAME: Gnaeus Silvius Amandus
BORN: Unknown
RULED: Western usurper, 285–286
DIED: Gaul, c. 286

FIFTY YEARS OF CONFLICT saw the peasantry crushed by oppressive taxes, barbarian raids and the devastation of their land. In Gaul especially, barbarians and deserters from the legions had forced many peasants off their lands. Convinced that the authorities were helpless, they rose up in revolt against Roman authority, raising one of their leaders, Amandus, to the position of emperor. He had a colleague, Aelianus, but it is uncertain whether he too accepted the purple.

The Romans called the rebels the Bagaudae, and Maximianus marched out to deal with them. They fought some engagements under Amandus's leadership but were poorly armed and disorganised. Maximianus easily suppressed the revolt, during which Amandus probably died.

JULIANUS

FIERY END

NAME: Julianus
BORN: Unknown
RULED: Western usurper, 286
DIED: Suicide, Italy, c. 286

WE KNOW VIRTUALLY NOTHING about this usurper. It seems that around the time of Maximianus's accession, a certain Julianus raised the standard of revolt in Italy. Eventually trapped in an unnamed city with the army of Maximianus breaching the walls, he stabbed himself with a dagger. Just to be sure of not falling into Maximianus's hands, he then flung himself into one of the fires raging in the city.

CARAUSIUS

JOINED THE CLUB

NAME: Marcus Aurelius Valerius Carausius
BIRTH NAME: Mausaeus Carausius
BORN: Belgica, northern Gaul, date unknown
RULED: Western usurper, 286–293
DIED: Murdered, Britannia, 293

THE CAREER OF CARAUSIUS demonstrates that perhaps there is a pirate in everyone. Growing up near the sea, he earned a living as a helmsman before enlisting with the Roman army. After serving with distinction in Maximianus's campaign against the Bagaudae, he was rewarded with the command of the North Sea, as well as the responsibility of clearing Frankish pirates who were raiding the coast of Gaul. Though he completed his commission with great speed and efficiency, it soon emerged that he had kept some of the pirate plunder for himself and possibly even allowed the pirates to carry on their work for a percentage of the booty. Maximianus ordered his arrest and execution, but Carausius fled to Britain, where he declared himself emperor.

Carausius's possession of the North Sea fleet, together with the support of his new best friends, the Frankish pirates, enabled him to retain the British provinces and control the northern portion of Gaul around the city of Boulogne. Maximianus's preoccupation with the Germans meant that it was not until 289 that he had a fleet ready to invade Britain, only to see it destroyed in a storm. The following year he launched a military campaign against Carausius's possessions in Gaul, but again without success. It was not until the arrival of the talented Caesar Constantius in 293 that there was headway in Gaul.

Carausius tried repeatedly to have his imperial claim recognised by Diocletian and Maximianus, adopting their names, as was customary, and issuing coins with all three displayed together, along with the inscription 'Carausius and his brothers'. It was all to no avail. Constantius recaptured the port of Boulogne, and Carausius was assassinated by his chief financial minister, Allectus.

ALLECTUS

QUIETLY OVERCONFIDENT

NAME: Allectus
BORN: Unknown
RULED: Western usurper, 293–296
DIED: Killed, possibly Calleva Atrebatum (Silchester), Britannia, 296

TO ALLECTUS FELL THE JOB of defending the rebellious British provinces against the formidable Constantius. Allectus was obviously a great believer in his own abilities, but his three-year reign was only possible because Constantius wanted to make sure that he got it right.

Even so, things did not go according to plan for Allectus. He used the time to strengthen Hadrian's Wall, enabling him to remove troops to defend the south. Yet when the invasion came, it caught him unprepared. Constantius was delayed by a storm, but his praetorian prefect landed and advanced towards London. Allectus rushed to meet him at Silchester and engaged his army in battle, but was defeated. Despite throwing away his imperial insignia, in the hope he would remain unidentified, Allectus was killed during the fight. The remainder of his troops, mostly Frankish allies, were trapped in London and killed, finally putting an end to the Gallic usurpers who had plagued the west for thirty-five years.

ROMAN EMPIRE AD 400

PROVINCES

PREFECTURE OF GAUL

Diocese of Spain
1. Galicia
2. Tarraconensis
3. Carthaginensis
4. Lusitania
5. Baetica
6. Mauretania Tingitana
7. Balearic Isles

Diocese of Gaul
1. Viennensis
2. Lugdunensis I
3. Germania I
4. Germania II
5. Belgica I
6. Belgica II
7. Maritime Alps
8. Pennine and Graian Alps
9. Maxima Sequanorum
10. Aquitaine I
11. Aquitaine II
12. Novempopulana
13. Narbonnensis I
14. Narbonennsis II

Diocese of Britain
1. Maxima Caesariensis
2. Britain I
3. Flavia Caesariensis
4. Britain II
5. Valentia

PREFECTURE OF ITALY

Diocese of Africa
1. Mauretania Caesariensis
2. Mauretania Sitifensis
3. Numidia
4. Byzacium
5. Tripolitana

Diocese of the City of Rome
1. Tuscany and Umbria
2. Picenum Suburbicarium
3. Valeria
4. Samnium
5. Campania
6. Apulia and Calabria
7. Bruttia and Lucania
8. Sicily
9. Corsica
10. Sardinia

Diocese of Italy
1. Venetia and Istria
2. Aemilia
3. Liguria
4. Flaminia and Picenum Annonarium
5. Cottian Alps
6. Raetia I
7. Raetia II
8. Pannonia II
9. Savia
10. Pannonia I
11. Dalmatia
12. Norium mediterraneum
13. Norium ripense
14. Valeria ripensis

PREFECTURE OF ILLYRICUM

Diocese of Macedonia
1. Macedonia Salutaris
2. Macedonia
3. Thessalia
4. Crete
5. Epirus Vetus
6. Epirus Nova

Diocese of Dacia
1. Moesia I
2. Dacia Ripensis
3. Dacia Mediterranea
4. Dardania
5. Praevalitana

PREFECTURE OF THE EAST

Diocese of Thrace
1. Moesia
2. Scythia
3. Haemimontium
4. Europe
5. Rhodope
6. Thrace

Diocese of Pontus
1. Paphlagonia
2. Pontus Polemoniacus
3. Armenia I
4. Armenia II

Diocese of Oriens
1. Eufratensis
2. Mesopotamia
3. Orshone
4. Syria Salutaris
5. Phoenicia Libani
6. Arabia
7. Palestine (Salutaris
8. Palestine
9. Palestine II
10. Phoenicia
11. Syria I
12. Cilicia II
13. Cilicia I
14. Isauria
15. Cyprus

Diocese of Asia
1. Caria
2. Phrygia Pacatiana
3. Phrygia Saluraris
4. Pisidia
5. Lycaonia
6. Pamphylia
7. Lycia
8. Lydia

Diocese of Egypt
1. Egypt
2. Augustamnica
3. Arcadia
4. Thebais
5. Lower Libya
6. Upper Libya

Cappadocia I
Cappadocia II
Galatia
Helenopontus
Galatia Salutaris
Honorias
Bythinia

ROMAN REFORM AND RECONSTRUCTION

DOMITIUS DOMITIANUS

JUMPED THE GUN

NAME: Lucius Domitius Domitianus
BORN: Unknown
RULED: Eastern usurper, 297
DIED: Possibly of natural causes, Alexandria, Egypt, 297

THE EAST WAS A DIFFERENT MATTER. The Persian invasion in 296 was initially successful and Domitianus, the prefect of Egypt, possibly believed it would cause Diocletian's downfall. Unwilling to wait, he declared himself emperor in 297, and then watched helplessly as Galerius rolled back the Persian advance while Diocletian marched down to deal with him. Luckily for Domitianus, he died just as he was preparing Egypt's defence and before the emperor's divine justice could catch up with him.

ACHILLEUS

LEFT IN THE LURCH

NAME: Aurelius Achilleus
BORN: Unknown
RULED: Eastern usurper, 297–298
DIED: Killed, Alexandria, Egypt, 298

ACHILLEUS, DOMITIANUS'S *corrector* of Egypt, was the man whom the rebel leaders turned to after their chosen emperor's unfortunate death. Things were not looking very good: Diocletian had recaptured most of Egypt and was now about to lay siege to Alexandria. Invested with the purple, Achilleus led a spirited defence, and for eight months he managed to hold Diocletian's best troops at bay, but in the end the citizens of Alexandria were no match for the hardened legions. Achilleus died when the city fell in March 298, ending the Egyptian rebellion.

EUGENIUS

SURPRISED BY RESISTANCE

NAME: Eugenius
BORN: Unknown
RULED: Eastern usurper, 303
DIED: Killed, Antiochia ad Orontem (Antioch), Syria, 303

EUGENIUS WAS A MILITARY tribune stationed at Seleucia Pieria in Syria. Bored by the dreary task of deepening the entrance to the harbour, he started daydreaming about attacking defenceless Antioch with his men, believing this to be an easy way to achieve a base from which he could pillage at will. He convinced the soldiers, who quickly declared him emperor, and this unruly gang descended upon Antioch, laying waste to the land as they passed.

What they had assumed was an easy target turned out to be a logistical nightmare. Led by the local aristocracy, the citizens of the city rose up against them. The Antiochans grabbed whatever implements they could lay their hands on and attacked the would-be invaders. Within a day the troops were trapped, and by the end of the second day, Eugenius and his band of five hundred were dead. For their efforts, Antioch's leaders were punished by the emperor with executions and confiscations: self-defence was no excuse to take up arms in the Roman Empire; if they could do it against a usurper, they might do it against the emperor.

CONSTANTIUS I CHLORUS

THE PALE

NAME: Marcus Flavius Valerius Constantius
BORN: Dardania, Upper Moesia, c. 250
RULED: Western emperor, 305–306
DIED: Of illness, Eboricum (York), Britannia, 306

PALE CONSTANTIUS WAS NOT a man who was afraid of a little hard work. Another Illyrian career soldier, he had proved himself repeatedly under Aurelian, Probus and Carus, before finally reaching the service of Maximianus as his praetorian prefect. He was, therefore, in the right place when Diocletian decided in 293 to establish the tetrarchy. As a reward for his devoted service, he became Caesar under Maximianus, and thus his nominated successor. To strengthen his new position, he left his mistress, Helena, with whom he already had a son, and married Maximianus's daughter, Theodora. This would have important consequences in the years to come when Constantius's bastard child became Roman emperor in his turn.

> You who had been false to your God are unworthy of my confidence; for how was it possible that you should preserve your fidelity to me, when you had proved yourself faithless to a higher power?
>
> CONSTANTIUS CHLORUS

Having been allotted Britain, Gaul and the Rhine frontier, Constantius hit the ground running, reclaiming northern Gaul and Britain from usurpers, while keeping the German tribes on the defensive. He carried out all his duties diligently, except for enforcing the edicts against the Christians—pulling down some churches was the extent of his participation in the Great Persecution.

Constantius became emperor on the abdication of Maximianus in 305 but he would not enjoy the purple for long. He was summoned to Britain to deal with a Pictish invasion from the north of the island and was joined there by his eldest son, Constantine, who had fled from the court of Galerius, where he had been a virtual hostage to ensure his father's good behaviour—none of the imperial college really trusted one another. Constantius was at York when he died in 306, mourned by his troops. By all accounts, Constantius was the calm and mild-mannered one of the imperial club. Under the terms of the tetrarchy, he was supposed to have been the senior Augustus, just as Diocletian had been; however, his temperament caused him to step back, allowing Galerius to exercise greater influence as both new Caesars were his creatures. Stories grew up around Constantius as Christian authors of subsequent decades declared him to have been a secret Christian. This was an invention: Constantius was a believer in the old gods, as was Constantine, his bastard son.

GALERIUS

TOP DOG ON THE BLOCK

NAME: Gaius Galerius Valerius Maximianus
BORN: Felix Romulianum (Gamzigrad), Moesia, c. 260
RULED: Eastern emperor, 305–311
DIED: Of illness, Nicomedia (Iznik), Bithynia, 311

DIOCLETIAN CHOSE HIS colleagues wisely, especially his groomed successor and understudy, Galerius, who strengthened his bonds to the emperor by divorcing his wife and marrying Diocletian's daughter. Diocletian put the tough Thracian, the most gifted of his colleagues, in charge of the difficult Danube frontier, and Galerius defended it with superb skill and panache.

The Persian invasion of 296 confronted Galerius with his greatest challenge. Though this area was nominally under Diocletian's direct control, he left it to his junior to handle the situation. After all, what was the point of having a Caesar if he did not deal with such problems? At first Galerius underestimated the enemy and, after suffering a severe defeat, he abandoned Mesopotamia. To improve his motivation, Diocletian forced him to march in front of his chariot before the citizens of Antioch. Humiliated, Galerius took out his frustrations on the Persians and in 297 thrashed the enemy in a number of battles, forcing them to sue for peace and reclaiming all the territory that had been lost, plus more.

> **It well becomes the Persians to dwell upon the fickleness of fortune.**
>
> GALERIUS

Diocletian's resignation elevated Galerius to the rank of emperor and, according to the rules established by Diocletian, two new Caesars were required to take his and Constantius's places. Usurping Constantius's right to select their imperial colleagues, Galerius further entrenched his power. His nephew Maximinus Daia became the eastern Caesar, while an old comrade in arms, Severus, was elevated in the west. Daia was readily accepted but two pretenders—Maxentius, son of the former emperor Maximianus, and Constantine, the son of Constantius—challenged Severus's position. By the time Maximianus came out of retirement to deal with Severus, the empire already had three Caesars and two Augusti running around, and Diocletian's carefully constructed edifice came crashing down. In an effort to save the deteriorating situation, in 308 Galerius called an imperial conference at Carnuntum, to which Diocletian was invited to hammer out a solution. The result was that Maximianus was forced to abdicate again, Constantine's position as Caesar (which Galerius had granted in 306) was reconfirmed, and Licinius, a loyal military companion of Galerius, was appointed Augustus in the west. Maxentius was declared a public enemy.

The close of Galerius's reign saw the decommissioning of his one major political act. He was the principal instigator of the Christian persecutions in 303 and applied pressure on them throughout his reign, but it was clear that the intended result—the extinction of Christianity—was never going to happen. It was from his sickbed—he was suffering from an ulcerated intestinal fistula that had opened onto the skin and turned gangrenous and maggot infested—that he issued an edict cancelling the persecution: perhaps he believed the Christian God was punishing him. In any case he did not obtain a miracle and died a few days later.

SEVERUS

TOO TRUSTING

NAME: Flavius Valerius Severus
BORN: Illyricum, date unknown
RULED: Western emperor, 306–307
DIED: Suicide, Rome, 307

SEVERUS PROBABLY CONSIDERED himself one lucky man. As a result of his friendship and military service with Galerius, he obtained the choice role of Caesar in the west when Constantius was elevated to the imperial throne in 305. His luck held when Constantius died a year later, making him emperor of the western provinces. Though his Caesar was Constantius's son, Constantine, who moved from Britain to Gaul to build a power base for himself, Severus probably thought things could not get much better.

He was right. Maxentius, son of the abdicated Maximianus, was in Rome and he rebelled against

Severus. The emperor marched down from Milan but found the city closed against him. Maxentius had asked his father to come out of retirement, and Maximianus used his contacts within Severus's army to get the troops to switch allegiance. Realising his support was withering away, Severus fled to Ravenna, where he remained until the soon to be re-crowned Maximianus convinced him to surrender. Escorted to Rome, he was soon imprisoned.

Galerius marched to Italy to free his imperial colleague but, seeing that his own troops were wavering in their loyalty, he promptly withdrew. Abandoned, Severus committed suicide, no doubt cursing his fortune.

MAXENTIUS
WANTED HIS DUE

NAME: Marcus Aurelius Valerius Maxentius
BORN: Place unknown, c. 278
RULED: Western usurper, 307–312
DIED: Drowned, Rome, 312

THE LAZY, FUN-LOVING and irresponsible Maxentius believed the western half of the empire was his birthright as the son of the emperor Maximianus. When his father abdicated the purple, he was persuaded, reluctantly, to retire to a villa, and he might well have stayed there had Constantine not declared himself

Campaign of Galerius against the Persians

emperor upon Constantius's death. Believing he had more right to the throne than a bastard, he used Galerius's imposition of a tax upon Italy to have himself declared emperor. While Italy south of the Po River and North Africa accepted his authority, Galerius demanded that Severus eliminate the upstart.

Devoid of real talent, Maxentius turned to the one man who could save him—his father. Maximianus forced Severus to retreat to Ravenna, where he was captured and soon afterwards killed himself. With no Augustus in the west, Maxentius officially elevated himself to the now vacant position but soon had to face Galerius, who was now marching against him. Again, he turned to his father, who successfully demanded he become Maxentius's co-emperor. Maximianus went north to Gaul and secured Constantine's support by giving him his daughter in marriage. Returning to Italy, he tried the same trick against Galerius that he had used against Severus, but Galerius was too wily an adversary to fall for it and quickly retreated northwards. Seeing that he was doing all of the work, Maximianus tried to overthrow his son in Rome, but he could not win the soldiers' approval. Fleeing to Constantine's court, he left Maxentius in charge of Italy.

Declared a public enemy by the other Augusti at the imperial conference at Carnuntum, Maxentius bunkered

MARTYRS OF THE GREAT PERSECUTION

For centuries, the Church has venerated a number of people martyred for their faith during the Diocletian persecutions. Many stories have grown up around them, usually focused on some miraculous event that transpired during their martyrdom.

ST CATHERINE OF ALEXANDRIA The daughter of the governor of Alexandria, she converted to Christianity but came to the attention of Maxentius, who lusted after her. When she refused to submit to him, he threw her into prison, where she converted many of her cellmates. Maxentius then tortured her on a 'breaking wheel', which broke apart when she touched it, before beheading her.

ST GEORGE The son of a military colleague of Diocletian, he was accepted into the imperial court as a military tribune but he refused to sacrifice to the gods as was required by all serving members of the army. Diocletian was loath to lose him, so he offered George land, money and slaves for his renunciation of Christ. George refused, whereupon Diocletian had him tortured repeatedly, including on a wheel of swords. Dying three times, he was miraculously resuscitated prior to his beheading before the walls of Nicomedia.

ST JANUARIUS The bishop of Naples during the Great Persecution, Januarius helped many Christians avoid capture before his eventual discovery. Placed in a furnace to be roasted alive, he came out unharmed, whereupon he was condemned to die at the hands of wild bears that had not eaten in days. Yet the animals refused to eat Januarius, choosing instead to lick his toes. The authorities finally beheaded Januarius for his belief.

ST ANTHIMUS OF ROME The priest responsible for converting a high level Roman prefect and for destroying pagan idols in Rome, Anthimus was captured and thrown into the Tiber with a stone around his neck. An angel came down and rescued him, whereupon he resumed his former work. Eventually recaptured, the consul Priscus avoided a repeat rescue by beheading him in 303.

down in Italy and waited, but his popularity rapidly waned as a result of food shortages and excessive taxation. With the deaths of his father in 310 and Galerius in 311, the situation changed rapidly. Painting the young Constantine as a murderer unfit to wear the purple, he aligned himself with Daia in the east, while Constantine joined up with the new western emperor, Licinius.

> **Why should he, the son of a harlot, enjoy such good fortune, while I, the son of so great an emperor, remain at home in indolence, as others enjoy my father's empire?**
>
> MAXENTIUS (referring to Constantine)

Constantine gathered what troops he could without leaving Gaul defenceless and marched south into Italy, eventually facing Maxentius at the battle of the Milvian Bridge, an old stone bridge across the Tiber River near Rome that he had destroyed to prevent Constantine's advance. Defeated, Maxentius and his army fled in disorder over a hastily made wooden bridge across the Tiber, only to have it collapse, drowning him and many of his troops. Constantine cut off Maxentius's head, displaying it in the provinces as proof of his death, while the Senate damned his memory.

DOMITIUS ALEXANDER

THE DEMANDS OF LOYALTY

NAME: Lucius Domitius Alexander
BORN: Phrygia, Asiana, c. 240
RULED: Western usurper, 308–310
DIED: Executed, Africa, 310

AFTER HE WAS DECLARED a public enemy at the imperial conference in 308 and fell out with his father, Maxentius became worried about the loyalty of his provinces. The *vicarius* of Africa, a timid old man by the name of Alexander, had consistently followed the commands of Maxentius. To ensure his continued loyalty, the emperor demanded that Alexander send over his son as security. Alexander refused and the African legions declared him emperor.

The revolt was short-lived. Maxentius sent over his praetorian prefect to take command of the assembled army. In the encounter, Alexander's soldiers put up a very poor fight, fleeing at the first charge. The usurper was captured and strangled.

MAXIMINUS DAIA

THE GREAT PERSECUTOR

NAME: Gaius Galerius Valerius Maximinus
BORN: Felix Romuliana (Gamzigrad), Moesia, c. 270
RULED: Eastern emperor, 310–313
DIED: Of poison, Tarsus, Cilicia, 313

MAXIMINUS DAIA WAS THE most enthusiastic of the imperial persecutors. Another peasant from that limitless supply pool in Illyricum, he had the good fortune to be the childless Galerius's nephew and closest living relative. Thrust from military obscurity, he became the new Caesar in the east upon his uncle's elevation in 305.

Daia had a peasant's attachment to the faith of his ancestors, and during his reign he was determined to defend his religion by drowning the Christians in their own blood. He demanded that everyone, including babies, attend the public sacrifices. He also possessed a peasant's cunning, and by distributing copies of the bogus *Acts of Pilate* sought to eliminate the sect through internal dissension.

After serving his uncle faithfully for some years, he was sorely annoyed by the outcome of the imperial council at Carnuntum that saw the confirmation of Constantine as Caesar and the introduction of Licinius as emperor in the west, a position he believed should have been his through seniority. Licinius earned Daia's hatred for the rest of his life and so in 310, when Galerius was clearly ill, Daia took the opportunity to claim the imperial title in the east. He consolidated this by taking the eastern provinces on his uncle's death, while Licinius retained Pannonia, the Balkans and Thrace, territory that he had gained after his elevation as Augustus of the west in 308. Daia and Licinius kept an uneasy eye on each other across the waters of the Bosphorus.

This state of affairs did not last long. The defeat of Maxentius in Italy in 312 left three competing emperors eyeing off each other—Constantine in western Europe, Licinius in eastern Europe and Daia in Asia. An alliance between Constantine and Licinius forced Daia's hand and he invaded the territory of his hated rival. It did not go well: crushed in battle, Daia had to flee to Asia dressed as a slave. Hot on his heels came Licinius, who besieged him in Tarsus. It was there that Daia swallowed poison and died an excruciating death.

The Diocletian persecution of the Christians was the most systematic attempt to destroy the sect in ancient times

LICINIUS

CHRISTIAN SUPPORTER

NAME: Gaius Valerius Licinianus Licinius
BORN: Upper Moesia (near modern Zaječar), c. 265
RULED: Western emperor, 308–313;
eastern emperor, 313–324)
DIED: Hanged, Thessalonica, Macedonia, 325

THE ELEVATION OF LICINIUS seemed to confirm that Galerius had an endless supply of drinking buddies with whom he wished to share his good fortune. Licinius appeared virtually out of nowhere to become emperor of the western provinces after the death of Severus, to the consternation of the other members of the imperial club. Given the fate of his predecessor, Severus, he did not attempt to remove Maxentius from his base in Rome. Instead, he concerned himself with a war against the Sarmatians, achieving some victories in the process.

The deaths of Galerius and Maxentius culled the numbers of emperors down to three, and Licinius strengthened his position by concluding a treaty with Daia in 311 and then marrying Constantine's half-sister in 313. His victory over Daia showed him to be a man with moderate abilities, but he would soon incur the jealous wrath of his ruthless brother-in-law. During the next ten years, the two imperial claimants would go to war three times, and on each occasion Licinius failed to prevail. In 314 Licinius just managed to hold his own, while in 316 Constantine mauled him badly, forcing him to relinquish his European provinces. Finally, in 324, Licinius was provoked into launching another war that ended in his humiliation. Abdicating the throne, he placed his faith in a most untrustworthy individual: Constantine. Though Constantine initially listened to his half-sister's pleas and agreed to spare Licinius, he had him executed on treason charges in 325, leaving the victor the sole emperor of the Roman world.

Part of Constantine's demolition of Licinius involved portraying him as a supporter of the pagan gods. This was not the case: contemporary evidence suggests that he was at least a committed supporter of Christians, co-authoring the Edict of Milan, which ended the Great Persecution, and re-affirming the rights of Christians in his half of the empire. He also added the Christian symbol to his armies' banners and attempted to regulate the affairs of the church hierarchy just as Constantine and his successors were to do. It is even possible that he converted to Christianity. However, Licinius had the misfortune to become the villain in Eusebius of Caesarea's works of historical revisionism, which turned someone who appears to have been a committed Christian supporter into a man who feigned sympathy for the sect before he showed his true bloodthirsty, pagan nature and was only stopped by the virtuous Constantine. He deserved to have a better reputation.

VALERIUS VALENS

CAUGHT IN THE MIDDLE

NAME: Gaius Aurelius Valerius Valens
BORN: Unknown
RULED: Eastern co-emperor, 316–317
DIED: Executed, place unknown, 317

AS THE FRAGILE PEACE between Licinius and Constantine broke down in 316, Licinius bolstered his position by promoting Valens, the *dux* of the frontiers, to be his co-emperor in the European provinces. Valens was an able military commander but this did not stop Constantine launching an aggressive campaign against Licinius. Together, Licinius and Valens raised an army to halt Constantine's advance, but they were defeated in two separate battles. Constantine made it clear there would be no peace while Valens was emperor, giving Licinius no choice but to execute his unfortunate colleague.

MARTINIANUS
DELAYING TACTICS

NAME: Sextus Martius Martinianus
BORN: Unknown
RULED: Eastern co-emperor, 324
DIED: Executed, Cappadocia, Pontus, 325

AS THE THIRD CIVIL WAR between Licinius and Constantine raged, things were looking bleak for the eastern emperor. To expand his options, he elevated his chief civilian official, Martinianus, to co-emperor, instructing him to stop Constantine crossing over into Asia at all cost. Failing, Martinianus was pulled back to join Licinius for one final battle. After their defeat, both were exiled, but not for long. Like his co-emperor, Martinianus soon suffered execution: the jealous Constantine would brook no rival, no matter how minor.

CONSTANTINE I THE GREAT
SAINT AND MURDERER

NAME: Flavius Valerius Aurelius Constantinus
BORN: Naissus, Upper Moesia, c. 274
RULED: Western emperor, 309–324; sole emperor 324–337
DIED: Of natural causes, Nicomedia (Iznik), Bithynia, 337

IF EUSEBIUS OF CAESAREA destroyed Licinius's reputation, he certainly gilded the lily when it came to Constantine, turning him into the new Moses, who triumphantly led his people from captivity. Not bad for the illegitimate son of a Roman general and a barmaid turned occasional prostitute.

Constantine's rise to power began with the death of his father, the emperor Constantius, at York in 306, when his troops raised him to the rank of Augustus. He had recently escaped from the court of Galerius, who had been afraid that Constantine would attract such support. Though only recognised by the other emperors as Caesar, he never relinquished the greater title, and in 309 he officially proclaimed himself Augustus. After establishing his court in Gaul, he eventually moved against Maxentius in Rome.

Invading Italy in 312, Constantine rapidly approached the army of Maxentius at Saxa Rubra, near the Milvian Bridge. The night before the battle, he reportedly had a dream directing him to place a sign on the shields of his soldiers, a monogram of the Greek letters chi (X) and rho (P), the first two letters of the name of Christ. Thus prepared, he defeated his rival's superior army and attributed his victory to intervention by the Christian God. It was a momentous event; for the rest of his reign he took a special interest in the affairs of the Christians, and one of his first acts was to stop the persecutions that Diocletian had introduced.

This relationship served Constantine well in the years to come, when he defeated his only surviving rival, Licinius, to become sole emperor of Rome, thirty-eight years after Diocletian's division of the empire. In Christianity's exclusivity, Constantine saw a religion that perfectly fitted his vision for the empire—one god, one emperor, one empire, one religion. There was one problem, however: the Christians, divided among themselves, fought over various arcane aspects of dogma, preventing them from presenting this united front. To overcome this, Constantine ordered Christian bishops to gather in 325 at Nicaea to develop articles of faith that would bind the church together. They were only partially successful, and doctrinal issues plagued the church for centuries to come.

Many mistakenly believe that Constantine converted to Christianity immediately after the battle of the Milvian Bridge. Though he tolerated Christianity, he still took part in the major functions of the pagan Roman

Constantine I

religion and the imperial cult. The army was intensely conservative and for them he maintained the cult of the unconquered sun, Sol Invictus. He did not undergo instruction in the Christian faith until the final years of his reign, being baptised on his deathbed. For the vast majority of his reign Constantine was a pagan emperor.

Yet he did show favouritism to the Christians, giving the Lateran Palace to the bishop of Rome and building a basilica next to it as the city's principal church. Because he was still a pagan emperor, he could not take the position of chief pontiff of the new religion but instead established the emperor as the secular defender of Christianity, with all ecclesiastical decisions handled by the church hierarchy. This separation of church and state was a historical first and the template would be followed by medieval kings in the west, who generally avoided the consequences of royal meddling in church affairs. Ironically, his imperial successors in the east would not follow his example, decreeing that they were the head of the church and Christ's representative on earth, qualified not only to enthrone and dismiss patriarchs, but also to intervene in the formulation of doctrine.

Constantine was a man of many contradictions—severe and impartial towards his subjects, vindictive and brutal when it came to any imperial rivals. On becoming sole emperor he butchered Licinius's family, and he raged with jealousy when his eldest son, Crispus, began increasing in popularity. In 326 he had Crispus killed. Rumour had it that Crispus had had an affair with Constantine's wife (his stepmother), who was also killed. More likely, Constantine was ridding himself of a popular young man who may have attracted ambitious people to him: sons had plotted against their fathers before. Yet the murder of Crispus is a dark stain upon the reputation of this supposedly Christian emperor.

Constantine's other major legacy was the establishment of Constantinople on the Bosphorus, conceived as the New Rome and the new capital of the empire. Though Rome had ceased to be the imperial capital in 286, everyone still held it in great esteem. However, for an empire under barbarian attack, it had the disadvantage of being too distant from the frontiers to be an effective seat of government. Constantinople, situated on the site of the old city of Byzantium, was within easy reach of both the Danube and Persian frontiers, and its natural attributes, including having only one landward-facing wall, meant it was virtually impregnable.

Constantine was serious when he declared the new city to be Rome's replacement—it too was built on seven hills and had a Senate, elected consuls and civic offices modelled on those of the old capital. It was from here that the eastern provinces would be ruled and, while Rome

ROMAN REFORM AND RECONSTRUCTION 127

THE COUNCIL OF NICAEA, THE NICENE CREED AND ARIANISM

Although Constantine I had placed enormous hopes in the ability of Christianity to unite his subjects, the reality at the time was that the early church was bitterly divided over the teachings of Arius, a Christian presbyter from Alexandria. His views, known ever since as Arianism, inspired a whole generation of churchmen and generated such heat that it threatened to rip apart the fragile unity of the church.

At the core of Arianism was a specific understanding of the relationship of Jesus Christ to God. According to Arius, Jesus as the Son of God was not of the same substance as God the Father: He was directly created by the Father out of nothing, and so followed the Father in time, that is, there was a point when the Son of God did not exist, and thus He was a finite being. Opposed to this was what became known as the orthodox view of Jesus. This maintained that the Son of God was both co-equal and co-eternal with God the Father, and of exactly the same substance as Him. To these churchmen, the teachings of Arius were heretical and endangered the salvation of souls.

As a result of the debate, in 323 Constantine sent letters to Arius and his principal opponent, Bishop Alexander of Alexandria, asking them to refrain from disturbing the peace. When this failed Constantine called the first Church Council in 325. It was held at Nicaea in Bithynia. Bishops were summoned from across the empire, and some three hundred, of whom the eastern bishops formed the great majority, attended the proceedings. Both Arius and Alexander were present, and both presented their arguments to the assembled throng, over which Constantine presided, although he did not vote during the debates.

Although the Council of Nicaea did debate other issues, such as the date for the celebration of Easter, the majority of its sessions were focused on the Arian question. The end result was that the council declared that the Father and the Son are of the same substance and are co-eternal, declaring that this was a formulation of traditional Christian belief handed down from the Apostles. This belief was articulated in what became known as the Nicene Creed, a statement of belief to which all Christian believers were to adhere. In it, Jesus Christ was described as 'God from God, Light from Light, true God from true God', emphasising His divinity. He was also 'begotten, not made, of one substance with the father', which declared His co-eternalness and his unity of being with God.

At the end of the proceedings, Constantine declared than anyone who refused to accept the creed would be exiled. Arius continued to reject it, and so was exiled to Illyria, as well as being excommunicated. His works were seized and burnt, while all persons found possessing them were to be executed. Yet the issue of Arianism would continue to plague the empire for over two centuries, as emperors such as Constantine's son Constantius adopted the outlawed creed.

In an attempt to bridge the divide, Arians came up with the term *homoiousios* or 'alike in substance', in an effort to counter the Nicene interpretation of *homoousisos*, 'of one substance'. The debates were so arcane that our modern expression 'there is not an iota's difference' originates here with the i, or the iota, being the only difference between these words. In the end, a Church council in 381 confirmed the Nicene creed. Yet this was not the end, as Arian missionaries spread their version of Christianity to the barbarians, who would bring it with them when they overran the western provinces of the empire.

declined in importance, Constantinople would survive as an imperial capital for a thousand years before finally coming under Turkish domination. All Constantine's achievements—his completion of Diocletian's military and judicial reforms, his victories over the barbarians and the recapture of lost provinces—were not enough to earn Rome's forgiveness for this abandonment. The church may have bestowed upon him the title of The Great in recognition of his role in Christianity's triumph, yet his elevation to sainthood in the Greek Orthodox Church, but not the Roman Catholic Church, speaks volumes about how the empire's two halves saw his legacy in the centuries after his death.

Constantine considered Diocletian's system of imperial division merely suspended during his reign. In accordance with the law, he decided to divide the empire between his three remaining sons and two of his nephews. These plans did not survive his death in 337.

CALOCAERUS

LORD OF THE SHEEP AND CAMELS

NAME: Calocaerus
BORN: Unknown
RULED: Eastern usurper, 333–334
DIED: Executed, Tarsus, Cilicia, 334

CALOCAERUS IS ONE of those individuals about whom we would like to know more. He was the *magister pecoris camelorum* in Cyprus, an impressive title that says he was responsible for managing the camels and sheep on the island. Just why he chose to rebel in 333 is a mystery. In any event, Constantine sent his half-brother, the censor Dalmatius, to deal with the problem. He quickly rounded up Calocaerus, who was taken to Tarsus for his trial and execution.

CONSTANTINE II

RESPECT MY SENIORITY

NAME: Flavius Claudius Constantinus
BORN: Arelate (Arles), Viennensis, 317
RULED: Western emperor, 337–340
DIED: In battle, Aquileia, Italy, 340

ON CONSTANTINE'S DEATH in 337, his three sons decided not to share their inheritance with anyone. Stirring up the troops, they massacred virtually all the remaining descendants of Constantius Chlorus. After finishing the bloody deed, they divided the empire between them: Constantine II received the prefecture of Gaul, which included Spain, Gaul and Britain.

Constantine and his brothers were the first emperors raised as Christians; undoubtedly, their teachers would have been sorely disappointed. Beginning their reigns bathed in their relatives' blood, they quickly turned on each other. The first fracture lines emerged over the newest church controversy about Arianism and Christ's nature as God and man, with Constantine II and Constans supporting the traditionalists while Constantius II adopted the Arian creed.

Constantine, as the eldest, also believed he deserved more than he actually got during the division of the empire. Rebuffed in his role as senior Augustus, he invaded the Italian territory of Constans, who was off defending the Danube frontier. Wheeling around, Constans confronted his brother at Aquileia, where an advanced scouting party ambushed and killed a surprised Constantine.

Constantine II wa a military man, pressed into military service by his father at a young age—he was thirteen when he went on a campaign against the Alamanni. Then in 332 he was made *magister militum* (commander of the army) of the Roman field armies during his father's campaign against the Goths. Used to giving orders, he carried this attitude into his reign.

CONSTANS I

ANNOYED THE ARMY

NAME: Flavius Julius Constans
BORN: Unknown, c. 323
RULED: Western emperor, 337–350
DIED: Murdered, Vicus Helena, Gaul, 350

CONSTANS, THE YOUNGEST of Constantine's sons, originally ruled the prefectures of Italy and Africa. He was unhappy with such a small amount of territory and the brothers met at Viminacium in 338 to discuss altering the boundaries. As a result, Constans gained the prefecture of Illyricum and the diocese of Thrace from his brother Constantius. This triggered Constantine's obsession about being sidelined as senior emperor, and as the situation deteriorated Constans handed Thrace back to Constantius to gain his support. Constantine's death in 340 gave Constans control of Gaul, Spain and Britain, as the Roman world saw another division between east and west.

In a sign of the changing times, the conflict between Constans and Constantius was not about border disputes or the exercise of sole power, but religion. By 343 the Christian world was tearing itself apart over the Arian dispute, taking the Roman *imperium* with it. Constans

Roman ships in Mainz (on the Rhine) harbour

supported the orthodox western view of the Trinity as outlined by the Nicene Creed; Constantius supported the views of Arius, that Christ was not God but merely the Son of God. By 346 the two brothers were on the verge of war over the matter, but both decided to avoid open conflict and, in the interim, supported the clergy of their preferred creed.

Constans may have been popular with western Christians for his support of orthodoxy; unfortunately, he was deeply unpopular with the military. His selling of government offices, domination by pampered favourites and open homosexuality all offended the officer class, leading to a rebellion in 350 by the commander of the Rhine armies, Magnentius. Very soon, the whole of the west supported the usurper. Fearing for his life, Constans fled towards Spain, but assassins sent by Magnentius tracked him down. Having sought refuge in a temple in a small town in the Pyrenees, Constans was dragged from the sanctuary by soldiers, who killed him without mercy.

MAGNENTIUS

UNGRATEFUL REBEL

NAME: Flavius Magnus Magnentius
BORN: Samarobriva (Amiens), Gaul, c. 303
RULED: Western usurper, 350–353
DIED: Suicide, Mons Seleucus, Gaul, 353

MAGNENTIUS, THE SON of a British father and a Frankish mother, was the first of a new breed of military commander—offspring of the barbarians who had been slowly seeded within the provinces of the empire. At one point Constans had rescued him from his subordinates, who were keen to kill their commanding officer. So imagine Constans's surprise when Magnentius expressed his gratitude by rebelling against him, donning the imperial purple at a birthday party, no less.

The army backed the rebel and very soon Constans suffered an ignominious death in an out-of-the way village. Magnentius gained control of Africa, Italy, Gaul and Spain and moved to consolidate his power over the remaining provinces. There were only two problems. The first was that the legions on the Danube did not recognise his authority, instead raising their own nominee as emperor, Vetranio. The second problem was much greater—Constantius, the surviving son of Constantine I. Though he was preoccupied with a drawn-out war against the Persians, by 351 Constantius had begun his march to reclaim the provinces of the west.

The two armies clashed at the battle of Mursa Major, the bloodiest battle of the fourth century, and for the first time heavy cavalry beat Roman infantry legions. Defeated, Magnentius spent the next two years steadily retreating from the advancing armies of the emperor. Fleeing first to Italy before moving to Gaul in 352, he waited for Constantius to make his move, so that it was not until 353 that the rivals fought at Mons Seleucus in Gaul. His troops soon surrendered to the son of Constantine and, seeing that all was lost, Magnentius fell on his sword to avoid the humiliation of capture.

NEPOTIAN

KING OF THE GLADIATORS

NAME: Flavius Julius Popilius
Nepotianus Constantinus
BORN: Unknown
RULED: Western usurper, 350
DIED: Killed, Rome, 350

THE DEATH OF CONSTANS opened the door for other would-be emperors, including his cousin Nepotian. Grandson of Constantius Chlorus and half-nephew to Constantine the Great, he was near Rome when news arrived of Magnentius's rebellion, and so he proclaimed himself emperor. Gathering a motley crew of gladiators, he attacked the former capital, successfully defeating Magnentius's praetorian prefect.

It was not to last. Twenty-eight days later he had been defeated by one of Magnentius's most trusted commanding officers, Marcellinus, and his head was adorning the point of a spear. Without the support of the army, even a connection to the great Constantine was no guarantee of success.

VETRANIO

NO STOMACH FOR A FIGHT

NAME: Vetranio
BORN: Moesia, date unknown
RULED: Western usurper, 350
DIED: Of natural causes, Prusa (Bursa), Bithynia, 356

IN THE CONFUSION surrounding Magnentius's usurpation, Constans's sister persuaded Vetranio, the commander of the Danubian legions, to assume the title of Caesar in order to block Magnentius. At first Vetranio assured Constantius that he would be a loyal deputy, and the sole remaining emperor confirmed him in the rank of Caesar. But the temptation proved too great. Assuming imperial honours, he made a pact with Magnentius in which the pair of usurpers asked Constantius to abdicate the throne.

Constantius's response was to confront Vetranio in late 350. When it became clear that the Danubian legions would support the emperor, Vetranio grovelled before him, agreeing to renounce his claims. Constantius led him away, allowing him to retire to private life where he was supported at taxpayers' expense. He died six years later.

SILVANUS

NEVER TURN YOUR BACK

NAME: Claudius Silvanus
BORN: Unknown
RULED: Western usurper, 355
DIED: Murdered, Colonia Agrippina (Cologne), Germania, 355

MAGNENTIUS'S USURPATION had one final act left to play. His fall opened the Rhine frontier and the Franks took advantage of the lack of Roman troops to invade Gaul. Constantius appointed Silvanus, a Frank and former officer of Magnentius, to deal with the crisis in 353. Silvanus's solution was to bribe the Germans to return to their homes.

Unfortunately, he had made some powerful enemies at court and they faked letters claiming that Silvanus was aiming for the purple. Initially persuaded by these, Constantius ordered his immediate recall. Silvanus, convinced he was a dead man, decided to take a risk and declared himself emperor. Soon his replacement arrived, assuring Silvanus that the emperor was unaware of his revolt. Relieved, he went to celebrate mass but to his great surprise he was dragged violently from the church by soldiers his replacement had bribed. They then butchered him.

CONSTANTIUS II

CHURCH MEDDLER

NAME: Flavius Julius Valerius Constantius
BORN: Illyricum, 317
RULED: Eastern emperor, 337–350; sole emperor, 350–361
DIED: Of fever, Mopsucrenae in Cilicia, Oriens, 361

UNDER CONSTANTINE the Great, the emperor was the defender of Christian orthodoxy. But what if the church could not agree what orthodoxy was? This was the chief domestic issue that plagued the reign of Constantius II.

The middle child, Constantius's subtle actions were driven by his relationship with his siblings. He orchestrated the massacre of his cousins, ensuring that the empire fell to the sons of Constantine. He also asked for the eastern provinces, ensuring that his elder and younger brothers would be the first to come into conflict over any issues of inheritance and pre-eminence.

In the burning question of the day, whether Christ was God or a divinely created creature, Constantius positioned himself with the Arians, who believed that Christ was not of the same substance as God. He spent his reign supporting Arianism, removing Trinitarian bishops and calling numerous church councils to get his version of Christianity accepted throughout the empire. His determination ultimately led him to interfere directly in church affairs. He orchestrated the condemnation of Bishop Athanasius and proclaimed a compromise theological position before exiling the orthodox Pope Liberius and enthroning an antipope, Felix II. Liberius, weakened by exile, agreed to the revised Arian position and his banishment was revoked in 357. He eventually recanted, but by that time some other problems had distracted Constantius.

One of these was the perpetually indecisive struggle with Persia. Constantius spent the first half of his reign on campaign in Mesopotamia and Armenia, and though he won some significant victories, he could not gain a decisive advantage over King Shapur. It was not until 350 that he was able to leave the Persian war in the hands of his Caesar, Gallus, and deal with the usurpers who had risen in the wake of Constans's murder. He spent the next ten years in the west, first defeating Magnentius and then fighting off the barbarians who were again terrorising the Rhine and Danube frontiers.

Yet his family troubles never seemed to go away. His nephew Gallus had managed to keep the Persians quiet while putting down some rebellions, but by 354 his conduct raised suspicions that he harboured imperial ambitions. Constantius recalled him and put him to death. Not having sons of his own, Constantius was forced to raise Gallus's half-brother, Julian, to the rank of Caesar and send him to deal with the tribes in Pannonia and along the Danube. Then the east erupted into war again. In 359 Constantius advanced to Antioch, where he failed to force the Persians back. He was about to start a new offensive when he received news that Julian had been proclaimed emperor. Gathering his troops, he marched to deal with his nephew but fell ill on the way; before dying, he named Julian as his successor.

JULIAN

THE APOSTATE

NAME: Flavius Claudius Julianus
BORN: Constantinople, 332
RULED: Sole emperor, 360–363
DIED: Killed in battle, Mesopotamia (modern Iraq), 363

MANY PEOPLE by the 350s were asking just why the empire seemed to be in such difficulties. To Julian, the answer seemed obvious—it was the fault of the Christians and their ability to cause civil unrest wherever they lived.

> **Thou hast conquered, Galilean!**
>
> JULIAN

Never considered imperial material, Julian had been locked away by the family in studious seclusion where, after discovering the joys of Plato and Aristotle, he secretly abandoned his Christian faith. And in seclusion he would have remained, had he and Constantius not been the last of Constantine's relatives still alive.

He was raised to the rank of Caesar in 355 and the emperor sent him to the Rhine frontier to fight the Germans. Astonishingly, Julian demonstrated a genuine skill in warfare, quickly gaining the affection of the legions, but his victories soon alienated Constantius, who was also being manipulated by officials whom Julian had offended. In 360 Constantius demanded reinforcements from Gaul to supplement his Persian campaign, though in reality it was to weaken Julian's position. This sparked a rebellion and the legions elevated Julian to the purple; luckily, Constantius's death spared the empire a new civil war.

Upon his accession, Julian attempted to turn back the clock and make paganism the dominant religion of the empire. Espousing religious toleration, he did not persecute the Christians but he removed the favoured financial status of the bishops and lower clergy, forced the surrender of pagan shrines they had occupied and sowed dissent among the various sects. At the same time, he used the Christian liturgy and clergy as a template to form a new pagan church. While intellectually dismissing the passive Christian philosophy, he could not forget that his Christian cousin had butchered his father, Julius Constantius, and most of his other relatives. Given time he may have won the battle against the Christians if it had not been for the Persian menace to the east.

Things had been quiet in the aftermath of Constantius's death, but the Persians were still in control of Upper Mesopotamia. So, in 363 Julian began his great offensive. Approaching the Persian capital, Ctesiphon, Julian crossed the Tigris River under heavy fire and defeated a Persian army encamped between the river and the city. He began besieging the city, but within a week he had abandoned his plans and started his retreat towards Roman territory, beaten by an impregnable city and the rapidly approaching army of King Shapur. Harassed by the Persians, Julian boldly counterattacked but was without his armour; on the cusp of victory he was struck by a spear. Carried from the field, he died that night, his great potential unfulfilled.

JOVIAN

PRESS THE RESET BUTTON

NAME: Flavius Jovianus
BORN: Singidunum (Belgrade), Pannonia, 331
RULED: Sole emperor, 363–364
DIED: Of food poisoning, Dadastana, Galatia, 364

A CENTURY BEFORE, Roman troops were stranded in Persia and deprived of their emperor. Then, as now, circumstances forced them to elect a general from the command staff to deal with the emergency. Their first choice, the praetorian prefect, declined the dangerous honour, citing old age. Therefore, the soldiers elected Jovian, son of the imperial bodyguard's commander.

His first task was to extricate the army from their current predicament. Arranging a peace treaty with King Shapur, Jovian surrendered all territory east of the Tigris and part of Mesopotamia. In the Romans' exposed position, it was the best he could hope for, but the empire reacted to the news with anger. Stopping at Antioch, Jovian quickly overturned Julian's pro-pagan laws and restored Christianity's privileges, but he knew his peace treaty was deeply unpopular and he wanted to get to Constantinople as soon as possible to consolidate his rule. He never made it, discovered dead in his tent after eating some particularly disagreeable mushrooms.

VALENTINIAN I

A VERY ANGRY MAN

NAME: Flavius Valentinianus
BORN: Colonia Aurelia Cibalae (Vinkovci), Pannonia, 321
RULED: Western emperor, 364–375
DIED: Of a stroke, Brigetio, Pannonia, 375

AFTER JOVIAN'S DEATH, it was to Valentinian that the army turned for leadership. Having risen through the ranks, he was a military man through and through. He also possessed a fearsome temper, which he proved incapable of controlling, to the detriment of those around him. On one occasion he even struck a priest who had tried to bless him with holy water.

Valentinian was a simple man, and he saw the imperial station as one of service to the state—in his case, military service. Following the example of Diocletian, he divided the empire administratively between himself and his brother Valens. Taking on the burden of the western provinces, Valentinian moved from city to city as he strove to halt the barbarian invasions that were now almost a yearly occurrence. His reign was one of frenetic military activity: fighting wars against the Alamanni from 365 to 370, clearing Britain of Picts, Scots and Saxons between 367 and 369, taking on the Sarmatians and Quadi from 372 to 375.

In this unceasing struggle to protect the provinces, Valentinian had to raise taxes to astronomical amounts, further harming an economy already crippled by perpetual barbarian invasions. He attempted to protect his subjects by establishing in every town public defenders, whose role was to prevent the oppression of the poor. He reorganised the administration of the empire, legislating to give imperial court officials and military officers equal ranking with civil officials. He dealt severely with members of the aristocracy who transgressed new laws dealing with magic, witchcraft, divination, adultery and the use of poison, and allowing the use of torture to obtain a conviction.

Valentinian's successful incursions into barbarian territory were halted by his death. The volatile emperor was so infuriated by the attitude of envoys from the Quadi, who had come to him to protest about the erection of Roman fortifications on their lands, that he lost control of his infamous temper, causing him to burst a blood vessel in his brain. He was the last of the victorious Roman emperors in the west. Very soon, the western provinces found themselves overrun by barbarian hordes, and it would take some four hundred years for another warrior emperor to arise. He would be born of those very barbarian tribes who had inflicted so much terror and destruction upon the empire.

FIRMUS

THE MOORISH PRINCE

NAME: Firmus
BORN: Unknown
RULED: Western usurper, 372–375
DIED: Suicide, North Africa, 375

BY THE END OF THE fourth century, the line between Roman and barbarian had started to blur. Firmus, the son of a Moorish prince in North Africa, was a former officer in the Roman army. He killed his brother over their inheritance, but this brother had been a favourite of the incompetent Roman military governor, who now pushed Firmus into rebellion.

After removing the governor, Firmus tried to make peace but Theodosius, the general sent by Valentinian to deal with the situation, rebuffed his overtures. Scorned, Firmus declared himself emperor and began a major uprising against Valentinian, uniting various North African tribes in an anti-Roman coalition. He also received support from local Romans and Donatists (a Christian group who maintained that priests or bishops who had apostatised could not be readmitted to the church) and spent the next three years engaging in a bloody war of attrition against Theodosius. Although he was quite successful, forcing Theodosius to withdraw several times in order to regroup, Firmus was eventually betrayed and captured by one of his allies. Before he could be delivered to Theodosius, he committed suicide.

VALENS

AGGRAVATOR OF THE GOTHS

NAME: Flavius Julius Valens
BORN: Colonia Aurelia Cibalae (Vinkovci), Pannonia, c. 328
RULED: Eastern emperor, 364–378
DIED: Killed, Adrianople (Edirne), Thrace, 378

WHERE VALENTINIAN HAD been a successful military officer, his brother Valens had enjoyed a quiet life of well-deserved obscurity. He possessed only one qualification that was of interest to Valentinian—he cheerfully acknowledged his brother's superiority as both man and emperor.

Where Valentinian was a dark and violent man, Valens was a timid creature, driven by his fears rather than his passions. His appointment may have spared the empire the spectre of civil war, but it exposed the eastern provinces to a man incapable of dealing with the problems facing the empire. Valens's first task was to manage a minor palace rebellion that turned into a major revolt due to his hesitant handling of the situation. He had departed for Antioch in 365, leaving Constantinople in the hands of his father-in-law, the praetorian prefect Petronius. Eager to convict anyone, guilty or innocent, and bankrupt his victims, Petronius was already widely loathed in Constantinople because of his greed, cruelty and ruthlessness, and Valens acquiesced to all his actions. With the emperor gone, the city rose up in rebellion, at the instigation of the usurper Procopius, and Valens was soon faced with a number of legions deserting his cause. He eventually regained control, but not before considering abdication and even suicide.

Things then started looking up. In 369 he overcame the Goths and then turned his attention to the Persians, defeating them and re-establishing Roman control over Armenia, though the peace treaty brought him no real advantage. By 376 he was about to undertake a new Persian expedition when he was summoned back to deal with a fresh crisis caused by the Goths.

The Goths had asked permission to settle on Roman territory south of the Danube and Valens had agreed, so long as they gave up their weapons and settled down as farmers. Unfortunately, Roman officials, who looked the other way when the Germans kept their weapons while simultaneously charging the barbarians exorbitant prices for necessities, undid the agreement. Close to starvation, the Goths rose up in rebellion, forcing Valens to return from the east. Not bothering to wait for the new western emperor, he rashly confronted some 200,000 Goths at Adrianople. In the ensuing battle, his cavalry fled and his infantry was cut to pieces; by the end of the carnage, two-thirds of the eastern army, numbering 40,000 men, were lying on the field of battle. Injured, Valens retreated to a small shack that the Goths quickly overran before setting it alight. The Romans never recovered his body.

PROCOPIUS

THE LAST OF THE FLAVIANS

NAME: Procopius
BORN: Corycus (Kızkalesi), Cilicia, c. 326
RULED: Eastern usurper, 365–366
DIED: Executed, Thyatira (Akhisar), Phrygia, 366

THE NEO-FLAVIAN DYNASTY did not perish with Julian. Julian had offered his maternal cousin, Procopius, the purple prior to his death, but Procopius declined it on Jovian's elevation. Retiring to private life, he was soon threatened by Valentinian, who was determined to prevent any challenge to his rule.

Procopius went into hiding, eventually turning up at Constantinople in 365. By this stage, Valens's popularity in the capital had plummeted as a result of the actions of his even more unpopular father-in-law,

Petronius. Using his relationship to the well-liked Julian to garner support, Procopius bribed two legions, which immediately acclaimed him emperor. Things got off to a splendid start as he quickly gained control of Thrace and Bithynia, defections from Valens's armies aiding his cause. When Valens was almost captured besieging one of the rebellious cities, Procopius believed that victory was within reach.

By 366, however, Valens had regained the initiative, slowly recapturing areas that had gone over to the usurper. Eventually, Procopius was defeated in battle and went to ground, but one of his former generals handed him over. Valens was not merciful: he had Procopius tied to bent trees, which, when released, ripped him in two.

Emperor Valens reaching his fatal accord with Gothic King Athanarich

ROMAN REFORM AND RECONSTRUCTION

MARCELLUS

DISTANT RELATION

NAME: Marcellus
BORN: Unknown
RULED: Eastern usurper, 366
DIED: Executed, place unknown, 366

WHERE PROCOPIUS USED his blood ties to Julian to gain the throne, Marcellus used his family relationship with Procopius. When he learned of the defeat and death of Procopius, he was in command of Nicaea. Using the city as his base, he captured Chalcedon, where his supporters named him Procopius's successor. Marcellus attempted to gain the support of the Goths, but troops loyal to Valens soon captured him. Taken into the emperor's presence, he was lashed and then executed for his presumption.

GRATIAN

THE INDOLENT EMPEROR

NAME: Flavius Gratianus
BORN: Sirmium (Sremska), Pannonia, 359
RULED: Western co-emperor, 367–375;
western emperor, 375–383
DIED: Assassinated, Lugdunum (Lyon),
Lugdunensis, 383

THERE IS NOT A LOT a seven-year-old boy can offer a militaristic empire. For the studious and unwarlike Gratian, Valentinian I's eldest son, the only thing he offered was the possibility of a smooth transition on the death of his father. To this end, he became co-Augustus in 367.

The transition was tested in 375 when the warrior emperor passed away and the soldiers beheld a quiet fifteen-year-old boy on the throne. They, therefore, proclaimed his four-year-old brother Valentinian co-emperor, to ensure that the military would continue to have some control over imperial decision-making. In any event, Gratian surprised everyone by repulsing an Alamanni invasion in 378 with speed, dexterity and skill. Since this campaign prevented him getting to his uncle in time to avert the disaster at Adrianople, he found himself senior emperor, responsible for dealing with the Goths who were rampaging through Thrace and the Balkans. Feeling unequal to the task, he summoned the exiled general Theodosius, whom Valentinian I had banished as a result of court intrigues, and offered him the purple and command of the eastern provinces.

> **I beseech you to wait a while for a partner in your dangers, and not rashly to expose yourself alone to serious peril.**
>
> GRATIAN (in a letter to his uncle Valens)

The appointment of the gifted Theodosius allowed Gratian to sink to his natural level of indolence, and he turned the empire over to his ministers, the Frankish general Merobaudes and the bishop of Milan, St Ambrose. Ambrose's influence meant that Gratian supported Nicean orthodoxy, speeding Arianism's decline. He also pushed the emperor to target other heresies and remove the pagan Altar of Victory from Rome. These actions increased Gratian's unpopularity with the Senate and the people. He then alienated the army by displaying a preference for his Alan bodyguards, with whom he went hunting—the Alans were one of the Sarmatian tribes who were now entering the service of Rome. The soldiers responded by raising a usurper, Magnus Maximus. Gratian was staying in Paris when Magnus marched to confront him. Finding that most of his troops had abandoned him in favour of the usurper, Gratian fled south, heading towards Italy and the relative safety of his brother's dominion. He had reached Lyon when his pursuers finally caught and killed him.

VALENTINIAN II

IN THE HANDS OF OTHERS

NAME: Flavius Valentinianus Iunior
BORN: Augusta Treverorum (Trier), Germania, 371
RULED: Western co-emperor, 375–388;
western emperor, 388–392
DIED: Hanged, Vienne (Vienna), Viennensis, 392

FROM THE MOMENT he was born until the day he died, Valentinian II was destined to be a pawn in the conflict between forces and individuals determined to control the empire. Surrounded by the daily routine of the imperial court, where his every move was tightly controlled and monitored, he was raised to the purple at the age of four at the request of the army, who were keen to have an emperor who they could easily control. After his elevation, he was taken from his father's camp and sent to the imperial residence in Milan, where he soon became the mouthpiece of his ambitious mother.

Though Valentinian was nominally given control of Illyricum, Africa and Italy, real authority for the western half of the empire rested with his brother Gratian until 383, and then with Theodosius until Valentinian came of age in 388. His first challenge was the rebellion of Magnus Maximus, which had seen the death of Gratian; remarkably, they came to an accommodation whereby Valentinian continued to rule in Italy while his new co-emperor managed the rest of the western provinces apart from Illyricum, which was transferred to Theodosius. The fight between Valentinian's Arian mother and the orthodox Bishop Ambrose of Milan dominated his reign. By Easter 386, it had reached the point where Ambrose had barricaded himself and his congregation in the main church in protest at Valentinian's pro-Arianism. The crisis was averted when Maximus invaded Italy, causing Valentinian and his mother to flee to Theodosius's court, where she soon died.

The last years of Valentinian's reign were spent at Vienna, first under Theodosius's watchful eye, and then under the thumb of his own *magister militum*, Arbogast. By the time Valentinian was twenty he acutely resented any limitation on his power. After his appeals to Theodosius were ignored, he tried to dismiss Arbogast in 392, but the Frankish general merely laughed at him. Valentinian grabbed a sword to attack him but was restrained by his courtiers. A few days later, they found the young man hanging in his quarters; Arbogast declared it suicide. However, St Ambrose gave him a Christian burial, indicating that the bishop, at least, did not believe the official story.

MAGNUS MAXIMUS

FRIEND OF THE FATHER

NAME: Magnus Maximus
BORN: Spain, c. 335
RULED: Western usurper, 383–384;
western co-emperor, 384–388
DIED: Executed, Aquileia, Italy, 388

PRIOR TO HIS REBELLION, Magnus Maximus had had a distinguished military career and had worked closely with Theodosius's father on a number of campaigns. By 383 he had been *comes Britanniae*, the commander of Britain, for three years, subduing the Picts and the Scots, but when he turned his eye to the political situation on the continent, two things jumped out at him—the unpopularity of Gratian, and the elevation of Theodosius to the eastern throne.

Believing his time had come, Maximus stripped the island of troops and crossed over into Gaul, where he dealt with the pampered and complacent Gratian, who was taken completely by surprise. Maximus then began preparations to march into Italy to overthrow Valentinian II, but Theodosius, mindful of his oaths to protect the young emperors, marched west to deal with him. The two rivals entered into negotiations, where

Theodosius blinked first, acknowledging Maximus as co-emperor in the west apart from the prefectures of Italy and Illyricum, which went to Valentinian and Theodosius respectively.

Maximus was quite pleased at first, ruling the western provinces efficiently so that some provinces experienced their first peaceful period in years. Unfortunately, he had a son to think of, so by 387 he was again in Italy, seeking to eliminate his only western rival. Valentinian fled east, asking for Theodosius's aid, and the emperor duly obliged. Maximus put up a good fight, but after losing a number of battles and seeing the Franks invade his realm during the chaos, he eventually surrendered to Theodosius. Maximus asked the emperor to spare his life, but sparing a defeated rival risked the possibility of the rival reclaiming what had been lost, and no emperor could take that risk.

VICTOR

FUTURE PLANS

NAME: Flavius Victor
BORN: Place unknown, c. 378
RULED: Western co-usurper, 384–388
DIED: Killed, Augusta Treverorum (Trier), Germania, 388

LIKE MANY AN EMPEROR before him, Maximus's plans involved securing the future for his son. Ensuring that neither Valentinian nor Theodosius had any objections, he made his young son co-emperor. The boy's future depended on his father's success, and by 388 that was looking grim. Maximus left Victor in his capital at Trier while he fought for his life, but he soon learned that Theodosius's *magister militum*, Arbogast, had quietly killed the young man.

FLAVIUS EUGENIUS

PAGANISM'S LAST STAND

NAME: Flavius Eugenius
BORN: Unknown
RULED: Western usurper, 392–394
DIED: Executed, Frigidus River, Dalmatia, 394

WITH VALENTINIAN II'S sudden death, the Frankish general Arbogast decided that now was the time to exercise direct power in the western empire. Having dealt successfully with the Frankish incursions in the wake of Maximus's fall, he was the most powerful minister of the western court. Only one thing stood in his way—he was a Frank, and his assumption of the purple would have aroused significant opposition. What he needed was a Roman puppet so that the Senate and people of Rome would believe they were still in control of the empire. The man Arbogast felt was most appropriate to inherit the throne of the Caesars was a former teacher of grammar, Eugenius.

The new emperor quickly realised he needed a substantial power base if he was to overcome his rivals. Though he was a Christian, it was to the pagan senatorial elite that he turned. By restoring some of the privileges the pagans had lost, he incurred the wrath of Bishop Ambrose, who demanded that Eugenius cease such evil acts. Ambrose fled when Eugenius and Arbogast marched into Italy, threatening to stable their horses in Milan's main church.

Being Theodosius's appointee, Arbogast may have felt safe to take this course of action, but he underestimated Theodosius's dynastic ambitions and support of Christianity. The eastern emperor marched west once again and defeated the usurpers. Arbogast committed suicide, while Eugenius threw himself on Theodosius's mercy. He was soon executed, and his head was stuck on a lance for good measure. Bishop Ambrose was overjoyed.

DIVISION AND DECAY

(392–491)

At a time when the only hope of delaying the ruin of the Roman name depended on the firm union and reciprocal aid of all the nations to whom it had been gradually communicated, the subjects were instructed to view each other in a foreign and even hostile light, to rejoice in their mutual calamities. The natives of Italy affected to despise the servile and effeminate Greeks of Byzantium, who presumed to imitate the dress, and to usurp the dignity, of Roman senators; and the Greeks had not yet forgot the sentiments of hatred and contempt which their polished ancestors had so long entertained for the rude inhabitants of the West. The distinction of two governments soon produced the separation of two nations.

EDWARD GIBBON
The Decline and Fall of the Roman Empire, 1880

FOLLOWING PAGE: Attila, King of the Hun, at the battle of Chalons, 451

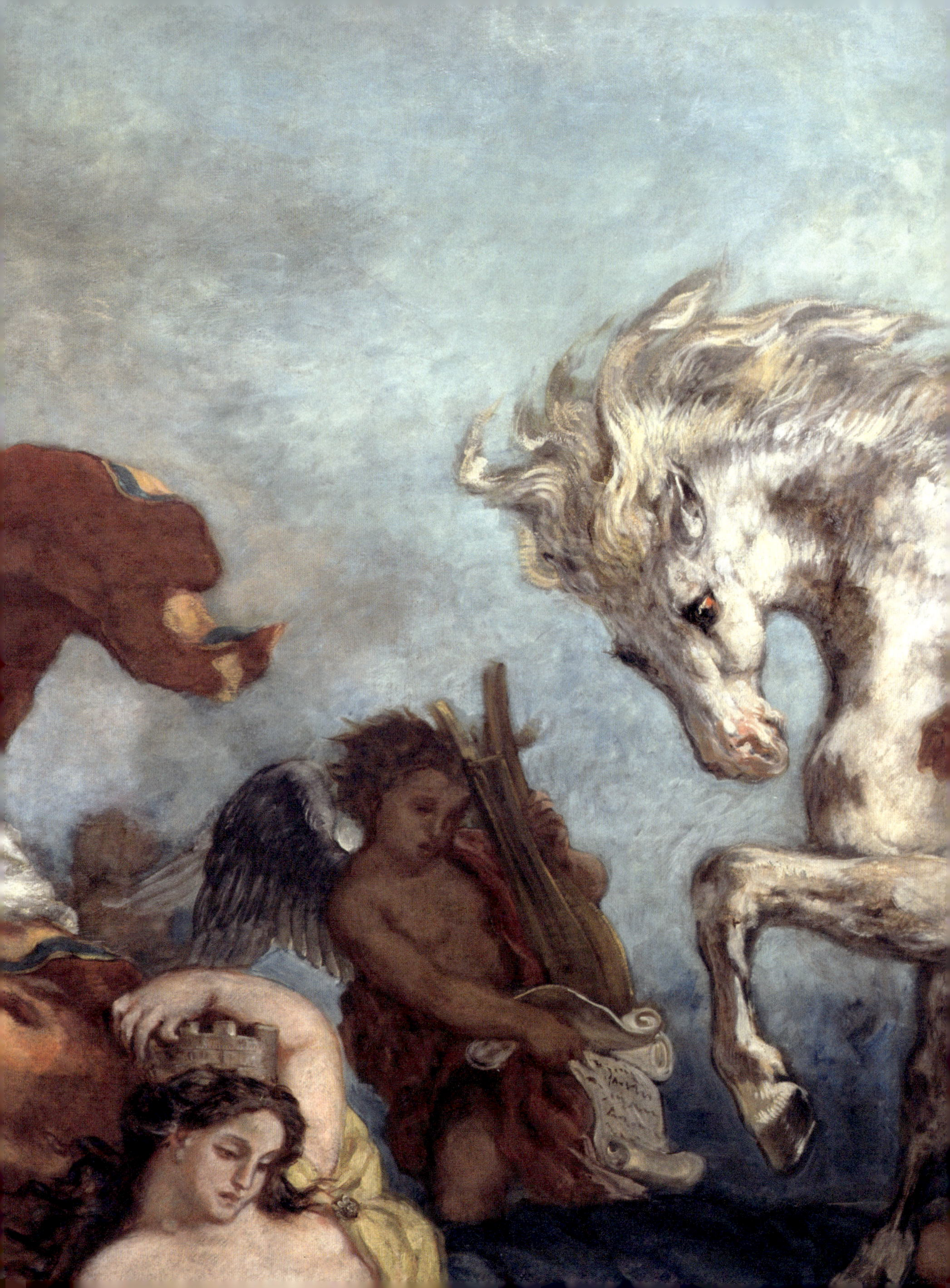

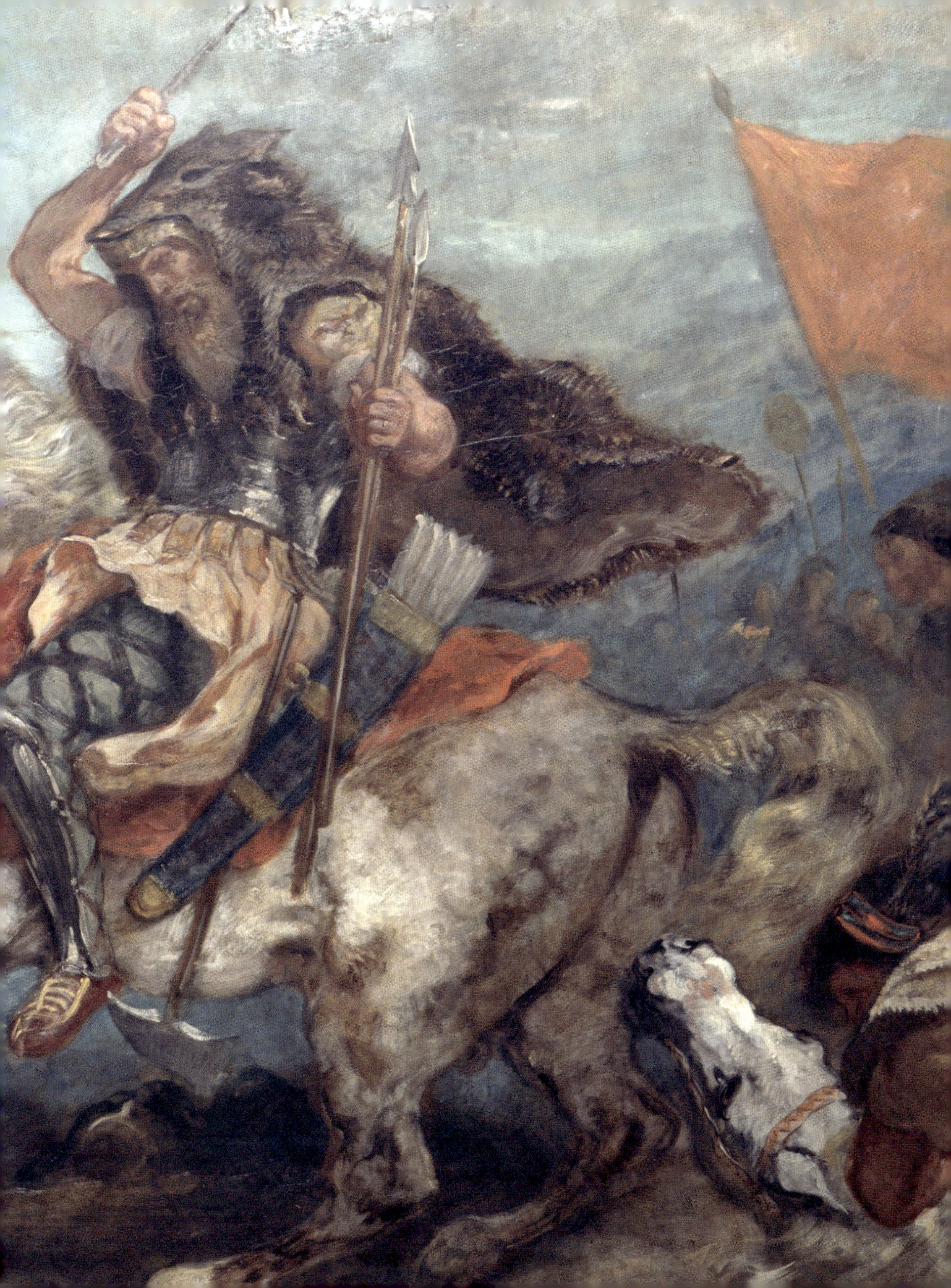

THEODOSIUS I THE GREAT

CHRISTIANITY'S CHAMPION

NAME: Flavius Theodosius
BORN: Cauca (Coca), Hispania, 347
RULED: Eastern emperor, 379–392;
sole emperor, 392–395
DIED: Natural causes, Mediolanum
(Milan), Italy, 395

THEODOSIUS HAD FIRST-HAND experience of Valentinian I's legendary wrath. His father, a victorious general with enormous experience, had lost two legions to the barbarians. His reward was execution, while his family, including his son Theodosius, the governor of Upper Moesia, went into exile. They would have remained in exile but for Valens's disastrous defeat in 378. Gratian, isolated and afraid, sought the one man who had demonstrated the military and administrative capacity to lead the empire in its time of need—Theodosius the Spaniard.

To Theodosius went the eastern provinces and the immediate task of dealing with the Goths, who were pillaging Thrace. Initially he pursued a military outcome, but a severe shortage of reliable troops forced him to develop a political solution, settling the Goths in the now devastated provinces. They were not part of the Roman Empire; they were a foreign nation within the empire, retaining their own kings and laws. In return, they were to furnish badly needed troops for Rome, not as part of the legions, but as separate military contingents. Though successful in the short term, this solution would destabilise the empire in the years to come.

By 383, Theodosius's major task was to deal with the usurper Magnus Maximus, who had murdered Gratian. Initially he was happy to see a capable military general in command in the west but eventually he had to deal with the threat Maximus posed to Valentinian II, ostensibly the true Roman emperor. Theodosius passed over to the west, killing Maximus in 387. It was at this time that he made contact with the most prestigious man of the age, Bishop Ambrose of Milan.

Theodosius had already demonstrated his support for the Nicene orthodoxy, declaring in 380 that the only legitimate religion in the empire was Catholic Christianity. Expelling Arian bishops from their sees throughout the empire, he also oversaw the death throes of paganism, closing temples, banning sacrifices and abandoning the Olympic Games. Yet even such a devout son of the church could incur its wrath, as Theodosius discovered in 390 when he responded to riots in Thessalonica. The death of the captain of the imperial guards angered Theodosius, who commanded the troops in the city to re-establish their control by whatever means necessary. Though he countermanded the order, it was too late; seven thousand citizens were slaughtered before the day was out.

> **We authorise the followers of this law to assume the title of Catholic Christians; all others we pronounce to be mad and foolish, and we order that they shall bear the ignominious name of heretics.**
>
> THEODOSIUS I

Bishop Ambrose was appalled; refusing to meet the emperor, he insisted that Theodosius would be excommunicated unless he performed a suitable public penance. At first Theodosius ignored the instruction, but within a few months he submitted. This was the first clash in the west between an emperor and a high ecclesiastical officer and, in a sign of things to come, the church emerged triumphant.

By 395 the conversion of the empire was nearly complete and Theodosius had done much to ensure Christianity's ultimate victory. For this, the church awarded him the title of The Great, as it had

St Ambrose and Theodosius

Constantine. Theodosius, however, was already close to death, and he bequeathed the empire to his two sons, Honorius and Arcadius.

ARCADIUS

THE LIZARD EMPEROR

NAME: Flavius Arcadius
BORN: Constantinople, 377
RULED: Co-emperor, 383–395;
eastern emperor, 395–408
DIED: Of natural causes, Constantinople, 408

RAISED TO THE PURPLE at a very young age, Arcadius never really got the hang of ruling. It did not help that he was so completely different from his energetic father—small and dark-skinned, slow of speech, weak-minded and indifferent to the necessities of leadership. Busying himself with trivialities, he was content to let others rule in his name. This was his father's legacy, as Theodosius gave Arcadius very little space for independent action, regardless of his nominal powers, while he was co-emperor.

Arcadius's first crisis after becoming eastern emperor at eighteen was a confrontation with the Huns, who were ravaging Syria and Asia Minor, while he also faced an invasion of the Balkans by the Visigoths under Alaric. Arcadius turned to Stilicho, the *magister militum* of the west, who skilfully and with great dexterity held Alaric in check. However, Arcadius's praetorian prefect, Rufinus, began whispering in his ear about Stilicho being a threat to his throne. Arcadius ordered Stilicho to withdraw and send his troops east to Constantinople and Stilicho complied, but his men were not happy and, on their arrival in the east, they murdered Rufinus in front of Arcadius.

There are always people who will take advantage of the simple-minded, and there were plenty to take advantage of

THE PARTITION OF THE EMPIRE

The death of Theodosius saw the implementation of a modified version of Diocletian's system of western and eastern imperial administration. From this time, the two administrations operated virtually uninterrupted for almost a hundred years. However, as had been the case under Valentinian I and Valens, this was not in any real sense a partition of the empire. The two co-emperors maintained imperial unity by the nomination of one consul in Rome and one in Constantinople, by the association of the statues of both Augusti in each part of the empire, and by the issuing of imperial enactments under their joint names. Laws enacted in one part of the empire were valid across its entirety. Additionally, the elevation of a new emperor had to be recognised by the existing one or, if necessary, he would raise one up himself. Upon the death of one of the Augusti, the imperial authority of the remaining emperor covered the whole empire until he nominated a colleague to fill the vacant throne.

The events of 476 are often referred to as the 'fall of the Western Empire'. This is incorrect: no empire fell in 476 since there was no 'Western Empire' to fall. There was only one Roman Empire, regardless of whether one or more Augusti ruled it. What did happen in 476—or more accurately 480, when the last legitimate Roman emperor in the west, Julius Nepos, died—was that the western provinces were again under the authority of the sole emperor reigning at Constantinople.

Arcadius. His reign saw the empire ruled by a succession of powerful individuals, starting with his chamberlain, the elderly eunuch Eutropius, who manipulated Arcadius into marrying Aelia Eudoxia. Her father had been a bitter enemy of Rufinus, and Eutropius hoped she would be grateful to him for making her the empress, but she engineered a revolt of the Gothic officials who were the mainstay of the Roman armies, forcing Eutropius into exile. The Gothic leader, Gainas, tried to emulate Alaric's success but was thwarted by Eudoxia, who organised a massacre of all Gothic officers and soldiers in the capital, ordering them chased through Thrace until they were all murdered.

> **The consulship befouled and defiled by a filthy monster is now delivered from the foul stain of his tenure.**
>
> ARCADIUS (on the fall of Eutropius)

Eudoxia ruled through her husband until she died from a miscarriage in 404. It was her suggestion that the new *magister militum*, Alaric, attack the western provinces. It was also during this time that she and Arcadius became the targets of the bishop of Constantinople, John Chrysostom. He condemned the imperial family for living in vulgar luxury while many of their subjects were suffering, before accusing Eudoxia of usurping Arcadius's role and using her wealth to achieve her own ambitions. Eventually she engineered his removal from office, but John appealed to the pope in Rome, further inflaming tensions between the two imperial courts. Yet Eudoxia did not enjoy her victory for long, as she died shortly afterwards.

For the remainder of Arcadius's reign, the emperor was controlled by the gifted praetorian prefect Anthemius, who did much to repair east–west relations. In this, as in all things, Arcadius barely participated; lizard-like, he was a passive observer, who retreated farther and farther into the background until he died in 408.

THEODOSIUS II
THE CALLIGRAPHER

NAME: Flavius Theodosius
BORN: Constantinople, 401
RULED: Co-emperor, 402–408;
eastern emperor, 408–450
DIED: Thrown from a horse,
Constantinople, 450

LIKE HIS FATHER, ARCADIUS, Theodosius II would be unable to shake off the domination of his officials, his wife and other family members. Inducted into the college of emperors at the tender age of one, he became sole eastern emperor at the age of seven, and the regency was placed in the hands first of Anthemius, the praetorian prefect, and then of his sister, Pulcheria. Throughout his reign he indulged his passions for reading and learning, in particular the art of calligraphy. Not inclined to be a military leader, he saw his role as a remote and untouchable ruler in communion with God and doing His will.

Theodosius's government renewed close ties with Honorius's western court, recognising the common threat faced by both administrations in the aftermath of Rome's sack in 410 by Alaric the Visigoth. Even so, Theodosius was unable to send military resources, being concerned with the large number of barbarians in his own armies. The fear that Constantinople would suffer a similar fate to Rome's forced Anthemius to begin the construction of the massive Theodosian Walls to protect Constantinople from barbarian attack, walls that contributed to the longevity of the Roman Empire in the east.

Lacking both independence of character and energy, Theodosius expressed no real desire to rule the empire; even his choice of wife he left to Pulcheria. These two women—his wife and his sister—would seek to control him, and their conflict would overshadow much of his reign, dividing the court and distracting the empire from the real problems it faced, in particular the threat from the Huns. From 434 the Huns, under their ruler, Attila, were a constant drain on the empire's resources, and when the eastern armies marched against them in 443, they were soundly beaten, forcing Theodosius to resort to annual tributes to keep the Huns from further damaging the provinces. By the close of his reign, not only was Attila openly boasting that he was Theodosius's overlord, but the Persians were beginning to stir again, while a new threat emerged in North Africa with the invasion of the Vandals.

Theodosius's only real contribution to the empire was the codification of Roman law into one body—the Theodosian Code. He was actively involved in taking all existing laws, from the reign of Diocletian onwards, and

Assassination of Stilicho

organising them in a coherent fashion to create a wholly new and up-to-date code of jurisprudence, using a system that allowed for the enlargement of the code as needed. Covering all aspects of Roman society, it stretched to sixteen books and was valid for the whole of the empire. It was a significant advance for the presentation of Roman law, becoming the basis both for Justinian's judicial reforms and for the Visigoth legal codification, the Lex Romana Visigothorum, in the next century.

> **Indeed, we believe it sinful that the enemies of the heavenly majesty and of the Roman laws should become the executors of our laws.**
>
> THEODOSIUS II

In July 450 Theodosius injured his spine after falling violently from his horse, and he died soon afterwards. His longevity provided some measure of stability for the east, but he had been fortunate that the western provinces provided a far easier target for the barbarians than his own, especially under the ineffectual rule of his uncle Honorius and cousin Valentinian III.

HONORIUS

A BOY DOING A MAN'S JOB

NAME: Flavius Honorius
BORN: Constantinople, 384
RULED: Co-emperor, 393–395;
western emperor, 395–423
DIED: Of natural causes, Ravenna, Italy, 423

WITH THE DEATH OF Theodosius I, the western provinces passed into the care of his eleven-year-old son Honorius. Though he had been made co-Augustus in 393, because of his youth no one expected the boy to do any actual ruling, Theodosius having placed him in the care of the new *magister militum*, Flavius Stilicho. Typical of the new breed of powerful individuals in charge of the empire, part Roman and part Vandal, Stilicho had the task of keeping the western provinces intact as the fifth century opened.

Honorius played no part in managing the affairs of the empire during these early years. He was stifled in the imperial court, continually told what commands to issue, and this formed the pattern of his adulthood. Later on, when he did act, it was always under advice from his favourites and ministers, and his decisions were invariably disastrous. Until 408 the western empire was in the hands of Stilicho, who was also Honorius's father-in-law. His arguments with Constantinople over disputed boundaries became less of a priority when the Visigoths invaded Italy in 402.

For the next six years, Stilicho fought battle after battle in a never-ceasing attempt to stem the invasions of barbarians. Having halted the Visigoths in 403, he then had to deal with the Ostrogoths, Vandals, Alans and Sueves, before the Visigoths returned in 408. Where he could win, he fought. Where the circumstances did not allow for a Roman victory, he did not waste Rome's precious military resources, instead bribing the barbarians to gain time to strengthen his military position. He alone preserved a semblance of imperial authority: Honorius's only contribution was to move the capital from Milan to the heavily fortified fortress of Ravenna.

By 408 Honorius was twenty-three and felt himself ready to govern independently. His first decision was to order Stilicho's death, and this murder began the slide into anarchy and chaos that would see the loss of Roman power in the west. Nearly all of his army defected to the Visigoths, who besieged Rome in 408 and installed a puppet emperor there in 409. Finally, in 410, Honorius decided, from the safety of Ravenna, to withhold tribute and try to kill Alaric. In retaliation, Alaric stormed the old capital and sacked Rome, the centre of the western world for over six hundred years, for three whole days.

> **What do you mean, Roma has perished? I have just finished feeding the bird out of my own hand!**
>
> HONORIUS

The rest of Honorius's reign was one of meek submission to the barbarians, who were rampaging across Gaul and Spain as usurpers sprang up, trying to do what the emperor would not. His principal general after Stilicho's death, Constantius, did his best, but the situation was too grave to do anything but take a defensive posture. By the end of Honorius's reign, Spain as well as northeastern and southwestern Gaul had essentially passed into barbarian control, while Britain was forced to look after its own affairs. By his indecisive and malleable nature, Honorius undid all that his father had spent his life achieving.

MARCUS
ABANDONMENT ISSUES

NAME: Marcus
BORN: Unknown
RULED: Western usurper, 406–407
DIED: Killed, Britannia, 407

AS STILICHO STRUGGLED to halt the barbarians, trouble was brewing elsewhere. Britain had long been overlooked by the court, especially when the heartland of the empire was threatened, but the troops there remembered when they had installed Magnus Maximus as emperor and finally become a centre of affairs in the empire. So, when Stilicho pulled significant numbers

Rome is plundered and burnt by Alaric I and his Visigoths, 410

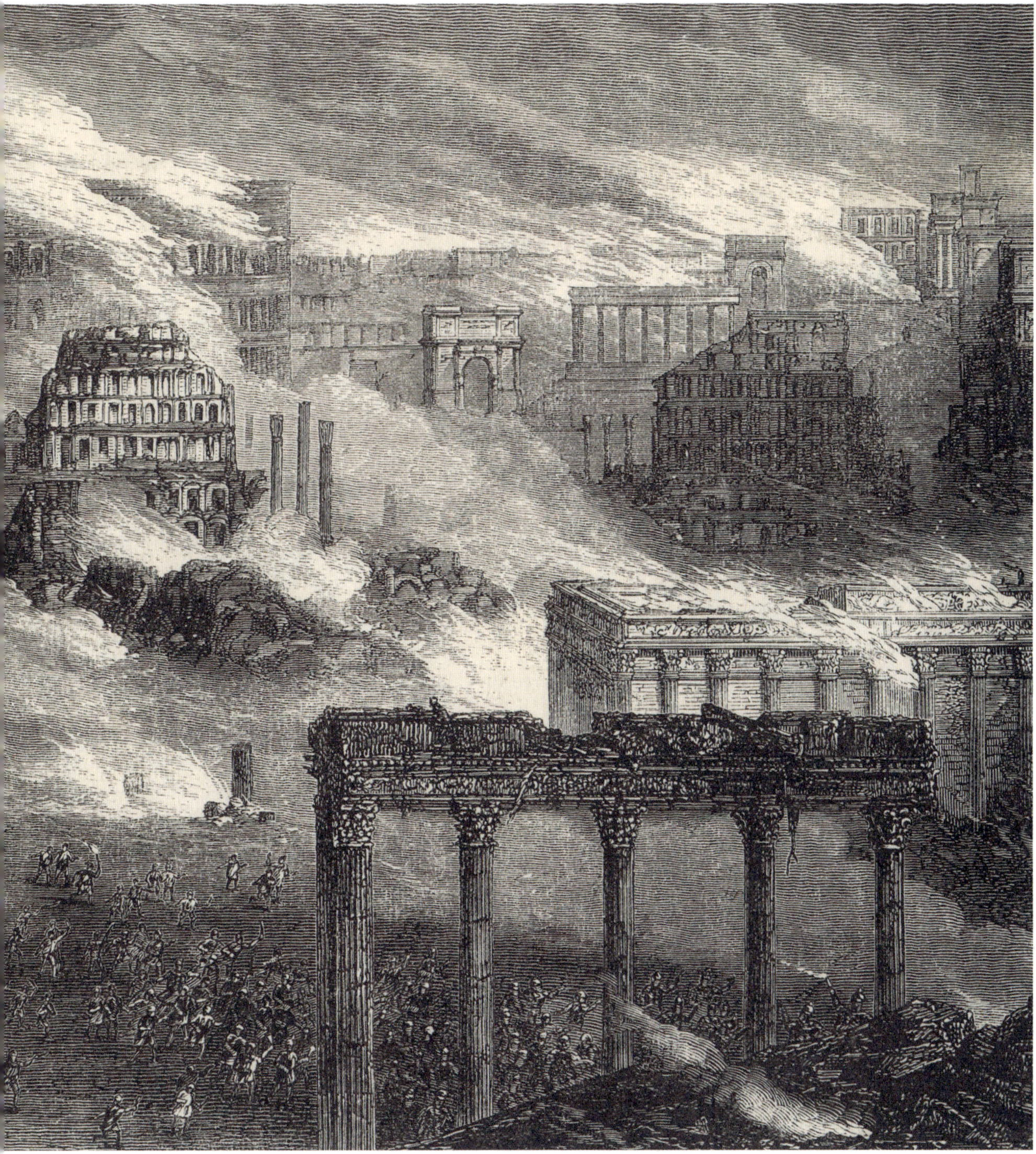

of troops from Britain to defend Gaul and Italy, they mutinied in 406, electing one of their own, Marcus, as emperor. He was evidently not a popular choice for long: he did something to annoy the soldiers who, ignoring their oaths of fidelity, killed him.

GRATIAN

THE BRITON

NAME: Gratian
BORN: Britain
RULED: Western usurper, 407
DIED: Killed, Britain, 407

MARCUS'S DEATH SAW an urgent need for a new emperor. The troops turned to Gratian, a Romano-British noble, deciding he had the appropriate bloodline. His short reign coincided with a massive invasion of Gaul by a host of different barbarians, many of whom were moving towards the Channel. Fearing an invasion, the commanders of the British legions demanded that they go across to intercept the invaders before they posed a threat to Britain. Gratian disagreed and ordered the army to remain on British soil. Seeing that a Romano-British noble might not have been the sort of ruler they wanted, the army mutinied and murdered him.

CONSTANTINE (III)

SOLDIER, EMPEROR, PRIEST

NAME: Flavius Claudius Constantinus
BORN: Unknown
RULED: Western usurper, 407–409; western co-emperor 409–411
DIED: Executed, place unknown, 411

NEVER SEND A NOBLE to do a soldier's job: that seemed to be the moral behind Constantine's elevation as emperor after Gratian's demise. A talented military man, Constantine was undoubtedly helped by the favourable omen of his names, reminiscent of the first Constantius and Constantine.

Quickly emptying the last of the legions from Britain, he had them ferried across to Gaul to secure the Rhine frontier, thus eliminating further barbarian invasions. In response, the legions in Gaul acknowledged his claim, realising that no help would be forthcoming from the fickle Honorius. Constantine's main threat was always going to be Stilicho, and so he was ecstatic when Honorius had his *magister militum* assassinated, leaving him the uncontested emperor of Gaul, Britain and Spain.

> **I beg forgiveness for having seized power, and I promise aid against the Visigoth Alaric.**
>
> CONSTANTINE (III)

By 409 Honorius was in trouble, without troops to confront Alaric, whose Visigoths roamed Italy at will. So when Constantine offered to eliminate Alaric in exchange for official recognition, Honorius agreed, even though the eastern emperor did not recognise Constantine's elevation. Up to now, Constantine had shown himself to be a capable general, and with Honorius's support he may have provided enough stability for the empire to catch its breath. However, the Romans were their own worst enemy.

By 410 usurpers in Spain, Gaul and Britain were rebelling against Constantine as well, distracting him from the main game. The barbarians overran the Rhine defences, adding to the chaos. In a final throw of the dice, Constantine invaded Italy, but a rebellion by his military commander in Spain forced him back. Finally, in 411 Honorius's new *magister militum*, Constantius, trapped him in his capital, Arles. In an act of desperation before the city fell, he resigned the purple and fled to a church, where he was consecrated a priest. It did not do him any good. Captured after receiving assurances that he would remain unharmed, he was beheaded en route to Ravenna.

CONSTANS (II)

TIME FOR A CAREER CHANGE

NAME: Constans
BORN: Unknown
RULED: Western co-usurper, 409–411
DIED: Executed, Vienne (Vienna), Viennensis, 411

CONSTANTINE'S SON, Constans, had apparently dedicated himself to God by joining a monastery. Just how seriously he took his vows can be gauged by the fact that he jumped at the chance to join his father in his quest to claim the purple.

Quickly elevated to the rank of Caesar, he was sent to relieve some of his father's beleaguered troops during their conquest of Gaul. He enjoyed his new rank and soon left his old life behind him, even taking a wife, as celibacy obviously did not suit him. His father then sent him to Spain along with his *magister militum*, Gerontius.

By 409 Constans was back in Gaul, where new barbarian invasions forced his father to make him co-Augustus, something not endorsed by Honorius. With Spain swamped by barbarians, Constantine ordered him to take over from the struggling Gerontius, but Gerontius refused to give up his troops, forcing Constans to abandon his planned expedition. Constans was trapped in Vienna as Gerontius's troops slowly closed in for the kill. After a successful siege, they captured and executed him.

MAXIMUS

PUSHED HIS LUCK

NAME: Maximus
BORN: Unknown
RULED: Western usurper, 409–411 and 420–421
DIED: Executed, Ravenna, Italy, 422

CONSTANTINE'S *magister militum*, Gerontius, employed a large group of individuals to do whatever chores he asked. One of these was his *domesticus*, or household manager, Maximus. An unassuming and retiring individual, it is doubtful that his job description ever spelt out the need to become Roman emperor. Yet this is what happened in 409 when Gerontius rebelled against the usurper Constantine.

Rather than placing the diadem on his own head, Gerontius gave it to the very surprised Maximus, swearing to serve him in all things. Gerontius then went on the offensive, killing Constans before besieging Constantine in Arles. Maximus was left behind in Spain to mind the fort, but word soon filtered back that Gerontius had retreated from Honorius's forces; his troops had mutinied; and he had been burnt alive while defending his home.

Pardoned by Honorius, Maximus went into exile in Spain to join a monastery. He should have counted his blessings and kept his head down, but an ex-emperor is a dangerous thing to leave lying around. By 420 much of Spain had come under the control of the Goths, who discovered Maximus in their midst. Having raised usurpers before, they bestowed on him the purple and started an unsuccessful rebellion in his name.

This time Maximus was not so fortunate. Captured and sent to Ravenna, he became the star attraction of the games celebrating Honorius's thirtieth year as emperor. In the middle of a crowd of bloodthirsty citizens, he was publicly executed.

ATTALUS
PUPPET OF THE VISIGOTHS

NAME: Priscus Attalus
BORN: Asiana
RULED: Western usurper, 409–410, 415–416
DIED: Cause unknown, Lipari Islands, Italy, date unknown

WHEN HONORIUS ABANDONED Rome to the fury of Alaric and the Visigoths in 408, the city's population suffered a horrific siege that would test the limits of their endurance. As the death toll mounted, they turned to august senators such as Priscus Attalus, a native of Ionia whose father had moved to be closer to the seat of power. One of the principal senators who negotiated with Alaric to lift the siege for a very large ransom, he was rewarded for his efforts with the position of urban prefect.

A self-professed cultured man, modesty was not Attalus's strong suit. Ignoring history, he was arrogant enough to believe he could dictate events. He again negotiated with Alaric during the Visigoth's next siege of Rome. Honorius in Ravenna alternated between conciliation and defiance, and so Alaric tried to force his hand by elevating Attalus to the purple (to which a desperate Senate agreed) and lifting the siege.

Alaric ends Attalus's reign as emperor

TRIUMPH AND TRAGEDY

Attalus was thanked by a grateful people who once again had food to eat. With Alaric following in tow, Attalus marched to Ravenna to overthrow the impudent Honorius. The emperor offered terms, agreeing to share power with Attalus, but the usurper, confident of the outcome, refused.

His pride was to be his undoing. The siege of Ravenna dragged on, as the city was reinforced by Roman troops sent from the east. Attalus, overestimating his power, then irritated Alaric by refusing to launch a military expedition to Africa. Alaric saw no further use for his puppet and, summoning him to the plains of Rimini, tore off his diadem and the purple in front of the assembled Romans and Goths. Attalus received a pardon from Honorius but he remained as a restricted guest of the Goths, accompanying them as they sacked Rome and travelled through Italy before returning to Gaul. His career hit a low point when he had to compose a celebratory speech for the wedding of the new Gothic king, Athaulf, in 414, but his fortune revived when Honorius's *magister militum*, Constantius, began a new offensive against the Goths.

> **I shall cut off his thumb and forefinger from his right hand, so that he will be unable to even draw a bow.**
>
> ATTALUS (threatening Honorius)

Athaulf again decided to raise Attalus to the purple, but the usurper proved even more ineffectual than last time. Abandoned by the Goths as they retreated into Spain, he was captured by Constantius and ended up in Ravenna. He was humiliatingly paraded in Honorius's Roman triumph of 416 and then exiled to the Lipari Islands after having his thumb and forefinger removed—a punishment he had promised to inflict upon Honorius.

JOVINUS
BARBARIANS EVERYWHERE

NAME: Jovinus
BORN: Gaul
RULED: Western usurper, 411–413
DIED: Executed, Narbo (Narbonne), Narbonensis, 413

THE DEATH OF THE USURPER Constantine saw a new usurper take his place—Jovinus, a Gallo-Roman senator with an impeccable aristocratic background, who tapped into the feelings of discontent directed at Honorius. Jovinus did not derive his authority from the Roman armies, but from the barbarians who were now making Gaul their own—in this case, Gundahar, king of the Burgundians, and Goar, the Alan chieftain.

Once the *magister militum*, Constantius, withdrew, other barbarian leaders also approached Jovinus to offer their services. The Visigoth king Athaulf quickly began negotiations, spurred on by Attalus, who still yearned to be useful. When a rival Visigoth chieftain entered into discussions with Jovinus, Athaulf crushed the newcomer, and a furious Jovinus, realising he needed a colleague to help manage the affairs of his empire, decided to elevate his brother Sebastianus to the rank of co-Augustus.

An aggravated Athaulf, frustrated that his puppet Attalus was not Jovinus's candidate for co-emperor, then communicated with Honorius: in return for an official appointment and marriage to the emperor's sister, he would eliminate the usurpers. Honorius agreed, and soon Jovinus found himself besieged in Valentia. Swiftly captured, transported to Narbo and executed, Jovinus's head was soon decorating the walls of Ravenna—a fitting tribute to Honorius's incredible ability to survive usurper after usurper.

SEBASTIANUS

THE CAUSE OF THE TROUBLE

NAME: Sebastianus
BORN: Gaul
RULED: Western co-usurper, 412–413
DIED: Killed, place unknown, 413

JOVINUS NEEDED A COLLEAGUE on whom he could rely, and so he selected his brother Sebastianus, who was weak and easily dominated and thus unlikely to be a glory seeker. Sebastianus's elevation started a chain of events that led to their deaths. King Athaulf decided to join Honorius and went to war against them. The Visigoth easily defeated the inexperienced Sebastianus in battle, an encounter that the co-usurper did not survive.

HERACLIAN

BROKEN PROMISES

NAME: Heraclianus
BORN: Unknown
RULED: Western usurper, 413
DIED: Executed, Carthage, North Africa, 413

THE ONE PERSON whom Honorius expected to remain loyal was the count of Africa, Heraclian. It was he who had wielded the sword that killed the great Stilicho, and he was among the few who protested when the Senate agreed to Attalus's elevation, even though he thus incurred Alaric's wrath. As a reward, Honorius gave him the consulship before posting him to the plum assignment in Africa.

In gratitude, Heraclian decided to make himself emperor. Amassing a fleet of seven hundred ships, he transported a three thousand-strong army to Italy. The result was a debacle. After disembarking at the Tiber, Heraclian's army was crushed while on the road to Rome by a small detachment of Constantius's troops. Commandeering a ship, Heraclian fled back to Africa but was surprised when the provinces there declared their loyalty to Honorius, refusing to welcome a defeated usurper. Heraclian was captured and executed at the Temple of Memory in Carthage.

CONSTANTIUS III

DEFEATED THE USURPERS

NAME: Flavius Constantius
BORN: Naissus (modern Niö), Dacia, date unknown
RULED: Western co-emperor, 421
DIED: Of pleurisy, Ravenna, Italy, 421

FEW DESERVE THE TITLE of preserver of the western empire at this time of crisis more than Constantius III. Where Honorius was timid and lazy, Constantius was energetic, focused and, above all, loyal. When Honorius realised what a mistake he had made in killing Stilicho, he turned to this grim soldier in one of the few inspired decisions of his reign.

Constantius was tireless in his pursuit of victories, crushing Gerontius and Constantine in Gaul before defeating Heraclian in Italy. He forced the Visigoths out of Italy into Gaul and then into Spain, and he captured Attalus in the bargain. To honour his service to the state, in 417 he received his long-held wish to marry Honorius's half-sister, Galla Placidia, whom the Goths had captured in the sack of Rome and whom he had rescued, over her protests. Though Constantius had loved her for some time, she apparently detested him. She did her duty, however, bringing forth a son who became Honorius's heir.

ADMINISTRATION OF THE EMPIRE IN THE FIFTH AND SIXTH CENTURIES

By the beginning of the fifth century the empire had been completely reorganised, transforming the simple administrative structure of imperial and senatorial provinces into a multilevel bureaucratic behemoth.

Where there had been some fifty provinces, there were now around 120 smaller provinces, each governed by a *proconsul, consularis, corrector* or *praeses*, according to the relative importance of the province.

The provinces were grouped together to form *dioceses*, of which there were fourteen, each under the command of a *vicarius*.

The dioceses, in turn, made up the four *prefectures* of Gaul, Italy, Illyricum and the Orient, which were under the administrative control of a praetorian prefect.

This formed the civil administrative structure of the empire. The prefects and their subordinates were in charge of raising taxes and the administration of justice in their respective jurisdictions, and the fifth century praetorian prefects—unlike their first, second and third century counterparts—had been stripped of their military functions.

Rome and Constantinople were exempt from the authority of the praetorian prefects; instead, they were each administered by a city or urban prefect (*praefectus urbanus*), who was responsible for maintaining order, supervising the police (*cohortes urbanae*), regulating and supervising all guilds and corporations, overseeing the city's grain imports, managing the sewerage system and public monuments.

The military system was separate. Under the old Augustan system, the legions were under the command of imperial legates and were stationed at strategic points along the frontiers. By the fifth century, the frontiers had been divided into military districts, corresponding with the provinces, and each district was under the command of a *dux* (from which comes the English word *duke*). The *duces* of the highest rank and importance were referred to as *comites*. These, in turn, were under the command of two commanders in chief—the master of the foot (*magister peditum*) and the master of the horse (*magister equitum*). Over time, these two positions were combined into one, which concentrated supreme military power in the hands of one master: the master of the soldiers (*magister militum*).

This system, already quite bloated, was further complicated by the rise of the officers of the imperial court. These were also given the title of *comites*, which translates as 'companions of the emperor'. They were the true bureaucrats of the empire, ministers responsible for the everyday running of the central government. These positions included the *comes domesticorum*, head of the imperial bodyguard, the *comes sacrarum largitionum*, the head of the treasury, and the *comes sacrae vestis*, head of the imperial wardrobe.

Finally, new titles and ranks that were largely honorific in nature were created. The new senatorial elite were those who possessed the title of *clarissimus*, and these were the ones who obtained the best posts in the imperial court. Above these were the *spectabiles* (the Respectables) and the *illustres* (the Illustrious), with the *illustriate* granted only to the great ministers of state. *Patrician* was another title of nobility, granted only to the highest public figures, such as the *magister militum*. Although it was attached to no specific post, it conferred a measure of official recognition, of being a highly placed and trusted representative of the emperor.

There was now pressure to make Constantius co-emperor. Honorius caved in, and in 421 Constantius was elevated to the purple. There was one hitch, however: the eastern emperor, Theodosius II, refused to recognise this upstart or his semi-barbarian wife, bringing the empire to the brink of civil war. It was only Constantius's declining health and death after a reign of seven months that averted this disaster. His was a lifetime of service to the empire, and he was one of the few men of his age worthy to bear the label 'Roman'.

JOANNES

GOOD GUYS FINISH LAST

NAME: Joannes
BORN: Unknown
RULED: Western usurper, 423–425
DIED: Executed, Aquileia, Italy, 425

HONORIUS'S DEATH BROUGHT a new period of confusion to Italy and the west. The eastern emperor, Theodosius II, now the sole recognised emperor of the Roman world, was keen to elevate a new colleague. However, he was in a bind. Amorous advances made by Honorius towards his sister after Constantius's death had forced her to leave for Constantinople in 423, along with her son, Valentinian. He was the obvious candidate but since Theodosius had rejected Constantius's claims, Valentinian was also officially unrecognised. For two years, Theodosius dithered, and in the meantime the western provinces, or more specifically the imperial bureaucracy, elected their own emperor.

A man of low birth, Joannes had climbed the ranks of the civil service, becoming head of the palace bureaucracy, the chief notary. Given the central place that the emperor held in the Roman constitution, the civil administration ground to a halt following Honorius's death and after three months, in a fit of desperation, the bureaucrats elected Joannes as emperor. By all accounts he was a moderate man, with a mild temperament and reasonable intelligence, and Italy, Spain and parts of Gaul soon recognised him. Moving the court to Ravenna, he was keen to come to terms with Theodosius.

It was not to be. Theodosius finally acknowledged Valentinian's claims and sent armies to deal with the usurper. At first luck favoured Joannes, for a storm hit the main eastern fleet and the general, Ardaburius, found himself a prisoner in Ravenna. Joannes now sent emissaries under the command of Aetius to the Huns, asking them for military help against Theodosius's armies. In the meantime, Valentinian and Galla Placidia had arrived with another army that had just captured Aquileia. It was now that they received an unexpected gift—Joannes. It turned out that Ardaburius had managed to suborn some of Joannes's troops; they opened the gates to let in a second army that Theodosius had sent, capturing Joannes in the melee.

Joannes was taken to Aquileia, where Galla Placidia ordered the amputation of his right hand. He was then tied to a donkey and paraded before the Roman citizens at the games, before being taken away and beheaded. Three days later the Huns arrived with Aetius—a potential crisis that was only averted by paying off the Huns with gold and offering Aetius the position of *magister militum*.

VALENTINIAN III

USELESS NONENTITY

NAME: Flavius Placidus Valentinianus
BORN: Ravenna, Italy, 419
RULED: Western emperor, 425–455
DIED: Murdered, Ravenna, Italy, 455

VALENTINIAN'S FATHER, Constantius III, was one of the great Roman generals; his grandfather was the capable Theodosius I; and his great-grandfather was the warrior emperor Valentinian I. With such a pedigree, everyone hoped that young Valentinian III would be the emperor to restore the greatness of Roman arms. Unfortunately for the empire, he took after his late, unlamented uncle, Honorius.

Coming to the throne at the age of six, Valentinian got off to an inauspicious start when his imperial cousin, Theodosius, refused to recognise him. Eventually relenting, Theodosius gave Valentinian's mother, Galla Placidia, an army to install her son. He was soon safely ensconced in the fortress city of Ravenna, where his mother dominated him before he came under the control of the western *magister militum*, Flavius Aetius.

Was not the death of Aetius well accomplished?'

VALENTINIAN III

Pope Leo I urges Attila the Hun to withdraw from Rome

Valentinian's reign was one of disintegration and collapse, as the invading barbarians slowly carved up the western provinces. Though Aetius had some success in holding the line in Gaul, he could not be everywhere. By the 430s, Africa had been lost to the Vandals, and while they were taking Carthage—some six hundred years after the Roman Scipio Aemilianus had finally vanquished the Carthaginians—Valentinian was busy expelling all Jews from the Roman army, part of his campaign to eliminate all pagans and Jews from government offices, as he was fearful of their potential to corrupt devout Christians.

With Spain virtually abandoned and a large part of Gaul no longer under direct imperial control, Valentinian's court was consumed by the rivalries of Aetius and Count Boniface, and the intrigues of his mother. Valentinian himself was obsessed with court magicians and astrologers; apart from this and church business, he spent the rest of his time seducing other men's wives, though his own wife was an amazing beauty. Such an emperor was ill prepared to deal with any crisis, let alone the greatest threat that the empire had yet seen—the rise of Attila the Hun.

The Huns had been plaguing the empire for some time, kept quiet only by Roman gold and other barbarian armies. This changed in 450 when the eastern emperor, Marcian, refused to continue paying protection money, setting the Huns on the move. Valentinian's sister made things worse by asking Attila to rescue her from a forced marriage to an elderly Roman senator. Interpreting this as a marriage proposal, Attila demanded half the western provinces as a dowry. Valentinian refused, bringing the whole Hun horde into the west.

In 451 Aetius forged an alliance of Romans, Goths, Franks and Burgundians and met the Huns in battle on the Mauriac fields, near Troyes in Gaul. Although this resulted in Aetius's greatest victory, Attila simply turned from Gaul and marched headlong into Italy, attacking Milan and Aquileia. The situation in Gaul meant that Aetius could not come to the rescue, while Valentinian shut himself in behind Ravenna's impregnable walls.

Only Pope Leo I, the sole remaining authority figure in Italy, was able to stop Attila outside Rome. After a private meeting between the two, Attila packed up his army and moved out of Italy. When a plague started ravaging the Huns, followed shortly after by Attila's death, the church declared it a miracle. Europe's greatest threat had been averted, and everyone gave thanks to Aetius—everyone, that is, except for Valentinian. The city prefect, Petronius Maximus, started whispering in the emperor's ear that Aetius, now Valentinian's newest brother-in-law, had designs on the throne. Frightened, Valentinian—in the only act of violence in his life—picked up a sword and killed the surprised Aetius during a council session.

Valentinian had removed the last man who could have kept what remained of the western provinces in Roman hands. For this base act, loyal supporters of Aetius killed him while he was practising archery in the following year. Amazingly, in a reign of thirty years, the feckless Valentinian was virtually the first emperor in two hundred years not to have had a usurper rise against him.

MARCIAN

A GOOD POLITICAL MARRIAGE

NAME: Flavius Valerius Marcianus
BORN: Thrace, c. 392
RULED: Eastern emperor, 450–457
DIED: Of gangrene, Constantinople, 457

THEODOSIUS II DIED without naming an heir and the choice of his successor was left to his sister, Pulcheria. She was interested in a consort who would convey the right image as emperor, and Marcian certainly fitted that requirement. He was handsome, strong and used to catching the ladies' eyes. He was also a successful military commander who had fought against the Huns and the Vandals, and had been promoted to personal assistant to Theodosius's commander-in-chief, Aspar. There was, however, a price on his elevation: Pulcheria made it clear that he was not to take away her virginity, a demand he respected.

Marcian's reign saw two key actions that provided stability for the eastern provinces. Firstly, seeing that he had inherited a bankrupt state, he stared down Attila the Hun, refusing to continue tribute payments. Attila decided the western provinces would provide easy pickings. Marcian sent troops from Constantinople to aid Valentinian, and soon Attila was dead. Reportedly, Marcian had a dream where he saw Attila's great bow broken before him.

> I have iron for Attila, but no gold.
>
> MARCIAN

Secondly, Marcian was a great defender of religious orthodoxy, summoning the Council of Chalcedon in 451 to define the basic creed of the Christian church. The council acclaimed him the new Constantine; it also fractured eastern Christendom when those churches that supported the rejected doctrine of Christ possessing only one unified nature broke off from the rest of the church, resulting in a permanent schism. Further, though the council supported the basic position of the church as outlined by Pope Leo I, it raised the patriarchal see of Constantinople to second place after Rome, a ruling that the pope rejected.

Overall, Marcian was an able administrator, and by the time he died the empire was in the best financial shape it had been in for some time. His prudence did have some unfortunate consequences, most clearly seen in his unwillingness to devote resources to helping the west deal with its next great crisis, the Vandals' sack of Rome in 455.

PETRONIUS MAXIMUS

MONEY CAN'T BUY YOU HAPPINESS

NAME: Flavius Anicius Petronius Maximus
BORN: Unknown, 396
RULED: Western emperor, 455
DIED: Murdered, Rome, Italy, 455

THE LAST GREAT DEFENDER of Roman honour, Aetius, was dead and two people moved to take advantage of the consequence—a weakened Rome. The first man to try his luck was the former city prefect Petronius Maximus. A man of obscure origin, he had attained the height of political power, becoming a senator and being twice elected consul. He was also extremely wealthy, and he used his riches to buy the imperial crown after Valentinian's murder. Knowing that he had not obtained Marcian's approval, he married Valentinian's widow to strengthen his claim to the throne. It was not a love match: she hated him and prayed daily for his death. She did not have long to wait.

The other man who rushed to take advantage of the situation was Gaiseric, king of the Vandals. Having established a base in North Africa, he had still kept an eye on the situation in Europe, especially on the one man capable of halting his plans—Aetius. When he heard of Aetius's death, he gathered his fleet and sailed towards the former capital, Rome. Maximus, who had engineered Aetius's fall, probably did not appreciate the irony in the situation. His first instinct, not being a military man, was to flee Rome. He never made it. He was accosted by the panicked Roman people, who stoned him to death, mutilated his body and flung the remains into the Tiber. Three days later Gaiseric entered Rome and sacked the city for two weeks.

Vandals plundering Rome, 455

AVITUS

UNPOPULAR GALLO-ROMAN

NAME: Flavius Maecilius Flavius Eparchius Avitus
BORN: Auvergne, Gaul, c. 395
RULED: Western emperor, 455–456
DIED: Of natural causes, Gaul, 457

ONE REASON MAXIMUS failed against the Vandals was that his *magister militum*, Avitus, was in Gaul seeking Visigoth support to bolster Maximus's claim to the throne. Avitus, with a distinguished civil and military career, had been an excellent choice for the post. Serving under Aetius, he had been instrumental in gaining Visigothic help in the desperate stand against Attila the Hun.

While in Gaul he learned of Maximus's death and the subsequent sack of Rome. The Visigoth king, Theoderic, urged him to take the purple; a reluctant Avitus agreed, and he was confirmed by the senators who had accompanied him to Gaul. Once installed in Italy, it was soon apparent he was deeply unpopular with the majority of the Senate and the people, who considered him a Gallo-Roman provincial with no claim to the throne, while Marcian also refused to recognise him.

To improve his position, he sent his newly installed barbarian *magister militum*, Ricimer, to deal with the Vandals. Ricimer met with some success but was unable to prevent food shortages and famine, which the people blamed on Avitus. When Avitus returned to Rome, Ricimer and another army commander, Majorian, revolted against him. The emperor looked for support from the Visigoths. He gathered what forces he could to march against Ricimer, only to be defeated. Stripped of the purple, he was forced to take priestly vows and become bishop of Placentia, where he would have stayed, but the Senate ordered his execution. He died while trying to flee to Gaul and his Visigoth friends.

MAJORIAN

ECHO OF THE PAST

NAME: Flavius Julius Valerius Majorianus
BORN: Unknown, c. 420
RULED: Western emperor, 457–461
DIED: Murdered, Liguria, Italy, 461

RICIMER, THE BARBARIAN *magister militum* of the west, was facing a dilemma—who was best equipped to become emperor for what remained of the western provinces and deal with the Vandal threat? Eventually he agreed to the elevation of Majorian, an officer who had served with him under the command of Aetius. This was Majorian's second attempt at the throne, the first having been after the death of Petronius Maximus, when Avitus outbid him. There was a delay before he achieved official recognition—upon Avitus's death in 456 the emperors in the east, Marcian and then Leo, assumed the overlordship of the whole empire—and it was only at the end of 457 that Leo finally recognised him as his co-Augustus.

Majorian was a throwback to an earlier age, when the empire spawned brave, talented men. Prior to his elevation, he had already seen military service against the Franks, only to be dismissed from active duty because Aetius's wife disliked him. He was soon promoted to the position of *comes domesticorum* (commander of the imperial bodyguards) under Valentinian III, a position he retained until his own elevation.

Determined to do whatever it took to halt the decline, he expanded the power of local officials, both in the gathering of taxes and the re-establishment of city administrators. Proceeding into Gaul, he dealt with the supporters of Avitus, crushing all resistance and once again dragging the Gallic provinces back under central control. He also defeated the Visigoths in Gaul and pursued them into Spain, where they became Roman allies and expanded Roman influence throughout the peninsula. Having stabilised Italy, Gaul and Spain, by 460 Majorian's next objective was Africa and the Vandals.

> Our own vigilance, and that of our father, the patrician Ricimer, shall regulate all military affairs and provide for the safety of the Roman world.
>
> MAJORIAN

King Gaiseric had felt Majorian's formidable skills at first hand when the Vandals had been thrust from Italy in 458. Observing the preparation of a great fleet to reclaim the African provinces, he struck while Majorian was busy securing Spain, launching a raiding party and destroying the anchored fleet in 461. His planned invasion halted for the moment, Majorian signed a truce with Gaiseric before returning to Italy to plan his next step. But he had not counted on his trusted ally, Ricimer.

Majorian's successes disturbed his barbarian sponsor, and Ricimer evidently decided that he did not want a man who would resurrect Roman power. As a barbarian he was content to see Rome under his domination, powerful enough to deal with local barbarian incursions but not wielding enough power to overthrow him and reassert itself. He incited a mutiny and, as Majorian passed through the town of Tortona, the soldiers forced him to resign the purple. Five days later, Majorian was dead. He had been both a warrior and a lawgiver; long gone was the era when such things could guarantee imperial safety.

LEO I

THE BUTCHER

NAME: Flavius Valerius Leo
BORN: Dacia, c. 400
RULED: Eastern emperor, 457–474
DIED: Of dysentery, Constantinople, 474

IN THE EAST, THE DOMINATION of the west by German military commanders, such as Stilicho and Ricimer, and the weakness of the western emperors had been observed carefully. However, the new eastern emperor, Leo, and his Alan *magister militum*, Aspar, drew very different conclusions from those events.

Originally from Dacia, Leo had had a long career in the military. He was serving as a legionary tribune when Aspar put him forward as the preferred candidate for the purple upon the death of Marcian. This excluded the expected successor, Marcian's son-in-law, Anthemius, but he took his demotion with good grace and Leo rewarded him when the imperial throne in the west became vacant, appointing him western emperor in 467.

What Aspar hoped to get was a grateful puppet; what he ended up with was an emperor determined to eliminate all Gothic and Alan control in the eastern provinces. This conflict between emperor and military commander would be the defining feature of Leo's reign. Determined to curb the pride and smash the power of the Germanic officers, Leo pursued a tactic of introducing a counterweight to them in the shape of the Isaurians, a tough and hardy mountainous people from what is now southeastern Turkey. Leo introduced these excellent, though highly undisciplined, soldiers into the imperial guard and obtained their loyalty by marrying his daughter to one of their chieftains, who took the name Zeno.

Recognising the threat that Zeno posed, Aspar succeeded in having his son marry Leo's youngest daughter, all the while trying to have the Isaurian killed. When it became clear that Aspar's son was negotiating with the Isaurians to change their allegiance, Leo struck first, butchering Aspar and his son in the imperial palace without warning.

Leo was a champion of Nicene orthodoxy. He was the first emperor crowned by the patriarch of Constantinople, and under him the empire showed a definite move away from military authority to religious authority. He often stood at the foot of a pillar outside Constantinople, taking foreign policy advice from a hermit who sat atop it, and he was a severe persecutor of Christian heretics and pagans. Aspar was an Arian, and his co-religionists suffered harshly after his fall.

Leo was also heavily involved in the affairs of the western provinces, organising a major military campaign against the Vandals of North Africa in 468 with the cooperation of the western emperor, Anthemius. Though it was initially successful, his decision to give overall command to his wife's brother Basiliscus was disastrous, and the expedition ended up an expensive failure. Yet even this debacle was not sufficient to kill his interest in the west. On occasion, the west recognised him as the sole emperor when the western emperor had died, and he was instrumental in assigning new emperors to the west when circumstances dictated. In fact, had it not been for the Huns and the Goths, who were still occasionally ravaging the Balkans, Leo might well have assumed the sole imperial position permanently. As it was, that step was left to his son-in-law Zeno.

THE BARBARIANS

By the beginning of the fifth century, the Roman world was awash with barbarian tribes, all eager to claim a piece of the empire to settle in and start their own kingdom. Population pressures and food shortages originally drove their migrations.

VISIGOTHS—One group of Goths, this East German people migrated from the Baltic coast down to the Black Sea. They poured into the province of Dacia, which became their first home. After sacking Rome in 410 they founded a kingdom in Spain and southwestern Gaul. The Christian Spanish kingdoms were descended from these people.

OSTROGOTHS—The other principal Gothic nation, they settled in the Pannonian provinces but soon migrated into Italy, where they set up their kingdom in the heart of the old empire. The Romans destroyed them during the wars of reconquest in the sixth century.

VANDALS—Made up of the Silings and the Asdings, these people began their migration from modern-day Poland and the Ukraine. They invaded the empire in 405 before settling in Spain. Forced out of Spain by the Visigoths, they migrated to North Africa, where they established their kingdom. A thorn in the side of the empire, they sacked Rome in 455 before also falling to the Roman reconquest.

FRANKS—Dwelling on the shores of the North Sea, the Salian Franks were a group of western Germans who crossed the Rhine and eventually settled in northern Gaul during the fifth century. They grew in strength as the decades wore on, forcing the Visigoths out of southern Gaul and conquering other Germanic tribes, such as the Alamanni and the Burgundians.

SAXONS—Another group of western Germans from the North Sea region, the Saxons travelled across the waters to settle in Roman Britain. Totally uncivilised, they alone of the barbarian invaders successfully obliterated the Latin language and Roman civilisation from the areas they conquered.

HUNS—A fierce people originating in Mongolia, the Huns eventually penetrated deep into the empire, occupying Dacia before moving on to Thrace and the Balkans. After the death of their king Attila, they scattered, most fleeing north and crossing the Danube River into Dacia and beyond, before eventually settling down, intermingling with other tribal groups and transforming into the Bulgars.

LIBIUS SEVERUS

SHADOW EMPEROR

NAME: Flavius Libius Severus Serpentius
BORN: Lucania, Italy, c. 420
RULED: Western usurper, 461–465
DIED: Of natural causes, Rome, 465

RICIMER HAD ELIMINATED Majorian because he was too capable and independently minded for the *magister militum*. When it came to elevating a successor, he would not make the same mistake again. After a period when he controlled the western provinces directly as the representative of the emperor Leo at Constantinople, he eventually selected Severus, a pious but obscure Italian senator, who became Ricimer's mouthpiece.

Severus's major problem was that Leo did not accept him as his co-emperor—not surprising given who had elevated him in the first place. Consequently, he remained unacknowledged in Gaul or Dalmatia, where the commanders declared their allegiance to Leo. Taking advantage of the situation, the Vandals also rejected Severus's imperial claims and began raiding the Italian coast at will. Ricimer was travelling between Gaul and Italy to deal with his numerous enemies and he now turned to Leo, asking for aid against the Vandals—it came, but not in the way he had expected.

> **We confirm that widows are not to alienate their betrothal gifts, which they hold in trust for their children.**
>
> LIBIUS SEVERUS

It says a lot about Severus that he reigned for four years but we know next to nothing about him. As a puppet, he did very little and did it very well, before he died in 465.

ANTHEMIUS

THE GREEKLING

NAME: Procopius Anthemius
BORN: Constantinople, c. 420
RULED: Western emperor, 467–472
DIED: Executed, Rome, 472

WHEN SEVERUS DIED in 465 the empire reverted to having one emperor, Leo. Ricimer was again confirmed to act in Leo's stead in the western provinces but he was unable to stem the Vandal incursions that were spreading farther east. Ricimer asked for aid, expecting some military support; what he got in 467 was a new emperor in the form of Anthemius.

Coming from an influential Constantinople family that had been at the centre of power for two generations, Anthemius believed he was destined for great things. His grandfather had been regent for the young Theodosius II, and both his father and he had achieved the rank of *magister militum*. The imperial throne seemed assured when he married Marcian's only daughter, but on Marcian's death the purple passed to another military man, Leo I. Disappointed, Anthemius returned to being *magister militum*, performing his duties admirably and securing victories against the barbarians along the Danube frontier.

Seeing that Anthemius was a capable general, and keenly aware that he was a potential rival, Leo granted him his long-held desire to be emperor, appointing him to the vacant position in the west. Anthemius was given two tasks to complete—firstly to neutralise the threat of Ricimer, which he achieved by marrying his daughter to the haughty Goth, and secondly to coordinate the western arm of the massive Roman offensive against the Vandals, something that Ricimer had been longing for since the early 460s.

The campaign began superbly, with a victorious eastern army crushing the Vandals in North Africa in 468 and a western army under the Dalmatian commander Marcellinus sweeping through Sardinia and Sicily. Nevertheless, luck still favoured the wily old Vandal king. For a second time Gaiseric destroyed the main Roman fleet while it was at anchor, a consequence of the incompetence of Leo's brother-in-law, who fled to Constantinople, and Marcellinus's military colleagues—possibly at the instigation of Ricimer, who detested him—murdered Marcellinus in Sicily. The campaign was an expensive disaster and, since he was Leo's nominee, the humiliation rebounded on Anthemius. His reputation took an additional beating in 469 when he failed to defeat the Visigoths, who by 471 would consolidate all their territorial possessions, virtually forcing the Romans out of Gaul. Anthemius's own son perished in these wars, adding a personal dimension to the failure of his armies.

> **What favours have we refused to this ungrateful man? What provocations have we not endured? Regardless of the majesty of the purple, I gave my daughter to a Goth; I sacrificed my own blood to the safety of the republic!**
>
> ANTHEMIUS (railing against Ricimer)

By this stage, relations between Ricimer and Anthemius had deteriorated to a point of no return. Ricimer was accustomed to exercising power through a weak and ineffectual emperor, while Anthemius was born to rule and unwilling to share his power. Considered by the Italians to be a Greek interloper, Anthemius had virtually no support in the west, and so when Ricimer turned on him, only the Senate sided with him. Consequently, Ricimer set up his court in Milan, while Anthemius continued to rule in Rome. Hearing about the breakdown in relations between the two men, Leo sent a senator by the name of Olybrius to try to achieve some sort of compromise amid the stalemate. After meeting the senator, Ricimer made him an offer he could not refuse and proclaimed the man emperor. They besieged Anthemius in Rome for three months, entering the city after a relief force from Gaul was defeated outside the walls.

The conceited Anthemius disguised himself as a beggar in order to escape from his enemies, but Ricimer's nephew found him hiding in what is now the Church of Santa Maria in Trastevere and had him beheaded. Though Anthemius had good intentions, his abilities were unequal to the task. By the end of his reign the western provinces had shrunk to consist solely of the Italian peninsula, and the capital was the plaything of barbarian kings.

ARVANDUS

POWERFUL FRIENDS

NAME: Arvandus
BORN: Unknown
RULED: Western usurper, 468
DIED: Unknown

ARVANDUS HAD BEEN the praetorian prefect of Gaul since 461 and by all accounts had performed his duties with care and due diligence. By the time of his reappointment in 467, however, he was no longer Gaul's golden boy. Heavily in debt and resorting to extortion and heavy-handed tactics, he all but ignored the looming Visigoth threat.

> **Begone, you and your nonsensical fears, degenerate sons of prefectorian fathers; leave this part of the affair to me; it is beyond an intelligence like yours.**
>
> ARVANDUS

Anthemius's unpopularity inspired Arvandus to write to the Visigoth king, suggesting that he declare war against Anthemius, attack the emperor's ally Riothamus, king of the Britons, and divide Gaul between his people and the Burgundians. Arvandus hoped to become emperor with Visigoth aid, seeing that men like Avitus had done the same thing. It was not to be. Discovering his letter, the Senate summoned him to Rome, ostensibly to grant him further honours. On arrival, they stripped him of his office before trying him and sentencing him to death. It was only through the influence of powerful friends that his sentence was commuted to exile. With that, Arvandus disappears from the historical record.

ROMANUS

NOT EVEN SORCERY HELPED

NAME: Romanus
BORN: Unknown
RULED: Western usurper, 470
DIED: Executed, Rome, 470

ROMANUS WAS A ROMAN senator who had strong links to Ricimer. Having served in a number of important posts, in 470 he attempted to have himself installed as emperor. Anthemius was suffering from an illness, widely believed to have been the result of sorcery, and during this time Romanus unsuccessfully attempted to wrest the throne from him. When Anthemius recovered, he killed a number of Ricimer's supporters, including Romanus, whom he beheaded for his impertinence. Whatever Ricimer's involvement, this plot certainly destroyed the emperor's relationship with his *magister militum* and eventually led to Anthemius's death.

OLYBRIUS

CHOICE OF THE VANDALS

NAME: Flavius Anicius Olybrius
BORN: Place unknown, c. 430
RULED: Western usurper, 472
DIED: Of natural causes, Rome, 472

ONE OF THE MOST POWERFUL and popular men in Italy during the second half of the fifth century, Olybrius hailed from the great senatorial family of the Anicii, which had been at the centre of western politics for over a hundred years. Marriage to Valentinian III's daughter in 454 meant he had some claim to the western throne after his father-in-law's murder in 455. By all accounts he was a very religious man, frequently visiting monks and hermits, such as Daniel the Stylite at Constantinople.

> I also have sent the patrician Olybrius to you; I wish you to kill him, so that you might reign as you should.
>
> LEO I (in a message to Anthemius)

Olybrius was on a mission to Constantinople when news arrived that not only had the Vandals sacked Rome, but that they had captured Valentinian III's widow and her daughters, including Olybrius's wife. When the Vandal king Gaiseric married his son to another of Valentinian's daughters, Olybrius became part of the same family. Seeing an advantage in the connection, Gaiseric demanded that Leo I appoint Olybrius emperor in the west after the murder of Majorian in 461, but Leo refused. Leo however did not forget this nomination, or the danger Olybrius presented.

Though it may have been his life's ambition to gain the purple, Olybrius did not live long enough to enjoy it, dying seven months later. The only notable event of his reign was the death of Ricimer, who had for so long been the power behind the throne. Ricimer's nephew, Gundobad, took his position as *magister militum*.

GLYCERIUS

SURRENDERED

NAME: Flavius Glycerius
BORN: Place unknown, c. 420
RULED: Western usurper, 473–474
DIED: Cause unknown, Salonae (Solin), Dalmatia, c. 480

OLYBRIUS'S DEATH MEANT that Leo I was again the sole ruling Augustus in the empire, but he had some difficulty finding a colleague. Dissatisfied by the eastern emperor's lack of attention to the situation, the new *magister militum*, Gundobad, elevated Glycerius, commander of the imperial bodyguard, to the imperial power.

> **Farewell, Himilco, most dear and beloved parent.**
>
> GLYCERIUS

A talented man of obscure origin, Glycerius successfully dealt with a Visigoth invasion and managed to avoid an Ostrogoth invasion through a combination of bribery and diplomacy. Yet regardless of Glycerius's abilities, Leo was never going to accept him as an equal and eventually dispatched his new co-emperor, Julius Nepos, to Italy with a large army to reassert imperial control in what remained of the western provinces.

Glycerius wanted to fight, but Gundobad chose this moment to return to Gaul to take up his inheritance as king of the Burgundians. Without a decent army, Glycerius was unable to defend Rome, quickly surrendering to Nepos. For his wise decision, Nepos spared his life; Glycerius was quickly consecrated as bishop of Salonae and, as far as we know, he remained there for the rest of his life. He would have his revenge against Julius Nepos, however.

JULIUS NEPOS

ONCE AN EMPEROR, ALWAYS AN EMPEROR

NAME: Flavius Julius Nepos
BORN: Place unknown, c. 430
RULED: Western emperor, 474–480
DIED: Assassinated, Salonae (Solin), Dalmatia, 480

JULIUS NEPOS OWED HIS RISE to family connections. His uncle was Marcellinus, who had ruled Dalmatia before his murder during the Vandal expedition of 468. Nepos inherited the position, governing the province on behalf of the eastern emperor. He had married the niece of Leo I's wife, and so it was to him that Leo turned when he was looking for a capable co-emperor to manage what remained of the west. Landing at the port of Rome, he overthrew Glycerius and the Senate soon confirmed his position.

> **But Nepos is still alive, and whilst he lives he is your lawful sovereign.**
>
> ZENO (to a delegation of Roman senators)

Nepos was not without military ability but he soon realised that the days of Roman power were long gone. When the Visigoths in Gaul finally declared their independence from Rome, he sent his *magister militum* in an attempt to deal with them. He was unsuccessful and turned to diplomacy, formally recognising their claim to most of Gaul and Spain, although he regained the southern regions of Gaul for the empire. For this failure, Nepos replaced him with the Germanic leader Orestes.

This was a mistake: Orestes turned on his new master and chased him from Rome to Ravenna. There, Nepos boarded a ship and fled to his old province of Dalmatia, still claiming the imperial title. His position as legitimate emperor in the west continued, though he was never to set foot in Italy again, ruling from Dalmatia through his appointed officers, including Odoacer, the man who would defeat Orestes in Italy. The western provinces still acknowledged Nepos as emperor, as did Odoacer in Ravenna and Zeno in Constantinople, and so Nepos bided his time. By 480 he felt strong enough to try to reclaim his imperial possessions, but a conspiracy among his officers, including former emperor Glycerius, saw him assassinated before the planned expedition could begin.

ROMULUS
THE LITTLE AUGUSTUS
NAME: Romulus Augustus
BORN: Place unknown, c. 461
RULED: Western usurper, 475–476
DIED: Cause unknown,
possibly Campania, Italy, c. 511

WITH NEPOS'S OVERTHROW, the *magister militum* Orestes wanted to rule the western empire, but it was illegal for a member of the Germanic tribes to elevate himself to the position of emperor. His son, however, was a Roman citizen; therefore, he petitioned the quarrelling eastern emperors, Zeno and Basiliscus, to acknowledge the young Romulus as their colleague in the west. Neither emperor recognised the usurper, declaring that Nepos was still the legitimate emperor, but Orestes went ahead and proclaimed the fourteen-year-old boy emperor in Ravenna.

By all accounts a very good-looking young man, Romulus took a back seat as his father grappled with the problem of what to do with the German mercenaries who were roaming all over Italy. For decades, the emperors had granted the German tribes federated status in the empire, given them lands to settle on where they could maintain their own laws under their own kings. Italy had so far been free of this burden, but in 476 the new *magister militum*, Odoacer, led an uprising of various German tribes after Orestes refused to hand over Italian land.

> **You shall spend the rest of your life in exile in the castle of Lucullus in Campania.**
>
> ODOACER (to Romulus)

Having captured and killed Orestes, Odoacer entered Ravenna and deposed Romulus formally, before sending the imperial regalia of the west back to Constantinople, confirming the Senate's decision that a western emperor was no longer necessary. Odoacer spared the boy's life because of his good looks, sending Romulus into a comfortable exile at Misenum in Campania. Granted a pension of six thousand solidi per annum, by all accounts he spent the remainder of his life there. Odoacer became the de facto ruler of Italy and swore allegiance to the reigning western emperor, Julius Nepos, indicating he would act as his personal representative. He transferred his oath to the emperor Zeno after Nepos's assassination in 480.

History has not treated Romulus well. His name, that of Rome's first king, invited mockery, especially when combined with his title of Augustus, the first Roman emperor. It was impossible not to make comparisons as the western provinces became the plaything of barbarians, and his name became twisted by succeeding generations. Romulus became 'Momyllus' (little disgrace), while Augustus morphed into 'Augustulus', or 'little Augustus'.

Deposition of Emperor Romulus Augustus by Odoacer

DIVISION AND DECAY 171

LEO II
THE LITTLE ONE

NAME: Flavius Leo Iunior
BORN: Constantinople, 467
RULED: Eastern co-emperor, 473–474
DIED: Of natural causes, Constantinople, 474

LEO I HAD NO SONS and succession problems as a result of the unpopularity of his Isaurian son-in-law, Zeno. To get around this issue, he elevated Zeno's son, also named Leo, as co-emperor prior to his death. With his grandfather's death, Leo II ruled as eastern Augustus alone for just three weeks before nominating Zeno as his co-emperor, and the Senate endorsed this. Leo did not last out the year, dying of some unknown ailment at the youthful age of seven. It says a lot about Zeno's unpopularity and the little esteem in which he was held that people, including his mother-in-law, readily accused him and his wife of killing their son to clear Zeno's path to the throne.

ZENO
DEEPLY UNPOPULAR

NAME: Flavius Zeno
BIRTH NAME: Tarasicodissa Rousoumbladeotes
BORN: Rousoumblada, Isauria, c. 430
RULED: Co-emperor, 474; eastern emperor, 474–475 and 476–491
DIED: Of an epileptic fit, Constantinople, 491

THE MOST UNPOPULAR group in Constantinople by the 470s were the Isaurians, violent, haughty, raucous, and regularly abusing their position as imperial guards. The people aimed their frustrations at the Isaurian chief, who had just been elevated to the purple—Zeno.

Originally known as Tarasicodissa, he had changed his name to the Greek-sounding Zeno when he married Leo I's daughter. A competent general who was known for his fleetness of foot, a result of his being born without kneecaps, Zeno's position as Leo's successor seemed assured when he successfully handled the Vandal invasion of Epirus in 469 and accepted Chalcedonian orthodoxy. Though originally passed over in favour of his son, he was eventually elevated to the purple and by the end of 474 was sole emperor in the east. Zeno's first act as emperor was to finally end the Vandal threat that had been a thorn in the side of the empire for the last thirty-five years, and he achieved this not by military conquest, but by a simple treaty that both parties respected.

Nevertheless, it was only a matter of time before someone took advantage of his increasing unpopularity. That someone was Basiliscus, Leo I's brother-in-law, whom Zeno had overshadowed after Basiliscus's poor handling of the campaign against the Vandals in 468. Alerted to the plot against him, Zeno fled to the mountains of his native land, where he remained for twenty months, biding his time and building up his forces, waiting for the danger to pass until Basiliscus was in his turn overthrown. Zeno returned to the capital along with Illus, the general who had been ordered to capture him.

Zeno's troubles did not end there. His mother-in-law, Verina, was a constant source of trouble; she instigated another revolt in 479, before conspiring with Illus, now eastern *magister militum*, to raise another usurper in 484. Though Zeno managed to overcome these threats, his popularity took an even bigger dive when he entered into arcane church debates about the nature of Christ. He issued the *Henoticon* in an attempt to heal the schism between the Chalcedonians (Christ had two unified natures, human and divine) and Monophysites (Christ had only one divine nature). It tried to paper over the differences between the two groups but, unfortunately, it only succeeded in alienating both and creating a schism with the west, and Zeno was condemned for entering into the religious sphere.

> **And if there be any man holding such [heretical creeds], we account him an alien. For, as we have already said, we are confident that this only preserves our kingdom.**
>
> ZENO

In fact, the west continued to occupy much of Zeno's time and energy. First, there was the final collapse of imperial authority in 476 when Odoacer overthrew Romulus. Informing Zeno that he was now the sole emperor of the Roman world, Odoacer declared he would be happy to rule Italy in Zeno's name, with the rank of patrician. Zeno was initially prepared to accept the new situation in the west—after all, barbarian generals had been the effective rulers there for nearly a hundred years, under the nominal leadership of the emperors, and so nothing much had changed, except the location of the universal emperor.

However, Zeno was not entirely satisfied with Odoacer, and so in 488 he asked Theodoric, king of the Ostrogoths, to take his people to Italy, settle there and govern the Italian provinces in his name. Raised in the court of Leo I, Theodoric was well versed in Roman manners and laws. He had helped Zeno put down the principal rebellions of his reign and been given the position of *magister militum* and even that of consul. He also terrorised various parts of the empire when he did not get his way. In short, he was the first truly Romanised Germanic barbarian, the perfect vehicle for ensuring a continuation of some form of imperial control in the west, short of the presence of the emperor himself. This also removed from the east a disruptive element that could turn on the empire at any time. Theodoric crossed to Italy and overcame Odoacer in 493. As the imperial viceroy, he robed himself in the imperial purple, while acting as the emperor's *magister militum* in the west. His laws, described as *edicta*, were subordinate to the imperial *leges*, and his coins bore a portrait of the current emperor, starting with Zeno.

Zeno ended his days paranoid and senile: convinced that a soothsayer had predicted the identity of his successor, he killed an innocent man to whom he believed the prophecy referred. After Zeno's death in 491, it was widely believed that his voice emanated from his tomb for three days after his internment, suggesting the gruesome possibility that they had buried him alive.

BASILISCUS

MORE EGO THAN TALENT

NAME: Flavius Basiliscus
BORN: Unknown
RULED: Eastern emperor, 475–476
DIED: Of starvation, Limnae, Cappadocia, Asiana, 476

IT SAYS A LOT ABOUT A MAN'S character if he can completely ignore his own manifest inadequacies. Such seems to have been the case with Basiliscus, Leo I's brother-in-law. Using his imperial connections, he became *magister militum* in Thrace before being given overall command of the expedition against Gaiseric and the Vandals in 468. Though his officers achieved victories on land and sea, Basiliscus threw it all away: having cornered Gaiseric at Carthage, he foolishly allowed him five days grace to regroup and let his own guard down. Gaiseric seized the opportunity to attack and destroy the Roman fleet at anchor.

Fleeing to Constantinople, Basiliscus sought sanctuary in the church of Hagia Sophia until he

Plan of Constantinople

received assurances for his life. Demoted and humiliated, at this point any other man would have disappeared off the stage, but not Basiliscus. He bided his time until Leo I's death brought the unpopular Zeno to the throne, and then—in league with his sister Verina and an up-and-coming Isaurian general, Illus—he launched a coup against the emperor. Zeno fled, and Basiliscus was crowned emperor to the acclamations of the people and Senate.

> It is the special task of kingly providence to furnish to their subjects, with forecasting deliberation, abundant means of security, not only for the present but for future time.
>
> BASILISCUS

Such an incompetent could not last long. Before he knew it, he had alienated Verina by killing her lover, whom she wanted to place on the throne. Being a firm Monophysite, he issued a circular that commanded the bishops to reject the pronouncements of the Council of Chalcedon, hardening their opposition to him. The pope condemned him, while the patriarch of Constantinople expressed his displeasure by draping the icons in Hagia Sophia in black. Even Daniel the Stylite, a hermit whom emperors occasionally consulted, descended from his column and proceeded to call down upon Basiliscus all sorts of divine punishments for his impious act. The people were outraged, even more so when he increased taxation to deal with a financial crisis. A destructive fire in the city was the last straw, and Illus asked Zeno to return to Constantinople, where he was welcomed with open arms.

Basiliscus again tried his old trick of seeking sanctuary in Hagia Sophia, refusing to come out until Zeno guaranteed his safety. Advised that Zeno had agreed not to execute him, he surrendered. Zeno was true to his word. He did not execute him: he exiled him and his family to Cappadocia and dropped them in a well, where they starved to death.

MARCUS

FEW CAREER PROSPECTS

NAME: Marcus
BORN: Unknown
RULED: Eastern co-emperor, 475–476
DIED: Of starvation, Limnae, Cappadocia, Asiana, 476

BASILISCUS WANTED TO MAKE it perfectly clear that he was in for the long haul and so, in the time-honoured imperial tradition, he elevated his son as co-Augustus. Unfortunately, the people were not interested in getting to know young Marcus, who was probably a Monophysite like his father. Trapped by his father's collapsing reign, he soon sought refuge in a church before ending up in Cappadocia, where he slowly starved to death and was quickly forgotten.

PROCOPIUS MARCIANUS

AGGRIEVED SON-IN-LAW

NAME: Flavius Procopius Marcianus
BORN: Unknown
RULED: Eastern usurper, 479
DIED: Unknown

FEW PEOPLE POSSESSED Marcianus's bloodline. The son of the western emperor Anthemius and another of Leo I's son-in-laws, he—more than most—resented the common Isaurian upstart who now possessed the throne. He watched as his mother-in-law Verina, itching to get back at Zeno for the death of Basiliscus, hatched plots against Zeno's chief military commander, Illus. When Verina's scheming was uncovered, Illus demanded that Verina be imprisoned. Zeno agreed, forcing Verina to become a nun.

Appalled at this treatment, Marcianus gathered loyal barbarian troops in the capital before marching on the imperial palace, gaining popular support from the citizenry who still detested Zeno. Declaring himself emperor, he almost captured Zeno in the palace, but the Isaurian escaped. For a day, the rebels held out against the imperial guards.

Illus quickly marched on the city and, under the cover of night, penetrated Constantinople. By morning it was all over. Captured, Marcianus took holy vows before his banishment to Cappadocia. Sometime later, he again rose in revolt and attacked the town of Ancyra, but he was quickly defeated, whereupon he spent the rest of his life imprisoned in an isolated Isaurian fortress.

LEONTIUS

KING OF ALL HE SURVEYED

NAME: Leontius
BORN: Dalisandus, Isauria, date unknown
RULED: Usurper, 484–488
DIED: Murdered, Seleucia ad Calycadnum (Silifke), Isauria, 488

LEONTIUS, ANOTHER OF the Isaurian commanders who appeared in Constantinople during these years, was a good-looking man whose diplomatic skills earned him elevation into the patrician class. Zeno sent him to deal with the latest rebel—Illus.

Illus had served Zeno faithfully for a number of years before earning the enmity of Zeno's wife, who instigated numerous attempts to assassinate him. When the emperor's brother took over his command, he rebelled and captured Zeno's brother.

> **Since Zeno's avarice is ruining the state, I have determined to transfer it to the pious Leontius.**
>
> EMPRESS VERINA

When Leontius arrived, Illus convinced him to abandon Zeno. The old empress Verina was dragged out of retirement and she was happy to strike out at Zeno by crowning Leontius emperor in 484. The rebels quickly captured Antioch, but that was the limit of their success. Imperial forces defeated Illus and Leontius, forcing them to take refuge in the fortress of Papirios in Isauria. Leontius served the rest of his reign there, trapped behind the walls of his only city, and after four miserable years the city fell after his sister-in-law betrayed it. His head soon graced the walls of Constantinople.

THE PRICE OF UNITY
(491–802)

An epistle was addressed, by their unanimous decree, to the emperor Zeno. They solemnly disclaim the necessity, or even the wish, of continuing any longer the Imperial succession in Italy; since, in their opinion, the majesty of a sole monarch is sufficient to pervade and protect, at the same time, both the East and the West. In their own name, and in the name of the people, they consent that the seat of universal empire shall be transferred from Rome to Constantinople; and they basely renounce the right of choosing their master, the only vestige that yet remained of the authority which had given laws to the world. The republic might safely confide in the civil and military virtues of Odoacer; and they humbly request that the emperor would invest him with the title of Patrician, and the administration of the diocese of Italy.

EDWARD GIBBON
The Decline and Fall of the Roman Empire, 1880

FOLLOWING PAGE:
Justinian I in Ravenna

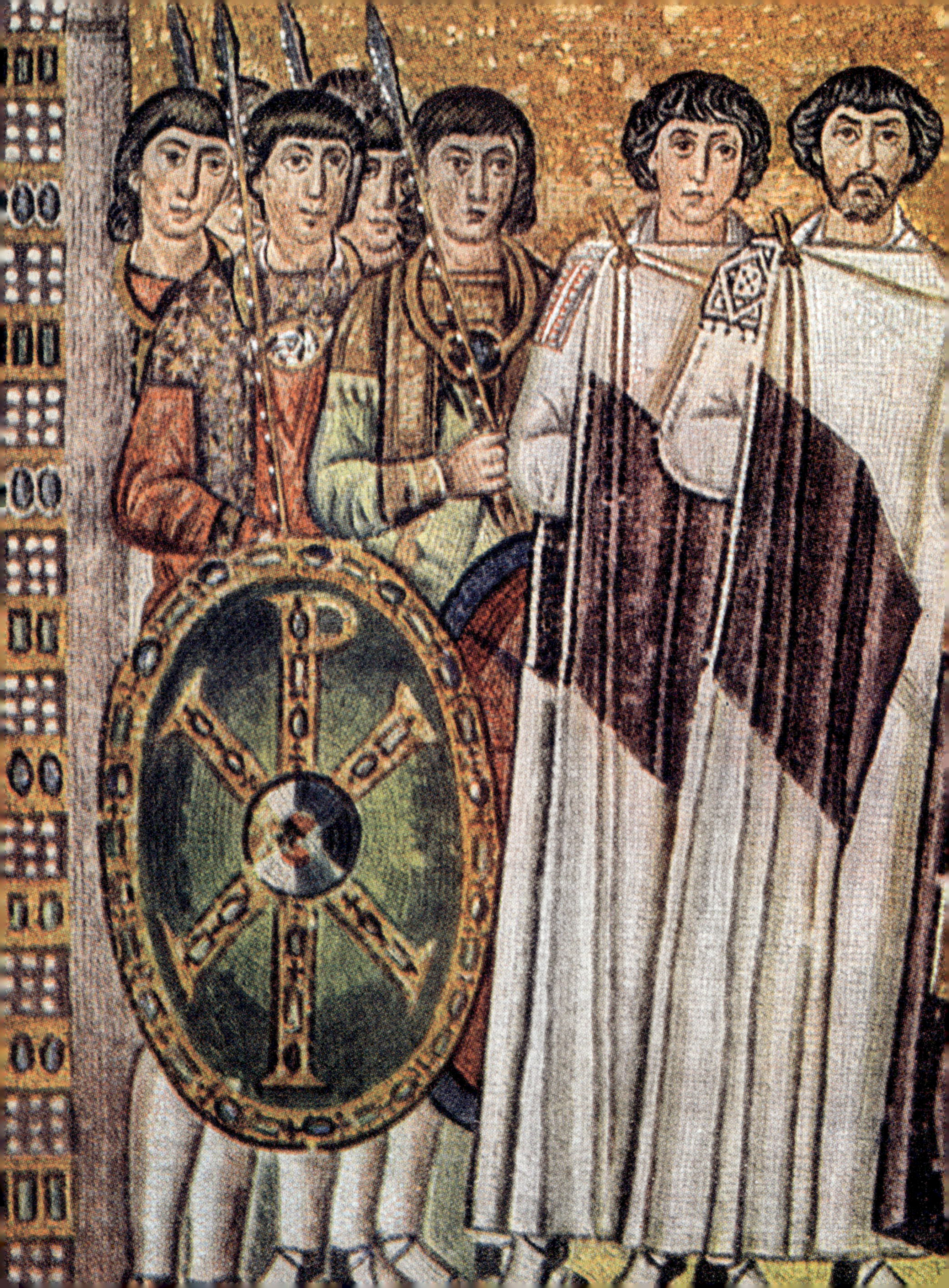

MAXIMIANVS

ANASTASIUS I

SEEING THE WORLD THROUGH DIFFERENT EYES

NAME: Flavius Anastasius
BORN: Dyrrachium (modern Durazzo), Illyricum, c. 430
RULED: Emperor, 491–518
DIED: Of natural causes, Constantinople, 518

ANYONE MEETING ANASTASIUS could not help but notice his eyes, one black and one blue, which earned him the nickname 'Dikoros'. It was symbolic of his reign, caught as he was in the middle of a religious clash between the Chalcedonians and the Monophysites. Tall, moderate and intelligent, he seemed the perfect choice to replace the childless Zeno, with his supporters claiming he was descended from Pompey the Great.

In fact, he was a minor palace official who had caught the empress Ariadne's eye. She married him to ensure a smooth succession and, though a Monophysite, he agreed to hold to Zeno's compromise before the patriarch crowned him. Immediately, there was an Isaurian uprising in support of Zeno's brother, Longinus. Like all his subjects, Anastasius was sick of the chaos created by these unruly mountain men, and so he took the opportunity to purge them. With Longinus defeated in 491, the rest of the rebel leadership hid in the mountains, and it was another seven years before they were subdued. To prevent further trouble, Anastasius transported much of the Isaurian population to Thrace.

Anastasius's religious sympathies soon caused problems. He made unpopular decisions to ban pagan dance festivals, gladiatorial combats and wild beast fights in the arena, and then the chariot races between the Blue and Green teams became rallying points for the Chalcedonian (Blue) and Monophysite (Green) causes. In 501 the emperor's illegitimate son was injured when

THE BLUES AND THE GREENS

Two great political factions dominated sixth century Constantinople: the Blues and the Greens, taking their names from the colours worn by the two chariot teams that raced in the Hippodrome. There had originally been four teams, but over the centuries the Reds and Whites had been absorbed into the two main ones.

The factions were part of everyday life in the capital. Their leaders were selected by ministers and given important tasks, such as maintaining public works. They also operated a primitive police force, though they were more than likely to form into militias and try to influence the political process as the Roman mobs used to do during the late republic.

The Blue and Green factions existed into the ninth century, although their form and functions became largely ceremonial, while their political affiliations would vary according to circumstances. During the height of their influence, the Blues represented the elite—landowners and the senatorial aristocracy, the bastions of religious orthodoxy. The Greens comprised members of the public service, as well as traders and manufacturers, and were likely to have been supporters of Monophysitism and other heresies. However, these affiliations were not fixed and members of both factions turned up in all levels of society throughout the empire.

Greens attacked Blues in the Hippodrome during a pagan festival. By now openly backing the Monophysites, Anastasius sacked two Chalcedonian patriarchs, replacing them with Monophysites. In 512 rioting began in Constantinople after Monophysite priests held masses in some of the main churches of the capital, offending the largely orthodox citizens, and the crowd demanded that the general Areobindus be crowned emperor. The general declined the offer, and the crowd only settled once Anastasius shocked them by offering to abdicate.

Reign as thou hast lived!

CROWD (presented with Anastasius I)

However, the danger was not over; Anastasius's slow movement towards Monophysitism alienated the influential Vitalian, count of the Bulgarian *foederati* (the barbarian tribes given federated status within the empire) in the Thracian army. Rebelling in 514 to force Anastasius's acceptance of the decrees of the Council of Chalcedon, Vitalian marched on Constantinople. Anastasius initially agreed to allow the pope's mediation but reneged on the deal, sending troops to deal with the rebel. His plan failed, however, and he was forced to pay off Vitalian as well as agree to convene a general church council to deal with the Monophysite question. Again, Vitalian accepted the concessions before the emperor broke his word. Marching a third time in 515, Vitalian was soundly beaten before fleeing into exile.

Though his religious policies caused no end of grief, Anastasius was a measured ruler, reducing taxation and government expenditure. He was interested in the affairs of the western provinces, giving Theodoric the imperial insignia that Odoacer had returned to Constantinople, and thus reinforcing his viceregal role. He also supported the claims of the Frankish king Clovis to Gaul by elevating him to the consulship. He was flawed as an emperor, but there were far worse.

JUSTIN I
PERSECUTOR OF HERETICS

NAME: Flavius Justinus
BORN: Bederiana, Illyricum, c. 450
RULED: Emperor, 518–527
DIED: Of an infected foot ulcer, Constantinople, 527

IT IS A CLICHÉ that the excitement of a big city draws young men from small country towns. Yet it was certainly true of Justin, a humble Illyrian peasant looking for opportunities, who travelled to Constantinople with nothing but the clothes on his back and some bread in his pocket. Strong and healthy, he and two friends enrolled in the palace guard, and he worked his way up the ladder to become head of the palace guards and a senator by Anastasius's reign. Although he was old, uneducated and illiterate, Justin used his influence in the guards to have himself elevated to the imperial throne on the death of the childless Anastasius.

> We have been elected to the Empire by the favour of the indivisible Trinity, by the choice of the highest ministers of the sacred Palace, and of the Senate, and finally by the election of the army.
>
> JUSTIN I

Coming from a Latin background, he was firmly in the Chalcedonian camp and quickly tried to eradicate Monophysitism in the empire. He recalled Vitalian from exile, using him to persecute Monophysite bishops, clergy and commoners in the Asian provinces until Vitalian's rival, Justinian, assassinated him in 520. Justin had, however, achieved reconciliation with the church in Rome, healing the schism begun by Zeno.

This reconciliation with Rome was important, since the Ostrogoth kingdom in Italy had taken advantage of the religious divisions between Rome and Constantinople to entrench itself firmly. Rapprochement would be the first step in attempting to return Italy and Illyricum to the emperor's direct control, especially as the Romans were orthodox and the Goths were Arians. King Theodoric suspected this, doing all he could to prevent direct Roman contact with the orthodox eastern emperor, but his death in 526 destabilised Italy, a situation the empire soon exploited. Though the elderly emperor died in 527, hopes for reunification would bear fruit under the reign of the man he made co-Augustus in the last year of his life, his nephew Justinian.

JUSTINIAN I THE GREAT

ON THE OFFENSIVE

NAME: Flavius Petrus Sabbatius Justinianus
BORN: Tauresium, Dardania, c. 482
RULED: Emperor, 527–565
DIED: Of natural causes, Constantinople, 565

JUSTINIAN BELIEVED IN DESTINY. Though born a Latin peasant, he was confident in his abilities, becoming the first emperor in nearly two centuries to reclaim territory that had been lost to the empire. That process again made Rome part of the empire, as it would remain for the next two centuries, until the empire's retreating boundaries radically altered the relationship between the western provinces and Constantinople.

Justin had ensured his nephew received the finest education available and Justinian's ability was evident during his uncle's reign, as he took over the reins of government during Justin's slow decline. Like his uncle, he was a firm Chalcedonian, who saw himself as Latin rather than Greek. Far more obsessed about this than his uncle, he was prepared to act upon it, especially in reclaiming the lost provinces of his Latin heritage from their Germanic rulers.

Yet he would have achieved little had it not been for two people who made his dreams reality—his wife, Theodora, and his general, Belisarius. In his personal life and in the framing of imperial policy, Theodora's influence was paramount. When Justinian fell in love with the professional actress and part-time prostitute, he was so smitten that he forced Justin to repeal a law that forbade the marriage of senators to actresses. Justinian fell completely under Theodora's spell, and she used her power over him to further her own interests, which were not necessarily synonymous with the empire's interests. Though her private life as empress was beyond reproach, she was jealous of the influence of others and vengeful towards those she believed had thwarted or insulted her. The one man who suffered her vindictiveness more than any other was Justinian's leading general, Belisarius.

Justinian's genius lay in choosing the right man for the required job, and it was to Belisarius that he entrusted the great plan of Roman reunification. Though Belisarius came to prominence during the Persian wars that began Justinian's reign, it was during the Nika riot of 532 that he demonstrated his invaluable service to the emperor.

The conflict between Green and Blue supporters that had troubled Anastasius I erupted into open warfare in the first years of Justinian's reign. Though Justinian was a supporter of the Blues, he attempted to punish the criminals from both sides who had taken advantage of the chaos, and this nearly cost him the throne. The two groups united to demand the release of their accused members, and within a day they had taken the whole city except for the palace and raised a usurper. Justinian decided to flee but Theodora refused to go, declaring 'Those who have reigned should never survive its loss'. Her influence and Belisarius's firmness convinced Justinian to stay. Belisarius bribed the Blues to desert the Greens and then slaughtered the Greens in their thousands as they sat in the Hippodrome.

Justinian with Theodora, Empress of the Eastern Roman Empire

THE PRICE OF UNITY

With Constantinople stabilised, Justinian sent Belisarius in 533 to reclaim the North African provinces, which he did in superb fashion, finally destroying the Vandal kingdom in 534. Then Justinian ordered Belisarius to reconquer Italy. Beginning in 535 with the conquest of Sicily, Belisarius reclaimed the south and occupied Rome in 536, driving the Goths into northern Italy. His crowning glory came in 540 with the capture of Ravenna, where he tricked the Goths into surrendering by declaring that he agreed to their proposal to crown him western Roman emperor.

Such victories unnerved Justinian, who began to distrust his general. On advice from Theodora and Belisarius's enemies, he recalled the general before he had secured Italy. As the Persian war had broken out again, the court dispatched Belisarius in 541 to deal with the escalating situation in the east but his success there only saw him recalled to the imperial court and castigated for

Theodora during the night of the Nika riots

his so-called disloyalty. Eager to prove his devotion to Justinian, and aware that the Goths had reclaimed much of their former territory, in 544 Belisarius returned to Italy to reverse the situation. However, years of endless campaigning and the stress of dealing with enemies at home had taken their toll on the general. Gone were his swashbuckling days, and he managed nothing except the recovery of Rome. In 548 he was replaced, and the new generals did manage to reconquer and hold Italy, as well as annexing parts of southern Spain.

> **We have good hopes that God will grant us to restore our authority over the remaining countries which the ancient Romans possessed to the limits of both oceans and lost by subsequent neglect.**
>
> JUSTINIAN I

By 554 the empire stretched from the deserts of Mesopotamia to the Pillars of Hercules (Gibraltar). It was a stupendous undertaking, but it came at a terrible cost. The conflict between Romans and Goths had ruined Italy, while the people endured crippling taxes to pay for the expeditions. Not only that, but in the late 550s the empire was afflicted with a plague that ravaged the provinces, further sapping what few resources remained. When he died, Justinian left an overstretched empire and an empty treasury.

But there was more to his reign than military exploits. His religious policies helped shape the future direction of the Christian world. Though he was a Chalcedonian, Theodora was a Monophysite, so he tried—but failed—to heal the breach between the two groups. Orthodox Chalcedonians rejected his compromise position, as did the Monophysites, who began establishing their own religious hierarchy. His attempts to force the pope to accept his formula of belief only confirmed the view that the emperors of the east were meddlers in church affairs and suspect in their devotion to orthodoxy. The split in Christendom had begun.

Justinian's other great achievement was the codification of Roman law, the *corpus iuris civilis*. A collection of all sources of law then in force, as well as the resolutions of debates resulting from jurists' interpretations and opinions, this compilation constituted the sole law of the empire. It formed the basis of Latin jurisprudence, including ecclesiastical canon law, and it ensured the survival of Roman law. Passed on to the states of western Europe, it became the basis for many of the European law codes.

Justinian's reign was a watershed in many respects. He was the last eastern emperor whose principal focus was the west, and the last whose native tongue was Latin and who used it as the language of government in Constantinople. He brought to a close six centuries of an Augustan imperial worldview, crystallised in his abolition of the annual consulship, which for a millennium had been the most recognisable symbol of those ancient Roman traditions from which the empire emerged. The eastern empire now began its journey towards becoming fully Greek—a journey that would lead to a permanent schism with the Latin west.

HYPATIUS

YOU'LL DO

NAME: Flavius Hypatius
BORN: Unknown
RULED: Usurper, 532
DIED: Executed, Constantinople, 532

A NUMBER OF ANASTASIUS I's nephews were overlooked when the throne passed to Justin and Justinian. Eager to retain their lives, they displayed no interest in being emperor, sparing themselves Justinian's fear and suspicion. It was during the Nika riots that the crowd and some opportunistic senators demanded that a nephew of Anastasius replace Justinian. Their first choice, Probus, had wisely fled the city, and so the mob set their sights on Hypatius.

A white-haired old man, this former consul and *magister militum* in Thrace had been disgraced when captured by Vitalian during the count's rebellion against Anastasius, and he had subsequently fallen foul of Justin as well. Hypatius did his best to hide from the rampaging mob but they tracked him down, wrenched him from the arms of his wife and crowned him with a golden chain in the Forum of Constantine. Setting up his court in the Hippodrome, he had begun to issue orders when word spread that Justinian had fled.

Long live Hypatius!
THE ROMAN MOB

It was a mistake. After Belisarius marched into the Hippodrome, he slaughtered the rioters and took Hypatius before the emperor. Justinian was sympathetic to the old man's plight, but Theodora demanded his execution. As always, Justinian bowed to her will, and Hypatius's body was thrown into the sea.

JUSTIN II
THE MADNESS OF EMPEROR JUSTIN

NAME: Flavius Justinus Iunior
BORN: Place unknown, c. 520
RULED: Emperor, 565–578
DIED: Of natural causes,
Constantinople, 578

LIKE HIS UNCLE, the great Justinian, Justin II believed that with his superior abilities he would defeat the empire's enemies and strengthen the state. Unfortunately, he lacked the services of a Theodora and a Belisarius, and his poor judgement saw the empire begin a slow decline that would continue through to the eighth century.

To some extent this was not his fault; like his uncle and his ministers, Justin believed that the empire could go on with its expansionist phase without consequences. The reality was that Justin faced a bankrupt economy and a severe manpower shortage, inhibiting any effective response to the problems now besetting the empire. What the empire needed was a period of consolidation; what it got was warfare on multiple fronts, all avoidable.

Justin's first act was to stop payment to the Avars, a Germanic tribe who began numerous incursions across the Danube, putting pressure on another Germanic tribe, the Lombards, who moved into northern Italy. Taking advantage of the removal of the general Narses, who had completed Italy's conquest, the Lombards flooded in, rapidly conquering areas that had so recently been in Roman hands. Justin tried to halt their progress, but these campaigns further sapped the empire's military strength and, by the time of his death, northern Italy was lost to the empire.

If that were not enough, peace with the Persians was shattered when Justin again refused to continue with agreed payments. Launching an invasion of Syria, the Persians captured a number of important military outposts. The Romans put up a good fight, winning some victories, but overall the Roman decline was steady. Though the war was costlier for the Persians, they had not exhausted themselves in almost continuous warfare for over forty years and thus were in a better position to weather the strain than the Romans.

The pressure of all these reverses was too much for Justin; in 573 the emperor's sanity snapped. Though he was occasionally lucid, from now until his death in 578 his wife, Sophia, and a leading general, Tiberius, handled the empire's affairs. The empress resumed payment of subsidies to foreign foes, resulting in a period of relative peace and consolidation, but Justin was too far gone to appreciate it. He spent his final years sitting in a cart, wheeled around by his carers while music played day and night. He would frequently bite at his keepers, who could protect themselves only by mentioning the name of the leader of a tribe known as the Ghassanids. Upon hearing the name 'Harith', the emperor would recoil in terror and become instantly quiet. Such was the state to which the ruler of the Roman world had degenerated, and it was to everyone's relief when he finally died in his palace cell.

TIBERIUS II
HEY, BIG SPENDER!

NAME: Flavius Tiberius Constantinus
BORN: Thrace, c. 520
RULER: Co-emperor, 574–578;
sole emperor, 578–582
DIED: Possibly poisoned,
Constantinople, 582

TIBERIUS WAS THE HANDSOME, popular and experienced commander of Justin II's imperial guards. He became co-emperor in 574 when Justin went mad and the empire needed a firm hand to deal with the enemies besieging it.

> What use is this hoarded gold, when all the world is choking with hunger?
>
> TIBERIUS II

Until Justin's death he ruled in tandem with the empress Sophia, who kept him under a tight leash, but in 578 he forced her out of power. Focusing on foreign threats, he was soon dealing with a massive Avar invasion, the continuing Persian war with its shifting fortunes and the increasing power of the Lombards. Unable to make headway, he found his only recourse was to hold the peace and pay large amounts of money to the various peoples he was fighting, adding to the financial problems crippling the state. Again a Roman emperor was forced to accept that there just were not enough troops to deal with both the eastern and western frontiers.

To boost his support, Tiberius gave some civil powers to the leaders of the Greens and the Blues, the factions that had been suppressed since the Nika riot, and to prevent the Greek Christian communities fracturing completely he stopped the persecutions of the Monophysites that Justin II had recommenced.

Tiberius was reportedly poisoned when eating a plate of juicy mulberries in 582, and he nominated one of his top generals—Maurice—as successor.

MAURICE
THE ORIGINAL SCROOGE

NAME: Flavius Mauricius Tiberius
BORN: Arabissus, Cappadocia, 539
RULED: Emperor: 582–602
DIED: Executed, Chalcedon (Kadıköy),
Bithynia, 602

A SOLDIER OF IMPRESSIVE ability, Maurice had shown his mettle during the seemingly endless Persian wars, winning a crushing victory in 582, and he had the good fortune to ascend the throne during a brief lull in that conflict. His family origins were Italian, and so it was natural for him to focus on the western provinces, where the empire lost Spain in 584 and the Lombards were strengthening their hold in Italy. In response, he created the system of exarchates, one in Ravenna (for Italy) and one in Carthage (for North Africa). The exarch, or military governor, represented the emperor and held combined civilian and military powers, marking a return to the old Roman style of governor that Diocletian and Constantine had overturned. This act alone saved Rome and the southern Italian possessions from falling into Lombard hands, by giving the exarch the authority to act decisively and providing a base for the imperial forces.

Maurice was also fortunate that a dynastic crisis in Sassanid Persia brought a more permanent peace to the east. He gave his support to one of the claimants, Khosrow II, who emerged victorious and married Maurice's daughter, and in 591 declared a lasting peace between Persia and Rome. It did not come a moment too soon.

Maurice's major problem was a lack of manpower. As he possessed only one principal army, the Persian threat had prevented his dealing with problems to the west. The Avars had been moving for some years, capturing a number of key cities as they advanced into the Pannonian provinces, while the Slavs had been migrating into the depopulated Balkan region for close to fifteen years. With the bulk of their troops engaged elsewhere, all the Romans could do was defend the Balkans.

Peace with Persia meant that Maurice finally had enough soldiers to launch a western offensive, and in 591 he did so. Though he was not able to defeat the barbarians, at least he brought the frontier under Roman control for the first time since Anastasius I.

Maurice's reign also marks the beginning of a schism between the eastern and western churches. With Maurice's support, the patriarch of Constantinople formally adopted the title of 'Ecumenical' in 588, thereby implying that his authority was superior to all other Christian prelates, including that of the pope. Rome rejected this, with Pope Gregory I seeing it as a brazen challenge to the status quo. The battle for supremacy in the church had begun.

Maurice's other problem throughout all this was a lack of money. Tiberius's approach of bribing the empire's enemies was expensive, and Maurice quickly discovered a depleted treasury. He was an honest and upright man, and his natural instinct was to be frugal with the state's money. Yet continual warfare meant that he was never able to replenish the coffers satisfactorily, making him thrifty to the point of being miserly. In the end, this was to be his undoing.

In 602 Maurice prohibited the army returning to their Pannonian base in winter, thus saving the cost of housing and feeding them. After eight months of fighting, the troops were physically and mentally exhausted and were looking forward to spending time with their wives and children. Declaring a centurion, Phocas, to be their leader, they marched on Constantinople and were at first content to dethrone Maurice and elevate either his son Theodosius or Theodosius's father-in-law as the next emperor. Yet when the rebels reached the capital, neither candidate was acceptable. Maurice approached the leaders of the Greens and Blues to provide men to defend him, but their 2400 men were never going to be enough. He fled with his family in the dead of night across the Bosphorus into Asia, allowing the centurion Phocas to be declared emperor and to begin eliminating any potential challengers.

By now quite ill, Maurice seems to have lost all his fight. When Phocas's troops ran him to ground, he made no effort to escape and watched impassively as they butchered his sons before his eyes, before he quietly offered his head for execution. The bodies of the imperial family were thrown into the waters of the Bosphorus and their heads taken to Constantinople, where they were exposed to the people's contempt or pity.

THEODOSIUS

AN UNKNOWN FATE

NAME: Flavius Theodosius
BORN: Constantinople, 583
RULED: Co-emperor, 590–602
DIED: Possibly in Colchis, Lazika, c. 602

YOUNG THEODOSIUS, named after the last emperor who had been born to a reigning emperor, was crowned emperor at the age of seven. Kept very much in the background by Maurice, he only came to prominence during the events that ended his father's rule.

When the army on the Danube demanded in 602 that Maurice step down, their two preferred candidates for his replacement were Theodosius and his father-in-law, Germanus. Both were away hunting at the time, and so Maurice summoned them to the capital where he accused them of treason. Germanus sought refuge in Hagia Sophia, while Maurice whipped Theodosius for his apparent betrayal. Maurice presumably repented, because the next thing we hear is that he sent Theodosius to obtain aid from the Persian king, Khosrow II, who owed his throne to Maurice.

In his depressed state, Maurice then ordered Theodosius to return. Although his message reached Theodosius in Nicaea, it is here that the fate of Theodosius becomes unclear. Did he return to die alongside his father in the slaughter that ended their male line? Or was he subsequently killed? Most of Maurice's contemporaries believed he was killed later. Yet his would-be murderer, Phocas, had one of his cronies, Alexander, executed on a charge of accepting a bribe from Germanus and helping Theodosius escape, and there were rumours Theodosius escaped to Colchis. If he did make it to Persian territory, it did him no good, as he disappears from the historical record while Khosrow took advantage of the revolution to launch a devastating attack on the Roman Empire.

PHOCAS

THE EARTHLY MONSTER

NAME: Flavius Phocas
BORN: Thrace, 547
RULED: Emperor, 602–610
DIED: Executed, Constantinople, 610

PHOCAS HAD TWO distinctive sides. One was a man full of energy and drive, determined to reassert Roman authority in the face of numerous enemies. The other was a depraved, paranoid monster, eager to kill and torture all those he suspected of trying to overthrow him—and he suspected almost everyone.

As a usurper, perhaps he had good reason to be paranoid. Rebelling against Maurice, he took advantage of a lack of suitable candidates to have himself crowned emperor when he entered Constantinople. His precarious position became clear during discussions with the Greens and the Blues when they warned him: 'Beware! Remember that Maurice is not dead!' Butchering Maurice's family and the main adherents of the old regime was a bloody start to a bloody reign.

Is it thus that you have governed the empire?

HERACLIUS (to the captured Phocas)

Phocas's appearance did not inspire confidence. With a mass of red hair, a thick and continuous eyebrow, and a scar that ran right across his face, he found it hard to gain legitimacy. The eastern general Narses rejected his authority; refusing to lift a finger to halt the Persian invasion, he entered into discussion with Khosrow to see if they could overthrow the tyrant.

Phocas reacted quickly, recalling Narses with promises of reconciliation, before changing his mind and burning him alive. This habit of dealing sadistically with his enemies caused the exarch of Africa, Heraclius, to rebel in 608. Until this point the Romans had kept the Persians at bay in the east, but the need to deal with Heraclius meant Phocas had to move many of his troops to the west. From 609 the Persians were able to overrun Mesopotamia, northern Syria and Asia Minor, while the Slavs poured into the undefended Balkans.

As the noose tightened around his neck, Phocas began to see conspiracies everywhere. Torture became commonplace in the capital, and he wreaked terrible vengeance on Maurice's female relatives. Adding to the chaos, he ordered the persecution and forcible conversion of all Jews throughout the empire. In the east, this degenerated into a civil war in many cities and resulted in the Jews welcoming the Persians as liberators.

Ironically, the only part of the empire that looked favourably on Phocas was Rome, where the pope was grateful for his adoption of key agrarian reforms, as well as his unwavering support of the papacy.

Yet the end was in sight. By 610 Heraclius had defeated the armies of Phocas in Egypt and moved on to Constantinople, which was suffering from famine and plague. Meeting no resistance, Heraclius's troops dragged Phocas out to meet his conqueror, who ordered that Phocas undergo his own tortures, before his body was mutilated and beheaded. His death came not a moment too soon.

HERACLIUS

THE NEMESIS OF PERSIA

NAME: Flavius Heraclius
BORN: Cappadocia, c. 575
RULED: Emperor, 610–641
DIED: Of natural causes, Constantinople, 641

IT SEEMED THAT the end had come for the Roman Empire. In the west, the Avars and Slavs had taken Illyricum and a large swathe of Thrace, with even Greece coming under threat, while in the east the Persians were knocking on Egypt's door. The empire was short of manpower and money, as everyone prayed for a miracle. This was the challenge laid down to Heraclius.

The exarch of Carthage was an able, fair-haired giant of a man with a reputation for bravery. Rebelling against Phocas's cruelty, he easily defeated the emperor's troops in Egypt before personally executing the detested emperor. Given the empire's health, Heraclius was in no position to take a stand against its enemies, even if he had wanted to. So for twelve long years he watched as Greece, Thrace and Egypt were lost, and the Persians rode within view of Constantinople. However, he used the time wisely, quietly reorganising the empire by creating new regional military administrative units, called *themes*, and creating a new currency that allowed payment to the military without straining the treasury. Although in 618 he did seriously contemplate abandoning the capital and re-establishing his court at Carthage, he decided to remain and fight to the end. Having bought off the Avars with an expensive peace treaty, by 622 he was ready to undertake the grand design of his reign—the destruction of the Persian Sassanids.

For the first time in centuries, an emperor marched at the head of his army, and not merely as a token gesture. Aside from the brief spell during the civil war against Phocas, this was Heraclius's first true experience commanding an army in war. Judging the Persians to be the greater threat, he trusted the capital to its mammoth fortifications and spent the next six years utterly crushing the once great Persian Empire.

It was a war to rival the exploits of Julius Caesar in scope and personal valour. Highlights included Heraclius's destruction of two combined Persian armies in 624, and the massacre of a third that stumbled onto the carnage. The following year he was crossing the Euphrates River when a Persian army surprised him and slaughtered his advance guard. Seeing an unmanned bridge, he led his troops over it, cutting down a Persian giant who stood in his path with a single sword stroke. Noticing what was going on, the Persian general ordered archers to sweep the bridge: arrows flew and still Heraclius pressed on, even with a number of arrow shafts embedded in his side. His courage saved the day.

The crucial year was 626. King Khosrow tried to force Heraclius's hand by forging an alliance with the Avars and making a joint assault on Constantinople itself. This presented the emperor with a dilemma: if he remained in Anatolia the capital might fall, but if he went back all of his hard-fought gains would be lost. Placing his faith in Providence and Constantinople's massive Theodosian walls, he remained in Azerbaijan and continued tightening the screws on the Persians. Constantinople survived, and Khosrow expressed his displeasure by ordering the body of his defeated general packed with salt and shipped to him so that he could have it flayed.

Battle of Heraclius against Khosrow II

THE PRICE OF UNITY

It was now only a matter of time. In 627 Heraclius grappled with Khosrow just outside the ruins of Nineveh. The battle was fierce and lasted all day. Challenged to single combat by the Persian general, the emperor charged at his rival, decapitating him with a single stroke. At sunset, the last Persian army in the east lay annihilated. By 628 the Persian king was overthrown and a peace treaty signed, returning all the territory the Persians had taken to the empire. When Heraclius returned to Constantinople, the entire population was there to greet the conquering hero, the empire's greatest general since Aurelian 350 years before. Yet the war had changed him. Gone were his youth and good looks; with his body bent and his grey hair falling out, all he wanted was to live out his life in peace and tranquillity, secure in the knowledge that his enemies had been broken before he himself was.

Will you govern any better?

PHOCAS (to his captor Heraclius)

It was not to be. Within six years, the armies of Islam burst forth from the sands of Arabia, swarming across all the territories so dearly gained. Neither empire nor emperor was in any condition to fight, one exhausted militarily, the other exhausted mentally. Within ten years, the Muslims had conquered Jerusalem, where the emperor had only recently marched barefoot along the Via Dolorosa carrying the True Cross for its triumphant return, and Heraclius had to watch as decades of hard work disappeared in a matter of a few years.

Believing God was punishing him for his marriage to his niece Martina, he spent his remaining years on religious questions, convinced that if he could heal the breach between the Chalcedonians and the Monophysites, God would stop punishing the empire. His first attempt was Monoenergism, the notion that while Christ had two natures—human and divine—he had only one 'energy' or active force. His second attempt, known as Monothelitism, stated that Christ possessed two natures joined in a single will. When the second idea was rejected, it was the last straw for a broken old man. His body bloated and near paralysed, forced to use a board to shield his face every time he urinated, he welcomed death.

Magnificent despite his end, Heraclius's reign was hugely important. His provincial reorganisation into *themes*, expanded by his successors, provided the backbone of the empire for the next six hundred years. Gone were Diocletian's praetorian prefectures; in their place there was a return to a much older Roman tradition—soldier-farmers, a throwback to the Italian farmers who made up the republican armies that had originally built the empire. Heraclius also replaced Latin with Greek as the official language of the empire's administrative and military branches. Within a generation, Latin would be extinct in the east, further dividing the eastern and western provinces. Finally, he abolished the old forms of imperial titles. Gone were *Imperator Caesar* and *Augustus*; in their place was the Greek word for 'king'—*Basileus*. The Roman Empire continued, but its forms and expressions had now become Greek.

ELEUTHERIUS

A STATE OF MY OWN

NAME: Eleutherius
BORN: Unknown
RULED: Usurper, 619
DIED: Assassinated, Ravenna, Italy, 619

GIVEN HERACLIUS'S unfavourable start, it is remarkable that his reign saw only one rebellion. That was the revolt of Eleutherius, exarch of Ravenna from 615. He had been sent to Italy by Heraclius to defend the province against the Lombards, but was defeated and forced to pay tribute of five hundred pounds of gold per year. Surprisingly, Eleutherius was also a eunuch, which would have precluded him from occupying the throne in Constantinople.

Regardless, the unstable situation facing the empire provided Eleutherius with an opportunity to declare himself emperor in Ravenna. Relying on Heraclius's unpopularity in Italy and his preoccupation with the Persians, Eleutherius set up his capital in Rome as western emperor. Buying off the Lombards with a yearly tribute, he was in the process of seeking the approval of Pope Boniface V when his own troops murdered him, sending his head to Heraclius as a new year's present.

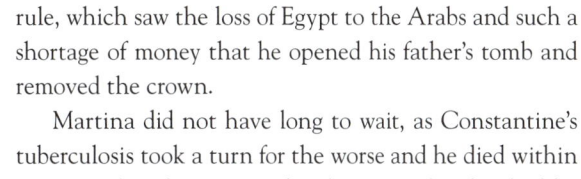

CONSTANTINE III

BEWARE A SCHEMING STEPMOTHER

NAME: Heraclius Novus Constantinus
BORN: Constantinople, 612
RULED: Co-emperor, 613–641;
senior emperor, 641
DIED: Of tuberculosis, Chalcedon
(Kadıköy), Bithynia, 641

CONSTANTINE, OR MORE accurately The New Constantine, was the receptacle of his father's hopes, and Heraclius raised him to imperial honours at the age of one. Unfortunately, Constantine soon showed the first signs of the tuberculosis that would eventually take his life. Though enthusiastic, he was always unwell and in need of supervision.

As a fourteen-year-old, he displayed conspicuous bravery during the Avars' siege of Constantinople, lifting morale and engaging the enemy on the walls of the capital, but his sickness eroded his father's confidence in him and his half-brother was elevated as co-emperor. Although he was twenty-nine when Heraclius died, his stepmother, Martina, tried to act as regent but was frustrated by ferocious opposition from the supporters of Constantine as well as the common people. Moving into the background, she tried to undermine Constantine's rule, which saw the loss of Egypt to the Arabs and such a shortage of money that he opened his father's tomb and removed the crown.

Martina did not have long to wait, as Constantine's tuberculosis took a turn for the worse and he died within four months of assuming the throne. Before he died he tried to head off Martina, by writing to the army, asking it to take care of his young son Constans.

HERACLONAS AND TIBERIUS

THE MEANS TO AN END

Names: Constantinus Heraclius; David Tiberius
BORN: Lazica (Egrisi), Georgia, 626; Unknown
RULED: Co-emperor, 638–641; co-emperor, 641
DIED: Cause unknown, Rhodes, 641; Unknown

THESE SONS OF HERACLIUS and his niece Martina had little chance to survive imperial politics. The elder, born during his father's Persian campaigns and named after him, was known by his nickname 'Little Heraclius', or 'Heraclonas'. He was the first of Martina's children born without deformity and she planned to rule the empire through him, convincing a failing Heraclius to nominate him as co-emperor with his stepbrother, Constantine. The two took over the reins of government in 641 but Martina soon made her presence felt, pushing Heraclonas into the background when Constantine died.

She replaced key supporters of Constantine, but they retaliated by implying that she had poisoned him. The army revolted, forcing Heraclonas to elevate his nephew Constans to the throne. Determined to remain in power, Martina raised another of her sons to the rank of emperor as a counterbalance—David, given the name Tiberius. It was not enough. Martina had made herself so unpopular that the Senate deposed her and her sons. Her tongue was cut out and Heraclonas's nose was amputated to prevent him ruling, the theory being that since the emperor was Christ's representative on earth, he should not have any physical imperfection. He was eventually exiled to Rhodes and perished soon afterwards. The sources remain ominously silent about young Tiberius's fate.

CONSTANS II
THE BEARDED ONE

NAME: Flavius Heraclius Constantine
BORN: Constantinople, 630
RULED: Emperor, 641–668
DIED: Murdered, Syracuse, Sicily, 668

THE ONE CONSTANT about Constans Pogonatus was that he seldom took advice. Stern and inflexible, he persevered with his chosen path no matter how fatal the

Emperor Constans gives orders for Abbot Maximus to be tortured for refusing to accept Monothelitism

consequences to others or even himself. His nickname, 'Pogonatus', came from his beard; in an era when everyone wore beards, his was excessive, stretching to his belly.

His reign was one of regular Roman retreats in the face of a triumphant Islam. By 645 Egypt and much of North Africa east of Carthage was lost. Firstly, there were Arab raids into the Anatolian and Armenia *themes*, followed by the creation of an Arab fleet that attacked Roman territory around the Mediterranean. The Arab ships eluded Roman patrols, and in 654 they took the strategically important island of Rhodes. Constans's humiliation was complete when he barely escaped with his life at the Battle of the Masts in 655—he swapped robes with his faithful servant and slipped away, while the enemy surrounded and slew his servant. What saved the empire from total extinction was a civil war in Arabia over the caliphate, which resulted in Islam's division into Sunni and Shi'a branches.

> **I therefore invite you to assist me by your advice and judgement in providing for the general safety of my subjects.**
>
> CONSTANS II POGONATUS

The gradual dismemberment of the eastern provinces forced Constans's attention to the west. Determined to reimpose control on what remained of the empire, he ordered all discussions about the nature, energy or will of Christ to cease. Without condemning his grandfather's Monothelite compromise, he hoped this would allow the supporters of orthodoxy and Monothelitism to coexist. When Rome condemned this command, he demanded that the exarch of Ravenna capture Pope Martin I. Brought in chains to Constantinople and charged with aiding and abetting the usurper Olympius in Ravenna, Martin ended up imprisoned, tortured and banished to the Crimea. Given this display of the imperial will, the pope's successors, though privately critical of Constans, did not publicly oppose him until after his death.

Constans's authority was secured, but he was unpopular in Constantinople, especially after he murdered his brother, whom Constans suspected, without any firm proof, of aiming for the throne. He crossed over to the west and began his campaign to preserve what remained of the western provinces. Pushing the Lombards from much of southern Italy, he headed up to Rome, becoming the first emperor since Julius Nepos to visit the ancient capital. The deteriorating situation in the east convinced him to move the imperial court from Constantinople back to Rome, though difficulties in continuing a campaign against the Lombards soon forced a change of plans. Moving his court down to the city of Syracuse in Sicily, he continued fighting both the Arabs and the Lombards.

Many were fearful of Constans's long-term plans, including the Franks, who believed the emperor coveted the lost Gallic provinces. However, most concerned were members of his court. Longing for the civilised pleasures of Constantinople, they listened with dread when, in 668, Constans announced plans to make Syracuse the new capital of the Roman Empire. In a panic, one of his Greek attendants smashed a soap dish across the emperor's head as he was bathing. He died instantly, ending the last serious attempt to reclaim the western provinces.

GREGORY

DISTRACTED BY RELIGION

NAME: Flavius Gregorius
BORN: Unknown
RULED: Usurper, 646–647
DIED: Killed in battle, Sufetula, North Africa, 647

THE PRICE THE EMPIRE paid for its distractions over obscure Christological debates was profound. Gregory's usurpation was a case in point. A relative of

Heraclius, he was appointed exarch of Carthage in the 630s, but instead of dealing with the looming Islamic threat he organised debates between orthodox Christian theologians and Monothelite clergy, trying to stem the religious conflict in his province. As a devout Christian, he thought he was doing the right thing. As a Roman commander, he could ill afford such a distraction.

Constans II's accession forced Gregory into overtly supporting orthodoxy. He donned the purple, citing the emperor's continuing support of Monothelitism, before confronting an Arab invasion from Egypt. He gathered an army but was defeated and killed in battle.

OLYMPIUS

IF YOU CAN'T BEAT THEM ...

NAME: Olympius
BORN: Unknown
RULED: Usurper, 650–652
DIED: Possibly of plague, Sicily, 652

CONSTANS GAVE OLYMPIUS one key task when he appointed him exarch of Ravenna: capture Pope Martin I and return him to Constantinople on charges of failing to gain the emperor's approval for his elevation, as well as rejecting Constans's religious solution to the Monothelitism controversy.

Olympius tried assassination; he tried bullying the bishops, to which the Latin Synod responded by condemning the emperor and the patriarchs. He then decided to throw in his lot with the pope, and so he declared himself emperor. Gathering an army, he marched into Sicily to disrupt any imperial preparations against his usurpation. He never made it back to Ravenna: his army was struck down by a mystery illness that killed many, including Olympius.

MEZEZIUS

BEING HANDSOME IS NOT ENOUGH

NAME: Mezezius
BORN: Unknown
RULED: Usurper, 668–669
DIED: Executed, Sicily, 669

CONSTANS'S MURDER opened up an opportunity for the court in Sicily to choose a successor. Their choice, Mezezius, had three things going for him. Firstly, he was a nobleman from Armenia and was believed to be descended from royalty. Secondly, he was a prominent patrician and the commander of the Opsikion *theme*. Thirdly, he was described as being very good-looking and handsome.

Regardless of his advantages, he was unable to gain enough support from the locals or the army to stabilise his rule. When Constans's son arrived with an army, he soon captured and executed the usurper along with his key supporters. The court returned to Constantinople with the new emperor.

CONSTANTINE IV

THE TURNING OF THE TIDE

NAME: Kōnstantinos
BORN: Constantinople, c. 650
RULED: Co-emperor, 654–668;
senior emperor, 668–685
DIED: Of dysentery,
Constantinople, 685

CONSTANTINE INHERITED much from his great-grandfather Heraclius. An able administrator, unafraid to challenge the status quo, he steadied the empire and provided the first serious check to the Islamic expansion.

Made co-emperor by his father, Constans II, at the age of four, and responsible for managing the eastern provinces during Constans's absence in Italy from 661, he was eighteen when he inherited an empire at war. Confronted with Caliph Muawiyah's plan to conquer Constantinople, he withstood the siege of 674. For the next five years, the Saracens returned each spring after quartering for the winter, but they fell back with heavy losses. This, plus their defeat by the Romans in Anatolia, forced the caliph to come to terms with Constantine, the first time a leader of the Islamic empire was not the victor when dealing with an enemy.

Constantine was far less successful against a new threat to the west, the Bulgars, who had settled in the former province of Moesia (modern Bulgaria and Romania). He led an army against them, but a case of acute gout forced him to halt his advance. Believing he had fled, the Bulgars swiftly butchered his army, forcing Constantine to come to terms.

Constantine's enduring achievement was finally to resolve the Monophysite and Monothelite problems. Aided by the fact that these groups were now occupying territory under Arab control, he convened the Sixth Ecumenical Council and presided over many of the sessions, but he refused to meddle in the theological

Caliph Muawiyah, governor of Syria, receiving the ruler of Egypt

discussions. The council condemned Monothelitic doctrine, confirming the orthodox teaching of Christ's dual natures, and resolving the struggle that had torn apart the church for over two centuries. His patience won the day; unfortunately for the empire, Constantine died in 685 at the age of thirty-five.

HERACLIUS AND TIBERIUS

TWO BROTHERS TOO MANY

NAMES: Heracleios and Tiberios
BORN: Unknown
RULED: Co-emperors, 659–681
DIED: Unknown

PRIOR TO HIS WESTERN expedition, Constans II elevated his two younger sons as co-emperors alongside Constantine to reduce the risk of another contender rising to take the throne. When the throne passed to Constantine in 668, he attempted to rule as sole emperor, but there was an uprising in Anatolia. The army demanded that his brothers be crowned equal co-emperors, based on the notion that since the Trinity ruled all of creation, three emperors should rule the empire.

Constantine captured and executed the leaders of the revolt. There was nothing to indicate that his brothers were involved in the conspiracy, but a seed of doubt seems to have entered Constantine's mind. Heraclius and Tiberius continued to be co-emperors, in name only, until 680 when something happened to raise Constantine's suspicions. He ordered the amputation of his brothers' noses, making them unfit to hold the office of emperor, before deposing them.

JUSTINIAN II

VENGEANCE IS MINE

NAME: Ioustinianos
BORN: Constantinople, c. 668
RULED: Co-emperor, 681–685;
sole emperor, 685–695 and 705–711
DIED: Murdered, Damatrys, Opsikion, 711

OF HERACLIUS'S DESCENDANTS, Justinian, the son of Constantine IV, most clearly inherited both his grandsire's virtues and his defects. Though driven and capable, Justinian was also mentally unbalanced, and this got worse as time went on. Made co-emperor on his uncles' fall, he became sole emperor at the age of sixteen. He was both determined to make his mark and desperate to ensure that his will prevail.

Justinian recaptured vital territory from the Bulgarians and Slavs but the campaign seemed to go to the young emperor's head, precipitating a renewal of the war against the Arabs that ended in a crushing defeat at Sebastopolis. It is here that we see the first example of Justinian's soon to be legendary cruelty. He had thousands of Slavs transported across to Anatolia to repopulate the devastated regions, foolishly expecting them to fight for him in return. They deserted during the battle, and Justinian, who had to flee to the province of Bithynia, blamed them for his defeat. In retaliation, he ordered the arrest of all the Slavs who had recently migrated to Bithynia—men, women and children—and massacred them by the thousands.

Hand in hand with this cruelty went his megalomania. During a synod he convened, his prelates tried to force some eastern traditions on the whole of Christendom and confirmed the equality of the patriarch of Constantinople and the pope in Rome. Pope Sergius refused to affirm these decisions, enraging Justinian, who ordered his arrest and then used violence to force the pope's agreement.

Also unhelpful was his choice of ministers, for they oppressed senators and commoners alike, acquiring money and land through extortion and torture. It was only a matter of time before his subjects revolted: in 695 adherents of the Blues invaded the palace and captured the angry and frightened emperor. Dragging him to the Hippodrome, they amputated his nose and sliced his tongue before exiling him to the town of Cherson in the Crimea.

Now mockingly referred to as 'Rinotmetos', the slit-nosed, he spent the next ten years plotting and scheming, and Cherson discovered there is nothing more dangerous than a former emperor seeking revenge. By 703 the fearful city magistrates planned to either kill Justinian or hand him over to the current emperor, Tiberius III. Justinian was forced to flee to the Khazars, a local tribe, where he attempted to gain the khan's support by marrying his sister. Tiberius now offered the khan a bribe to have Justinian killed. Learning of his danger from his wife, Justinian murdered the would-be assassins with his bare hands before fleeing to the Bulgars. Justinian then made a deal with the Bulgar king, who became his son-in-law, and in 705 Justinian appeared before the walls of Constantinople at the head of a Bulgar army. After three days, he and some soldiers entered the city in secret through an unused water conduit, quickly gaining control of Constantinople.

With his rivals lying prostrate in chains before him, Justinian, wearing a fetching silver nasal prosthesis, trod upon their necks before executing them. A six-year reign of terror followed, as Justinian took bloody revenge against all those who had opposed him. People were hanged, beheaded or enclosed in sacks and drowned, while others were tied to spits and roasted over an open fire.

In particular, Justinian singled out Cherson for special treatment, having never forgiven the town's betrayal. He dispatched a fleet there, and his forces occupied the town but did not destroy it, forcing the emperor to send another fleet to finish the job. The city rebelled, and the fleet, under the command of Bardanes, joined the revolt. Justinian then gathered an army and marched to crush the rebellion, but Bardanes instead occupied Constantinople and was crowned emperor under the name Philippicus. Justinian was on his way back when his troops deserted, butchering him and sending his head to Bardanes as a trophy.

A man with Justinian's drive could have achieved much; instead, all he achieved was the empire's hatred for his bloody misdeeds.

LEONTIUS

THE PRICE OF FAILURE

NAME: León
BORN: Constantinople, 669
RULED: Emperor, 695–698
DIED: Executed, Constantinople, 706

NOT EVEN JUSTINIAN'S generals avoided his wrath, with failure punished severely, as Leontius discovered. Hailing from the mountainous regions of Isauria, he had achieved military success under Constantine IV who, recognising his ability, appointed him *strategos* (military governor) of Anatolia. He won even more victories early in Justinian's reign, but Justinian held him accountable for the disastrous battle of Sebastopolis, jailing him for two years.

Released in 595 and appointed *strategos* of Hellas, Leontius was naturally fearful of again falling foul of Justinian's tempestuous rages. With the patriarch's backing, he organised a coup in Constantinople and gained control of the city. He then had Justinian brought before him, before mutilating and then exiling him.

Leontius very soon faced the continuing Arab threat and concentrated on retaining the exarchate of Carthage. However, the Arabs captured it in 698, and the Romans withdrew to Crete. There, fearful of returning home with news of their defeat, the army elevated Apsimarus as emperor. The fleet then continued to Constantinople, but Leontius was confident he could hold out. He did not expect Apsimarus to bribe the imperial officers to allow the army into the city. They captured Leontius, amputated his nose and forced him to take monastic vows.

A monk he would have remained but for the near miraculous return of Justinian in 705. The old emperor had not forgiven those who rose up against him. Dragging the unwilling Leontius from his cell, Justinian humiliated him before finally beheading him.

TIBERIUS III

WE DON'T LIKE YOUR NAME

BIRTH NAME: Apsimarus
BORN: Constantinople, 669
RULED: Emperor, 698–705
DIED: Executed, Constantinople, 706

IT SEEMED THAT APSIMARUS had everything going for him. A naval officer of Germanic origin, he earned his appointment as admiral on merit. Only one thing was against him—his name. So, when he was elevated to emperor by the army, he adopted the more imperial sounding name of Tiberius before moving against Leontius in Constantinople.

He was preoccupied, like his predecessor, with the Arabs, but his efforts were much more successful. Aggressive where Leontius had been defensive, he was determined to stem the losses in Asia. Though resigned to the temporary loss of North Africa, he launched attacks in Syria and Armenia, defeating a number of Saracen armies during his reign.

However, his greatest threat was not external enemies, but the former emperor Justinian. Hearing of Justinian's plans to return to the capital, Tiberius attempted to capture him, but the old emperor managed to elude his grasp. The next time Tiberius beheld him, it was at the head of a Bulgar army outside the walls of Constantinople. Betrayed from within the city, Tiberius fled to Apollonia, but he could not evade capture. Justinian paraded him before the citizens of the city, who pelted him with rubbish, before he was taken away and executed.

TIBERIUS

A LAMB TO THE SLAUGHTER

NAME: Tiberios
BORN: Crimea, c. 705
RULED: Co-emperor, 706–711
DIED: Murdered, Constantinople, 711

DURING HIS EXILE, Justinian spent some time with the Khazars, a barbarian tribe in the Crimea. Their chief liked the former emperor, even without his nose, and gave his sister to the widowed emperor in marriage. When Tiberius III pressured the chief to kill Justinian, he abandoned his new wife, but his return to the throne changed everything. Learning his barbarian wife had given birth to a son, he asked his brother-in-law to send them to Constantinople. Justinian named his son Tiberius and associated him with the purple.

The boy was six when news came of his father's death and Bardanes's plan to eradicate the Heraclian line. The assassins found the child seeking refuge in a church near the Blachernae Palace, clinging with one hand to a leg of the altar, his other hand holding a piece of the True Cross and holy relics hanging around his neck. They were undeterred. Dragging Tiberius away from the altar, they removed the sacred objects before carrying him outside. There, they cut his throat like a sheep's, watching as his blood poured onto the ground.

PHILIPPICUS

ADDICTED TO PLEASURE

BIRTH NAME: Bardanes
BORN: Pergamum, Thrakesion, date unknown
RULED: Emperor, 711–713
DIED: Of natural causes, Constantinople, 714

THE SON OF AN ARMENIAN patrician, Bardanes was born in one of the Armenian colonies in Anatolia. He had been banished by Tiberius III for desiring the throne, but Justinian recalled him to help in the destruction of Cherson. Appalled by the emperor's madness, he rebelled and sought the aid of nearby Khazar tribesmen, who sheltered him from Justinian's fury. As the rebellion spread, he changed his name to the more suitable Philippicus before marching to Constantinople. Discovering Justinian had left to attack him, he was crowned emperor, and soon after Justinian was killed by his own troops. It would be the highlight of Philippicus's brief reign.

Philippicus quickly proved to be addicted to pleasure, with no real desire to deal with the challenges facing the state. With the empire under attack from the Bulgars and Saracens, Philippicus focused on the one thing guaranteed to cause conflict at home—religion. Ignoring the rulings of the Sixth Ecumenical Council, he ordered the recognition of Monothelitism as the true expression of Christ's nature, sending the church into schism.

The army once again intervened to overthrow an unpopular monarch. The commanders of the Opsikion troops stationed in Thrace decided to send some soldiers to deal with Philippicus. The emperor was resting after a

THE EARLY CHURCH COUNCILS

Given the complex theological arguments that sprang up over the centuries, the church needed a way to define what was orthodox and what was heretical. To preserve the unity of the church and empire, the church convened a number of church (or ecumenical) councils to settle controversial matters decisively.

FIRST COUNCIL OF NICAEA (325) Convened by Constantine I, it refuted Arianism, adopted the original Nicene Creed and set Easter day.

FIRST COUNCIL OF CONSTANTINOPLE (381) Convened by Theodosius I, it rejected Arian doctrines and revised the Nicene Creed about the Holy Spirit.

COUNCIL OF EPHESUS (431) Convened by Theodosius II, it repudiated Nestorianism and Pelagianism, and reaffirmed the Nicene Creed.

COUNCIL OF CHALCEDON (451) Convened by Marcian I, it anathematised Monophysitism and adopted the Chalcedonian Creed.

SECOND COUNCIL OF CONSTANTINOPLE (553) Convened by Justinian I, it declared the 'Three Chapters' as Nestorian, and decreed the Theopaschite Formula.

THIRD COUNCIL OF CONSTANTINOPLE (680–681) Convened by Constantine V, it disavowed Monothelitism and Monoenergism.

SECOND COUNCIL OF NICAEA (787) Convened by Constantine VII, it restored the veneration of icons and refuted iconoclasm.

morning banquet when they dragged him off to a quiet change room and blinded him. They then exiled him to a local monastery, where he died the following year in anguish and misery.

ANASTASIUS II

PREPARING FOR WAR

BIRTH NAME: Artemios
BORN: Unknown
RULED: Emperor, 713–715
DIED: Executed, Constantinople, 719

MUCH TO THE ANNOYANCE of the Opsikion rebels, the next emperor elected by the Senate was the imperial secretary, Artemios. Crowned by the patriarch with the name Anastasius, he soon demonstrated great foresight and potential, quickly restoring stability to the church and state by again outlawing the Monothelite doctrine. Foreseeing a new Arab offensive, he spent time restoring the capital's defences, as well as storing enormous quantities of grain to withstand any siege. Nor was he prepared to wait for the inevitable. A large fleet was prepared, rendezvousing at Rhodes to carry the army to Phoenicia.

> **Each citizen is to provide himself with means to procure sustenance, sufficient to last for three years, and that all who are too poor to compass this are to leave the city instantly.**
>
> ANASTASIUS II

Unfortunately, Anastasius had made enemies along the way. His decision to execute the leading Opsikion rebels caused resentment, as did his desire to reform the military command structure. Deciding they had had enough of this bureaucrat, the Opsikions rebelled at Rhodes and marched to Constantinople, dragging with them their imperial nominee, Theodosius. Anastasius fled and shut himself up in Nicaea, hoping for the best. Constantinople was betrayed to Theodosius, who offered Anastasius his life if he surrendered. Agreeing, Anastasius took holy vows, becoming a monk at a monastery in Thessalonica in 715.

But former emperors do not take their degradation lightly. In 719 he tried to regain his throne from the newest emperor, Leo, but though he had Bulgar aid, he was defeated outside the capital. This time there was no mercy for Anastasius, who was executed on Leo's order.

THEODOSIUS III

THE TAX COLLECTOR

NAME: Theodosios
BORN: Unknown
RULED: Emperor, 715–717
DIED: Unknown cause, Ephesus, Thrakesion, c. 754

THE OPSIKIONS, who were unhappy with Anastasius, decided that they would pick the next emperor. They selected a tax collector named Theodosius from the city of Adramytteion in Asia Minor, though he was so frightened at the idea that he ran away and hid in a nearby forest. However, the rebels were determined, carrying Theodosius into Constantinople and crowning him emperor.

Though filled with the best of intentions, Theodosius lacked the ability to rule an empire. Consequently, the next two years became chaotic as the Arabs penetrated deep into Anatolia, while the Bulgars pushed from the west. As things spiralled from bad to worse, Theodosius freely acknowledged his unfitness to reign, helped by the fact that the only capable general in the empire, Leo, had captured his son and was making his own play for the throne. Resigning the purple, Theodosius lived out his life as a clergyman, possibly becoming bishop of Ephesus, a position more suited to his talents.

LEO III

THE SARACEN-MINDED

NAME: Konon
BORN: Germanikeia, Anatolia, c. 685
RULED: Emperor, 717–741
DIED: Of natural causes, Constantinople, 741

A GENERAL OF OUTSTANDING ability, Leo became one of the most important of the 'middle period' Roman emperors. Both Justinian II and Anastasius II recognised his skill, appointing him general of the Anatolican *theme*. Hearing of Anastasius's fall, Leo used his province as a base to launch his bid for the empire, taking Constantinople in 717 and marching through the Golden Gate in a triumphal procession, one of the few traditions persisting from the empire's past.

Luckily for the empire, he arrived just in time. That year, the long-awaited Saracen siege of Constantinople began, with the city's survival due to Anastasius's preparations as well as Leo's military training and skill. The Arabs wore themselves out assaulting the walls of the city, as defeats on the waters, a harsh winter and the unexpected intervention of the Bulgars destroyed the majority of the eighty thousand troops gathered to sack Constantinople. So complete was their defeat—reinforced by Leo's victories later in his reign—that it would be another three hundred years before Islamic armies again seriously challenged the Roman Empire in the east.

Leo also commenced the next round of imperial reconstruction, strengthening the civil, legal and military arms of the state. Restoring army discipline and reorganising the *themes*, he encouraged settlers to move to the eastern provinces, reinvigorating areas of the empire recently depopulated by war. Abolishing serfdom, he introduced a new class of free tenants to work the land. The provinces would not see peasants and serfs again until that system was reintroduced by the Franks after Constantinople's conquest in 1204.

Roman law, like Latin, was no longer used in the empire. As the empire's borders now encompassed almost exclusively Greek-speaking peoples, Justinian's Latin laws were incomprehensible, forcing Leo to introduce a revised law code, the *Ecloga*, a Greek handbook outlining the empire's most important laws. The *Ecloga* no longer had any relationship to the old imperial laws and jurisprudence; rather, it was law based on interpretation of scripture, a religious legal framework that saw no need for a secular legal system based on precedent and interpretation of law. Now, the state's wellbeing depended on the union and harmony of the emperor and the patriarch. In this sense, the empire was now not so much a Roman Empire as a Christian Empire. However, if it were indeed a Christian Empire, what would happen if differences of doctrine and dogma arose between what the emperor declared and what the religious hierarchy believed? What would be the price of unity? Such questions began to surface when Leo III introduced legislation to ban the use of religious imagery, leading to what is known as the iconoclast controversy.

I am an Emperor and a priest.

LEO THE ISAURIAN

Iconoclasm (literally, the breaking of images) originated for two reasons. The first cause was Islam's proximity and the profound influence its prohibition of graven or painted images had on the empire's Asian provinces. The Muslims' accusation that Christians worshipped idols and images was one that Leo wanted to refute, and by doing so prevent the apostasy of Christians and their conversion to Islam. The second root cause was ongoing support in the east for Monophysite doctrine—since for the Monophysites Christ was only divine, he should not, indeed could not, be portrayed in any form, particularly one that represented him as a human being.

Leo was not always averse to holy images. During the siege of Constantinople there were regular processions taking an icon of the Virgin Mother around the walls of the beleaguered city. Yet by 726 the emperor had decided that the cause of the empire's ills, including some recent earthquakes, was God's anger at the breaking of the Second Commandment. So he ordered the removal of an enormous golden icon of Christ that surmounted the gate that led to the palace of the emperors, replacing it with an unadorned cross. The capital erupted in protest, while Greece elevated a usurper in response. This outcry forced Leo to tread more carefully; in 730 he made his next move, summoning a conclave that condemned iconolatry and replaced the patriarch with an iconoclastic nominee.

This time opposition centred in the west, as monks and clergy fled to Italy to preserve their precious relics and avoid arrest. The entire west refused to follow the edict, and the exarchate of Ravenna flared into revolt. The pope condemned the legislation outright, excommunicating emperor and patriarch. Leo tried to arrest the pope, but the fleet he sent foundered at sea. By the end of Leo's reign, the emperor had removed from the pope's jurisdiction the dioceses of Sicily, Calabria and Illyricum, as Ravenna became an isolated outpost under the ecclesiastical control of Rome and besieged by the Lombards, who took advantage of the Roman divisions to capture more imperial territory.

Leo's death in 741 left an empire that, while relatively free of external problems, had deep internal divisions, with the emperor focused on suppressing the iconodules. It saw the beginning of the final separation of the western half of the empire, which in the fullness of time would seek its own path forward with the elevation of a rival emperor.

TIBERIUS
JUMPED TO CONCLUSIONS

BIRTH NAME: Basileios Onomagolos
BORN: Unknown
RULED: Usurper, 718
DIED: Executed, Sicily, 718

DURING CONSTANTINOPLE'S fateful siege many were convinced that Leo III was doomed. In Sicily, news arrived that there had been massive reinforcements for the Arab besiegers and, thinking the emperor was as good as dead, the *strategos* of Sicily, Sergius, renounced his allegiance to Leo and nominated one of his officers, Basil, for the purple.

Renamed Tiberius, Basil was shocked to discover that Constantinople had not fallen; worse, Leo sent a reliable general, Paul the Patrician, to quell the revolt. When Paul

Byzantine Emperor Leo III the Isaurian

arrived in Sicily, the army declared its undying loyalty to Leo. Sergius fled to Benevenetum, while the unfortunate Tiberius literally lost his head.

COSMAS

DEFENDER OF ICONS

NAME: Cosmas
BORN: Unknown
RULED: Usurper, 727
DIED: Executed, Constantinople, 727

BY THE LATE 720s, Leo's excessive taxation and religious reforms were throwing the empire into ferment. Greece was where his changes were felt most keenly, and the province rebelled, elevating one of the commanders stationed there, Cosmas, to the position of emperor. The rebel army sailed towards Constantinople with the intent of overthrowing Leo, but it was no match for the imperial navy, which easily defeated it. After capturing Cosmas, Leo ordered his execution.

CONSTANTINE V

THE ICONOCLAST

NAME: Kōnstantinos
BORN: Constantinople, 718
RULED: Co-emperor, 720–741;
senior emperor, 741–775
DIED: Of fever, Strongylon,
Peloponnese, 775

THERE IS A CHARMING story about the infant Constantine V, son of Leo. As he was being baptised by the priest, he proceeded to defecate in the baptismal font, earning him the name 'Kopronymos'. Not a true story, unfortunately, but one that shows just how hated the emperor became over his one obsession—the abolition of religious imagery.

Constantine was a highly strung and nervous individual, suffering from bouts of depression and chronic ill health that would occasionally nearly incapacitate him. Nevertheless, he was implacable to his enemies, both external and internal, pursuing them with an energy that belied his physical imperfections.

> **He cannot be depicted. For what is depicted in one person, and he who circumscribes that person has plainly circumscribed the divine nature which is incapable of being circumscribed.**
>
> CONSTANTINE V KOPRONYMOS

He was not the natural soldier his father had been, but he was able to defend the empire with enormous skill, even enlarging it when possible. Targeting the Arabs, who were distracted by a civil war, Constantine invaded northern Syria and defeated them, while further attacks on Armenia and Mesopotamia increased pressure on the collapsing Umayyad Caliphate. The Ummayads' successors, the Abbasids of Baghdad, concluded a truce with the Romans, freeing Constantine to deal with the problems in the west. When the Bulgars attacked in the 750s, Constantine himself took the field, and in the course of nine campaigns he proceeded to deal death and ruin to them. Evolving into a master tactician and a superb leader of men, he routinely crushed the Bulgar armies sent against him, but he was not able to stop their incursions and he was still on campaign in 775 when he died from his chronic illnesses.

Such a man was deserving of the people's praise; he did not receive it, as he pushed the war on images to its extreme. While he shared the imperial throne with his father, he had been heavily involved in implementing Leo's limited iconoclastic laws. He detested what he saw as the people's stupidity and credulity; his subjects inevitably reciprocated his contempt. His obsession went way beyond the simple desire to remove pictorial representations of Christ: he was determined to crush any devotion to the Virgin Mother and the saints, forbidding the use of the term 'saint' when referring to churches or people. If a courtier uttered a religious exclamation, Constantine mocked and ridiculed him.

What pushed Constantine over the edge was the attempted usurpation of the throne in 741 by his brother-in-law, who promised an end to the attack on icons. Constantinople rejected Constantine, closing its gates on him, and all the icons believed to have been destroyed suddenly reappeared. This ingratitude and betrayal were to have a profound influence on Constantine once he retook the capital. Where his father trod carefully, he decided to push through or crash.

In 754 he convened a synod that formally declared as blasphemous any depiction of Christ; further, it forbade people to venerate or manufacture images of Mary or the saints. This council did not include representatives from Rome, Alexandria, Antioch or Jerusalem because of their opposition to iconoclasm.

The monks resisted the council's decree, and they bore the full brunt of Constantine's fury. There were extended persecutions during the 760s, when monks were blinded, burnt, had their noses amputated and were killed. Constantine appointed governors who fully participated in the repression of the monasteries and were sometimes quite sadistic. Yet for Constantine it was not just about religion. Mixed in with his prejudices was a perception that the monasteries were consuming the empire's wealth and manpower. With plague and warfare crippling the empire's capacity to sustain itself, it must have seemed criminal to Constantine to have such productive members of society locking themselves away, leaving regions dangerously underpopulated and the armed forces unable to find able-bodied men. Such considerations meant that the battle went from icon suppression to monastic suppression. It was a fight that would outlast Constantine.

Iconoclasm could not be enforced in the west, where the emperor's authority was nominal at best, and it contributed to the fact that there was little love there for the empire or its outpost at Ravenna. When Ravenna fell to the Lombards in 751, Rome was again independent of the empire, but also under imminent threat. Nevertheless, the popes refused to deal with Constantine, whom they regarded as a heretic, and they were forced to look elsewhere for protection—in this case to the Franks. The Franks swept down into Italy, crushing the Lombards and freeing the exarchate of Ravenna. Yet rather than return these dominions to Constantine, the Frankish king, Pepin, declared that they were under the direct control of the papacy. Thus were born the Papal States, rising from the ashes of the former imperial province.

Such an outcome, though insulting, would not have bothered Constantine too greatly; after all, there would be time enough to reclaim the former provinces later. However, what he did not foresee was the eventual elevation of a rival western emperor claiming dominion over the old provinces, one whose commitment to orthodoxy would force the west to relinquish its allegiance to the heretical emperors in the east. Very soon, two Augusti would again rule the world.

ARTABASDUS AND NICEPHORUS

BEWARE OF BROTHERS-IN-LAW

NAME(S): Artavasdos and Nikephoros
BORN: Unknown
RULED: Usurper and co-usurper, 742–743
DIED: Unknown

ARTABASDUS WAS STRATEGOS of the Armenian *theme*. Having given Leo his full support when Leo took the throne, he gained the emperor's daughter in marriage and a promotion to *kouropalatēs*, or major-domo, of the palace. On Leo's death, he took advantage of the unpopular iconoclast laws, as well as Constantine Kopronymos's absence, to launch his own bid for the throne.

Artabasdus mounted a surprise attack and entered the capital amid scenes of jubilation, where icons suddenly reappeared. Constantine fled to Amorium, where he set up a temporary court, and Artabasdus and his elder son, Nicephorus, were crowned co-emperors, declaring the iconoclast heresy over.

Having secured Constantinople, Artabasdus took his armies east to deal with the young and sickly Constantine, leaving Nicephorus to rule in the capital city. However, to everyone's surprise, Constantine demonstrated military abilities no one had suspected. Artabasdus and his younger son, Nicetas, were crushed in two battles, and Artabasdus found himself trapped in Constantinople. When another army under Nicetas was defeated, Artabasdus and his sons fled to Nicaea, but they were captured, blinded and forced to spend the rest of their lives in a monastery. In

EMPEROR AND CO-EMPEROR

A common feature of the imperial system as it developed at Constantinople from the seventh century onwards was the elevation of one or more of the emperor's sons as co-Augustus while their father still lived. Although this development stems from the introduction of the Tetrachy under Diocletian, it differed from the older Roman co-imperial tradition of the fourth and fifth centuries in a number respects. Firstly, the older tradition was primarily concerned with the administration of an empire that required the presence of two or more Augusti. Its development was driven by the need of the empire to respond to crises. The later version was not about the management of the provinces: it was about rank and prestige, about demonstrating the continuity of the ruling dynasty. It was also the mechanism by which a regent would rule when the individual who was supposed to be emperor was still too young to assume the position.

This new system differed from the older one in terms of authority. In the older imperial tradition, all the co-emperors exercised full power and *imperium* in their respective provinces. In Constantinople, although the theory still held, in practice the young co-emperor had no real power or authority. It all rested with his father as senior emperor, although the emperor was generally never termed as such. He, along with his sons, was crowned simply as emperor, although on occasion the senior emperor could be designated as *megas Basileus* and his co-emperors as *symbasileus*. The emperor's seniority was implied either through age, when the co-emperor was a minor, or because he was already the emperor when he crowned his colleague.

This elevation of the sons as emperors during their father's lifetime meant that the older imperial title of Caesar (in Greek, *kaisar*) soon lost its traditional meaning of indicating the successor to the emperor. Gradually, the title became an honorific one, usually restricted to members of the imperial family, although it could be granted to important members of the nobility and occasionally to foreigners (such as when Justinian II named Tervel, khan of the Bulgars, *kaisar* in 705).

a macabre postscript, Constantine later forced his sister to dig up her husband's bones and throw them into a common grave for criminals.

LEO IV

THE KHAZAR

NAME: Leōn
BORN: Constantinople, 750
RULED: Co-emperor, 751–775;
senior emperor, 775–780
DIED: Of fever, Strongylon, Thessaly, 780

LEO IV, CONSTANTINE Kopronymos's eldest son, was quite unlike his father. By nature indolent rather than fierce, he was also far more balanced, sharing only his father's ill health. From his barbarian mother, he gained the nickname 'The Khazar', a sign of contempt for his somewhat uncouth origins. Though he, too, was an iconoclast, his wife, Irene, was a committed iconophile, and she managed to temper Leo's natural inclinations. He still employed iconoclasts in positions of authority, but he also appointed monks as bishops and removed some of the harsher restrictions that had been imposed on the monasteries.

> **Was this what you swore to my father the Emperor upon the fearsome and pure mysteries of our faith?**
>
> LEO THE KHAZAR (to Irene, on discovering some icons under her pillow)

Early in his reign Leo survived a conspiracy to elevate one of his half-brothers, Nicephorus, to the throne. Leo took the precaution of forcing all five of his half-brothers to become monks.

It is suspected that Leo suffered from tuberculosis, and so it was not unexpected when he died at the age of thirty, though a rumour suggested that he became ill after daring to wear the crown of the Great Church, causing boils to appear on his head.

CONSTANTINE VI

MOTHER ISSUES

NAME: Kōnstantinos
BORN: Constantinople, 771
RULED: Co-emperor, 776–780;
sole emperor, 780–797
DIED: Unknown cause, Principo (Büyükada, Princes Islands), Sea of Marmara, c. 802

CONSTANTINE WAS TEN when his father, Leo IV, passed away, and two issues—the ongoing iconoclast conflict and his struggle for supremacy against his mother Irene—would dominate his reign. Not that the latter was much of a contest, given his weak and vacillating nature: his only hope lay in the support of those who rallied about him in opposition to Irene.

Given Irene's support of icons, it was inevitable that within weeks of Constantine's elevation there would be an iconoclast conspiracy to elevate one of his uncles to the throne. When it failed, the iconoclasts placed their hope in Constantine, waiting for him to achieve maturity before they struck at his mother. It was a vain hope.

Until he reached the age of eighteen, Irene dominated all aspects of her son's life, even his choice of bride. However, her decision in 790 to become the senior Augustus offended just about everyone. Constantine tried to remove her, but she struck first, imprisoning him. The army, mostly iconoclast, rallied around Constantine, who escaped from prison and overthrew Irene. The future was his, if only he had known how to take it.

Mother and son—Irene and Constantine VI

Within two years, he had disappointed all his supporters. The army was disgusted when he fled a battle against the Bulgars, abandoning the army to its fate. His worthless ministers advised him to reappoint Irene, and this antagonised the iconoclasts, who again turned to his uncle Nicephorus as a potential emperor. Though his uncle had no knowledge of the plot, Constantine (on orders from his mother) had Nicephorus's eyes ripped out and, as a precaution, had his four other uncles' tongues removed. Finally, when he also offended the monastic party by divorcing his wife on Irene's advice so that he could marry his mistress, his mother knew it was time to strike.

In 797 Constantine marched at the head of his troops to intercept a Saracen invasion of Anatolia, hoping to retrieve what remained of his reputation. Receiving faulty intelligence from Irene's spies that the enemy had withdrawn, Constantine returned to the capital only to discover the Saracens were still ravaging the empire. New accusations of cowardice were levelled at the emperor, and a party of soldiers attacked him while he was taking part in a procession. He managed to flee from Constantinople, but his mother's agents hunted him down. He was returned to the palace and taken to a private room, where, on Irene's orders, he was blinded and deposed. He spent the rest of his days in darkness and in exile on the island of Principo.

IRENE

THE MOTHER FROM HELL

NAME: Irene Sarantapechaina
BORN: Athens, Hellas, c. 752
RULED: Emperor, 797–802
DIED: Of natural causes, Lesbos, 803

MAN OR WOMAN, few could compete with the ambitious and duplicitous Irene, who schemed and maimed her way to the highest position in the land. Seeing herself as the equal of any man, she eschewed the title of Augusta: she was the Augustus of the Roman Empire.

Hailing from a noble Athenian family, Irene was elegant and beautiful. Nevertheless, as an iconophile she was a curious choice for Leo IV's wife. Her husband enthralled by her charms, she persuaded him to relax the iconoclast laws and upon his death assumed the regency for her young son, Constantine. Overturning decades of iconoclast legislation, she earned the undying enmity of the die-hard icon-haters. A purge of the army sparked rebellions throughout the empire, usually in favour of her brothers-in-law, who suffered mutilation at her hands.

During the regency, she sought to renew ties with Rome by convening another council to end the iconoclast controversy, and it should come as no surprise that the Seventh Ecumenical Council decreed that the veneration of icons was permissible. This victory only served to increase her desire for power, as well as her conviction that she alone was qualified to wield it. Only one thing stood in her way—her son, Constantine.

In 790 her plan to become the senior Augustus failed and she was banished for two years. Upon her return she spent the next five years plotting to bring down her son, finally succeeding in 797 when she blinded and exiled him. Such an act of callous brutality, carried out in the very room where she had given birth to him twenty-six years before, removed all legitimacy from her rule and blighted the remainder of her reign.

> **That which Leo the emperor had formerly cast down, Irene has re-erected here.**
>
> IRENE OF ATHENS (inscription over the icon of Christ on the Chalke Gate, Constantinople)

Resistance began almost immediately. Rumours that she had been responsible for the death of her infant grandson were followed by plots to elevate one of Leo IV's brothers, forcing Irene to grant extensive remission of taxes to gain popularity. As the Saracens overran Anatolia and the treasury rapidly emptied, people looked for some form of deliverance. Rumours that her eunuch advisors had recommended she marry the newly created western emperor only hastened her end. She was taken captive during a palace coup one night in October 802 and ended up on the island of Lesbos, occupying her time by spinning cloth until her death a year later.

Irene's reign, though brief, did have one lasting effect. The sight of a woman on the throne in Constantinople horrified the west, rupturing the last, tenuous lines of loyalty to the eastern emperors. Never before had the Roman world beheld a woman wielding the authority of the Caesars. Though queens were not unusual in the Greek east, the Latin west absolutely rejected the notion that a woman could be an emperor.

Refusing to recognise Irene, the pope declared the imperial throne vacant, and the western provinces turned towards the one man in Europe capable of wielding power across the Roman *imperium*—the king of the Franks, Charles, or as he became known to history, Charlemagne. His elevation as western emperor begins a new chapter in the history of the Roman Empire, taking the Roman name and ideal to new heights and in a very different direction. A new world had begun, and the empire would never be the same.

RESTORATION AND RENEWAL
(802–1028)

The dignity of Charlemagne, the length of his reign, the prosperity of his arms, the vigour of his government, and the reverence of distant nations, distinguish him from the royal crowd; and Europe dates a new era from his restoration of the Western empire. That empire was not unworthy of its title; and some of the fairest kingdoms of Europe were the patrimony or conquest of a prince, who reigned at the same time in France, Spain, Italy, Germany, and Hungary.

EDWARD GIBBON
The Decline and Fall of the Roman Empire, 1880

FOLLOWING PAGE: Charlemagne is received at Paderborn, Germany

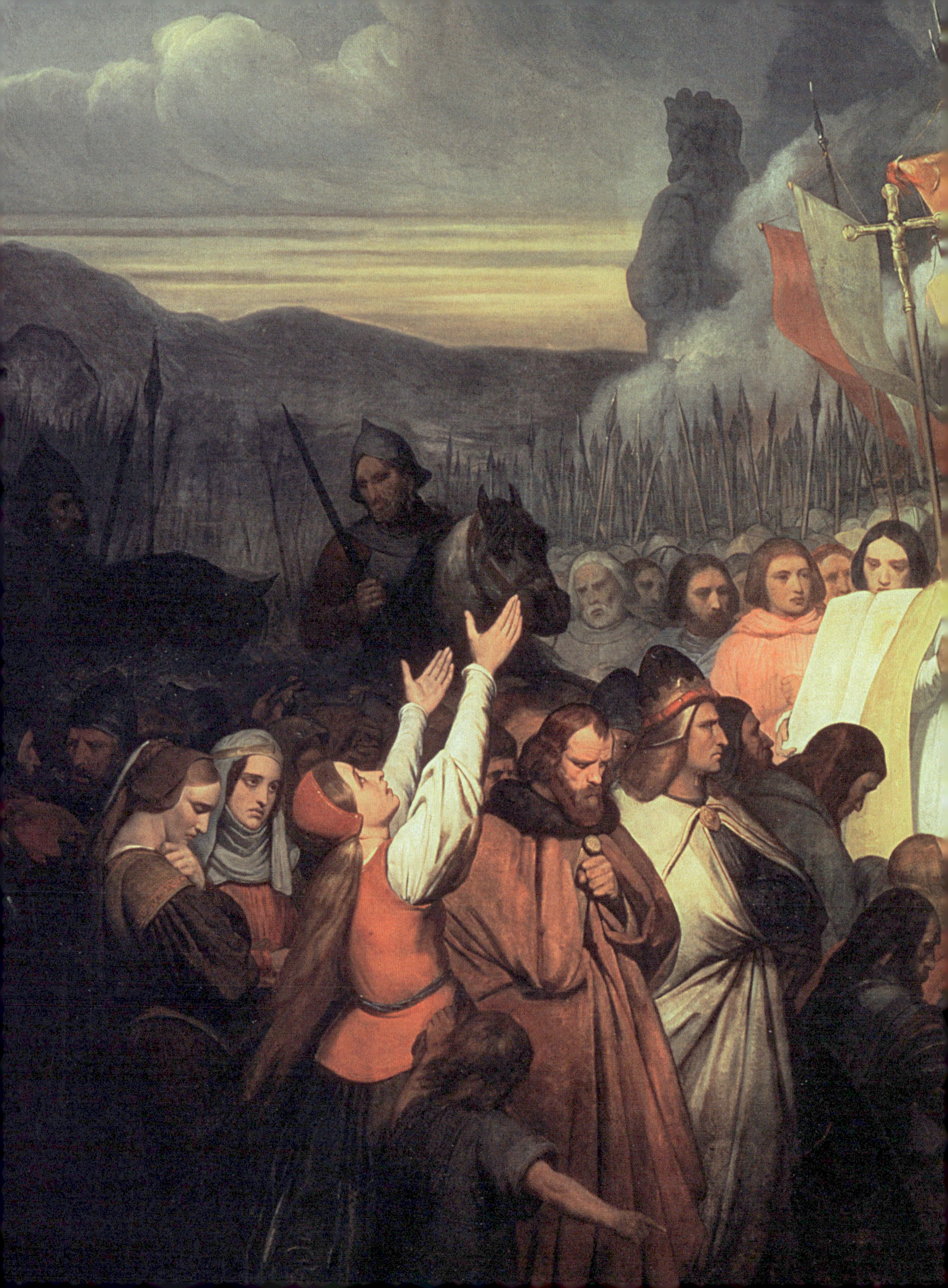

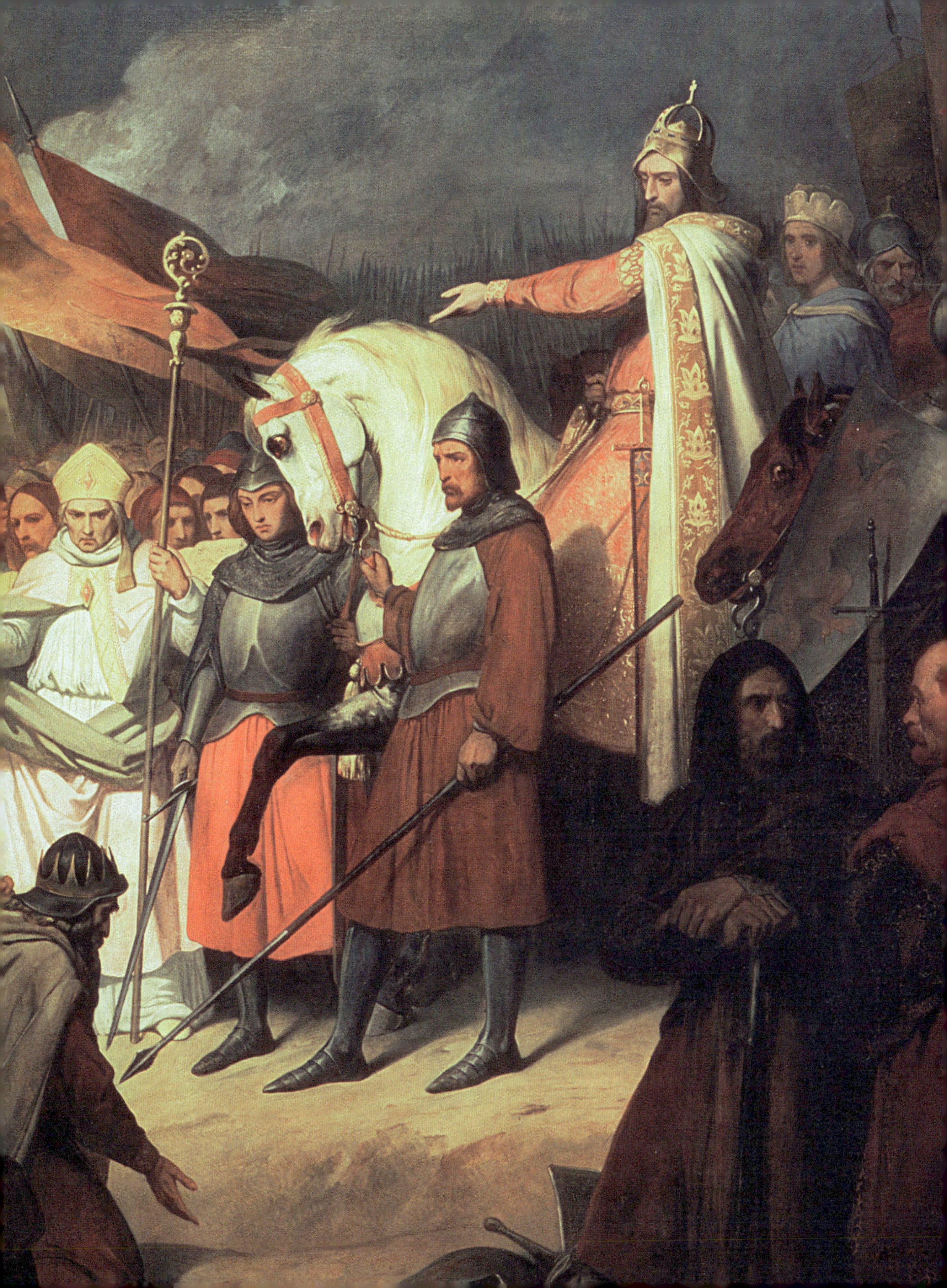

THE WESTERN EMPERORS

CHARLES I 'CHARLEMAGNE'

A NEW WESTERN EMPEROR

NAME: Karl
BORN: Herstal, Francia, 742
RULED: Emperor, 800–814
DIED: Of pleurisy, Aachen, Francia, 814

AFTER JULIUS NEPOS'S DEATH in 480 the provinces of Gaul, Illyricum and Italy all professed their continued allegiance to the empire. Though Rome returned to the imperial bosom, Gaul passed into the hands of the Franks. Their kings acknowledged the overlordship of the Eastern emperors, and in return were granted the title of Patrician of the Romans, with the authority to rule Gaul in the emperor's name. By 771 this title belonged to Charles, the newest of the Frankish kings.

The man who became the first Western emperor in three hundred years was tall, fair-haired and majestic. Courteous and easygoing, Charles was a man of dynamic energy and intense charisma. This fearsome warrior spent most of his reign engaging in warfare, determined to expand his realm to the widest possible extent. His father, Pepin III, had taken the kingdom, which roughly corresponded to the provinces of Gaul as well as Upper and Lower Germania on the right bank of the Rhine, from the Merovingian kings. Charles ascended the throne in 768 along with his brother, whose premature death in 771 left Charles in sole charge. His first important campaign was the conquest of Lombardy in 774.

> **By the King of Heaven, I take no account of your noble birth and your fine looks, though others may admire you for them.**
>
> CHARLEMAGNE

The Franks had become the papacy's protector when the fall of Ravenna in 751 exposed Rome to the fury of the Lombards. Though Charles's father had crushed the Lombards, they were once again encroaching on the former exarchate of Ravenna that the Franks had handed to the papacy. Pope Adrian I asked Charles for assistance and Charles marched into Italy and overthrew the northern Lombard kingdoms, adding half of Italy to his realm.

Charles then focused on his eastern borders, spending his youth and energy in a twenty-five-year war against the Saxons. Over eleven campaigns, highlighted by numerous victories and blood-chilling massacres, he imposed his will upon an undisciplined and implacable enemy. In between these campaigns, he extended his kingdom to the Ebro River in Spain at the expense of the Moors, and reclaimed the Roman province of Pannonia from the Avars and Huns who had settled there and fought in southern Italy against the Roman Empire. By 799 he was able to rest, but his once fair hair had by this time turned snow white.

The year 800 was momentous for Charles and the empire, as Pope Leo III fled Rome after an uprising and sought his protector's help. Returning to Rome with Leo, Charles restored him to the throne of St Peter; in gratitude, Leo crowned him Emperor of the Romans, an act ratified by the venerable Roman Senate. By all

Charlemagne at his court c. 800

THE *FILIOQUE* CLAUSE AND THE GREAT SCHISM

By the beginning of the eleventh century, the increasing tensions between the eastern and western halves of the old empire, though occasionally patched over, were about to erupt into open conflict. The gradual disappearance of imperial authority in the west, the language barrier between the Greek east and Latin west, and the emergence of the medieval papacy, which claimed universal jurisdiction over all churches, steadily drove the two regions in different directions.

For the west, the major point of contention was the east's regular lapses into heresy and the intervention of the emperor in promoting these errors. Whether it was Arianism, Monophysitism or Monothelitism, by the year 800 the popes had had enough, and the century-long iconoclast controversy was the last straw. Their solution was to elevate an emperor in the west, a Catholic emperor in the shape of Charlemagne. In the east, concerns were primarily about papal supremacy and the enforcing of the Latin customs in southern Italy, which was nominally under the authority of the eastern emperor. But for the Orthodox Church, the issue that was to bring everything to a head was the debate over the *filioque*.

The *filioque* is an addition to the authorised Nicene Creed that discusses the procession of the Holy Spirit from God. In the original Creed, the Holy Spirit is described as proceeding from God the Father alone. This was the Orthodox position. In the west, Charlemagne's court introduced the *filioque* clause, which stated that the Holy Spirit proceeds from both God the Father and God the Son. Although the popes originally refused to accept this addition, by the eleventh century, they had adopted it and insisted that it be used by the whole church.

In 1054 a delegation was sent from Rome to Constantinople to settle the matter. Centuries of antagonism erupted when two bigoted old men, Michael Cerularius, patriarch of Constantinople, and Cardinal Humbert, the papal legate, clashed over simple matters of protocol and civility. Cerularius was a man who detested and was suspicious of the Catholics, and he hated the notion of papal supremacy, while Humbert was bigoted, opinionated and fanatically anti–Eastern Orthodox. The end result was that both men excommunicated the other, resulting in the Great Schism that still divides the Catholic west and the Orthodox east a thousand years later. Although the excommunications were directed personally at the offending individuals, not at the respective churches, it did not matter. It gave the churches the excuse they needed to exercise complete authority over their spheres of influence, without interference by the other. Church unity was sacrificed on the altar of political expediency, and Christendom has haemorrhaged ever since.

accounts, this gift surprised Charles: while he was kneeling in prayer in St Peter's Basilica, the pope crowned him with the jewel-encrusted diadem that Charles had somehow failed to notice sitting on the altar. This papal coronation was an innovation, as traditionally only the Senate or army could acclaim an emperor, but as the patriarchs of Constantinople had been crowning Eastern emperors for centuries, this was merely an extension of the privileges granted to the church.

However it happened, Charles was now a Roman emperor—the only Roman emperor according to the west, which rejected Irene's claims to be an emperor in her own right. While the east dismissed Charles as an uncouth barbarian, not worthy of serving in the imperial court, let alone ruling the empire, his vigour and military exploits showed him to be a worthy successor of the Caesars. Arrogantly, he offered to marry Irene and reunite the two halves of the empire, but during negotiations Irene was dispatched to a monastery. Her successor, Nicephorus I, though happy to recognise Charles's title in 803, strove to maintain two separate states within the one *imperium*.

Charles's final years saw the first appearance of the Vikings in the empire, but it was clear that the emperor was no longer capable of marching at the head of his army, especially as the deaths within a year of each other of two of his sons, Pepin and Charles, had sapped his enthusiasm for reigning. To ensure the succession, he elevated his surviving son, Louis, to the purple in 813, not long before he died in January of 814.

Charles's achievements were impressive, including the reunification of many of the former western provinces of the empire (Pannonia, Illyricum, Gaul, parts of Spain and Italy) together with the addition of new lands in upper and eastern Germany. He was the first ruler in the west for many years to undertake monetary reform and, though illiterate, he was also a great patron of education, founding schools throughout the empire, purchasing books and educating his sons with the best teachers available. In religious music, writing, the arts and architecture, his kingdom was the first in western Europe to resurrect something, however dim, of Roman civilisation. Occasionally his attempts to appear learned would backfire—one such instance was his insistence on the insertion into the Nicene Creed of the *filioque* clause, which the popes initially rejected. Yet he fully merited the name that posterity bestowed on him—Charlemagne, or Charles the Great.

LOUIS I
THE PIOUS

NAME: Louis
BORN: Chasseneuil, Francia, 778
RULED: Emperor, 813–833 and 834–840
DIED: Of natural causes,
Ingelheim am Rhein, Francia, 840

LOUIS'S REIGN IS a melancholy tale of rebellion, civil war and family discord, as Charlemagne's successors fought for supremacy. Louis was a gentle man, the least ruthless of Charlemagne's sons, and he lacked his father's panache for warfare and statecraft. With the empire surrounded by enemies—Normans to the north, Bulgars to the east and Saracens in Spain—it was unfortunate that family struggles consumed his energies.

His empire had one missing chunk—Italy, which Charlemagne had passed to his bastard son Bernard. Bernard tried unsuccessfully to overthrow his half-brother, and in retaliation Louis put his eyes out, causing his death. Guilt stricken and accused of murder by a clergy who resented his clerical reforms, Louis performed penance before the church and the people and received absolution, but he had now shown his weakness to his most determined rivals—his sons.

In 817 an accident almost claimed Louis's life. Concerned for the future, he divided his realm between his sons, proclaiming them kings of various parts of the empire. In this, he was following a Frankish custom where sons split their father's inheritance. Charlemagne had avoided doing this, and in the case of Louis it plunged the empire into a series of civil wars. These were triggered when another son was born to him and he wanted to take back territory to provide for him. His elder sons, led by Lothair, rebelled in 830 and again in 833, protesting against their stepmother's interference. Louis was reluctant to challenge Lothair, who had the pope's support, and he was soon abandoned by his army and deposed as emperor, at Lothair's request, by a synod of bishops. However, discord between his sons saw Louis restored to the imperial throne, with the church's consent.

Louis's love for his children meant he was unable or unwilling to punish his tormentors. Further concessions to the eldest and youngest saw a final rebellion by another son in 839. While marching with his troops to put down the revolt, he was struck down by a serious illness. He declared Lothair to be his imperial successor, the ruler of a divided empire.

LOTHAIR I

NO ONE STANDS IN MY WAY

NAME: Lothar
BORN: Place unknown, 795
RULED: Co-emperor, 817–831;
senior emperor, 840–855
DIED: Of natural causes,
Prüm, Middle Francia, 855

LOTHAIR INHERITED Charlemagne's ruthless ambition but not his ability to inspire loyalty. Though his father crowned him co-emperor early in his reign, he showed his ingratitude by being the chief instigator of the rebellions against Louis. Impatient and consumed by the need to preserve his inheritance as eldest son, he had the pope crown him emperor in Rome in 823.

Unfortunately, he lacked that killer instinct needed to achieve his aims. He always acted in concert with his two brothers, but they were never willing to go as far as he was prepared to. His first rebellion saw him fight the partitioning of the empire in favour of his half-brother, Charles. Louis I fled, but a withdrawal of fraternal support saw Lothair make terms with his father, who downgraded him from the rank of emperor. Lothair travelled to Italy and again rebelled, this time obtaining papal support before capturing his father. He used psychological and physical abuse to try to force Louis to renounce the crown, but Louis refused to crack. Meanwhile, his brothers, feeling that Lothair was becoming too powerful, decided to side with their father, and so Lothair gave in.

His next chance was in 840: learning of Louis's death, he attempted to seize those parts of the empire inherited by his brothers. Civil war erupted, with Lothair defeated in 841 at a battle involving 100,000 men. He capitulated and divided the empire, losing Francia forever. His imperial territory now encompassed just Germany, Switzerland and Italy.

Lothair's remaining years saw him come to terms with his diminished empire. After dividing his lands between his three sons, he abdicated the throne in 855, only days before he died in a monastery, trying to expiate his sins.

LOUIS II

SARACEN HUNTER

NAME: Louis (The Younger)
BORN: Place unknown, 825
RULED: Co-emperor, 850–855;
sole emperor, 855–875
DIED: Of natural causes, Ghedi, Italy, 875

LOUIS WAS CONTENT with his reduced patrimony of Italy, which he received while his father, Lothair, was still alive, though he did eventually also gain Alsace and parts of Provence. A man of energy and few vices, he lacked his father's devouring ambition and focused on fighting the Saracens, who had conquered Sicily and were ravaging the Italian coast. This concern for Italy continued when he became sole emperor on his father's death, and in 871 he threw the Saracens out of Bari with help from the Eastern emperor, Basil I.

Louis's rule was not without problems. Simmering tensions between the heirs of Charlemagne consumed much of his attention, while Pope Nicholas I, keen to demonstrate the pope's superiority over the emperor, forced Louis to walk before Nicholas's horse, leading it while the pope rode. It was a humiliating act of submission, one that clearly showed the emperor's powerlessness. That imperial weakness was also evident during Louis's campaigns against the Saracens, when he was captured in Beneveneto by his Lombard vassal, who held him for some weeks. In the face of further Saracen incursions, Louis was released, on condition that he swore not to retaliate. Once he gained his freedom, he had the pope release him from that oath, but ill health and death prevented his vengeance.

CHARLES II

THE BALD

NAME: Karl
BORN: Frankfurt am Main, Francia, 823
RULED: Emperor, 875–877
DIED: Poisoned, Brides-les-Bains, Francia, 875

LOUIS II LEFT NO MALE HEIR, beginning a furious competition between his surviving uncles for the vacant imperial crown. It was to Charles, the youngest son of Louis I and Lothair's detested half-brother, that the imperial prize finally fell, when he marched into Italy and secured Pope John VIII's approval.

> **What separates a Scot from a sot?**
>
> CHARLES THE BALD (having a joke with John the Scot, the Irish theologian)

Devious, like most of Charlemagne's descendants, Charles fought vigorously to secure the throne of West Francia after the civil war that saw Lothair's failure to reunite the empire. He was surrounded by ambitious and untrustworthy relatives, and his thirty-year reign was a

Charles the Bald seated on his throne

constant struggle against his half-brother Louis, king of East Francia, not to mention disaffected nobles, rebellious vassals and Vikings, who were ravaging the north.

Once he gained the imperial throne, Charles tried to establish his claim on German Lorraine, which his nephew Louis had inherited. Marching north, he unexpectedly lost Italy to another nephew, Carloman, who assumed the title of king of Italy. Charles died soon after, reportedly of poison.

CHARLES III
THE FAT

NAME: Karl
BORN: Bavaria, East Francia, 839
RULED: Emperor, 881–888
DIED: Of illness, Reichenau Island, East Francia, 888

FOAMING AT THE MOUTH in church and so being accused of demonic possession is not a good way to begin a career, as Charles the Fat discovered. This unfortunate incident in his youth coloured everyone's attitude towards him and fuelled the impression he was unable to control anything, as his constant illnesses saw him focus on religion rather than politics.

As Louis I's grandson, he was in the right place at the right time. Although he was the youngest son of

Norman attack on Paris led by Rollo in 885, which cost Charles III his crown

Louis the German, the first king of East Francia, deaths in the imperial line meant that France, Germany and Italy—almost all Charlemagne's mighty empire—came into his possession without him having to lift a finger. Yet when the pope crowned him in 881, he entrusted the empire to a feeble individual, ill equipped to deal with the Viking threat.

Under Viking siege in 885, Paris desperately called on Charles for help. He marched up at the head of his troops but refused to give battle, instead purchasing a Viking withdrawal with a hefty tribute. When he returned to East Francia, he found the empire in uproar over his craven actions, and by 887 the West and East Francians had renounced their allegiance to him and elected their own kings from Charlemagne's other descendants. He retained the imperial crown but ruled Italy only with the support of his nephew, the new king of East Francia, and was dead the following year.

GUY

FIGHTING FOR THE THRONE

NAME: Guido of Spoleto
BORN: Unknown
RULED: Emperor, 891–894
DIED: Of illness, Taro River, Italy, 894

THE AFFAIRS OF THE EMPIRE began to resemble those of a petty state as the crown passed to Duke Guy of Spoleto in 891. The duchy of Spoleto, recently enlarged by Guy, was a state in central Italy used by the Franks as a buffer against the Eastern Empire as well as the Saracens. As his mother was Charlemagne's granddaughter, Guy had hopes of acquiring the West Francian throne following Charles the Fat's deposition. He did not succeed but he had better luck elsewhere, first obtaining the Italian crown by defeating the current king, Berengar of Friuli, in 889 and then being given the imperial crown by Pope Stephen VI, an enthusiastic supporter who described Guy as his only son.

Like all his cousins, Guy was preoccupied with Frankish politics, as rulers and popes continually intrigued against each other. Pope Formosus, the new pope, was fearful of Guy's interference in the Papal States and so gave support to the German king Arnulf of Carinthia. By the time Guy died in 894, he was fighting Berengar as well as Arnulf for control of the Italian peninsula.

LAMBERT

BRING OUT YOUR DEAD

NAME: Lambert of Spoleto
BORN: San Rufino, Italy, c. 880
RULED: Co-emperor, 892–894;
sole emperor, 894–898)
DIED: Falling off his horse, Marengo, Italy, 898

DESPITE HIS YOUTH, Lambert was a fearsome adversary, determined to wrest the empire from those who opposed him. His father, Guy, forced Pope Formosus to crown Lambert co-emperor, though Formosus asked King Arnulf of Carinthia to save him from them. Guy's death made Lambert sole emperor under the tutelage of his mother, who detested the Germans.

Lambert was forced out of Rome in 896 when Formosus crowned Arnulf emperor, and he never forgave the insult. Upon Arnulf's retreat, Lambert approached Rome, only to discover Formosus had died. Determined to have his revenge, he ordered the exhumation of the body. In 897 he put the corpse on trial and, finding it guilty, had it stripped of its papal robes, mutilated and cast into the Tiber. Lambert was still trying to impose order on other rebellious Italian principalities when he died on a hunting trip in 898, throwing the Western Empire into chaos.

ARNULF

WARRIOR KING

NAME: Arnulf von Kärnten
BORN: Carantania, c. 850
RULED: Emperor, 896–899
DIED: Of a stroke, Bavaria, 899

ARNULF WAS THE bastard son of Carloman, Charles III's brother, who bequeathed to Arnulf the duchy of Carinthia. The East Francian nobility compared this successful warrior favourably with Charles III, whose humiliation at the hands of the Vikings was the last straw, and Arnulf took advantage of the situation. Marching into East Francia he deposed Charles, who bitterly reproached his nephew.

> Up and at them, soldiers!
> You see the criminals before you.
> I will get from my horse and carry
> the flag before you. After me!
>
> ARNULF OF CARINTHIA

Arnulf ignored all criticism and his acclamation as king in East Francia went unopposed. He took to the field, crushing an invading Viking army, enhancing his reputation and bringing himself to Pope Formosus's attention. The pope, afraid of the emperors Guy and Lambert and trapped in Rome, offered the imperial crown to Arnulf, who marched into Italy to free him. In 896 Formosus crowned Arnulf emperor, and he went on the attack, forcing Lambert back towards his duchy of Spoleto. Victory was within reach when Arnulf suffered a stroke that left him partially paralysed. Unable to continue, he returned to his German territories where he lingered, frustrated and impotent for three years, until his death.

LOUIS III

THE BLIND

NAME: Louis
BORN: Provence, 880
RULED: Emperor, 901–905
DIED: Of natural causes, Vienne, Provence, 929

IN A TIME OF DYNASTIC chaos, the last thing the divided Italians needed was for the Magyars of Pannonia to uproot themselves in 900 and fall upon them. Looking for a saviour to rescue them, the Italian nobles chose Louis, king of Provence.

Another petty Frankish king descended from Charlemagne through his mother, Louis had been successful against the Saracens in Provence, and so many hoped that he would repeat his success against the Magyars. There was just one problem: Italy already had a king—Berengar, who had attained the position on the death of Charles III. His defeat by the Magyars had triggered the SOS to Louis, and he quickly fled to Germany to avoid Louis's approach. Settling affairs in northern Italy, Louis was in Rome by 901 to receive the imperial title from the pope.

However, Berengar soon returned to Italy with fresh troops, defeating Louis in 902, but sparing his life on condition that Louis not set foot in Italy again. The emperor agreed, returning to Provence where he stayed until 905, when a powerful Italian noble invited him to invade Italy. He was briefly successful but Berengar soon had him seeking sanctuary in a church, before he was dragged out, forced to abdicate as emperor and then had his eyes gouged out to ensure that he would not trouble Berengar ever again.

Louis was led back to Provence and remained nominally king, although Hugh, count of Arles, exercised all royal power as Louis languished in darkness before dying in obscurity in 929.

BERENGAR

EASILY THWARTED

NAME: Berengario of Friuli
BORN: Cividale, Italy, 845
RULED: Emperor, 915–924
DIED: Murdered, Verona, Italy, 924

BERENGAR WAS YET another prince descended from Charlemagne through the female line, and he inherited the March of Friuli at the age of thirty. He saw this as a stepping-stone to greater things, especially with the overthrow of Charles III in 887. Failing to become king of West Francia, he successfully asserted his claim to the Italian throne upon Charles's death.

All too quickly, Berengar was fighting to keep the throne as Guy of Spoleto contested it, but with Arnulf of Carinthia's help Berengar was confirmed as king of Italy, although this remained a side issue as Guy, Lambert and Arnulf struggled to be Western Emperor. Though Berengar was eventually dragged into the mess, he managed to outlive his rivals, and by 900 was again the undisputed ruler of Italy.

> We reject the barbaric, surreptitiously obtained anointing of Berengar.
>
> THE COUNCIL OF ROME (898)

However, when the Magyars invaded, he was unable to stop them and fled to East Francia. Louis of Provence came to the rescue of Italy and was made emperor, making this the fourth time the popes had overlooked Berengar for the honour. Berengar returned and, despite his relative lack of military ability, successfully drove Louis out of Italy in 902, and he again prevailed when Louis returned in 905.

Berengar was desperate to become emperor, but the popes made him wait ten long years, making it clear exactly what they thought of him and his abilities. However, increasing pressure from the Saracens gave him his opportunity. He promised to defeat them and, in return, Pope John X crowned him emperor in Rome, amid splendour and rejoicing. Yet despite the alliance, it was not the emperor but the pope who led the armies.

The rest of his reign saw Berengar dealing with the Magyar problem, but his policy of buying them off, as well as his obvious nepotism, saw his popularity slide. Turning on him, the Italian nobles asked Rudolph of Upper Burgundy to take the Italian throne. A defeated Berengar fled to Verona, where his own troops dethroned and killed him.

OTTO I THE GREAT

CHURCH REFORMER

NAME: Otto von Sachsen
BORN: Place unknown, 912
RULED: Emperor, 962–973
DIED: Of natural causes, Memleben, Germany, 973

WITH BERENGAR'S DEATH, the western provinces fell into chaos, constantly attacked by the Magyars and distracted by the rivalries of petty princes. Forty years would pass before one arose with the ability to re-establish the Western Empire—Otto.

Otto, king of Germany (formerly East Francia), had the blood of emperors running through his veins. Descended from Louis I and Arnulf via his grandparents, he was tall and possessed a commanding presence. Though impulsive and violent when aroused, he was generous to his friends and enemies. His father defeated the Magyars, but at the cost of building up the power of the nobility, who rebelled when Otto took the throne. Not until 942, after six years of fighting, was his position secure, whereupon he inflicted a humiliating punishment in the form of the *Harnescar*, forcing each of the rebels to walk for almost ten kilometres (six miles), carrying a dog upon their shoulders.

Subsequent victories over France, Denmark, Bohemia and the Magyars saw Otto turn his eye towards an even greater prize—the Italian provinces. Taking advantage of the chronic chaos in the peninsula, he married Adelaide, heir to the Italian throne (a result of her being the daughter, daughter-in-law and widow of the last three kings of Italy), and in 951 marched south to claim the throne from a usurper, Berengar of Ivrea. Forced to return home to deal with a rebellion instigated by his son, Liudolf, Otto confirmed Berengar's title, but on condition that he became Otto's vassal. This arrangement continued until Berengar invaded the Papal States, causing Pope John XII to ask for Otto's aid. Marching into Italy in 962, Otto deposed Berengar, and in gratitude the pope crowned Otto Roman emperor, setting the stage for a new conflict, this time between emperor and pope.

> **It is better to die in battle than to live shamefully in slavery.**
>
> OTTO THE GREAT

The origins of the conflict lay in Otto's need to curb the power of the nobility. To do so, he planned to control the only organisation that had the necessary resources and structures to withstand the nobles—the church. In pursuit of this vision, of a theocratic imperial power, Otto began conducting royal investitures of bishops and abbots to gain their spiritual and temporal allegiance, essentially making them his vassals. He provided the bishoprics and abbeys with vast tracts of land, and because he personally appointed the higher clergy, the upper ranks of the German church became virtually part of the imperial bureaucracy. As landowners dependent upon the king, they became the perfect counterbalance to the nobles.

By these actions, Otto was not subjugating the church to the state so much as making the church political. The clergy were the king's officials first, and their membership of an ecclesiastical order came a distant second. As emperor, he believed he had absolute control over the church, with even the pope being his vassal, meaning the German clergy could not divide their loyalty between pope and emperor.

Of course, Pope John XII did not see it quite that way, and for the next six years papal rebellions consumed Otto's energies. John XII quickly contacted the Magyars and the Eastern emperor to help him overthrow Otto, who responded by convening a synod of bishops and deposing John XII in 963. The Romans drove out Otto's nominee, Leo VIII, when Otto returned to Germany, forcing him to return to reinstate Leo. They then renounced their allegiance to the emperor and, declaring their intent to revive the ancient Roman Republic, forced out Leo's successor, John XIII.

Otto's vengeance was swift. Returning to the empire's ancient capital, he had John XIII reinstated in the Lateran Palace, before pronouncing judgement on the guilty. He scourged and jailed the city prefect after making him ride naked on a donkey. He drove the consuls into exile and hanged the tribunes, while killing or banishing many others. Otto then made the Romans promise to resurrect the custom of requiring imperial authorisation to elect a pope, while conceding that the King of the Romans (king of Germany) could not call himself a Roman emperor unless he received the imperial crown from the pope.

The pinnacle of Otto's career came in 972 when—after a brief war (sparked by the sons of Berengar being guests at the court of the Eastern emperor) against the Eastern Empire in southern Italy—the Eastern emperor, John I Tzimisces, recognised Otto's right to call himself Roman emperor in the west. Yet within a year Otto was dead, mourned by the Germans, unloved by the Italians. From Otto's reign onwards, German kings wore the purple of the Caesars, and the Romans acknowledged emperors who were strangers to their country and customs, and

Otto I and his victory over the Magyars at the battle of Lechfeld, 955

whose brief sojourns in Italy generated no loyalty between the emperor and his people. The German nobles elected the king-emperor, but his imperial crowning could only happen at the pope's hand, a division that sowed the seeds of a conflict that would destabilise the Western Roman Empire.

OTTO II

THE RED

NAME: Otto
BORN: Place unknown, 955
RULED: Co-emperor, 967–973;
sole emperor, 973–983
DIED: Of unknown causes, Rome, 983

A WELL-EDUCATED BRUTE, Otto II received the imperial crown during his father's occupation of Rome in 967, where he received first-hand experience of how to treat the untrustworthy Italians. His admirers claimed that his nickname of The Red stemmed from his reddish complexion; his enemies said that he earned it after inviting his Roman enemies to a party and butchering his defenceless guests.

Like his father, Otto had to put down rebellions. He dealt first with his cousin, Henry, duke of Bavaria, before dealing with a French annexation of Lorraine. Invading France, he took his armies to the very walls of Paris and, though he was driven back and defeated, he did regain control of the disputed territory.

> I have lost the best of my kingdom,
> and stung with sorrow and pain
> I will no more tread the land nor see
> the friends of the dead.
>
> OTTO THE RED

Although he was married to a niece of Emperor John I Tzimisces, relations with the Eastern Empire were not good, especially after he invaded southern Italy. Unable to deal with this unexpected attack, Tzimisces called on Saracen help to defeat Otto's forces and, in 982, they wiped out the German army. Otto just managed to escape the field of battle and fled on a Greek ship, but the captain was loath to release him once he discovered who he was, and so Otto was forced to jump overboard and swim ashore. This defeat allowed the Eastern Empire to strengthen its position in southern Italy as Otto made extensive preparations to avenge his defeat. He travelled as far as Rome before dying unexpectedly in 983.

OTTO III

DREAMS OF EMPIRE

NAME: Otto
BORN: Kessel (near Goch), Lorraine, 980
RULED: Emperor, 996–1002
DIED: Of malaria, Paterno
(near Civita Castellana), Italy, 1002

THE EMPIRE OF the Caesars was now in the hands of the mother and grandmother of Otto II's four-year-old son, Otto III. Though Henry of Bavaria quickly abducted Otto to push his own imperial claim, this time the other great dukes did not follow him and he had to back down.

Immersed in Greek and Roman culture, Otto III spoke three languages, becoming so learned that as a child he was described as the Wonder of the World. To him the empire was Roman, and he ended up despising the rough Germans who were his chief subjects. His dreams were of an idealised empire and a perfect church. Rome, not Aachen, was the centre of his empire, and Italy the focus of his ambitions.

He eagerly accepted Pope John XV's invitation in 996 to come to Rome and receive the imperial crown. His mother's influence was clearly visible in his court ceremonials and the many names and customs he introduced from Constantinople. Planning to restore the Roman Senate and consulate, and revive the office of patrician, which by the tenth century had been transformed from a social class to a leadership position, he began calling himself the 'consul of the Roman senate and people'. Such actions disturbed Germany's nobility, who were concerned about Otto's increasingly erratic behaviour. Once, while visiting Charlemagne's tomb, he opened the great vault to discover the emperor still sitting on his throne, exactly as he had been buried centuries before, minus his nose. Prostrating himself before the dead emperor, he ordered a golden nose be placed on Charlemagne's face before he took a tooth from his hero's mouth as a relic.

Though Otto loved Rome, it had no great love for him. In 1001 he was driven from Rome after he showed leniency towards the town of Tibur, which had rebelled, angering the Roman citizens who had wanted their old rival destroyed. He was returning with a new German army to reconquer his capital when he died. The mundane reason for his death was malaria; the more sensational explanation was poisoning by the widow of a leading Roman citizen Otto had beheaded.

HENRY II

THE CHASTE

NAME: Heinrich of Bavaria
BORN: Abbach, Bavaria, 973
RULED: Emperor, 1014–1024
DIED: Of natural causes, Göttingen, Saxony, 1024

HENRY, FIRST ROMAN EMPEROR but second German king of that name, was a man surrounded by problems, new and old. His newest foes were the Poles, whose annexation of Bohemia in 1004 triggered a fourteen-year conflict that saw the Polish king keep much of his conquests in return for becoming Henry's vassal. The old problem was the troublesome Italian kingdom.

When Otto III died childless in 1002, the Germans crowned his cousin, Henry, while the Italian nobles and bishops elected their own king—Arduin of Ivrea. To receive the imperial crown, Henry needed to be in possession of the Italian kingdom. He marched into Italy, Arduin's army fled before the advancing Germans, and Henry was crowned king of Italy in the city of Pavia in 1004.

> **Best of fathers, you have done this to teach me most practically how I ought to rule.**
>
> HENRY THE CHASTE (to Pope Benedict VIII)

His reign got off to an inauspicious start when a fire started after fighting broke out between Henry's troops and Arduin's supporters. As Pavia burned, Henry had to leap from a palace window to save himself, injuring his leg so that he limped for the rest of his life. These conflicts with Arduin and his supporters continued for years—usually occurring when Henry had been forced to return to Germany—even after Henry was crowned Emperor of the Romans in 1014 and King of the Romans the following year.

Italy proved to be an ongoing distraction. In 1021 the pope asked Henry to deal with the expanding power of the Eastern Empire in Italy's south. Campaigning with the assistance of Norman mercenaries, he was forced to abandon his plans when the plague struck, and he died before he could continue the fight.

Henry felt great affection for the church. He was exceedingly generous to the upper clergy, granting them large estates while expanding their role in governing the state at the nobility's expense. This, along with his vow of chastity, pious nature and many charitable works, led to his being declared a saint after his death. Future emperors would rue his generosity.

ATLANTIC OCEAN

NORTH SEA

BALTIC SEA

IRELAND

ENGLAND

BRITTANIA
NEUSTRIA
SAXONIA
WEST FRANCIA
EAST FRANCIA
ALAMANNIA
BAVARIA
Vienna
CARINTHIA
Aquitania

WEST ROMAN EMPIRE

MIDDLE FRANCIA
PROVENCE

Oviedo

KINGDOM OF ASTURIA

Lisbon
Saragossa
Toledo

EMIRATE OF CORDOVA

Cordova

Corsica
Italy
Dalmatia
Rome
ADRIATIC SEA
Sardinia

EAST

Sicily

0 — 500 miles
0 — 500 kilometres

CALIPHATE OF

EAST AND WEST EMPIRES NINTH CENTURY AD

- KINGDOM OF THE KHAZARS
- ARAL SEA
- LAND OF THE TURKS (MAGYARS)
- KINGDOM OF THE AVARS
- CASPIAN SEA
- CRIMEA
- Danube River
- KINGDOM OF THE BULGARIANS
- BLACK SEA
- MACEDONIA
- THRACE
- Dyrrachion
- Thessalonica
- Constantinople
- OPSIKION
- ARMENIAKON
- Manzikert
- Armenia
- ROMAN EMPIRE
- ANATOLIKON
- Azerbaijan
- THRAKESION
- Aleppo
- Antioch
- Emesa
- Euphrates R
- Tigris R
- Baghdad
- Crete
- Cyprus
- Damascus
- MEDITERRANEAN SEA
- Jerusalem
- Alexandria
- PERSIAN GULF
- THE ABBASIDS

THE EASTERN EMPERORS

NICEPHORUS I

THE TAXMAN

NAME: Nikēphoros Logothetes
BORN: Seleukeia (modern Bucakşihler), Kibyrraioton, c. 760
RULED: Emperor, 802–811
DIED: Killed in battle, Verbitza, Bulgaria, 811

NICEPHORUS I, the descendant of an Arab king, was the *logothetēs tou genikou*, the minister responsible for taxation, during Irene's reign. He and his fellow bureaucrats looked on in horror as Irene's government became the plaything of eunuchs and monks, while the empress contemplated marriage to Charlemagne. Determined to restore the empire to its former vigour, Nicephorus deposed Irene, becoming emperor in 802.

He was immediately confronted with a number of problems, the first being what to do about Charlemagne. Luckily, the Romans in the east had recovered from their incredulity that a barbarian claimed to sit on the throne of the Caesars. Nicephorus did eventually recognise Charlemagne as Western emperor, and they entered into an agreement whereby the east ruled Venice, Istria, the Dalmatian coast and south Italy, while Rome, Ravenna and the Pentapolis (a region on the Adriatic coast, encompassing Rimini, Pesaro, Fano, Sinigaglia and Ancona) were included in the western realm.

Nicephorus's second problem, the dire state of the empire's finances, forced him to revoke Irene's ill-conceived tax concessions and tax the church, causing the monkish chroniclers to blacken his reputation. His third problem involved revolts against his rule, first by Bardanes, who was declared emperor, and then by Arsabar, whose plot was uncovered before he could claim the purple.

> **If the Basileus wishes to rule effectively, he must permit no one to be more powerful than himself.**
>
> NICEPHORUS I LOGOTHETES

Though possessing sufficient energy, Nicephorus lacked military experience. In 808 the Bulgar invasion under the leadership of Krum made this abundantly clear. After the Bulgars destroyed a Roman army and sacked the city of Sardica, Nicephorus's furious subjects goaded him to take the field. To his great surprise, he managed to destroy Krum's capital and rebuild Sardica without loss, returning to Constantinople somewhat redeemed. Believing his own propaganda, he marched out again in 811 with an enormous army, determined finally to crush the Bulgars. Krum tried to sue for peace, but Nicephorus seemed a man possessed, killing everyone in his path, including women and children. Rejecting any offer of peace, he pursued Krum until he fell into a trap at Verbitza and Nicephorus and his army were massacred. Krum ordered the imperial corpse brought to him, and he had Nicephorus's skull lined with silver and used it as a drinking cup until the day he died.

BARDANES
SHOULD HAVE LISTENED TO THE HERMIT

NAME: Bardanes Tourkos
BORN: Unknown
RULED: Usurper, 803
DIED: Unknown

BARDANES, AN ARMENIAN with the curious surname of Turk, became the *monostrategos* (the commander-in-chief) of the five eastern *themes* in Anatolia to prosecute the Saracen war. The army's discontent over Nicephorus's financial rigour persuaded him to accept the imperial purple from their hands, and for seven weeks he dreamed of being emperor.

Among his commanders were the future emperors Leo V and Michael II, who at the beginning of the rebellion supposedly accompanied Bardanes to see a prophetic hermit. Unfortunately, he predicted Bardanes's doom. When it became clear the emperor had far greater forces at his disposal, Bardanes's commanders deserted. Unable to establish a base of operations, and obtaining no support in Constantinople, Bardanes surrendered without a fight. Initially, Nicephorus's only revenge was to force Bardanes into monastic life, where he took the name Sabbas, but Nicephorus later changed his mind, sending trusted men to the island monastery to blind the usurper.

STRAURACIUS
UNLUCKY SURVIVOR

NAME: Staurakios
BORN: Place unknown, c. 794
RULED: Co-emperor, 803–811;
sole emperor, 811
DIED: Of an infected wound,
place unknown, 812

'PHYSICALLY AND INTELLECTUALLY unfit for the position' was a contemporary's opinion of the young man made co-emperor early in the reign of his father, Nicephorus, and there were accusations that he raped two girls in his youth. He accompanied Nicephorus to that fateful battle against the Bulgars in 811 and survived, but only just, suffering a wound to his neck that left him paralysed and in constant agony. Rescued from the battlefield, he was crowned at Adrianople to ensure stability, but it was soon obvious that he could not defend the empire in his condition.

> **You will not find a better friend than me.**
>
> STRAURACIUS

The only man available to assume the throne was his brother-in-law, Michael Rhangabe, whom Strauracius detested. He alternated between declaring his wife, Theophano, empress and, improbably, re-establishing the republic, until the issue was forced by Michael's supporters. Hearing that Michael was about to be blinded, they acted swiftly, crowning him in secret before forcing Strauracius to become a monk. The unfortunate man spent his last few months in a monastery, slowly dying from his infected wound.

MICHAEL I
ANYONE CAN BE A GENERAL
NAME: Mikhaël Rangabe
BORN: Unknown
RULED: Emperor, 811–813
DIED: Of natural causes, Princes Islands, Sea of Marmara, 844

MICHAEL I, DESCENDED from a Semitic family, was young, handsome and good-natured. Luck had him become Nicephorus's son-in-law; luck saw him escape the bloodbath at Verbitza; and luck (together with Strauracius's incapacity) brought him the imperial crown. Unfortunately, he was an incompetent general and a weak administrator who exhibited a poor grasp of financial matters.

He overturned Nicephorus's financial reforms, especially with regard to the church, and spent money as if it grew on trees. He also reintroduced the iconoclast persecution that his father-in-law had allowed to lapse and gave formal recognition of Charlemagne's title as western emperor, something that had only been tacitly acknowledged by Nicephorus I. However, his main task was to defeat the Bulgars and here his lucky streak failed, though it is likely that his overwhelming defeat at the battle of Versinikia was due to a treacherous general, Leo, who ordered the retreat of most of the army. Leo was now moving rapidly towards Constantinople, demanding to be crowned emperor.

Fleeing the battle, Michael at first resisted calls to abdicate. However, hearing of Leo's coronation, and with the Bulgars heading towards the capital, he and his children swiftly became monks and nuns. Leo spared Michael's life, sending him to a monastery where he adopted the name Athanasius. Eking out a meagre existence, he survived for thirty years before death claimed him.

THEOPHYLACTUS
NO CHANCE FOR CHILDREN
NAME: Theophylaktos Rangabe
BORN: Unknown
RULED: Co-emperor, 811–813
DIED: Of natural causes, Princes Islands, Sea of Marmara, 849

THEOPHYLACTUS WAS JUST a boy when his father placed the imperial diadem upon his fragile head in Hagia Sophia on Christmas Day, 811. Michael had great plans for him, even contemplating asking Charlemagne for one of his daughters for the young man to marry. It was not to be.

With Leo advancing rapidly on the capital, Michael forced his son to become a monk in a desperate attempt to save his life. It worked, but Leo took an extra precaution, castrating the youth to ensure he could never father an emperor. Changing his name to Eustratios, the poor lad ended up, like Michael, on a rocky island near Constantinople. Upon his death many years later, they buried his body next to his father's.

LEO V
THE ARMENIAN
NAME: Leōn
BORN: Armenia, c. 775
RULED: Emperor, 813–820
DIED: Murdered, Constantinople, 820

DUPLICITOUS AND DETERMINED, Leo the Armenian was a low-born but gifted general who gave outstanding service in many campaigns while being drawn to rebellion like a moth to a flame. Short in stature, with a booming voice, he was a key supporter of

Bardanes; that and his marriage to the rebel Arsabar's daughter saw him exiled by Emperor Nicephorus I. Recalled by Michael I, he rewarded his emperor by orchestrating his defeat by the Bulgars. As Michael fled to Constantinople, Leo gathered what remained of the shattered Roman army, marched towards the capital and, after promising to support orthodoxy, was crowned emperor.

He now needed to defend Constantinople against Krum and the victorious Bulgars. The mighty city walls kept Krum out, but he ravaged the countryside, sacking other, more vulnerable cities. Leo opened negotiations with him, but a botched assassination attempt demonstrated Leo's untrustworthiness. Swearing revenge, Krum was planning to launch a new assault on the empire when he died. Without his leadership, the Bulgars were defeated.

> **Wife, you have released my soul from sin today; perhaps it will soon cost me my life.**
>
> LEO THE ARMENIAN

Intriguingly for such a consummate liar, Leo was dedicated to the administration of justice, promoted military and public efficiency, and was generally

Elevation of Leo V as emperor in the traditional Roman method—by the army on a shield

RESTORATION AND RENEWAL   233

considered an able ruler. Yet it was his religious beliefs that forged his reputation. A closet iconoclast, he ignored his promises of orthodoxy and reintroduced legislation to outlaw the veneration of images. He convened a synod, which quickly agreed with his position, and he used its decision to close down his opponents' monasteries.

Leo's suspicion of one of his leading generals, Michael the Amorian, was to be his undoing. Furious that such a trusted servant was plotting treason, Leo ordered him burnt alive in a furnace, but the hasty intervention of Leo's wife saw him imprison Michael instead. Uncertain about the security arrangements, he went that night to check on Michael, only to discover he was free of his cell and sleeping next to the jailer. Concerned, he quietly slipped out, but someone noticed him. When they woke, Michael and the jailer decided to kill him. At daybreak Michael's followers, dressed as monks, entered the church where Leo was praying. He tried to flee and called for his guards, but the doors were locked and his guards had been disposed of. Unarmed, Leo defended himself with a large wooden cross in one hand and an incense burner in the other until he was overpowered and butchered.

SYMBATIOS CONSTANTINE

TRAUMATISED BY THE EXPERIENCE

NAME: Symbatios Kōnstantinos
BORN: Unknown
RULED: Co-emperor, 814–820
DIED: Of unknown causes, Princes Islands, Sea of Marmara, date unknown

LEO V CONSIDERED SYMBATIOS an uncouth name for a prospective co-emperor. As a sign that the iconoclasts were back, he named his son after Constantine V, whose father was also a Leo.

Like so many co-emperors, Symbatios Constantine was trapped by his father's fall. Michael the Amorian had the young man castrated; this, plus the trauma of seeing his father's mutilated corpse, caused him to become mute, though legend says that with St Gregory's intercession he regained his speech. Becoming a monk, he lived out his remaining days in prayer and solitude.

MICHAEL II

THE STAMMERER

NAME: Mikhaël
BORN: Amorion, Anatolikon, 770
RULED: Emperor, 820–829
DIED: Of kidney disease, Constantinople, 829

MICHAEL II WAS ANOTHER general whose climb to the top was a tribute to his ambition and energy. An illiterate peasant, ill mannered and superstitious to boot, he was also a second generation Christianised Jew, attracting all the ninth century prejudices that entailed. Standing out like a sore thumb among Constantinople's cultural elite, this rural career soldier never bothered to hide his contempt of Greek culture. The elite hated him for it, mocking his slow and rustic speech with the nickname 'the Stammerer'.

> *I know the greatness of your sorrow and the ocean of your distress.*
>
> MICHAEL II PSELLOS (to Leo V's nephew)

Like Leo V, he betrayed Bardanes and then helped Leo overthrow Michael I; as a reward, he was made chief commander of the imperial armies. However, during Leo's final days, he was charged with treason. After he arranged Leo's assassination, his supporters escorted him from his cell to the imperial throne, still wearing ankle shackles, which had to be broken with a hammer.

His reign opened with Thomas the Slav's uprising. By the time that was over, three years had passed; the Asian provinces were in ruins; the small farmers were devastated; and the army was severely weakened. Consequently, the empire was unable to deal with a Saracen invasion of Crete. Michael sent three expeditions to dislodge them, but to no avail. Crete was now lost to the empire, though Sicily was saved.

Michael's other preoccupation was the continuing iconoclast dispute. Given his Judeo-Christian heritage, he was sympathetic to the anti-image faction. However, while officially supporting iconoclasm, he would not force the iconophiles to comply with the law: toleration and gentle persuasion were his preferred methods. He approached the Western emperor, Louis I, to hold a western synod in support of iconoclasm and remove Rome's support of the iconophiles, but although a committee of Frankish bishops ended up supporting a limited iconoclastic interpretation, its recommendations were rejected by Rome. Yet he stuck to his policy of moderation until his death in 829.

THOMAS

THE SLAV

NAME: Thomas of Gaziura
BORN: Place unknown, c. 760
RULED: Usurper, 821–823
DIED: Arcadiopolis (modern Lüleburgaz), Thrace, 823

OF THOSE WHO PLEDGED their loyalty to Bardanes, only a Slavonic commander, Thomas, kept his oath. Fleeing to Syria on his patron's fall, Thomas stayed with the Saracens until the accession of Leo V who, remembering his old comrade at arms, gave him a military command, even though he had a lame leg. However, the disturbances of Leo's iconoclast revival saw Thomas prepare to challenge for the throne and he launched his revolt once Michael II, a bitter rival, killed Leo and assumed the purple.

Thomas announced that he was, in fact, Constantine VI, the deposed son of Irene. Under this assumed name, he gathered an army of persecuted and disaffected heretics, draining the eastern provinces of soldiers and allowing the Saracens to raid the empire. Forced by his men to take action against the Saracens, he confronted the Caliph Mamun, but they came to an agreement whereby Mamun recognised Thomas as Roman emperor, while Thomas became the caliph's vassal. Moving to Antioch, Thomas dropped his fake name and the patriarch of the city crowned him.

Pity me, O thou who art true Emperor!

THOMAS THE SLAV (to Michael II)

Nearly all of the eastern provinces had recognised Thomas when he crossed into Europe, where thousands of iconophiles flocked to join the rebellion, and it was with an army of eighty thousand that he besieged Constantinople in December 821. For a year, Thomas unsuccessfully launched wave after wave against the land and sea walls, until declining morale in the city forced Michael II to seek help from the Bulgars. Marching south, they forced Thomas to lift the siege and do battle in Thrace, resulting in the destruction of the rebel army. Thomas fled and a subsequent defeat by the emperor in 823 had him seeking refuge in Arcadiopolis. Trapped there for five months, Thomas's followers ended up eating the rotting flesh of dead horses before he surrendered. His fate was unpleasant. Led in chains before Michael, he had his hands and feet amputated before he was impaled alive on a stake. His rebellion died with him.

EUPHEMIUS

UNINVITED GUESTS

NAME: Euphemios
BORN: Messina, Sicily, date unknown
RULED: Usurper, 826–827
DIED: Killed in battle, Enna, Sicily, c. 827

IF YOU FORCE A NUN to marry you, either you surrender to the local governor and await certain death, or you declare yourself emperor. Unsurprisingly, the Roman admiral Euphemius, stationed in Sicily, decided that option two was preferable. After he was dismissed from his post, he killed the governor and declared himself emperor in Syracuse. His position was very insecure and loyal imperial forces soon drove him out. Crossing over to North Africa, he asked for help from the Arab emir of Kairouan. Having agreed to pay the emir an annual tribute, Euphemius returned to Sicily with ten thousand Arab soldiers, and though he did not survive long—he was killed in a skirmish with Roman troops at Enna—this invitation opened Sicily up for the Arab conquest.

THEOPHILUS

LAST OF THE ICONOCLASTS

NAME: Theophilos
BORN: Place unknown, 812
RULED: Co-emperor, 821–829;
senior emperor, 829–842
DIED: Of dysentery, Constantinople, 842

THEOPHILUS WAS THE COMPLETE antithesis of his father, Michael II. Witty, urbane, learned and obsessed with theology, he was the quintessential Eastern Roman emperor. His years as co-emperor are obscure, though he did lead a procession involving the True Cross during the siege of Constantinople in 822.

Theophilus seemed to possess the common touch, regularly touring the capital and talking directly with the common people, a practice that was unheard of. His concern for the administration of justice (even his family were not exempt) and easy approachability ensured that he was a much loved emperor during his lifetime, though one piece of literature written some three hundred years later depicts him as a judge in Hell. To his credit, he also restored and enhanced the city's sea walls, which were Constantinople's one great weakness.

> **What? Has my wife made me, the Emperor, a merchant?**
>
> THEOPHILUS

Though an able administrator, he was not fortunate in military matters. He was not a naturally gifted military leader, but his training was superb and he gave as good as he got in the endless wars against the Saracens, although his victories were inevitably followed by heavy losses, negating all forward momentum. In one celebrated campaign, Theophilus destroyed the caliph's home town, only to have the same fate inflicted upon his own home town. His approach to Louis I, the Western emperor, to form an alliance and launch a dual assault against the Saracens, was unsuccessful.

Theophilus was severe in one matter—the prosecution of anyone who broke the iconoclastic laws. He tortured and imprisoned many outspoken monks and clergy who defended icons. However, his severity was limited to the capital. Elsewhere within the empire, he tended to ignore the majority support for icons, so that his persecutions were very limited. However, the iconoclast movement was by now almost a spent force, and it would not survive the death of Theophilus.

CONSTANTINE
THE INFANT

NAME: Kōnstantinos
BORN: Constantinople, 833
RULED: Co-emperor, 833–835
DIED: Of natural causes, Constantinople, 835

CONSTANTINE, THEOPHILUS'S first-born son, was, in traditional style, crowned co-emperor within months of his birth. He died in infancy.

MICHAEL III
THE DRUNKARD

NAME: Mikhaël
BORN: Constantinople, 840
RULED: Co-emperor, 840–842; senior emperor, 842–867
DIED: Murdered, Constantinople, 867

WHEN YOUNG CONSTANTINE died the succession was in doubt for some five years until the birth of Theophilus's second son, Michael, who was also crowned co-emperor before he could crawl.

Michael III was weak and easily dominated by those around him, and so it was lucky that he was initially guided by individuals of great ability, principally his mother, Theodora, and then his uncle, Bardas. Theodora was the one who finally settled the iconoclast controversy by replacing the iconoclastic patriarch John with the iconophile Methodios, and she chose Michael's wife, forcing him to abandon his preferred mate. Michael, as in most things, acquiesced, but he did rebel to some extent, fathering no children on his wife and instead keeping a mistress and siring bastards.

THE IMPERIAL BRIDE SHOW

One tradition that is said to have been prevalent in the Eastern Empire during the ninth century was the method of choosing the new bride for the imperial heir—the bride show. It was organised by the groom's mother, who would send out agents throughout the empire to seek beautiful and well-bred young women who met certain exacting standards. These agents carried with them specifications for foot and height measurements, as well as an idealised image of the future empress.

In Theophilus's case, they escorted the girls into the palace and paraded them before the young man. His stepmother gave him a golden apple to bestow upon the woman who took his fancy. The first woman he chose tried to be witty, which he did not appreciate, so he gave the apple to another young woman, who was both quiet and demure.

Although there is some debate as to whether these shows actually occurred, or were just a literary invention, the fact that they were believed to have occurred gives us some insight into ninth-century life.

In 856, with help from Bardas, he overthrew Theodora, thus beginning a resurgence of Roman fortunes against the Saracens. Both Michael and Bardas started aggressively attacking Saracen and Bulgar outposts, as Roman arms began to be victorious on a regular basis. Yet by 865 Michael had become a hopeless and chronic alcoholic. While his armies continued to conquer, a fight between pope and patriarch over supremacy in the church distracted him, with a synod in Rome in 863 declaring the patriarch Photios deposed and ordering the reinstatment of his predecessor, whom Michael had dismissed. Michael refused to dismiss

Basil the Macedonian being attacked by a stag

Photios, launching an aggressive campaign to spread Constantinople's religious authority over the newly Christianised Bulgar kingdom and causing a schism that was exacerbated by the west's addition of the *filioque* clause into the Nicene Creed.

> **I made you emperor, and have I not the power to create another emperor if I choose?**
>
> MICHAEL THE DRUNKARD (TO BASIL THE MACEDONIAN)

It was now that Basil, the gifted but ambitious high chamberlain, began his play for power. Murdering the *kaisar*, Bardas, in 866, he convinced Michael to elevate him to the rank of co-emperor, but an injudicious comment from Michael convinced Basil that the emperor was planning to kill him, so he struck first. He gave a dinner party where Michael got drunk as usual. He then led Michael to his bedroom, having arranged for his men to burst into the bedchamber and butcher the slumbering emperor.

BASIL I

THE MACEDONIAN

NAME: Basileios
BORN: Macedonia, 835
RULED: Co-emperor, 866–867;
senior emperor, 867–886
DIED: Of fever, Constantinople, 886

BASIL THE MACEDONIAN—well, not quite. His parents were Armenians who had been forced to relocate to the *theme* of Macedonia, while he himself was a brutish illiterate peasant who spoke barely comprehensible Greek. Coming to Michael III's attention because of his great strength and ability with horses, he rose steadily until he became Michael's *parakoimomenos* (or high chamberlain). From there it was a short step to becoming co-emperor after he killed Bardas, and then emperor after murdering Michael.

It was a bloody path to the throne, and Basil resolved to make the most of it. Dismissing Patriarch Photios, he reinstalled the man who had been deposed, thereby conciliating the pope. This was important since Basil was keen to recapture the western provinces of the empire.

His generals were unable to recapture Crete or hold Sicily, but they managed to reclaim southern Italy and eagerly pushed north. In the east, Basil was successful against the Saracens, reclaiming territory that had been lost for over a century. And not content with military matters, he introduced administrative reforms, while producing an extensive revision of the law, basing it on Justinian's code. This was all the more remarkable given that he had had no military or administrative roles prior to becoming emperor.

> **Lord, you have given me the crown; I place it at your feet, pledging myself to your service.**
>
> BASIL THE MACEDONIAN

Yet Basil's final years saw a gradual descent into depression and madness, caused by the loss of his eldest son, Constantine. He cruelly tortured and executed suspected traitors. He also detested his second son, Leo, flogging him with his own hands on one occasion and eventually throwing him into prison. Basil's death came after a hunting accident; his final order was to kill the guard who had used a knife to free him (his belt had become entangled in the antlers of a deer he had been chasing), declaring that none should live after raising a weapon against their emperor.

CONSTANTINE
APPLE OF HIS FATHER'S EYE

NAME: Kōnstantinos
BORN: Place unknown, c. 861
RULED: Co-emperor, 868–879
DIED: Of unknown causes, Constantinople, 879

CONSTANTINE WAS THE SON of Basil's first wife, Maria, whom Basil had been forced to divorce in order to marry Michael's mistress, Eudocia—Michael was unwilling to divorce his current wife and needed a way to keep Eudocia around. Consequently, Constantine was Basil's beloved son and was soon crowned co-emperor. Ruggedly handsome, with an athletic build, he cut quite the dashing figure, accompanying his father on campaign dressed in golden armour and sitting atop a white horse. He was betrothed to the daughter of Louis II, the Western emperor, but the arrangement was never concluded. He died suddenly in 879, leaving his father an emotional and mental wreck.

LEO VI
THE WISE

NAME: Leo
BORN: Constantinople, 866
RULED: Co-emperor, 870–886;
senior emperor, 886–912
DIED: Of natural causes, Constantinople, 912

OFFICIALLY, LEO VI was the son of Basil and his second wife Eudocia; unofficially, he was the son of Michael III, who was sleeping with Eudocia, and this fact embittered Leo's relationship with Basil, who resented having been forced to divorce his beloved first wife, Maria. The situation was so poisoned that Basil almost blinded Leo during a ferocious argument when Leo was a teenager. It was from spite that Basil forced Leo to abandon the love of his life, Zoe, to marry the devout and morbid Theophano. Leo returned the favour by reburying his real father in the Church of the Holy Apostles, the resting place for many of the emperors.

Leo was so unlike Basil that no one could ever mistake them for father and son. Leo was cultured, mild tempered, charming and a renowned scholar, with interests in philosophy and theology, quite unlike the down-to-earth Basil. The only part of Basil's program that Leo continued was Roman law reform, which he expanded considerably. It was during Leo's reign that one of the last vestiges of the old Roman state disappeared—the Senate, or at least the Senate as a body that the constitution recognised as authorised to wield power.

> **If you wish to marry you must observe the laws of marriage. Do not adulterate marriage.**
>
> LEO THE WISE

Leo's antipathy towards Basil's legacy was detrimental to the empire in one key area—it led to a reduction in military power. Bulgar invasions and Saracen incursions in the east and southern Italy proved difficult to stop, and Saracens were even able to sack the great city of Thessalonica with very little resistance. Leo resorted to the tactic of paying tribute to relieve the pressure.

Leo's greatest concern was with the succession. His first marriage had been an unmitigated disaster from start to finish: Theophano had locked herself into a monastery after the death of their only child, and he was relieved when she finally died in 897. Quickly summoning his beloved Zoe to the capital, he married her and they were blessed with a daughter. Within two years she, too, was dead, leaving the emperor grief-stricken but aware that he needed a son. This was problematic since, according to his own legislation, an individual could not marry more than twice. Prior to his reign, although a church wedding was an ancient practice, there had been no legal requirement to have one. Leo changed this, and he also tried to align civil laws with church teachings, including the instruction that, although a second marriage was permissible, a third was only allowed under the most extraordinary of circumstances. However, he persuaded the patriarch to agree to a third marriage, but when this wife died giving birth to a son who also died it left Leo in a greater mess than before, since a fourth marriage was absolutely prohibited. Soon a new mistress, another Zoe, gave birth to an illegitimate son, Constantine. Leo married his lover in secret before obtaining the pope's approval. This caused the patriarch and the general Andronicus Ducas to conspire against him, but the plot was uncovered during the planning stage. Quashing all resistance (and agreeing to outlaw all future fourth marriages), Leo managed to secure the succession before he died.

ALEXANDER

INCOMPETENT DRUNK

NAME: Alexandros
BORN: Constantinople, c. 870
RULED: Co-emperor, 879–912;
senior emperor, 912–913
DIED: Of a burst blood vessel, Constantinople, 913

LIKE HIS FATHER, BASIL I, Alexander loathed his half-brother, Leo VI. Kept out of any position of power, Alexander spent the tedious years of Leo's reign hunting, drinking and whoring to excess, to the point where it was destroying him physically and mentally. When he came to the throne, he tried to undo all Leo's achievements. Quickly banishing the empress Zoe, the patriarch and many of Leo's advisors, he promoted Leo's enemies and his own drinking buddies. Abrogating Leo's treaty with the Bulgarians, he started a new and bitter war the empire could ill afford. Luckily for everyone, he died while playing polo.

CONSTANTINE VII

BORN TO THE PURPLE

NAME: Kōnstantinos Porphyrogennētos
BORN: Constantinople, 905
RULED: Co-emperor, 908–913; sole emperor, 913–920; co-emperor, 920–945; senior emperor, 945–959
DIED: Of natural causes, Constantinople, 959

CONSTANTINE'S PRIMARY LESSON in childhood was that if he wanted to stay alive, it was best to stay as much as possible in the background. From the death of his father, Leo VI, until he reached the age of forty, his fate was in the hands of others, beginning with his uncle Alexander, who contemplated castrating him. Upon Alexander's death, power was held by a regency council under the leadership of the patriarch, before Constantine's banished mother, Zoe, returned, much to the relief of the young emperor, who had wandered the corridors crying out for her. She became regent, but failed attempts to deal with the Bulgarians, culminating in a humiliating defeat of the imperial army, saw her replaced as regent in 919 by the general Romanus.

Constantine was still only fifteen when Romanus assumed power, first becoming his father-in-law and then his nominal co-emperor, although in reality Romanus was to rule as the senior emperor for the next twenty-five years. During this time, Constantine grew up to be a tall, broad-shouldered man, fair skinned and with a glowing complexion. Everyone spoke of his fair speech, his generosity and his voracious appetite for reading and writing. Apart from the required ceremonial duties, he lived in enforced isolation, during which he developed a love of books and fine food. Like his father, he used his spare time to write historical, geographical, medical and natural science works, but his two most important books were a manual on court ceremonies and a handbook for running the empire.

After being forced to participate in the posthumous condemnation of his father's fourth marriage (and thus his own birth), he was given the mocking nickname Porphyrogenitus, 'born in the purple', highlighting the irregularity of his birth. Such humiliations he bore patiently, waiting until 944 when Romanus was overthrown by his sons. Their promotion ahead of Constantine made them unpopular, allowing Constantine to use his newfound support to remove his brothers-in-law and take over the throne for himself.

Yet the habits of a lifetime are hard to break. For the remainder of his reign he allowed the civil service, his generals and his wife to administer the empire, and they managed quite well. His rule was steady and moderate, keeping up the pressure on the Saracens and winning some key victories, though Crete's recapture eluded him. As he continued Romanus's policy of strengthening the landed peasantry against the aristocracy, the people said goodbye to him with great sadness after a short illness.

CONSTANTINE DUCAS

LACKED RECENT INFORMATION

NAME: Kōnstantinos Doukas
BORN: Unknown
RULED: Usurper, 913
DIED: Murdered, Constantinople, 913

ONE PERSON EAGER to see Alexander's death was a key general in Anatolia, Constantine Ducas. He was the son of Andronicus, who had rebelled against Leo VI, but had remained behind when his father fled to the Saracens. For this Leo rewarded him with a high military command, and he served with distinction.

Prior to Alexander's death, the patriarch had approached Constantine with an intriguing offer—to take the throne and prevent the former empress Zoe becoming regent on behalf of her infant son. The general agreed, and at the prearranged time his supporters stormed the palace and proclaimed him emperor. He was surprised when no one else came out; unbeknown to him, it was the patriarch, not Zoe, who ended up on the regency council. The guards halted Constantine's supporters, while Constantine's horse slipped on the bloodied pavements, throwing him to the ground, where the guards killed him.

ROMANUS I

THE KINDLY USURPER

NAME: Romanos Lekapenos
BORN: Lacape, Anatolia, c. 870
RULED: Senior emperor, 920–944
DIED: Of natural causes, Princes Islands, Sea of Marmara, 948

ROMANUS, SON OF an Armenian peasant, was an uneducated military commander who rose to power during Constantine Porphyrogenitus's minority. A schemer, his abandonment of an imperial army crushed by the Bulgarians enabled him to engineer the downfall of Empress Zoe. Claiming to be Constantine's protector, he gained control of the government while Constantine lost his heart to Romanus's daughter and became his son-in-law. To smooth his way to the throne, he summoned a church council to declare all fourth marriages illegal, thus casting doubts on the legitimacy of Constantine's possession of the throne. Seeing where things were heading, Constantine made Romanus *kaisar*, before crowning him emperor in 920. This enabled Romanus to elevate his three sons to the rank of co-emperor and fully exclude his son-in-law from all imperial business.

Romanus had to deal with the Bulgars, who were destroying Thracian towns at will. As a military solution had failed, he negotiated a way out of the problem, overawing the Bulgar king with the majesty of the empire, together with a large sum of money. A marriage between his granddaughter and the next Bulgar king cemented the peace, leaving Romanus free to deal with the Saracens. Here he was very successful, as his brilliant general, John Curcuas, routed the divided and weakened Saracens, even reincorporating the Arab emirate of Melitene, lost during the first century of Muslim expansion, into the empire in 934.

These victories did not bring the ageing Romanus any comfort, however. With his eldest son's death, he began to feel guilt about his treatment of Constantine, contrasting Constantine's respect for him with the way his own sons treated him. With age and illness wearing him down, he could not prevent his sons recalling John Curcuas from the Saracen war, with disastrous results. Disappointed by his children, he placed Constantine ahead of them in

THEMES OF THE BYZANTINE EMPIRE AD 950

944, but his sons acted decisively, capturing Romanus in the dead of night and sending him to a monastery. Here he lived out his life, tormented by his sins and dreams of his descent into hell. The one attempt to restore him to the throne quickly came to nothing, and to the sound of monks praying for his soul, Romanus finally passed away on 15 June 948.

CHRISTOPHER

FAVOURED SON

NAME: Christophoros Lekapenos
BORN: Unknown
RULED: Co-emperor, 921–931
DIED: Of natural causes, Constantinople, 931

CHRISTOPHER WAS ROMANUS'S favoured son. Nothing could change that, not even his involvement in a plot instigated by his father-in-law to overthrow Romanus. His crowning as co-emperor in 921 was a clear demonstration that the Lecapeni were the new imperial dynasty. Romanus confirmed this in 927, when Christopher gained precedence over Constantine at the insistence of the Bulgarian king, who took offence that his new father-in-law was the most junior of the three emperors. Though talented, Christopher was never in the best of health and he died a few years later, to Romanus's great grief.

BASIL

THE COPPER-HANDED

NAME: Basileios
BORN: Macedonia, date unknown
RULED: Usurper, 932
DIED: Executed, Constantinople, 932

THE IRREGULARITY OF ROMANUS'S accession inspired a number of people to conspire against him. The most inventive of these was Basil, appearing in Opsikion under the assumed name of the usurper Constantine Ducas. Though he attracted a following, imperial officials arrested him and sent him to Constantinople where he had his right hand amputated, which should have been the end of the matter. However, Basil was persistent.

Returning to Opsikion, he had created a copper hand holding an enormous sword, and he attached it to his arm. Proceeding to gather a crowd of peasants, he launched a second rebellion against the empire. After initial success, an imperial army defeated him and returned him to Constantinople in chains. To save his life, he falsely accused many nobles of being involved in his rebellion, to no avail. To ensure there would be no third performance, he was burnt alive in the Forum Amastrianum.

STEPHEN AND CONSTANTINE

NOT VERY POPULAR

NAMES: Stephanos and Kōnstantinos Lekapenos
BORN: Unknown
RULED: Co-emperors, 924–945
DIED: Of natural causes, Lesbos, 967; murdered, Samothrace, 946

THESE TWO CORRUPT and pampered co-emperors were their father's worst nightmare. Showing Romanus no love or loyalty, their only thought was to become senior emperor and enjoy themselves. To their great shock, it appeared that after Christopher's death, the grief-stricken Romanus was going to leave the throne to their bookish half-brother, Constantine Porphyrogenitus.

Determined to prevent this they captured Romanus, forcing him into exile. But they badly overplayed their hand: with Romanus gone, the people transferred loyalty to Constantine Porphyrogenitus. The brothers, forced against their will to name Constantine Porphyrogenitus the senior emperor, soon began to conspire against him. However, Constantine struck first, exiling them in 945 to join their father as monks.

It was inevitable that plots would develop around the former emperors. With encouragement from his supporters, Constantine Lecapenus repeatedly tried to escape. In 946 his luck ran out: when he killed the captain of the guards during an escape attempt, the guards chased him down and killed him. Stephen was also a focus of plots, yet none came to fruition and he remained in relative obscurity, outliving Porphyrogenitus by a number of years.

ROMANUS II

TO ENJOY LIFE

NAME: Romanos Porphyrogennētos
BORN: Constantinople, 939
RULED: Co-emperor, 945–959;
sole emperor, 959–963
DIED: Of natural causes, Constantinople, 963

IN LOOKS, MILDNESS of character and love of fine foods, young Romanus was the spitting image of his father, Constantine Porphyrogenitus. Growing up, he was fond of hunting and playing polo, but hopes were high that he would become a fine emperor.

For dynastic purposes, he married quite young, but his wife died before he became sole emperor. He was pressured to marry the niece of the Western emperor, Otto I, but his heart settled instead on the beautiful daughter of a Greek innkeeper, Theophano. She was to dominate Romanus's reign, banishing his mother and forcing her five sisters-in-law to take the veil and retire to monasteries; Romanus said not a word. She then replaced all of Constantine's ministers with her own appointees.

> **Nicephorus Phocas is not to be removed from the command of the army employed against the Saracens.**
>
> ROMANUS II

The highlight of Romanus's reign was the reconquest in 961 of Crete, which had been held by the Saracens for nearly 150 years. Romanus did not participate in the campaign, leaving it to the great Roman general Nicephorus Phocas. The celebrations in Constantinople were barely over when Romanus's decadent lifestyle caught up with him and he died at the age of twenty-five.

NICEPHORUS II

THE PALE DEATH OF THE SARACENS

NAME: Nikēphoros Phōkas
BORN: Cappadocia, Anatolia, c. 912
RULED: Senior emperor, 963–969
DIED: Murdered, Constantinople, 969

ROMANUS II'S DEATH left his wife Theophano in a precarious situation. Her two infant sons needed a protector, and the man she turned to was the empire's leading general, Nicephorus Phocas. With his accession vigorously contested, he married the widowed empress to solidify his claim to the purple. For this young and beautiful woman, it was a choice of last resort.

A monstrous dwarf was how one contemporary described Nicephorus, and he was not far wrong. Short, swarthy, with a thick neck and small, deep-set eyes under thick eyebrows, Nicephorus was stupendously ugly, certainly not the sort to attract a beautiful woman. Then there was his quasi-monastic lifestyle, with daily prayers, a vow of celibacy and a hairshirt worn to mortify his flesh. But more important was the fact he was one of the most gifted generals the Romans ever

Forces commanded by John I capture the Bulgarian capital of Preslav, 971

produced. Cool, calm and collected under fire, fearless in combat and quick to seize the initiative, he was loved by his soldiers.

Quickly discovering he had no desire to play emperor in the capital, Nicephorus returned to doing what he loved—destroying the Saracen threat to the east. From Tarsus to Antioch, city after city fell to him, and he was seriously contemplating the invasion of Egypt. The most successful general since Heraclius, he should have been the most popular in generations. Unfortunately, his personality let him down.

You are not Romans, but Lombards!

NICEPHORUS II PHOCAS (to Emperor Otto I's representatives)

Dark, morbid and morose, he was a poor diplomat, offending everyone he dealt with. His negotiating skills caused war to erupt on the Bulgarian and Italian frontiers while his armies had their hands full in the east. Add his blatant favouritism to the soldiers, his excessive taxation to fund his military ventures, and his criticism of the church over its apparent wealth, and all that was needed for Nicephorus to lose the throne would be for Theophano to transfer her allegiance elsewhere. Sure enough, she had fallen for the emperor's nephew, the dashing young general John Tzimisces. Together they plotted the old man's death.

Though he had been warned about an assassination attempt, the conspirators had reassured him, and he was sleeping on the floor in his hairshirt when he awoke to find Tzimisces and his colleagues entering the room. They slashed the face of the cowering emperor with a sword and beat him savagely, breaking his jaw and numerous other bones, before finally ending his agony with a sword thrust. It was an unjust end for a man who had sworn to defend the empire to his dying breath.

JOHN I
CONQUEROR OF PALESTINE

NAME: Iōannēs Tzimiskēs
BORN: Chozana, Armenia, c. 925
RULED: Senior emperor, 969–976
DIED: Poisoned, Constantinople, 976

JOHN TZIMISCES AND NICEPHORUS Phocas were like chalk and cheese. Devastatingly handsome, with piercing blue eyes under reddish blond hair, John was generous to a fault, easy going and able to charm women who, like the empress Theophano, found him irresistible. She hated being married to the morbid religious bore Nicephorus and plotted to elevate John to the throne. Yet once he was emperor, he was cautious of her—after all, she had turned on Nicephorus, why not on him? Therefore, he had the patriarch 'force' him to send her to a monastery, ignoring her bitter tirade. Freed from a potential threat, he legitimised his position by marrying Romanus II's sister, becoming an uncle to Basil and Constantine, the child emperors.

Stained as he was with his uncle's blood, his reign was at first disrupted by rebellions instigated by the Phocas family, starting with Leo, Nicephorus's brother, who attempted a coup, and then his son Bardas, who declared himself emperor. Yet soon enough the rest of the empire forgot about his crime. Giving away a great portion of his fortune to help the people suffering a devastating famine and making regular visits to hospitals, he was soon one of the most loved emperors ever to sit on the throne. His diplomatic skills were also renowned, and he solidified an alliance with the western emperor Otto I by marrying off an imperial princess to the future Otto II.

In John Tzimisces, the empire traded one soldier-emperor for another, continuing the Eastern Empire's resurgence. Nicephorus's bungle in Bulgaria had seen it swallowed by the militaristic Russians, who were about to launch an assault on the empire. John headed off the threat by crushing them in two campaigns, restoring their territory to the Bulgarians, but as a province of the empire.

When he turned his attention eastwards, his victories surpassed even those of Nicephorus. From 974 Armenia was subdued; then, marching into Syria, Lebanon and Palestine, he captured Damascus, Nazareth and many other cities and planned to conquer Jerusalem the following year. Remarkably, he extended Roman control to areas that Heraclius had abandoned centuries before.

> **Roman emperors toil like mercenaries to add to the riches of an insatiable eunuch!**
>
> JOHN I TZIMISCES

Unfortunately, death curtailed his plans. On his way back to Constantinople, he commented on the wealth of his chief minister, Basil Lecapenus, who had been purchasing large estates through suspect means. Suddenly fearful, Basil had the emperor poisoned, and by the time John returned to Constantinople he was clearly dying. Most remembered him as a just and wise man, compassionate to all and eager to serve the empire. His own prayers indicated he had not forgotten beating the unarmed, cowering and bloodied Nicephorus to death.

BARDAS PHOCAS

LUCK OF THE DUEL

NAME: Bardas Phōkas
BORN: Unknown
RULED: Usurper, 971 and 987–989
DIED: Of a stroke, Abydos, Opsikion, 989

BARDAS PHOCAS, Nicephorus II's nephew, inherited his uncle's gloominess and his military skill. After his father's aborted coup, John Tzimisces had exiled him, along with his older brother, while castrating his younger brother. Bardas, though, soon escaped and marched south to Caesarea, where his supporters proclaimed him emperor. The revolt quickly spread to Thrace, where his uncle and brother joined him.

Tzimisces sent his best remaining general, Bardas Sclerus, to deal with the threat. Sclerus sent in spies to weaken the morale of his opponent's troops and was so successful that Phocas found himself deserted by the majority of his army. Fleeing to a nearby fortress, he surrendered on condition his life was spared. Good to his word, Tzimisces sent Phocas to a monastery, where he would have stayed but for a strange twist of fate.

Tzimisces's death offered a usurper the chance to gain control of the Eastern Empire. In this case it was Bardas Sclerus who decided to rebel. After the new emperor, Basil II, had suffered two defeats, in desperation he recalled Phocas from his monastic cell to deal with the deepening crisis. Cherishing this opportunity to gain revenge on the man who had crushed his own imperial ambitions, Phocas abandoned his monastic vows and raised an army from his old power base at Caesarea. Over the next three years, he doggedly battled against Sclerus without achieving a substantial victory. Finally, in 979, the two armies met for one final encounter. Phocas, seeing the battle was again slipping away, challenged Sclerus to a duel and was accepted. It was an epic encounter, and as both men charged at each other, Phocas struck Sclerus down.

Phocas was restored to favour and Basil II made him *doux* of Antioch, a command that he managed skilfully. However, he still hungered for greater things, and news of Basil II's humiliation at Trajan's Gate in 986 in Bulgaria prompted him to action. Once acknowledged emperor throughout the *themes* of Anatolia, he secured his position by imprisoning Sclerus, who was also making another play for the throne. For a year, Phocas was unable to attack Constantinople and, growing complacent in the belief that Basil was in no position to threaten him directly, he split his forces. One group, which was sent to the Bosphorus, was caught unawares by Basil's army

OFFICES OF THE EASTERN EMPIRE

Although the titles had changed from Latin to Greek, the offices of the Eastern empire originally reflected the purpose for which they were created in the days of Diocletian and Constantine. However, by the eleventh century many more positions and ranks had been created, reflecting the Eastern empire's love of bureaucracy and court ceremonials, and all designed to reflect a person's standing at court. Some of these titles included:

DOUX The Greek version of the *dux*, the *doux* was originally responsible for the military, but not the civil, administration of a province. By the eighth century it had been transformed into a lower military commander under the authority of the *strategos*, and by the tenth it was assigned to the military commander of a larger district, the *doukaton*. The *doux* of Antioch was an example of this later designation.

STRATEGOS In the eighth century, this was the military governor of a *theme*, a province of the empire. The *strategoi* were originally also responsible for local financial and judicial administration, but by the eleventh century their role had been significantly reduced, with the civil administration passed on to the thematic judges.

MONOSTRATEGOS This was an overall commander of the armies across two or more *theme*s. They were appointed during times of crisis.

MEGAS DOUX (Grand Duke) This was the admiral (or overall commander) of the navy, a position created when the naval forces were stripped from the *theme*s during the tenth century.

MEGAS DOMESTIKOS (Grand Domestic) The overall commander of the army, this position was created by the end of the tenth century and outranked the *strategoi* and the *doux*.

EXARCHOS The exarchs were the governors of the remote western provinces of the empire, Italy and Africa. They acted as the personal representative of the emperor in those regions.

PROTOVESTIARIOS This was usually a minor relative of the emperor who took care of the emperor's personal wardrobe and finances, especially on military campaigns. He eventually gained more authority, so that by the tenth century it was not unknown for the *protovestiarios* to command armies, conduct peace negotiations and conduct inquiries.

ORPHANOTROPHOS He was the official responsible for the care of orphans. As a member of the secular hierarchy, this official wielded significant influence.

PARAKOIMOMENOS The highest office conferrable on a eunuch, this was the imperial high chamberlain, who slept in the emperor's bedchamber. His proximity to the emperor gave him enormous clout.

MEGAS LOGOTHETES (Grand Logothete) The head of the imperial bureaucracy, this official was personally responsible for the legal system and treasury.

LOGOTHETĒS TOU GENIKOU This was the secretary responsible for finance and taxation. He managed a large number of subordinates.

SEBASTOKRATŌR This was a rank given to close family members of the emperor, such as a brother. Translated as August Ruler, it had no function attached to it.

KOUROPALATĒS From the sixth to the twelfth centuries, this was one of the most important positions. Originally given to the official in charge of running the imperial palace, by the eleventh century it had become mostly honorific, the functions of the office having been taken over by the *protovestiarios*.

of Russianised Vikings, who proceeded to annihilate them. Phocas himself was preoccupied with the siege of Abydos and soon had to contend with the approaching emperor. Leaving part of his forces to continue the siege, he prepared for battle just outside Abydos. Not willing to chance it all on a risky engagement, and seeing the emperor nearby, he tried to emulate his previous success by charging at his enemy. Closer and closer he rode, sword at the ready, only to fall off his horse just metres from the waiting Basil after suffering a stroke.

BARDAS SCLERUS

TOO OLD TO CONTINUE

NAME: Bardas Skleros
BORN: Unknown
RULED: Usurper, 976–979 and 987–990
DIED: Of natural causes, Thracia, 991

BARDAS SCLERUS WAS among the best generals of his generation. A meticulous planner who had crushed the Russians in 970 at Arcadiopolis, he was ordered by the emperor John Tzimisces to quash the rebellion of Bardas Phocas. It was a feat he would achieve without a pitched battle.

With Tzimisces's death, the chief minister, Basil, tried to eliminate potential rivals, ordering Sclerus's removal as general of the eastern armies. Sclerus showed his contempt by securing the support of bordering eastern states to declare himself emperor. After some initial failures, he achieved two comprehensive victories over the imperial armies, only to encounter a released Bardas Phocas, eager for revenge. They met in two indecisive encounters, and on the third he rashly decided to fight the giant, brutish Phocas one on one. He charged and slashed at Phocas, who deflected his attack. Phocas struck him across the head, knocking him unconscious. When he came to, his men were fleeing the battlefield and, using the chaos as cover, Sclerus also fled, taking refuge in Baghdad.

After a seven-year exile, Sclerus—like Bardas Phocas—decided to take advantage of Basil II's failure against the Bulgarians and fulfil his thwarted imperial ambitions. With Saracen help, he returned to the eastern provinces, but discovered the Anatolian nobility mostly supported Bardas Phocas. Phocas lulled him into a false sense of security and, during a meeting to discuss a division of the empire, captured him. Sclerus was incarcerated until Phocas's death in 989, when Phocas's wife freed him, urging him to seek revenge against Basil II. But by now he was old and rapidly going blind, and instead he threw himself on the emperor's mercy. Basil, for once magnanimous, agreed to spare his life, though during the interview Sclerus committed the ultimate faux pas of wearing socks in the imperial purple. Death was a welcome release from his failed ambitions.

BASIL II

THE BULGAR-SLAYER

NAME: Basileios
BORN: Constantinople, 958
RULED: Co-emperor, 960–976;
senior emperor, 976–1025
DIED: Of natural causes,
Constantinople, 1025

BASIL, THE ELDER SON of Romanus II, was nothing if not patient. His stepfather and his step-uncle, crowned senior emperor in turn, dominated most of his first seventeen years. After their deaths, he became senior emperor, but rebellions by the Anatolian aristocracy consumed the following fourteen years. It was only in 991 that he finally emerged, no longer constrained by senior co-emperors or rebellious warlords, and determined to remake the world.

A man of boundless energy, with an iron will, brave and stern, Basil was contemptuous of the imperial court. Though he lived the life of a pampered noble in his youth, upon his accession in 976 he foreswore all pomp. Wearing simple clothes, eating and drinking very ordinary fare in small amounts and living a life of austere simplicity, he even swore off women for the whole of his reign. He maintained this austerity for nearly fifty years without ever 'falling off the wagon', so indomitable was his willpower. Over time, however, these virtues changed and hardened, becoming crueller as his reign progressed.

> **And is this the man who has so long been the object of our terror?**
>
> BASIL THE BULGAR-SLAYER
> (referring to Bardas Sclerus)

Two key events demonstrated Basil's single-mindedness. The rebellions of Bardas Phocas and Bardas Sclerus showed just how independent the Anatolian aristocracy had become, especially in their control of the army. To ensure they could not undertake such rebellions again, he took personal control of the army, preventing further mischief by having it on permanent campaign. He then passed a law in 996 that restored to the peasantry all the property the nobles had acquired over the past forty years. At a stroke, he crippled the nobility's power, and it was only when a new generation arose that they dared to take on the emperor again, in 1022.

The second defining event of his reign was his defeat at the hands of the Bulgarians. Having studied under Nicephorus Phocas and John Tzimisces, he was eager to emulate their feats. The Bulgarians had rebuilt their power and expelled the Roman authorities from their lands, and so Basil led the army against them. It was his first command, but he almost died and most of his army were butchered in an ambush at Trajan's Gate in 986.

Humiliated, he swore that he would have his revenge against the Bulgars and their king.

Beginning his campaign in 991, he did not let up for the next twenty-seven years; unlike other generals, he did not lead his troops back to camp for the winter, but stayed in the field pursuing his enemies, living the life of the common soldier. Though he would occasionally return to the capital for administrative purposes, he spent most of these years on campaign, conquering town after town, destroying army after army. After one comprehensive victory in 1014, he ordered the blinding of fifteen thousand prisoners, leaving a single eye to the leader of each group of one hundred. When the Bulgar king saw what had happened, he collapsed with rage and grief, dying two days later. By the time Basil had finished, he had restored the ancient frontiers at the Danube and had received the name by which history remembers him—the Bulgar-Slayer.

Though pitiless and inhuman, he was one of the most successful emperors the Romans had ever beheld. In only one area was he deficient: he never married and thus left the empire to his indolent brother, who would begin the decline that would see Basil's efforts turn to dust.

NICEPHORUS PHOCAS

IN HIS FATHER'S FOOTSTEPS

NAME: Nikēphoros Phōkas
BORN: Unknown
RULED: Usurper, 1021–1022
DIED: Murdered, Anatolia, 1022

NICEPHORUS WAS THE SON of Bardas Phocas, who had rebelled early in Basil II's reign. His father's disgrace did not hamper Nicephorus's career prospects, and by the 1020s he was one of Basil's generals stationed in

Anatolia. Despite Basil's many victories, the aristocracy still resented the elderly emperor, and so in 1021 they took advantage of his problems with the Armenians to launch a rebellion, declaring Nicephorus emperor.

Nicephorus's main backer was the *strategos* of Anatolia, Nicephorus Xiphias, and together they made Cappadocia their base as they tried to incite the Armenians to join their cause. However, Basil was too wily an opponent. He secretly sent letters to both Nicephori, offering a pardon to the man who would kill the other. Phocas, proud and honourable, went to his colleague and showed him Basil's letter. Xiphias did not let on that he, too, had received a letter and soon after assassinated Phocas during a private interview between the two. The rebellion died with Phocas's death, as the troops were loyal to him to a man and refused to serve under his murderer.

CONSTANTINE VIII

PLEASURE SEEKER

NAME: Kōnstantinos
BORN: Constantinople, 960
RULED: Co-emperor, 962–1025;
sole emperor, 1025–1028
DIED: Of natural causes, Constantinople, 1028

CONSTANTINE WAS A GIANT of a man and a reasonably decent horseman. Unfortunately, they are the only good things anyone could say about the Bulgar-Slayer's brother. Possessing neither any interest in warfare nor any ability statecraft, he spent the majority of Basil's reign in cheerful obscurity, living a life of luxurious ease.

You must either ascend the throne or lose your eyesight.

CONSTANTINE VIII (to Romanus Argyrus)

He saw no reason to change when he assumed sole power in 1025 and he continued to play dice and chequers, go hunting and indulge his sexual fantasies, though his increasingly painful gout limited these. Like his brother, he possessed a cruel temperament, executing and mutilating any noble accused of treason, even if only on the basis of a rumour. Constantine regularly removed men of ability from the military and civil service, replacing them with weak individuals who owed their position to his favour. A multitude of eunuchs replaced the military aristocracy, so long the bedrock of the empire. His foreign policy, as far as one existed, was to bribe the enemies of the empire; war was something to avoid, as it would only result in more comparisons to his brother, the Bulgar-Slayer.

Constantine died after a three-year reign, leaving the empire to three daughters, whose jealousies, rivalries and disastrous marriages saw the Eastern Empire eaten away from within, oblivious to the enemies that were circling, waiting for their moment to strike.

THE CRUSADES
(1028–1204)

The power of the sultans was shaken by the victories and even the defeats of the Franks; and after the loss of Nice they moved their throne to Iconium, three hundred miles from Constantinople. Instead of trembling in their capital, the Comnenian princes waged an offensive war against the Turks, and the first crusade prevented the fall of the declining empire.

EDWARD GIBBON
The Decline and Fall of the Roman Empire, 1880

FOLLOWING PAGE: Procession of crusaders around Jerusalem, 1099

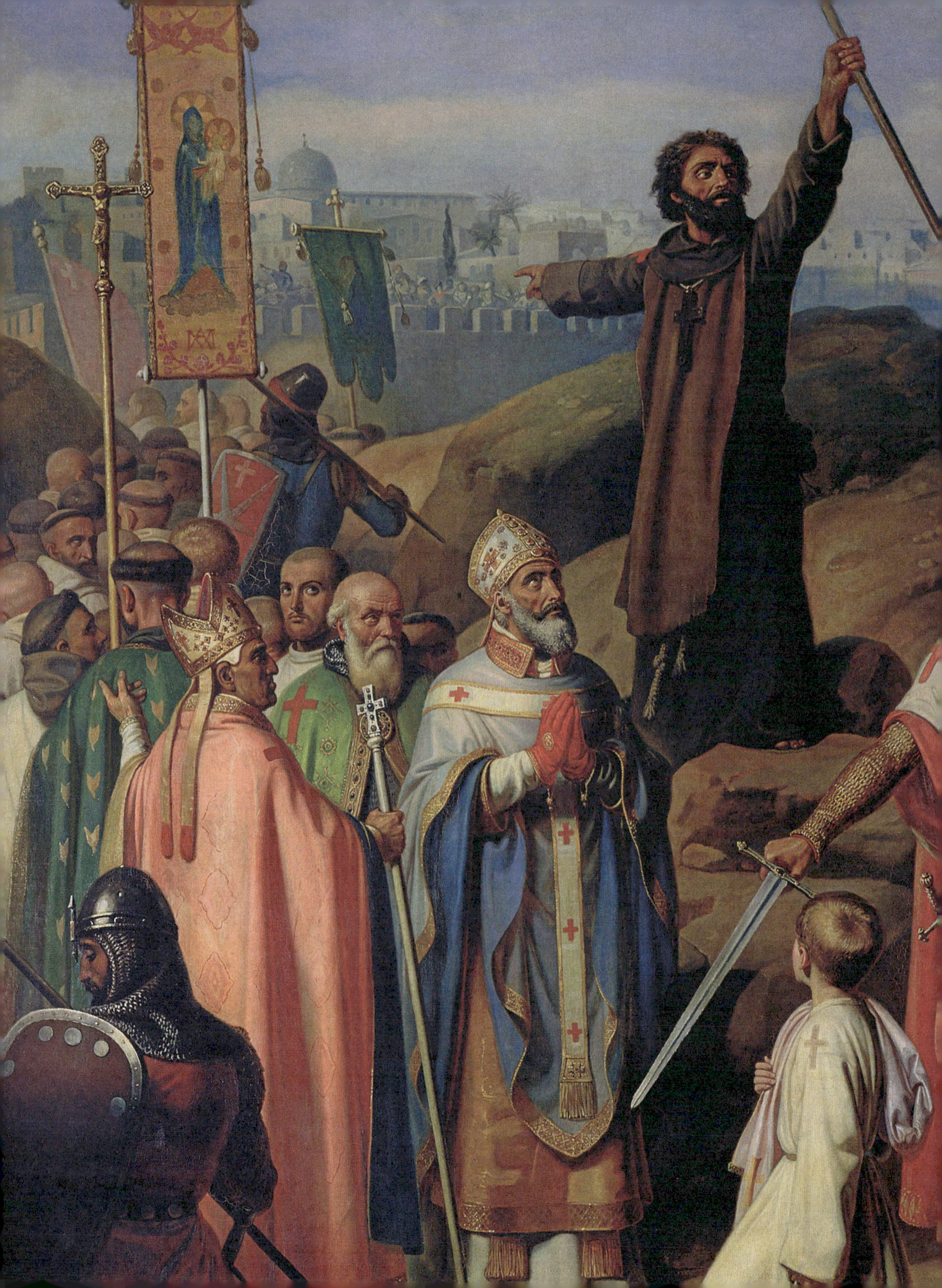

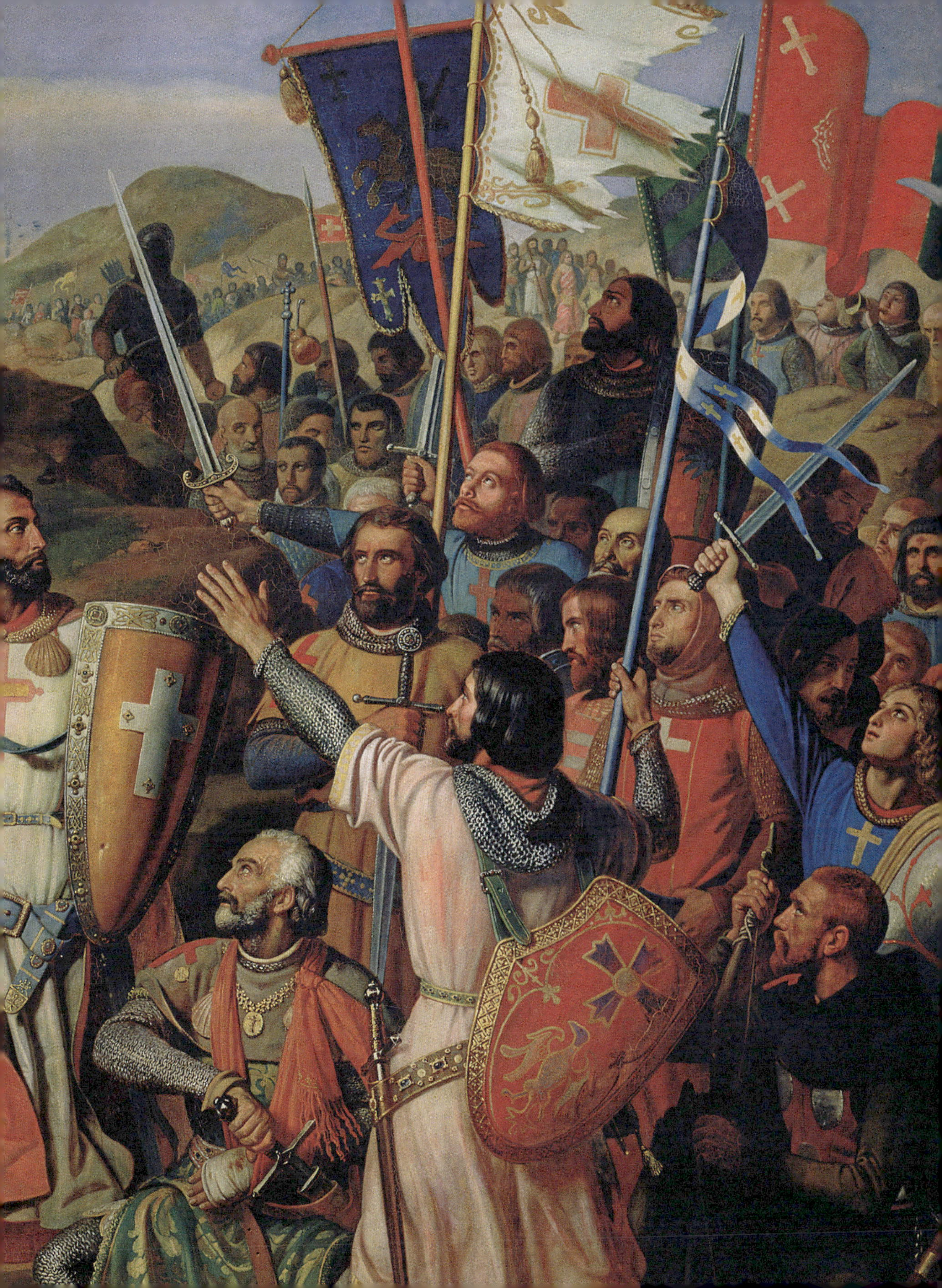

THE WESTERN EMPERORS

CONRAD II

ITALIAN CHAOS

NAME: Konrad of Speyer
BORN: Franconia, c. 990
RULED: Emperor, 1027–1039
DIED: Of gout, Utrecht, Friesland, 1039

SINCE HENRY II had died childless, the German nobles gathered on a plain in the Rhine valley between the towns of Mainz and Worms to elect Conrad, duke of Franconia, as King of the Romans. As usual, the Italians rebelled against their German overlords, though no one they approached accepted the offer to be king of Italy, being fearful of Conrad. This accounted for the relative short period between his becoming German king in 1024 and his crowning as emperor in 1027, an event at which the kings of England and Burgundy were present.

Though Conrad had the requisite bloodline, being the great-great-grandson of Otto I through Otto's daughter, Liutgarde, his family was quite poor compared with the great noble houses, and this deprivation meant he was cautious with the empire's wealth. He was also concerned for the application of justice throughout the realm. In fact, during his coronation parade, he stopped proceedings to listen to the grievances of the poor—who cast themselves at his feet, crying aloud for justice—annoying the bishop, who was keen to proceed. During his reign he issued an edict stopping superior lords depriving their vassals of their lands without judgement by their peers.

> **It is a heavy office that I have taken up, and surely I must walk in the paths of righteousness.**
>
> CONRAD II

His major preoccupation involved the frequent rebellions of his stepson, Ernest of Swabia, who resented Conrad after the emperor obtained the throne of Burgundy in 1032, something that Ernest believed he had more right to, since he was more closely related to the last king of Burgundy, Rudolph. After a number of insurrections, the rebel became the first prince to incur the Ban of the Empire, which deprived him of his dukedom. He was excommunicated and proclaimed an outlaw and enemy of the empire, and all swore not to avenge any harm that might befall him, and not to punish any who might strike him.

Like his predecessors, Conrad was constantly required to intervene in the endless internecine conflicts of the Italian states. Civil war erupted in Lombardy in 1035, continuing through to Conrad's death in 1039, and his attempts to end the strife were ignored. His final major expedition was to southern Italy, where he was asked to adjudicate in a dispute over Capua: he found in favour of Prince Guaimar IV of Salerno and chased out the rival disputant, Pandulf. A year later, Conrad was dead.

HENRY III

THE BLACK

NAME: Heinrich
BORN: Unknown, 1017
RULED: Emperor, 1046–1056
DIED: Of natural causes,
Bodfeld (Harz Mountains),
Saxony, 1056

LIKE HIS FATHER, Conrad, Henry was tall, reputedly standing far above his nobles. Surnamed The Black because of his dark complexion, he was brave, generous and pious, and was often seen on the battlefield kneeling in prayer. After a victory, he would dress in a hairshirt and walk barefoot from church to church, giving thanks to God.

Thanks to the Truce of God (see page 264), the empire's interior was at peace during Henry's reign, but he frequently marched out to deal with enemies on the borders. Successful expeditions into Bohemia, Hungary and Burgundy meant that by 1046 he had managed to quell most of the threats to his power.

Henry's focus soon shifted to Italy and the sorry state of the papacy. The church was in schism as three popes claimed the throne of St Peter. Keen to begin a renewal of the church, Henry marched south and summoned the claimants. Holding court over them, he deposed them all, stating that their elections had been invalid and that the pontificate was, therefore, vacant. Henry then nominated a new pope, Clement II, formerly the bishop of Bamberg, who crowned him emperor in Rome, to the people's acclamations.

> **I as King will show you the example and forgive all those who have done aught against me.**
>
> HENRY III

Henry enforced his right to nominate the pope, and the next three popes owed their elevation to him. These German popes, supported by the Western emperor, were able to emancipate themselves from the quagmire of local Italian politics. Focusing on reform and the rectification of abuses that had been rife within the church for more than two centuries, these popes began expanding papal authority and prestige, and introduced the notion that no earthly authority, not even the emperor, should control the church.

In the meantime, Henry joined the popes to handle a new threat in Italy's south—the Normans. Originally given imperial approval to settle there and attack the Eastern Empire, they rapidly conquered large swathes of territory, becoming a threat to both pope and Western emperor. A coalition in 1054 attempted to halt their expansion, but a Norman victory and Pope Leo IX's capture saw their territorial acquisitions confirmed. By now, however, Henry's focus was back north. Lorraine, Hungary, Poland and Bohemia all flared into war, while German princes began rebelling, darkening the final years of his reign. He managed to quell them before dying on campaign against the Slavs.

Henry was the most powerful Western Roman emperor since Otto I, perhaps even Charlemagne. By the standards of the time, few questioned his authority as emperor and king, and the popes openly acknowledged their vassalage. However, by the end of his reign a new and far more formidable force had joined his old enemies—the renewed papacy, ironically the very entity he had helped create.

HENRY IV

THE EXCOMMUNICATED KING

NAME: Heinrich
BORN: Goslar, Saxony, 1050
RULED: Emperor, 1084–1105
DIED: Liège, Lorraine, 1106

AT THE START OF HENRY IV'S reign, the Western Empire was at the height of its power. By its end, civil war and a drawn-out fight with the papacy had ruined the emperor's authority. Henry III's youngest son and Germany's king at the age of six, he became the pawn of the nobility and the ever more powerful archbishops. Rebellions were common as these groups fought for supremacy, and at one point the twelve-year-old Henry was captured to use as a bargaining chip. Taking these lessons to heart, he would ruthlessly impose royal authority, setting the scene for a confrontation with the church and the nobility.

His first independent action was to impose royal control by building castles throughout Saxony, which was a hotbed of rebellious activity. This, along with a decision to depose certain influential nobles, caused a general uprising. Henry had to flee for his life and wandered the woods for three days before reaching safety. He was only able to crush the revolt when the rebels began to perform acts of sacrilege and brutality, forcing the other German nobles reluctantly to join Henry's side.

Having just managed to regain control of the situation in Germany, Henry became embroiled in a new conflict with the papacy. Since the time of Otto I, the popes had been obliged to have their election confirmed by the emperor, something they resented. During Henry's minority, a number of popes had been crowned without seeking his approval, pointing out that he was German king but not yet emperor, and thus in no position to impose the right of confirmation. Henry, of course, did not see it that way, believing that as King of the Romans and, therefore, emperor-elect he did possess the right. The situation finally exploded with the election of Pope Gregory VII in 1073. Gregory summoned church councils to rule that kings could not elect bishops, and that no payment should go to the king for the right of nomination to the see. This hit Henry hard, removing at one stroke a key source of royal revenue, as well as meaning he now had prince-bishops in his realm who owed their allegiance to the pope, not to him

> **I, Henry, King by God's grace, cry to you with all my bishops, 'Abdicate! Abdicate!'**
>
> HENRY IV (TO POPE GREGORY VII)

Henry went on the offensive, summoning a council in 1076 to declare Gregory's election to the chair of St Peter as illegal. Gregory struck back, declaring Henry excommunicated from the church and, therefore, deprived of his crown. This was unprecedented in the annals of the Western Empire and threw Germany into chaos. The nobility rebelled, forcing Henry to travel to Italy and ask for the pope's forgiveness. Gregory was surprised to see the king outside the walls of the town where he was staying and for three days Henry waited, deprived of all signs of royalty, without food in the cold mountains. Gregory did not want to reconcile with Henry, since he was keen to overthrow the stubborn and authoritarian king. However, as pope, he had to forgive a penitent, and so he reluctantly came out and allowed Henry to embrace his feet in abject humiliation before restoring Henry's right to the crown.

Henry III, inadvertent creator of the medieval papacy

THE CRUSADES

Unfortunately, the German nobility were not so forgiving, crowning a rival, Rudolf, as German king. Henry expected the pope to support his position, but when Henry was defeated by the rebels in 1080 Gregory acknowledged Rudolf. Furious at such a betrayal and bitter about his earlier humiliating backdown, Henry pronounced Gregory deposed and replaced him with Clement III. Few could stand against Henry when he was roused and he killed Rudolf in battle before marching on Rome, besieging it three times before entering the city in 1084. He officially installed Clement as pope and he, in turn, crowned Henry Western emperor, while Gregory remained trapped in Hadrian's Tomb. Henry was forced to flee when the Normans intervened, though Gregory died shortly afterwards.

Gregory's successors maintained Henry's reimposed excommunication and this led to continued revolts in Germany throughout his reign. Then came the rebellions of his two sons. The elder, Conrad, went over to the papal camp in 1093. He was crowned king of Italy and was promised the imperial crown upon his father's defeat. In 1098 Henry disinherited Conrad, and he was confined to Italy before dying, deserted and despised, at Florence in 1101. Then Henry's younger son, also named Henry, rebelled with Pope Paschal II's support. This time all Germany rose up, and Henry IV resigned the purple in 1105 after his son tricked him into disbanding his armies. He fled to Liège and was attempting to reclaim his crown when death overtook him in 1106.

HENRY V

LIKE FATHER, LIKE SON

NAME: Heinrich
BORN: Goslar, Saxony, 1086
RULED: Emperor, 1111–1125
DIED: Of natural causes, Utrecht, Friesland, 1125

GIVEN HENRY V'S ALLIANCE with the papacy, Pope Paschal II expected to deal with a dutiful son of the church. He misjudged Henry's imperious and unforgiving personality. Upon his father's death in 1106, Henry fought for his rights more fiercely than Henry IV ever had. The conflict dragged on for four years before Henry forced the issue by marching to Rome. The sight of thirty thousand Germans worked wonders, and Paschal agreed (on the clergy's behalf) to relinquish everything the emperors had bestowed on the church since Charlemagne's time, as well as agreeing to an imperial coronation, in return for Henry giving up his claims to royal investiture of bishops.

St Peter has chosen King Henry!

THE ROMAN PEOPLE
(greeting Henry V on his approach to Rome)

It was a debacle: the bishops refused to endorse the transfer of their property to the king. Furious, Henry declined to hand over his rights and captured the pope. Under duress, Paschal agreed to allow him to retain his right of investiture of German bishops and crowned him as Roman emperor.

No sooner had Henry returned to Germany than Paschal reneged on the agreement, and by 1114 civil war once again engulfed Germany. As the secular and spiritual nobles strove to destroy the emperor, Henry's only safe haven was Italy, but when he returned there, the new pope, Calixtus II, excommunicated him in 1119. To save his crown, Henry held a council at Worms in 1122, finally agreeing to abandon the royal right of investiture of bishops, though he retained the right to grant imperial estates to the candidate, along with the imperial sceptre.

Henry's final years saw him deal ruthlessly with the aftermath of the recent rebellions. Consequently, the people hated him: to them he was a hard and severe ruler, and when he died in 1125 few mourned his passing.

LOTHAIR III

UNPOPULAR CHOICE

NAME: Lothar von Supplinburg
BORN: Unknown, 1075
RULED: Emperor, 1133–1137
DIED: Of natural causes,
Breitenwang, Bavaria, 1137

HENRY V DIED CHILDLESS, and so in 1125 the German princes gathered to elect a new king. They chose Lothair, a minor noble whom Henry V had made duke of Saxony after he helped him defeat his father.

Lothair was reluctant to take the German crown because of the rival claims of Frederick and Conrad Hohenstaufen and his reign was a constant battle against them. Using their inheritance of lands held by Heny V as a pretext, Frederick dedicated himself to stirring up trouble in Germany, while Conrad marched into Italy, becoming king of Italy in 1128. Conrad's departure weakened Frederick's position at home, and Lothair was able to defeat him within seven years.

Meanwhile, Pope Innocent II was threatened by Conrad to the north, Roger, the Norman king of Sicily, to the south and the antipope, Anacletus, and he needed Lothair's help. Marching into Italy with a small force, since the bulk of his troops were containing Frederick, Lothair installed Innocent in Rome and, in return, Innocent crowned him Roman emperor. Within two years, Conrad would rejoin his brother, and both submitted to the emperor.

Lothair returned to Italy in 1136 to deal with King Roger and, having successfully pushed the Normans out of southern Italy, was contemplating an invasion of Sicily when his dissatisfied troops confronted him and demanded to go home. Turning around, Lothair made it only to the Alps before, stricken by disease, he passed away suddenly.

FREDERICK I 'BARBAROSSA'

RED BEARD

NAME: Friedrich von Hohenstaufen
BORN: Waiblingen, Swabia, 1122
RULED: Emperor, 1155–1190
DIED: Drowned, Saleph River,
Cilicia, Anatolia, 1190

AFTER LOTHAIR'S death, there was no emperor for over seventeen years. Conrad of Hohenstaufen, though he had been elected King of the Romans, was never crowned Roman emperor, and upon his death the German nobility elected his thirty-year-old nephew, Frederick, as king.

Blessed with great physical prowess, Frederick's forceful personality enabled him to dominate almost everyone around him. Charismatic and egotistical, his ambition matched his abilities, and though he was surrounded by implacable enemies, he used any advantage he could to ensure he came out on top.

> **By heaven, if we were not in a church you would feel how sharp is a German sword for these words!**
>
> FREDERICK I BARBAROSSA

Frederick was fortunate that for much of his reign Germany was at peace. Though facing a formidable rival in the shape of Henry the Lion, duke of Saxony, he managed to contain the struggles between the Ghibellines and the Guelfs. It was very different in Italy. The continuing conflict between pope and emperor, as well as half a century of German civil wars, had prevented the emperors paying attention to northern Italy. By the time Frederick assumed the crown, Italy's cities were civilised, prosperous and independent, and

Pope Alexander III hands the holy sword to the Doge of Venice, sailing with his fleet to fight against Frederick I

unlikely to submit to an emperor in far-off Germany. The attempts of these rebellious city-states to throw off the imperial yoke would see Frederick repeatedly attack them and it was they, the first to feel Frederick's wrath, that nicknamed him Barbarossa, or Red Beard, as a mark of their fear and respect.

This spirit of republicanism also infected Rome, where the citizens hoped to resurrect the ancient and glorious Roman Republic, and they threw out Pope Adrian IV, who then asked for Frederick's help. He marched into Italy, but things got off to a rocky start when he neglected to hold the pope's stirrup as a sign of submission. Eventually he gave in and preparations began for his imperial coronation after his German troops had dealt with the republican forces within the city. However, they left such ill feeling among the populace that once Frederick was crowned emperor, the Romans rose up and attacked the German troops, who turned around and massacred thousands. Frederick had to leave Rome because of the unhealthy Roman summer and was soon back in Germany.

Frederick spent the next thirty years trying to enforce his authority on his Italian subjects, a task made even harder by the ever-shifting alliances. Anti-imperial leagues were formed and did occasionally inflict substantial defeats on Frederick's troops. Nevertheless, the emperor gave as good as he got, ruthlessly sacking cities such as Milan. His treatment of conquered cities was quite lenient for the times: on one occasion, he forced the citizens of a defeated city to march out of their city to him with bridles around their necks, ashes on their heads and crosses in their hands to acknowledge his supremacy.

Frederick had an elevated opinion of himself and his place in the world and once invaded Italy just because the pope implied that the empire was a fief of the papacy, making him the pope's vassal. He believed he was the sole Roman emperor, lord of all his subjects' properties throughout the ancient boundaries of the empire, a belief made explicit because he did not recognise the Eastern emperor, Manuel I. Frederick believed he was the chief defender of Christendom, and so when news came of Jerusalem's fall to Saladin in 1187, he knew what he had to do. Taking the crusader oath, Frederick joined Richard I of England and Philip II of France on the Third Crusade.

Of the three, Frederick was the monarch Saladin feared most. Easily defeating the Turks who had overrun Anatolia, he captured a number of cities on his way south. However, fate was to intervene decisively. Crossing the Saleph River in Cilicia, he drowned without achieving his goal of recapturing Jerusalem. His soldiers could not preserve his remains, but they bore him onwards, interring his heart and internal organs in Tarsus, his flesh in Antioch and his bones at Tyre.

Under Frederick Barbarossa's reign, imperial authority regained respect. His control of the German princes was no mean feat, while his control of the Italians, though maintained only by decades of warfare and bloodshed, was an achievement few of his successors matched.

HENRY VI

GRANDIOSE DREAMS

NAME: Heinrich von Hohenstaufen
BORN: Nijmegen, Lorraine, 1165
RULED: Emperor, 1191–1197
DIED: Of malaria, Messina, Sicily, 1197

HENRY VI, SON OF FREDERICK Barbarossa, was twenty-five years old and already crowned king when Barbarossa died. Like his father in many ways, Henry was also hard and cruel, but he lacked Frederick's generosity of spirit and thus was not as loved or admired.

Frederick had found a way to eliminate the Norman kingdom in the south by marrying Henry to Constance, the aunt of the childless King William of Sicily and his heir presumptive. After William died, it was Tancred, the bastard son of the duke of Apulia and William's cousin, who usurped the throne, forcing Henry to spend the rest of his life pursuing his claims in Sicily. Marching into Italy in 1191, he stopped off at Rome to be crowned emperor by Pope Celestine III, who, in a fit of pique, kicked the crown off Henry's head immediately after placing it there. Henry only got as far as Naples when a plague forced him back to Germany, with the added humiliation that his wife was captured by forces loyal to Tancred.

Tancred's death in 1193 saw Henry once again on the offensive. This time he was successful, and by 1195 had reunited southern Italy with the Western Empire, the first time it had been under the Western emperor's authority since Julius Nepos's reign in 473. Yet his humiliation in 1191 had rankled in Henry's mind, and now he indulged in the utmost brutality. He desecrated Tancred's tomb, stripping the body of any sign of royalty. As for Tancred's son, Henry had him blinded and castrated, before he burnt a number of Norman nobles alive. Returning north, he attempted to formalise the hereditary succession for Germany and the empire. He had visions of a worldwide empire: not content to claim that England, France and Spain were under his authority, he was even planning to conquer Constantinople itself, though initially he was happy to accept a large bribe from the Eastern emperor, Alexius III. Before he could act on his plans, Sicily flared into revolt against his brutal and tyrannical rule. Having reached Messina, he was engaged in more cruel reprisals when he died of malaria, to the relief of the local population.

GHIBELLINES, GUELFS AND THE TRUCE OF GOD

The origin of the conflict between Ghibellines and Guelfs lay in the rivalry between the Welfs, the family of the dukes of Bavaria, and the Hohenstaufens of Swabia that arose during the twelfth century and troubled the reigns of the German king Conrad III and his son, the emperor Frederick I. The term 'Guelf' was an Italian corruption of Welf, while 'Ghibelline' came from Waiblingen, a Hohenstaufen castle. Both terms were originally battle cries used by the respective armies during the German conflicts, but eventually they came to denote the northern Italian factions that supported either the pope (the Guelfs) or the Roman emperor (the Ghibellines).

The Truce of God was an attempt to curtail the prevalence of private wars in feudal society, such as were rampant in the Western Roman Empire at this time. Through this mechanism, violence between the nobility was prohibited on Sundays and Holy Days, and over time this was extended to all of Lent, and then every week from Wednesday evening to Monday morning. Although it was first introduced in France in 1027, it was the emperor Henry III who, seeing how well it worked there, decided in 1048 to enforce it throughout Germany. He summoned all his nobles and, using a combination of threats and gentle persuasion, forced them to swear an oath that they would keep the truce and not engage in acts of feudal warfare against each other. Although initially quite successful, the practice began to wane by the thirteenth century, due in no small part to its ineffectualness at curbing the conflict between the Guelfs and the Ghibellines.

THE EASTERN EMPERORS

ROMANUS III

THE EGOTISTICAL EMPEROR

NAME: Rōmanos Argyros
BORN: Place unknown, 968
RULED: Emperor, 1028–1034
DIED: Poisoned, Constantinople, 1034

BASIL II'S SUCCESSES had turned the Eastern Empire into Europe's most powerful state. Its future depended upon the calibre of emperor sitting on the throne, yet court intrigues saw the elevation of men incapable of defending the empire. The first of these was Romanus Argyrus.

Because he did not have a male heir, the dying Constantine VIII was persuaded to marry off one of his daughters to the sixty-year-old Romanus. Of those available, forty-four-year-old Theodora refused outright and so he turned to forty-eight-year-old Zoe. A respectable member of the non-military nobility, Romanus was well versed in literature and learning. He was also married and not eager to leave his wife, and so Constantine threatened to blind him. Unsurprisingly, he agreed to the marriage and, within a week, he was emperor.

Romanus was a vain man, supremely confident in his own abilities. Determined to start a royal dynasty with his aged wife, he took massive amounts of aphrodisiacs, hoping to enhance his fading performance, but they only resulted in extreme hair loss. He spent a fortune on new and useless building works, squandering the empire's precious resources. He also dreamed of being a warrior-emperor like John Tzimisces, though he had never marched into battle in his life. Provoking a fight with the Saracens to show his mettle, he walked straight into an ambush near Antioch. At the first Saracen charge, he fled, taking his troops with him. He never marched out of Constantinople again.

> My most faithful servant.
>
> ROMANUS ARGYRUS (referring to Michael the Paphlagonian)

Zoe, in the meantime, had grown to detest her husband and started an affair with one of her servants, Michael, the brother of the chief court eunuch, John the *orphanotrophos*. Romanus was suspicious, but when he confronted Michael the young man denied any wrongdoing. Eager to reward her young lover, Zoe slowly poisoned Romanus, who died while taking a bath.

MICHAEL IV
THE GOLDEN ADONIS

NAME: Mikhaēl Paphlagōn
BORN: Paphlagonia, Anatolia, 1010
RULED: Emperor, 1034–1041
DIED: Of natural causes, Constantinople, 1041

MICHAEL, A YOUNG peasant from Paphlagonia, had two things going for him. His brother John was the court's chief eunuch, and he himself was a living Adonis—muscular, ravishingly handsome and graceful. John got him a menial job in the imperial household; his looks won him the empress's heart. Soon this former forger was sitting on the throne of the Caesars.

Zoe may have hoped for a puppet to manipulate, but Michael soon dashed her hopes. At twenty-four, he did not love the older empress and Romanus's murder gave ample proof she could not be trusted, and so Michael quickly locked her in the palace. Against all expectations, he turned out to be a conscientious emperor, dedicated to strengthening the empire and providing justice for the people. His major problem was that he was an epileptic, whose fits grew worse throughout his reign. The government was managed by his brother, John the *orphanotrophos*, who was appointed chief minister. Though he was competent, John's nepotism and excessive taxation meant he was the target of numerous plots.

During Michael's reign, the empire managed to hold its own. Saracen incursions in the east were halted, while in the west the brilliant general George Maniakes almost reconquered Sicily single-handedly before his recall squandered all his gains. John's financial excesses then saw the Bulgarians rebel. In the final act of his reign, the declining Michael—bloated, almost paralysed, with gangrenous legs and in constant agony—marched at the head of the Roman army and crushed the rebellion. By the end of the campaign he was clearly dying. Returning to Constantinople, he resigned the purple and, taking monastic vows, spent his final few days on earth seeking forgiveness for his role in Romanus's death.

MICHAEL V 'CALAPHATES'
THE CAULKER

NAME: Mikhaēl Kalaphatēs
BORN: Place unknown, 1015
RULED: Emperor, 1041–1042
DIED: Of natural causes, Chios, 1042

WITH MICHAEL IV obviously unwell, John the *orphanotrophos* began his search for a successor. Since his remaining brothers were either dead or eunuchs, he turned to his nephew, another Michael, to carry on the imperial bloodline. He was a poor choice.

> **Look—if you see me struggle, nail me down!**
>
> MICHAEL V CALAPHATES (about to be blinded)

Michael V was the son of Stephen, a former caulker who had replaced George Maniakes to lead the humiliating Sicilian expedition of 1040. Michael was completely untrustworthy, without morals or scruples. Prior to his uncle's death, he had become the adopted son of Zoe, who was recalled just for this ceremony, and having been crowned emperor in late 1041, he promised to rule in conjunction with Zoe, under the guidance of John. He quickly broke both promises, banishing both to separate monasteries in 1042 and even claiming that Zoe was trying to kill him. This, together with an ill-advised frontal assault on the aristocracy, roused the people of Constantinople to a fury. They marched on the palace, demanding the restoration of Zoe as well as the crowning of her sister, Theodora. Michael tried to placate the crowd but soon fled, seeking sanctuary in a monastery along with another uncle, Constantine. When both were dragged out to be blinded, the frightened emperor insisted that Constantine go first. He was then forced into taking holy vows but was dead before the end of 1042.

ZOE

UNLUCKY IN LOVE

NAME: Zōē
BORN: Constantinople, c. 978
RULED: Sole empress, 1041; co-empress, 1042
DIED: Of natural causes, Constantinople, 1050

ZOE, CONSTANTINE VIII'S middle daughter, was a pleasure seeker whose importance depended on her uncle and father not producing any sons. Considered the most beautiful of Constantine's daughters, she was promiscuous in an age that frowned on such activities. Quick witted, with a lively disposition but slow in speech, she was seen by men as the means by which they could attain the purple.

She was forty-eight when forced to marry the elderly Romanus, whom she enjoyed until he restricted her spending in order to control the imperial budget. When Romanus refused to share her bed, her attentions wandered to her beautiful servant, Michael. Falling head over heels in love, she showered the twenty-something with kisses and caresses, openly flaunting him as her lover. He, on the other hand, felt nothing for Zoe, now fifty-five years old, seeing her as his ticket to imperial glory. She poisoned Romanus and he was barely cold when Michael became her husband and emperor. She bitterly regretted her folly when Michael confined her to the palace under the strictest security, and his visits became ever more infrequent until they stopped altogether.

Zoe stayed in the palace until the eve of Michael's death in 1041. Summoned to adopt the nominated heir, Michael Calaphates, she begged to be allowed to see her husband, but Michael refused to see her, shamed by his actions and grotesque illness. With his death, she became empress of the Romans for three days, during which time she discovered she did not want the burden of running the empire. She had Calaphates crowned and he promised to respect her; her banishment again showed how gullible she was when it came to dealing with men. Yet before long she was back in Constantinople. To her surprise, the people wanted her as their empress, but they insisted that she reign with her sister Theodora, whom she loathed.

Their joint rule lasted under two months and it was an unmitigated disaster. Holding separate courts, they intrigued against each other until Zoe, seeing no other way out, looked for another husband. After her first choice rejected the offer and her second choice died in mysterious circumstances, she married Constantine Monomachus, who was crowned emperor. By this stage Zoe was in her mid sixties and was no longer interested in dominating events. Within a few months of remarrying, she retired from public life. Though she was forced to share her position with Constantine's mistress, she did not seem to mind, enjoying her imperial status until her death eight years later.

CONSTANTINE IX

REJECTING THE SWORD

NAME: Kōnstantinos Monomakhos
BORN: Constantinople, c. 1000
RULED: Emperor, 1042–1055
DIED: Of natural causes, Constantinople, 1055

WITTY, POLISHED AND URBANE, Constantine Monomachus appeared to be the perfect ruler for an empire at the centre of culture and learning during the eleventh century. Seeking pleasure in elaborate court ceremonials, he surrounded himself with scholars and

Constantine's reign also saw the final split between the eastern and western churches. Long-standing tensions erupted in 1054, with protests lodged against the imposition of Latin usages in Greek churches in Italy's south. Pope Leo IX sent legates to Constantinople to resolve the issue, and Constantine was keen to placate the pope in order to keep pressure on the Normans. Unfortunately, the anti-Greek attitudes of the legates and the patriarch's well-known anti-western feelings resulted in petty bickering where all the old wounds (the *filioque* clause, papal supremacy and the subservience of the eastern church to the emperor) were exposed. The session ended in mutual excommunication of the participants, and the final separation of the churches. Constantine attempted to mediate, but the conflict drained his fading strength and he passed away early in 1055.

Constantine IX

intellectuals on whose book-bound advice he increasingly relied. Their opinion? Control the military aristocracy by reducing the army's strength and remove the civil administration of the provinces from military governors to deskbound bureaucrats. The empire's subsequent decline begins with Constantine.

Unconcerned with military matters, pampered in his palace, Constantine watched with complete indifference as the Pechenegs, a Turkic people on the northern shores of the Black Sea, overran the newly acquired Bulgarian provinces, while the Normans took what little territory remained in southern Italy. However, the main disaster was to the east, where Constantine's foolish destruction of the independent Armenian kingdoms opened the door for the introduction of the Seljuk Turks, who launched their first major attack against the empire in 1048.

GEORGE MANIACES

END OF AN ERA

NAME: Georgios Maniakes
BORN: Unknown
RULED: Usurper, 1042–1043
DIED: Killed in battle, Ostrovo (modern Arnissa), Thessalonike, 1043

GEORGE MANIACES, last of the talented generals schooled by Basil II, was a reminder of the empire's glory days. A giant of a man, stupendously ugly and violent, he dominated the pygmies who controlled the court and the military. He left them in no doubt as to his opinion of them, in particular his bitter enemy, Romanos Skleros.

As *strategos* of Telouch, he came to prominence in 1030 during Romanus Argyrus's reign, with an audacious attack on the Saracens who were besieging the fortress he was manning. When Michael IV gave him command of Sicily's reconquest, he took to the task with gusto, by 1039 forcing the Saracens out of the island and crushing a new invasion in 1040. It was unfortunate that his ferocious temper ruined his imminent victory, as he rashly struck Stephen, Michael IV's incompetent brother-in-law, who had him recalled to Constantinople and cast into prison. This resulted in the Romans being expelled from the island by 1041.

Released after the fall of John the *orphanotrophos*, he returned to Bari to hold what little imperial territory remained. His time in prison had not improved his mood; finding the province in rebellion, he felt drastic measures were needed. Systematically crushing all resistance, he butchered whole towns, not even sparing children, monks or nuns. The few who survived shuddered at the mention of his name. Then his progress was halted by Constantine IX, who listened to the advice of Skleros's sister and ordered his recall.

George was furious. Gathering his troops, he declared himself emperor and killed his designated successor after filling his mouth, nose and ears with manure. Marching towards Constantinople, he destroyed an army sent to intercept him but, on the cusp of victory, was killed by an arrow shot by the retreating imperial army. Thus died the one man capable of arresting the empire's slide towards ruin. He deserved a better fate than having his head paraded on a lance in Constantine's ill-deserved triumph.

LEO TORNICIUS

ALWAYS TAKE YOUR CHANCES

NAME: Leōn Tornikios
BORN: Adrianople (Edirne), Macedonia, unknown date
RULED: Usurper, 1047
DIED: Unknown

LEO TORNICIUS, the *strategos* of Iberia and Constantine IX's ambitious nephew, was extremely popular at court. Consequently, the emperor was jealous of him, using every opportunity to humiliate him. When Constantine tried to force Leo to become a monk, after a failed revolt, he fled to Adrianople where, having declared that Constantine was dead and that he had married the empress Theodora, he was raised to the purple by the army.

Leo swiftly besieged Constantinople, which, through Constantine's distrust of the military, was short of troops. A skirmish saw Constantine's troops flee, leaving the city wide open for Leo. He did not advance, hoping for Constantine's overthrow from within, but it never happened and the defenders eventually secured the gates against him. It was his only chance. The next day he launched an unsuccessful assault against the walls and was forced to raise the siege and retreat to Arcadiopolis. Subsequent defeats saw him deserted by his followers and so he took refuge in a church. Forcibly removed, he wound up before Constantine in chains and was then blinded.

THEODORA

SPINSTER EMPRESS

NAME: Theodōra
BORN: Constantinople, c. 981
RULED: Co-empress, 1042; sole empress, 1055–1056
DIED: Of natural causes, Constantinople, 1056

THEODORA, CONSTANTINE VIII'S youngest daughter, was intelligent, steady and thrifty, with an excellent grasp of the government's needs. Her ability was one reason her sister Zoe detested her. The other was that she was Constantine's first choice as wife for Romanus Argyrus. Happy to be single, she refused, forcing Constantine to choose Zoe instead, but Zoe never forgave the insult. During Romanus's reign Theodora was accused of conspiring against the emperor, and Zoe forced her to take monastic vows.

Thus the situation remained until 1042, when the people of Constantinople demanded she become co-empress along with Zoe in the days leading up to the deposition of Michael V. She resisted, but eventually they forced her to wear the imperial crown. Her first decision showed her mettle: she ordered the blinding of Michael when Zoe looked like she was wavering.

During their joint reign, though Zoe had official precedence, all the decisions were made by Theodora, including reorganising government administration and correcting the abuses from previous reigns. This only served to alienate the jealous Zoe, whose marriage to Constantine Monomachus forced Theodora from all imperial duties. Theodora again disappeared into the background until the deaths of Zoe and her husband altered the situation and left her the sole surviving member of the imperial family.

At the age of seventy-four Theodora took over, ruling with singular capacity and effectiveness, and many commented on the unfortunate circumstances that had prevented her assuming the purple until so late in her life. Her superstitious nature stopped her from nominating a successor before she died in 1056.

MICHAEL VI

THE AGED

NAME: Mikhaēl Bringas
BORN: Unknown
RULED: Emperor, 1056–1057
DIED: Of natural causes, Constantinople, 1059

THEODORA'S DEATH ended the Macedonian dynasty and, with it, whatever loyalty the military aristocracy felt towards the emperors. The first to feel their indignation was Michael Bringas, contemptuously known as Michael the Warlike, but more commonly as Michael the Aged.

An elderly court bureaucrat selected by other bureaucrats, he symbolised everything the military believed had gone wrong with the empire. He survived a laughable attempt by Monomachus's nephew, Theodosius, to topple him from the throne, a plot that involved the release of prisoners who fled at the sight of the imperial guards. The next rebellion was much more serious.

The nobility's growing discontent, their public humiliation at the emperor's hands, and the loss of their perks triggered a civil war. The Asian provinces rallied around Isaac Comnenus, declaring him emperor, while Michael, urged on by his eunuch supporters, summoned the European armies. Defeated, Michael tried unsuccessfully to encourage his supporters, berating them for their lack of honour. When the patriarch finally moved to support Isaac, Michael realised all was lost. He resigned the purple and lived out his life in retirement, undisturbed by his successor.

ISAAC I

FAILED REFORMER

NAME: Isaakios Komnēnos
BORN: Place unknown, c. 1007
RULED: Emperor, 1057–1059
DIED: Of natural causes, Constantinople, 1061

ISAAC COMNENUS'S ABILITIES saw him promoted at an early age as Basil II's personal bodyguard. Having climbed the military ladder, by 1057 he was an important army commander in Anatolia. The nobility were fed up with Michael VI and Isaac became their candidate for emperor, though he was very reluctant to accept the burden and it required a military delegation to help convince him. His victory over Michael's forces assured him of the crown, but initially he was happy to become the *kaisar*. However, a push to overthrow Michael from within saw Isaac made emperor.

Throwing himself into reinvigorating the empire's military and administrative functions, long neglected by Basil II's successors, Isaac abolished useless court offices and reclaimed land that royal favourites had accumulated, pouring the money saved back into the military. This and his attacks on wealthy monasteries made him very unpopular, but his justification came when he won an impressive victory against the Hungarians.

Unfortunately, Isaac, like many of his contemporaries, was deeply superstitious. He was already deeply shaken after narrowly avoiding being struck by lightning while he was leaning against a tree, and when he fell ill he saw it as a sign of God's displeasure. Court bureaucrats convinced him that he was dying, and the depressed emperor abdicated the purple and took monastic vows. Instead of passing the diadem to his capable brother, he gave in to pressure from the bureaucracy to name one of their own—Constantine Ducas—as his successor. Isaac recovered from his illness but he remained depressed. Refusing to reclaim the throne, he preferred to end his days as a doorkeeper in a monastery.

CONSTANTINE X

PRELUDE TO DISASTER

NAME: Kōnstantinos Doukas
BORN: Paphlagonia, Anatolia, 1006
RULED: Emperor, 1059–1067
DIED: Of natural causes,
Constantinople, 1067

MODEST, KIND, FAIR-MINDED and thrifty, Constantine Ducas also possessed the characteristics of a classic bureaucrat—he was a time waster and his energy was consumed with endless discussions about abstruse points of law, philosophy and theology. An army of bureaucrats, who paid no attention to the real issues, strangled the management of the empire.

Constantine's only proactive endeavours were to limit the military's power by replacing standing soldiers with mercenaries, leaving the frontier fortifications unrepaired and the army without decent arms or artillery. The generals were so isolated that their only attempt to assassinate the emperor failed miserably in 1061.

Constantine's reign saw further losses in southern Italy, while the savage Uzes crushed a Roman army in the Balkans and captured its general, Nicephorus Botaniates. Yet the east was where the real trouble lay, as Constantine's religious, financial and military policies saw Armenia exposed to the predatory ambitions of the Turks. Having invaded that province, they used it as a springboard to launch raids into Anatolia, the Eastern Empire's heartland. Constantine by now was clearly dying. His final act was to demand that only his sons succeed him, and that his wife not remarry.

ROMANUS IV

BETRAYED IN BATTLE

NAME: Rōmanos Diogenēs
BORN: Cappadocia, c. 1030
RULED: Emperor, 1068–1071
DIED: Of an infected eye wound,
Kınalıada, Princes Islands,
Sea of Marmara, 1072

WITHIN HOURS OF Constantine Ducas's death, his widow, Eudocia, was searching for ways to break her oath not to remarry. The perilous state of the empire, as well as her own tenuous hold on the regency, meant she needed a strong man to run things. She chose Romanus Diogenes. Though he had previously been charged with conspiring to overthrow her children, his charm and beauty had captured her heart. The patriarch declared her oath invalid, and on 1 January 1068, Romanus was crowned emperor and took Eudocia as his wife.

The Turkish capture of Caesarea had convinced the court to recognise the elevation of Romanus, a member of the military aristocracy, to the throne. He was not devoid of military ability but his main flaw was impetuosity. Despite opposition from the Ducas family, who continually intrigued against him, for the first two years of his reign he achieved some success in limiting Turkish advances into the empire. However, the year 1071 saw the destruction of the eastern army at Manzikert and the humiliating capture of Romanus himself by the Seljuk Turks. Though the emperor fought like a lion, a member of the Ducas family betrayed him by spreading rumours of the emperor's death and then fleeing the battle.

> **As emperor, I promised you a ransom of a million and a half. Dethroned, I send you all I possess as proof of my gratitude.**
>
> ROMANUS IV DIOGENES

The Turkish sultan treated Romanus with great respect, releasing him on condition that a huge ransom would be paid, but on his way back to Constantinople he discovered the Ducas family had overthrown him and sent his wife to a monastery. He had never been popular with the people, the bureaucracy or the aristocracy because of his reforming zeal and so no one tried to defend him. Romanus collected what troops he could and fought the Ducas army at Doceia, but his confidence had been shattered. Defeated, he fled to a mountain fortress where he remained until he received reassurance of his personal safety. He came out, resigned the purple and settled down in monastic exile, but the enmity of the Ducas family pursued him. They blinded him and allowed his wound to fester, so that he endured a lingering death.

LEO AND NICEPHORUS

DISINHERITED SONS

NAMES: Leōn and Nikēphoros Diogenēs
BORN: Constantinople, 1069; 1070
RULED: Co-emperors, 1069–1071; 1070–1071
DIED: Killed in battle, Balkans, 1090; unknown

CROWNED CO-EMPERORS during their father's reign, Romanus IV's two sons were banished in 1071 to a monastery, along with their mother, on the order of John Ducas, Constantine X's brother. They returned to favour in 1081 when Alexius Comnenus came to the throne. Taking them into the palace, he raised them like his sons and they soon obtained important commands.

Good-natured Leo was content with his lot; he died in Alexius's campaigns against the Pechenegs in 1090. Handsome and athletic, Nicephorus was a different character, and though Alexius had appointed him governor of Crete, he began planning Alexius's murder. While on campaign with Alexius in 1094, he entered the tent of the emperor one night, carrying a sword that he intended to use. However, the presence of a maid scared him off. When he tried again at the house of Constantine Ducas in Macedonia, he was caught, sword in hand. Later, when questioned under torture, he named all his accomplices. Alexius then commanded that he be blinded, after which he dedicated himself to study, though he continued to yearn for the throne.

> **For this sword here I prepared for thy murder, I fetched it from home and came here to plunge it into thy heart. Once, twice, nay thrice!**
>
> NICEPHORUS DIOGENES (to Alexius Comnenus)

MICHAEL VII
MINUS A QUARTER

NAME: Mikhaēl Doukas
BORN: Constantinople, 1050
RULED: Co-emperor, 1060–1071;
senior emperor, 1071–1078
DIED: Of natural causes, Constantinople, 1090

MICHAEL PSELLUS, TUTOR to young Michael Ducas, declared the emperor to be a 'prodigy of our generation, and a most beloved character'. To almost everyone else, he was despicable and incompetent, surrounded by sycophantic court officials, all blind to the empire collapsing around them.

This son of Constantine X resented his mother and Romanus for overlooking him and eagerly listened to advisors who persuaded him to depose both after the disaster at Manzikert. He felt no obligation to honour the agreement struck by Romanus and the sultan, refusing to pay the ransom. His vindictive short-sightedness saw the loss of Anatolia, as the Turks used the dispute to pour into the defenceless provinces. Michael had no army worthy of the name, and usurpers began fighting each other instead of the Turks.

Meanwhile, the last imperial possession in Italy was lost; the Balkans erupted in revolt; and the Bulgarians were again on the march. Rampant inflation required Michael to debase the empire's currency by a quarter, giving him the nickname Parapinakes ('minus a quarter'), and adding to the people's misery. There was no forward planning, only panicked reactionary policy on the run. By 1074 the sheer number of rebels forced him to acknowledge the Turkish conquests. He even asked for help from the Turks to secure his throne, thereby encouraging the sultan further. By the end of his reign, Michael watched impotently as two usurpers fought for

Seljuk Sultan Malik-Shah, who captured Romanus IV at Manzikert

the throne, and the people dethroned him in favour of Nicephorus Botaniates. He took monastic vows, later becoming the bishop of Ephesus before dying in relative peace and tranquillity around 1090.

CONSTANTIUS AND ANDRONICUS

INCOMPETENT BROTHERS

NAMES: Konstantios and Andronikos Doukas
BORN: Constantinople, 1060; c. 1055
RULED: Co-emperors, 1060–1078; 1068–1077
DIED: Killed in battle, Dyrrhachion (modern Durrës), Albania, 1082; of unknown causes, Constantinople, c. 1077

MICHAEL VII HAD two brothers who became his co-emperors: Constantius, elevated at the same time as Michael, and Andronicus, elevated by Romanus IV eight years later. Neither possessed any great ability and both were happy for the bureaucrats who dominated Michael's reign to manage them. Andronicus's love of hunting consumed much of his leisure time before he died during the chaos of Michael's final years.

Unlike his brothers, Constantius was born *porphyrogenitus*. Though he was a useless dullard, Michael VII abdicated in his favour in 1078. Initially he was supported by the army in Anatolia, but his complete inability to rule was so manifestly evident, he was handed over to Nicephorus Botaniates, who forced him to become a monk. Recalled into active service by Alexius Comnenus, he perished in battle against the Normans at Dyrrhachion in 1082.

PORPHYROGENITUS

By the seventh century, the Roman Empire had well and truly embraced the principle of hereditary succession, overturning the tradition of the emperor being selected by the Senate or the army based upon their ability and authority. Yet it was still a real possibility that an army could raise up an *autokrator* and thus dethrone an existing emperor. To shore up the legitimacy of a ruling dynasty, great emphasis was laid on individuals who were born while their father ruled as *basileus*. These sons were given the honorific title of *porphyrogenitus* (or *porphyrogenita* in the case of a daughter).

Although the concept has its origins back in the sixth century, the term did not come into existence until the ninth century at the latest. The term itself has two co-equal meanings: firstly, that the child was 'purple-born', that is, was born after their father had been crowned emperor and, secondly, that the child was born as dictated by imperial custom in the *Porphyra*, a free standing purple-decorated pavilion located within the imperial palace at Constantinople.

The Romans in the east saw something mystical and pre-ordained in the person of the *porphyrogenitus*, a gift anointed by God to become the next emperor. Such mystical connotations were useful in ensuring a stable succession, although the powerful military governors held far less reverence for the imperial successor than did the common people of the capital.

PHILARETUS
SURVIVOR OF MANZIKERT

NAME: Philaretos Brachamios
BORN: Unknown
RULED: Usurper, 1071–1078
DIED: Of unknown causes, Germanikeia,
Anatolia, c. 1087

IN MANZIKERT'S AFTERMATH, the only general left in southeastern Anatolia was an Armenian who had accompanied Romanus on that ill-fated trip—Philaretos. On Romanus's death, Philaretos's troops declared him emperor, and he created an independent kingdom stretching from Cilicia to Edessa. Noted for his cruelty and greed, he finally agreed to abandon his imperial claims when Nicephorus Botaniates made him *doux* of Antioch in 1078. He then lost everything when the Turks captured Antioch in 1084 and Edessa in 1087. Retreating into inaccessible Germanikeia, he died soon afterwards.

JOHN DUCAS
CRAFTY INTRIGUER

NAME: Iōannēs Doukas
BORN: Unknown
RULED: Usurper, 1074
DIED: Of natural causes,
Constantinople, c. 1088

JOHN DUCAS, CONSTANTINE X'S brother, was the leader of the court faction opposed to Romanus Diogenes. Because of his constant intriguing he had been forced to retire to his estates, but the disaster at Manzikert saw him return with all haste to the capital, where he was instrumental in dethroning Romanus and removing the empress. It was John who spitefully blinded Romanus after giving him assurances of his safety, and he then sent the former emperor a letter as he lay dying, congratulating him on the loss of his eyes.

Made *kaisar* during his brother's reign, John continued to hold that title throughout the rule of his nephew, Michael VII, until he was sidelined by Michael's favourite eunuch minister. He spent the next few years hunting on his great estates, until he obtained command of an army to deal with Norman mercenaries who had betrayed their allegiance to the empire and allowed the Turks to strengthen their grip on Anatolia. After Nicephorus Botaniates's shameful retreat, John was defeated and captured by the Normans. Their leader convinced him to become Roman emperor and overthrow Michael and his overpowerful eunuchs.

Michael asked the Turkish Sultan Suleiman to help defeat his uncle and his Norman supporters, and the sultan was very willing to do so. Soon John found himself a Turkish prisoner. Michael secured his release on condition that he become a monk and John did so, but he still managed to influence events at court. He advised Michael to resign the purple in 1078, and in 1081 advised Alexius Comnenus to make his play for the throne. Having married his granddaughter to Alexius, he remained part of the court until his death.

NICEPHORUS III
EMPIRE IN CHAOS

NAME: Nikēphoros Botaneiatēs
BORN: Place unknown, c. 1002
RULED: Emperor, 1078–1081
DIED: Of natural causes,
Constantinople, 1081

FEW THOUGHT IT possible that anyone could outdo Michael VII; Nicephorus Botaniates proved them wrong. Claiming descent from the ancient Roman Fabii family, he had been considered for the throne by the empress Eudocia before she selected Romanus Diogenes. A competent general in the past, Nicephorus was humiliated by his capture in the Balkans by the Oghuz Turks during Constantine X's reign but this did not stop him becoming *strategos* of Anatolikon, from which position he launched his bid for the throne in the chaos of 1078.

> **I merely ask to retain the name of Emperor, public acclamations and the red buskins, and further the permission to live quietly in the palace.**
>
> NICEPHORUS III BOTANIATES

A coup in the capital and help from Turkish troops—in exchange for his recognition of Turkish conquests—ensured Nicephorus's accession. The next three years saw scenes of utter chaos as he abandoned himself to the pleasures of the palace while the empire collapsed into anarchy. His favourites pillaged the provinces, he debased the coinage to the point of worthlessness, and he married the ex-empress Maria while her husband, Michael VII, still lived, dragging her out of the Petrion monastery to do so. Rebellions sprang up everywhere, and his plan to promote his worthless nephew Synadenos as co-emperor over his stepson Constantine Ducas was the final straw. The Normans of southern Italy, under Robert Guiscard, invaded the Balkan provinces, ostensibly to support Constantine's rights, and easily defeating the imperial armies. Then a conspiracy involving the empress, the *kaisar*, John Ducas, and others saw the elevation of the empire's up-and-coming general, Alexius Comnenus, as Constantine's co-emperor. Abandoned, and unable to obtain the support of the Seljuk Turks, he was forced to abdicate and take monastic vows in 1081. Nicephorus's humiliation was brief as he was dead within the year.

NICEPHORUS BRYENNIUS, NICEPHORUS BASILAKES AND NICEPHORUS MELISSENUS

NO CHANCE AGAINST ALEXIUS

Names: Nikēphoros Bryennios;
Nikēphoros Basilakes; Nikēphoros Melissenos
BORN: Unknown
RULED: Usurpers, 1077–1078; 1079; 1080–1081
DIED: Unknown

NICEPHORUS BRYENNIUS was the best strategist the empire still possessed. The only general who performed well at Manzikert, he enhanced this reputation as *doux* of Bulgaria and then Dyrrhachion. Michael VII's mismanagement of the empire roused him to declare himself emperor at Adrianople and within a week he was pressing his claims at Constantinople. His troops behaved badly, alienating the people, who refused to overthrow Michael for him. Hearing of Botaniates's approach, he withdrew, only to see this rival steal the throne. When Bryennius rejected the position of *kaisar*, Botaniates sent his best general, Alexius Comnenus, to defeat him and cast him into prison, before he was blinded and exiled to Adrianople. Though blind, Bryennius was still active in 1094 when he led the defences of that city against a Cuman attack.

All this time, another rebel emperor was sitting in Thessalonica, waiting to see who would emerge victorious between Botaniates and Bryennius. This was Nicephorus Basilakes, the current *doux* of Dyrrhachion, and his one weakness was an overestimation of his abilities. Tricked by Alexius Comnenus into fighting an engagement, he was defeated. His soldiers then betrayed him, sending him to the emperor for blinding.

Next to try his luck was Nicephorus Melissenus, an aristocratic general who had opposed the elevation of Botaniates. Having promised to concede more territory to the Turks in exchange for a large body of troops, he entered into discussions with Botaniates to partition what remained of the empire. As Alexius Comnenus's brother-in-law, Melissenus thought he had all bases covered but did not count on one thing—Alexius declared himself emperor and took Constantinople. With support slipping away, Melissenus accepted the position of *kaisar*, along with the tax revenues of Thessalonica. He continued to serve Alexius, helping the emperor defeat the Pecheneg threat in 1091.

CONSTANTINE DUCAS

IMPERIAL PAWN

NAME: Kōnstantinos Doukas
BORN: Constantinople, 1074
RULED: Co-emperor, 1074–1078 and 1081–1088
DIED: Of unknown causes, Constantinople, 1095

CONSTANTINE DUCAS, Michael VII's eldest son and co-emperor, stood no chance against the forces ranged against his father. To shore up his position, Michael betrothed Constantine to the daughter of the Norman Robert Guiscard, duke of Apulia, but, nevertheless, Constantine was demoted when Nicephorus Botaniates assumed the throne.

The plotters who overthrew Botaniates justified their action as protecting Constantine's rights, and so Alexius betrothed him to his daughter Anna and again made him co-emperor. He was again demoted after the birth of Alexius's son John but he did not protest, possibly because his own health was quite fragile, and he remained loyal to Alexius until his death during the 1090s.

ALEXIUS I

SAVIOUR OF BYZANTIUM

NAME: Alexios Komnēnos
BORN: Constantinople, 1057
RULED: Emperor, 1081–1118
DIED: Of natural causes, Constantinople, 1118

ALEXIUS COMNENUS WAS the empire's last hope of avoiding imminent ruin. He had been Nicephorus III's general of choice to suppress his rivals before he himself assumed the purple at the age of twenty-four. Though courageous, his gifts as a general were not his strong suit; rather, his talents lay in deceiving his enemies and using cunning stratagems. The perilous state of the empire made him reactive rather than proactive, and pragmatism was the order of the day. Though vain and arrogant, he was a competent administrator and brilliant diplomat, and it was only his diplomatic skills that prevented the Eastern Empire's complete collapse.

Alexius's reign did not begin well, with the partial sack of Constantinople by his troops. It was days before he could stop the raping and pillaging. Requiring the Ducas family's support, he married John Ducas's granddaughter to ensure his survival on the throne. It was a wise choice: their adherence to his cause preserved his throne against rebels and he was well aware of the debt he owed them.

Alexius's first task in 1081 was to deal with the long-threatened Norman invasion, led by the brilliant Robert Guiscard. Taking advantage of Alexius's absence in Constantinople, Robert captured Dyrrhachion and marched into Thessaly, defeating Alexius's increasingly desperate attempts to halt his advance. Alexius saved the situation by bribing the Western emperor, Henry IV, to

Turks attack the army of Bohemund I while crossing the Vardar River

attack the Normans in Calabria, forcing Robert to return home. He left his son Bohemund in charge of the army, but though Bohemund was initially successful, Alexius finally managed to halt the Norman advance in 1084. A new offensive collapsed with Robert's death in 1085, and by the end of that year Alexius had recovered everything that Robert had spent three years claiming.

You die as you have lived: a hypocrite.

EMPRESS IRENE (to Alexius I Comnenus)

This victory was easy, however, compared with the herculean task that lay before the empire—the reconquest of Anatolia from Turkish hands. Knowing this was beyond the empire's current capacity, in 1095 Alexius sent envoys to Pope Urban II seeking a substantial body of mercenaries to fight for the empire. Instead, what Urban preached was a call to arms to liberate the Holy Land from the Muslims—the crusades. By 1096 the first rabble led by Peter the Hermit had made its way across Europe. Alexius, though horrified, was flexible enough to manage the logistical challenges. The peasant army was ferried across the Bosphorus and the Turks swiftly annihilated them.

It was not until 1097 that the First Crusade finally made its way to Constantinople, led by the nobility of western Europe. Alexius distrusted its leaders, in particular the Norman contingent led by his old enemy Bohemund. In exchange for supplies and military assistance, the crusaders swore an oath to hand over all conquests to Alexius. Taking them across to Anatolia, he watched as they took Nicaea, which they resentfully handed over. By late 1097 the crusaders had reached Antioch, which they besieged for seven months under enormous hardships. Alexius had sent an army to help but, hearing that the besiegers were about to be destroyed by the Turks, he had it turn around; when news filtered back of the crusader victory, it was too late. Declaring their oaths to Alexius void, the crusaders set up kingdoms for themselves, the first going to Bohemund who became prince of Antioch. By the time Jerusalem fell in 1099, Palestine was once again in Christian hands, for the first time in four hundred years.

The success of the crusade caught Alexius by surprise, and he spent the remainder of his reign fighting not only against the Turks, but also with the crusader kingdoms, principally Bohemund's. Achieving victories against the Turks from 1110 to 1116, he reclaimed much of western Anatolia, which had been lost after Manzikert. By the time he returned to Constantinople, he was clearly beginning to fade, and his final year was consumed by family struggles as his daughter Anna and her husband tried to become his successors. These struggles darkened his final days, but by his usual deceptions he ensured that his eldest son, John, would become the next Roman emperor.

REBELLIONS AGAINST ALEXIUS I

Alexius I was plagued by a large number of rebellions against his rule. The rebels included:

- a monk masquerading as the emperor Michael VII
- Constantine Humbertopoulos, who had helped Alexius gain the throne
- John Comnenus, *doux* of Dyrrhachion
- Tzachas, a Turkish pirate who declared himself emperor
- Karykas, a rebel in Crete
- Rapsomates, a rebel in Cyprus
- Michael Taronites, Alexius's brother-in-law
- an imposter claiming he was Constantine Diogenes, eldest son of Romanus IV
- Salomon, a wealthy senator
- two governors of Trebizond, Gregory Tironites and Theodore Gabras.

JOHN II
THE BEAUTIFUL

NAME: Iōannēs Komnēnos
BORN: Constantinople, 1087
RULED: Co-emperor, 1092–1118; senior emperor, 1118–1143
DIED: Of an infected wound, Selelicia, Anatolia, 1143

JOHN COMNENUS, KNOWN to his contemporaries as John the Beautiful, was very ugly. Short and dark, his physical features hid the soul of a pious and gentle man, generous and charitable, who disliked excessive displays of luxury. He was also lenient to rebels, a fact that saved his sister Anna on a number of occasions when she plotted to elevate her husband to the throne. Their mother, Irene, tried to exclude John from the throne, and he had to gain access to his dying father secretly in order to obtain the imperial ring. His coronation by the patriarch occurred while the empress's back was turned. Anna hated John all her life, detesting his magnanimity when he refused to kill or blind the conspirators who plotted his death during his first year as emperor and limited himself to confiscating their property.

John, unlike his father, tended to exclude family from the most important governmental posts, and generally appointing men of integrity and ability so that he was free to pursue the restoration of the empire's eastern provinces. Overall, he was successful in extending his hold over western Anatolia and pushing further into Turkish-held lands. His tactics of avoiding pitched battles whenever possible and concentrating on sieges allowed him to reclaim territory slowly without overextending his armies. Yet there were distractions. The Normans were a continual thorn in his side, requiring his diplomatic skills to convince Lothair III, the Western emperor, to threaten them in Italy. Additionally, his attempts to motivate the crusader states to take a more coordinated approach against the Turks failed because of their mistrust of him and each other.

John's successes against the Turks strengthened the empire by building on Alexius I's foundations. To everyone's great regret, he died prematurely after receiving a wound in the hand while hunting. His plans included the reconquest of Antioch, as well as pushing deep into Syria and Palestine; with another ten years, he might have actually done so. As it was, he left a resurgent empire in the hands of his youngest son, Manuel.

ALEXIUS
A FLEETING GLIMPSE

NAME: Alexios Komnēnos
BORN: Balabista, Macedonia, 1106
RULED: Co-emperor, 1119–1142
DIED: Of fever, Attalia, Kibyrraioton, 1142

THERE IS A LACK of contemporary sources for John Comnenus's reign, and so history records very little about his eldest son, Alexius. Made co-emperor by his father very shortly into his reign as a deterrent to his Aunt Anna's ambitions, he stayed within John's shadow, accompanying him on his eastern campaigns. It was during one of these, late in his father's reign, that he was afflicted by a mystery illness that killed him within days, to his father's great grief.

MANUEL I
MASTER DIPLOMAT

NAME: Manouel Komnēnos
BORN: Constantinople, 1118
RULED: Emperor, 1143–1180
DIED: Of fever, Constantinople, 1180

THE UNEXPECTED DEATH of John's eldest son, Alexius, saw John wrestling with the issue of succession and he eventually passed the crown to his youngest son, Manuel, whose attributes he thought were what the empire needed. Courage, ability and force of character were Manuel's strengths, and he possessed a calmness that his older brother, Isaac, lacked. Tall and handsome, Manuel's keen intellect saw opportunities everywhere. Where his father was slow, steady and deliberate, Manuel was more surefooted and quick, seeking to exploit advantages when they arose without giving thought to longer-term objectives. Therefore, while Manuel was more frenetic than his father, his achievements were much more transitory.

Manuel's reign saw the empire become increasingly dependent on mercenaries to fight its wars and diplomacy to achieve its aims. In one way or another, Manuel greatly influenced European affairs, but such a strategy was expensive and impossible to sustain in the long term. His reign also saw a far more complex international situation than John had had to manage, when the Second Crusade was launched as a result of the fall of Edessa in 1144.

Unlike his grandfather at the time of the First Crusade, Manuel had to deal with kings, who were far pricklier to manage than the leaders of the First Crusade had been. The first, Conrad III of Germany, was initially suspicious of Manuel, and there were unpleasant confrontations between Romans and Germans during the crossing of the Bosphorus. Nevertheless, after Conrad fell ill he received treatment at Constantinople, with Manuel personally ministering to him during his recuperation. Conrad stayed for a year, developing a firm friendship with Manuel.

The other king, Louis VII of France, was quickly ferried across to Anatolia, but his campaign was an unmitigated disaster. Ignoring Manuel's advice, he attacked Damascus, the only sympathetic Muslim state. Manuel's decision to withhold troops aggravated Louis, who saw it as an attempt to hinder the crusade. He blamed the Second Crusade's failure squarely on Manuel and shared this view across Europe, building up resentment against the Eastern Empire.

Next to be dealt with was Frederick I, who became the Western Roman emperor in 1155 and whose ambition was to become the sole Roman emperor of the world. The majority of Manuel's reign was devoted to stopping Frederick one way or another, by siding with the pope and using vast quantities of gold to stir up the Italian city-states, keeping Frederick too busy to attack the Eastern Empire directly.

> **I present you with all these treasures so that you may know my generosity and munificence and that he who is lord over such wealth is he who grants so much to one man.**
>
> MANUEL I COMNENUS

Manuel continued to fight the Turks in Anatolia with a measure of success, but there was never a sustained effort against them on the part of the empire, due in no small part to his habit of being distracted by the next opportunity that presented itself. Whether it was against the Normans in Sicily, the Hungarians and the Serbs in the Balkans, the Russians, the Saracens or the Crusader states, he spread the empire's resources too thinly, so that his successes were ethereal at best, and the empire's many enemies were able to weather his uncoordinated assaults against them. Of these distractions, two events would be the key to the empire's future. The first was his decision in 1171 to arrest all Venetians throughout the empire on the pretext that they had attacked a Genoese settlement at Galata, near the capital. The Venetians declared war, but Manuel managed to outmanoeuvre them and sent their fleet back home in humiliation. Venetian anger remained, but they were a patient people.

The second event was Manuel's humiliating defeat at Turkish hands at Myriocephalon in 1176, a blow from which he never fully recovered. This more than anything demonstrated the real weakness of the empire, which no amount of diplomatic manoeuvring could fully mask. Manuel's skill was to hide this weakness from the world and present a face of power and influence. His incompetent successors would not be able to continue the charade.

ALEXIUS II

IN THE WAY

NAME: Alexios Komnēnos
BORN: Constantinople, 1169
RULED: Co-emperor, 1171–1180;
senior emperor, 1180–1183
DIED: Murdered, Constantinople, 1183

MANUEL'S DEATH BROUGHT his vain eleven-year-old son Alexius to the throne. Alexius did not undertake any imperial duties but spent his time hunting and attending chariot races. Consequently, his reign was dominated by competing groups, each determined to control the immature emperor. On one side there was his mother, Maria of Antioch; on the other, his half-sister. Fighting erupted in the capital, but the arrival of Alexius's cousin, Andronicus, swept the factions away.

Andronicus's march on Constantinople scared everyone, and the boy-emperor tried to bribe him to turn around. He refused, and before long he was Alexius's co-emperor. Alexius's precarious position was made clear when Andronicus made him sign his mother's death warrant. His own death was only a matter of time, and he ended up strangled with a bowstring before being decapitated. Andronicus contemptuously kicked the corpse in the side before having the body thrown into the sea.

ANDRONICUS I

GIFTED MONSTER

NAME: Andronikos Komnēnos
BORN: Place unknown, c. 1118
RULED: Co-emperor, 1183;
senior emperor, 1183–1185
DIED: Murdered, Constantinople, 1185

ANDRONICUS COMNENUS was one of the most amazing characters ever to grace the imperial stage. Like most of the Comneni, he had a first-rate mind and an impressive physique. Tall, handsome, courageous and eloquent, he was the most gifted of his family, and so when he put his mind to it, there was no better general or able administrator. His flaw was that his abilities were always at the mercy of his passions.

Jealous of his cousin Manuel, he spent many years plotting against him and was imprisoned on a many occasions, though he usually broke out of the prisons. His exploits were legendary. One time he found a secret underground passage under his cell. As he hid there, the guards came across what appeared to be his empty cell. Raising the alarm, they immediately arrested his wife on suspicion of aiding his escape and brought her into the cell. Andronicus soon emerged back into his cell, where he slept with his wife, and since the guards believed he had fled, they relaxed their watch, allowing him to break out of the prison. On another occasion, he faked an attack of diarrhoea, manufactured a dummy of himself defecating to deceive the guards and then made his escape. His travels across the empire and the Middle East saw him take up residence with foreign princes, though he inevitably had to flee after engaging in another amorous exploit. In between these adventures, he served under Manuel in various posts, and usually performed quite well when he was not actively conspiring against the emperor.

His opportunity came with Manuel's death and Alexius's accession. Leaving his place of exile, he recruited an army and began a leisurely march towards

Constantinople. The chaos in the capital meant that the people welcomed him; their dislike of the Latin empress, Maria of Antioch, allowed him to gain control of the government, while they rose up and massacred all the Latin inhabitants of the city they could find, including thousands of Venetians.

Andronicus as emperor was a monster. The murder of his opponents, including young Alexius, triggered a bloody reign of terror. He married Alexius's twelve-year-old bride, reportedly consummating the marriage. Though he tried to curb abuses by royal officials and the nobility, he blinded, burnt, amputated, impaled and hanged everyone he considered a traitor. Such actions triggered more plots, and as Andronicus descended into paranoia, the empire fell into a nightmare. The Normans, accompanied by Manuel's nephew Alexius, sacked Thessalonica, while Andronicus considered executing every prisoner accused of sedition in the empire.

It took a popular uprising in support of Isaac Angelus to overthrow the tyrant. For over two days, the people beat and tortured their emperor. They cut off his hand, gouged his eyes out, poured scalding water over his face, burnt his genitals off, and beat him repeatedly before hanging him up by his feet and killing him.

JOHN COMNENUS

DISTRACTED BY HUNTING

NAME: Iōannēs Komnēnos
BORN: Place unknown, 1160
RULED: Co-emperor, 1183–1185
DIED: Murdered, Philippopolis (Plovdiv), Bulgaria, 1185

JOHN WAS CONCEIVED DURING one of Andronicus's incarcerations in prison. He was one of the conspirators who sought to overthrow the empress Maria and was involved in the battles to secure control of the young Alexius. Imprisoned for his trouble, he was then released in an attempt to appease his father, who was marching towards the capital. Soon he was appointed Andronicus's co-emperor.

With Andronicus's regime collapsing in 1185, the emperor ordered John to lead a division of soldiers to stop the Norman advance on Thessalonica. However, John was enjoying the hunting at Philippopolis and did not go, refusing to believe the city would fall. Within ten days, Thessalonica had fallen; within the month, Andronicus was dead. When the news arrived at Philippopolis, the army seized John and gouged his eyes out, causing his long, painful death.

ISAAC COMNENUS

CRUEL AND VINDICTIVE

NAME: Isaakios Komnēnos
BORN: Place unknown, c. 1155
RULED: Usurper, 1184–1191
DIED: Poisoned, Iconium (Konya), Anatolikon, 1196

ISAAC COMNENUS WAS unpleasant, quick to anger and extraordinarily violent, even in such a violent age. The maternal grandson of Isaac Comnenus, who was passed over in favour of Manuel I, he had the misfortune of being captured by the Armenians while governor of Cilicia. His imprisonment lasted nearly five years, which soured his relationship with his extended family. Though Andronicus freed him, Isaac repaid his benefactor by taking over Cyprus, and crowning himself emperor. Andronicus did not have time to deal with him and though his successor, Isaac II, did send a fleet, it was defeated with the help of Sicilian pirates. This left Isaac Comnenus in peace while he raped, looted and pillaged at will, alienating the local Cypriots to the point of revolt. Their salvation came from an unexpected source.

Isaac had captured the shipwrecked sister of King Richard I of England. Richard, on his way to Palestine for the Third Crusade, exacted retribution by conquering the island. Isaac surrendered on condition that Richard not place him in irons. Richard agreed, instead imprisoning him with chains of silver. He was then incarcerated by the Knights of St John for three years, but after his release he tried to intrigue his way back to power. The new emperor, Alexius III, wanted nothing to do with him, and so he took up residence with the Turkish sultan, but shortly afterwards was found poisoned.

ISAAC II

THE BLIND EMPEROR

NAME: Isaakios Angelos
BORN: Place unknown, 1156
RULED: Sole emperor, 1185–1195; co-emperor, 1203–1204
DIED: Of a heart attack, Constantinople, 1204

ANDRONICUS'S DETESTATION of the nobility saw him eliminate bureaucratic corruption; with Isaac Angelus's accession, corruption again dominated the running of the state. This red-headed son of a cowardly general was weak, conceited, rude, mean, greedy and vicious. Andronicus thought so little of Isaac that in the days leading to his overthrow, when one of his ministers wondered if Isaac would start a rebellion, as he had already participated in a revolt alongside his father and brothers at Nicaea some months before, Andronicus laughed himself silly over the thought, describing Isaac as a pathetic coward. However, when that minister tried to arrest Isaac, Isaac grabbed a sword and killed him. Fleeing to Hagia Sophia, he roused the people of the capital, who overthrew Andronicus and elevated Isaac in his place.

Almost immediately, Isaac's lack of attention to foreign and domestic affairs saw the empire attacked on all sides, while usurper after usurper attempted to win a throne held by so feeble a hand. He was plagued by numerous pretenders claiming to be Alexius II, the murdered son of Manuel I, plagued him. There were rebellions by Basil Chotzas at Tarsia; Isaac Comnenus, who incited a riot in the capital; and Constantine Tatikios, who gathered a group of five hundred to overthrow the emperor. All ended up blind or dead.

Then, in 1187, Jerusalem fell to Saladin, bringing about the Third Crusade. Unlike Alexius and Manuel Comnenus, Isaac actively hindered the progress of the crusaders, especially the Western emperor Frederick Barbarossa. Isaac issued contradictory orders, and the Germans became ever more frustrated with a lack of provisions. Isaac's conduct saw the two imperial armies come to blows, forcing him to back down and agree not to delay the crusaders any longer. His actions further poisoned east–west relations, adding another element to the storm brewing in the west that would be unleashed in the Fourth Crusade.

Isaac's greatest threat came from a Bulgarian revolt against excessive imperial taxes. By the end of his reign, Bulgaria was effectively lost, and the enemy was approaching the walls of Constantinople. In 1195 he took to the field, along with his brother Alexius, but while he was off hunting, the army proclaimed Alexius emperor. Captured and blinded, Isaac ended up in prison and remained there for eight years, living on bread and water.

Isaac was released in 1203 as the Fourth Crusade was preparing to attack Constantinople. Officially, the crusaders were there to place Isaac's son Alexius on the throne, and so to prevent the assault Isaac was again crowned. He immediately ordered the hanging of all those who had participated in his blinding. During this second reign, Isaac's blindness and debilitation saw Alexius IV appropriate all power. Crippled by gout, Isaac consorted with astrologers and monks, living long enough to see Alexius overthrown before he died of shock.

ALEXIUS BRANAS

A HEAD FOR FOOTBALL

NAME: Alexios Branas
BORN: c. 1166
RULED: Usurper, 1187
DIED: Beheaded, Constantinople, 1187

ALEXIUS BRANAS WAS ONE of the few outstanding late–twelfth century generals in the Eastern Empire. Holding the rank of *protosebastos*, he was related through blood and marriage to the Comneni, and was virtually the only general who stood by Andronicus and he campaigned successfully in Hungary. Isaac II gave him a command against the Normans and he threw them out of the Balkans with great slaughter, by 1186 reconquering almost everything the empire had lost there.

In 1187 Alexius successfully repelled the Bulgarians from Thrace, and it was at this point that he began marching towards Constantinople. He declared himself emperor and expected the city to fall at his approach; that it did not was due to Isaac's brother-in-law, the Caesar Conrad of Montferrat. Gathering a ragtag group of Latins, Greeks and Turks, he attacked Alexius. The rebel army scattered, and while Alexius was trying

Siege of Jerusalem by Saladin, which precipitated the Third Crusade

to restore order, Conrad threw him off his horse and ordered the removal of his head. It was presented to Isaac and he and his courtiers played football with it in the imperial palace.

THEODORE MANKAPHAS

THE FOOL

NAME: Theodoros Mankaphas
BORN: Unknown
RULED: Usurper, 1188–1189 and 1204–1206
DIED: Unknown

A NOBLEMAN FROM LYDIA Philadelphia, in the *theme* of Samos, Theodore Mankaphas decided to overthrow Isaac II and gained followers from around his town. Isaac trapped him in Philadelphia but was unable to deal with him because of the arrival of Frederick Barbarossa. Eager to remove a potential troublemaker, he pardoned Theodore, making him governor of Philadelphia on condition he renounce his imperial claim. Thus it was Governor Theodore who greeted Frederick on his way to the Holy Land. By 1193, however, Theodore's former supporters, with the help of Basil Vatatzes, the *doux* of Thrakesion, had chased him out of the city. Joining the Turks, Theordore began attacking the empire until Isaac bribed the sultan to hand over the troublemaker. Imprisoned, Theodore earned the nickname The Fool.

Theodore managed to regain control of Philadelphia but was defeated in 1204 by Henry of Flanders, the Latin ruler of Constantinople. He retreated to the city, where he remained until Theodore Lascaris finally overpowered him.

CONSTANTINE ANGELUS DUCAS

YOUTHFUL AMBITION

NAME: Kōnstantinos Angelos Doukas
BORN: Place unknown, c. 1173
RULED: Usurper, 1193
DIED: Unknown

CONSTANTINE ANGELUS DUCAS, Isaac II's cousin, gained command of the Bulgarian war during its later stages. He was only a young man when entrusted with this command and the honour seemed to go to his head. He trained his troops to obey him without question and his native fierceness had the Bulgarians fearing his advances. Though his military advisors initially kept his impetuosity in check, a string of successes saw Constantine don the imperial purple over their objections. While he was marching with his army towards Adrianople, his former comrades-in-arms imprisoned the usurper and handed him over to Isaac, who blinded him for his youthful ambition.

ALEXIUS III

COWARDLY EMPEROR

NAME: Alexios Angelos Komnēnos
BORN: Place unknown, c. 1153
RULED: Emperor, 1195–1203
DIED: Of natural causes, Nicaea (Iznik), Opsikion, 1211

ISAAC WAS A FEEBLE EMPEROR, but at least he tried; his older brother Alexius did not even do that. Though in manners and education Alexius appeared to be superior to his younger brother, he was a born intriguer. He had fled to the court of the Sultan Saladin after an aborted attempt to overthrow Andronicus I and was returning home in 1186 when he was captured and imprisoned in Tripoli in 1186 by Raymond, the Latin count. After his release, Alexius rode on Isaac's coat tails, before betraying and blinding him. His reign, too, was plagued with rebels, including even more pretenders claiming to be Alexius II, and so, to legitimise his reign, he added the name 'Comnenus' to his birth name.

> **I have a better right to the throne, as I am the one holding the sceptre of the Roman Empire.**
>
> ALEXIUS III ANGELUS COMNENUS

Alexius III's crowning was marred when his horse refused to be mounted and his crown fell off. His first imperial action was to empty the treasury and distribute generous parcels of land to reward his supporters. Bankrupted, Alexius disbanded the army that Isaac had gathered for the Bulgarian war and retreated to his palace to enjoy the imperial lifestyle. In doing so, he left the empire defenceless and ruined what remained of its finances. The Turks swarmed all over the eastern provinces, while Henry VI, the Western emperor, threatened to invade. Luckily, political instability in Bulgaria and the use of diplomacy saw the northern border of the empire eventually stabilise.

By now the Fourth Crusade was heading towards Constantinople, ostensibly to replace Alexius with his nephew, also named Alexius, whom the emperor had foolishly allowed to escape from prison. Making no preparations for a siege, though he had ample warning that the crusaders were coming, Alexius led a numerically superior army against them. At the first charge by the crusaders his troops fled back into the city. Eventually the crusaders entered the city as Alexius, cowardly as always, took a boat and lots of gold and fled to Thrace.

After the fall of Constantinople, Alexius tried to destabilise the newly established Latin kingdom of Thessalonica. He then joined forces with a rival former emperor, Alexius V Murtzuphlus, but became jealous and blinded him, before being captured himself by the crusaders. Released in 1209, he made his way to the court of his son-in-law, Theodore Lascaris, at Nicaea. Unable to stop intriguing, Alexius began plotting with the Turkish sultan to overthrow Theodore and re-establish himself as emperor. Joining up with the Turkish forces, he and the sultan attacked Theodore, who killed the sultan and captured Alexius. Sent to a monastery, Alexius soon died, despised by all who knew him.

ALEXIUS CONTOSTEPHANUS

STARGAZER

NAME: Alexios Kontostephanos
BORN: Unknown
RULED: Usurper, 1195 and 1200
DIED: Unknown

EVERYONE IN THE CAPITAL accepted Isaac II's overthrow in 1195, except for the artisans. Instead, they chose for their emperor a nobleman, the former governor of Crete and part-time astrologer Alexius Contostephanus, who had yearned for an opportunity to become emperor. He was acclaimed in the agora with the mob declaring their refusal to be ruled by the Comneni ever again, but was attacked by supporters of the empress, and after a brief skirmish he was captured and imprisoned. He managed to return to try his luck in 1200, again without success.

JOHN COMNENUS AXUCH

THE OBESE

NAME: Iōannēs Komnēnos Axouchos
BORN: Unknown
RULED: Usurper, 1200
DIED: Executed, Constantinople, 1200

THE GREAT-GRANDSON of John II Comnenus, John was an unpleasantly obese nobleman. His Asian habits offended everyone and he was always perspiring and out of breath. Nevertheless, he was supported by much of the nobility, including the future emperor Alexius Murtzuphlus, and they accompanied him as he stormed Hagia Sophia and proclaimed himself emperor. A mob sacked the imperial palace and the treasury, while the patriarch of Constantinople hid in a broom closet. The coup failed as a result of his incompetence, and his fickle supporters quickly melted away once Alexius III moved against him. He surrendered and was immediately executed.

ALEXIUS IV

PLAYED WITH FIRE

NAME: Alexios Angelos
BORN: Constantinople, c. 1182
RULED: Emperor, 1203–1204
DIED: Murdered, Constantinople, 1204

THE BLINDED ISAAC II'S son was an ignorant, immature youth, lacking comprehension or insight. Cast into prison with his father by order of his uncle Alexius III in 1195, his escape in 1201 had more to do with the prison's pathetic security than any skills Alexius possessed. Fleeing to his brother-in-law, King Philip of Germany, he soon met the leader of the Fourth Crusade, Boniface of Montferrat.

Believing he could use the crusaders to overthrow his uncle, Alexius offered to bring the Greek Church under the pope's authority, as well as providing 200,000 silver marks and ten thousand troops for the crusade. Gaining agreement, he joined the crusaders on their march towards Constantinople, where a successful assault saw Alexius crowned emperor alongside his father, Isaac.

> **For in the day of mine afflictions he hid me in his tabernacle.**
>
> ALEXIUS IV ANGELUS (thanking Alexius V for apparently rescuing him)

Alexius now discovered that through his uncle's ineptitude he had no money or soldiers to hand over to the crusaders, while the Greek Church absolutely rejected Rome's supremacy. He was soon in desperate straits, as the crusaders would not move until they received their money, while the people refused to co-operate with an emperor who destroyed church treasures to pay off the Latins. Inevitably, he lost the confidence of both parties, and a fire lit by the crusaders was the last straw. A party of crusaders had secretly decided to attack a mosque within the city and steal whatever treasures they could find. The Greeks within the city came to the rescue of the Muslim traders and drove the crusaders back, but not before the Latins had set some buildings alight. Within minutes, the city was ablaze. The fire burned for two nights, destroying large swathes of the city in a direct line from north to south, including the Forum of Constantine and the hippodrome. Constantinople began preparing for resistance by expelling the crusaders from the city, while Alexius and his father were dethroned in favour of Alexius Murtzuphlus, who ordered the young man's strangulation in prison.

NICHOLAS CANNAVUS

A DANGEROUS REFUSAL

NAME: Nikolaos Kannabos
BORN: Unknown
RULED: Usurper, 1204
DIED: Murdered, Constantinople, 1204

AMID DESPERATE SCENES, the Senate, clergy and people began looking for a replacement for the incompetent Alexius IV and Isaac. After three days, they selected a young nobleman, Nicholas Cannavus. Gentle and intelligent, he was proclaimed emperor over his objections, and he refused to leave Hagia Sophia, sensing the crisis was beyond his abilities. His refusal saw Alexius Ducas Murtzuphlus begin to take control of the situation, and very soon Nicholas's adherents had gone over to the rising power. Alexius was proclaimed emperor and immediately he sent armed men to overpower Nicholas. Without support, Nicholas was trapped and soon was thrown into prison, where they probably killed him at the same time as Alexius IV.

Crusaders under Baudouin take Constantinople, 1204

ALEXIUS V

BUSHY EYEBROWS

NAME: Alexios Doukas Mourtzouphlos
BORN: Unknown
RULED: Emperor, 1204
DIED: Executed, Constantinople, 1204

WITH ALEXIUS DUCAS, the Eastern Empire finally had a man of ability and courage on the throne. Unfortunately for the empire, it was already too late.

Given the name Murtzuphlus for his bushy and overhanging eyebrows, he was clever and arrogant, and he believed he was the only person capable of saving the city from the crusaders. A member of the nobility, and possibly related to the Ducas emperors, after the fall of Alexius III he had been appointed by Isaac II to the position of *protovestiarios*, a high office responsible for the emperor's private wardrobe and treasury. A stint in prison for his part in John the Obese's usurpation had done nothing to quench his spirit, and he was the only one who fought the crusaders before the walls of Constantinople after the expulsion of the crusaders from the city.

The unpopularity of Isaac and Alexius IV gave him the opportunity to gain the throne, which he did by tricking Alexius IV into accompanying him in the dead of night from his imperial quarters to a supposed place of safety, claiming there were plots against his life. There were: Murtzuphlus had him imprisoned and killed.

The next day he put on the imperial insignia and by February 1204 was crowned emperor. By now Murtzuphlus was focused on defending the city. Closing it off, he prepared as best he could, strengthening defences and patrolling the walls in person. Morale improved and the city put up a determined fight, but to no avail. Constantinople fell in April 1204 and was brutally sacked, while Alexius Murtzuphlus fled into Thrace.

Here Murtzuphlus joined forces with the deposed Alexius III, even marrying his daughter. However, the older Alexius, jealous as always, turned on his son-in-law, assaulting him in the bath and blinding him before setting him loose. The Latin rulers of Constantinople soon captured him, and they put him on trial before throwing him off the Column of Theodosius in December 1204.

> **Despair not! I will go and attack the Franks!**
>
> ALEXIUS V MURTZUPHLUS (rallying the defenders before fleeing the city)

The Eastern Empire was now no more. Defeat at the hands of the crusaders saw it fracture into smaller principalities and kingdoms, each at war with the other. Nevertheless, the Eastern emperors did survive, and within sixty years they would once again rule from Constantine's city.

FALL OF THE EASTERN EMPIRE

(1204–1453)

It was thus, after a siege of fifty-three days, that Constantinople, which had defied the power of Chosroes, the Chagan, and the caliphs, was irretrievably subdued by the arms of Mahomet the Second. Her empire only had been subverted by the Latins: her religion was trampled in the dust by the Moslem conquerors.

EDWARD GIBBON
The Decline and Fall of the Roman Empire, 1880

FOLLOWING PAGE: Conquest of Constantinople by the Turks under Mehmet II

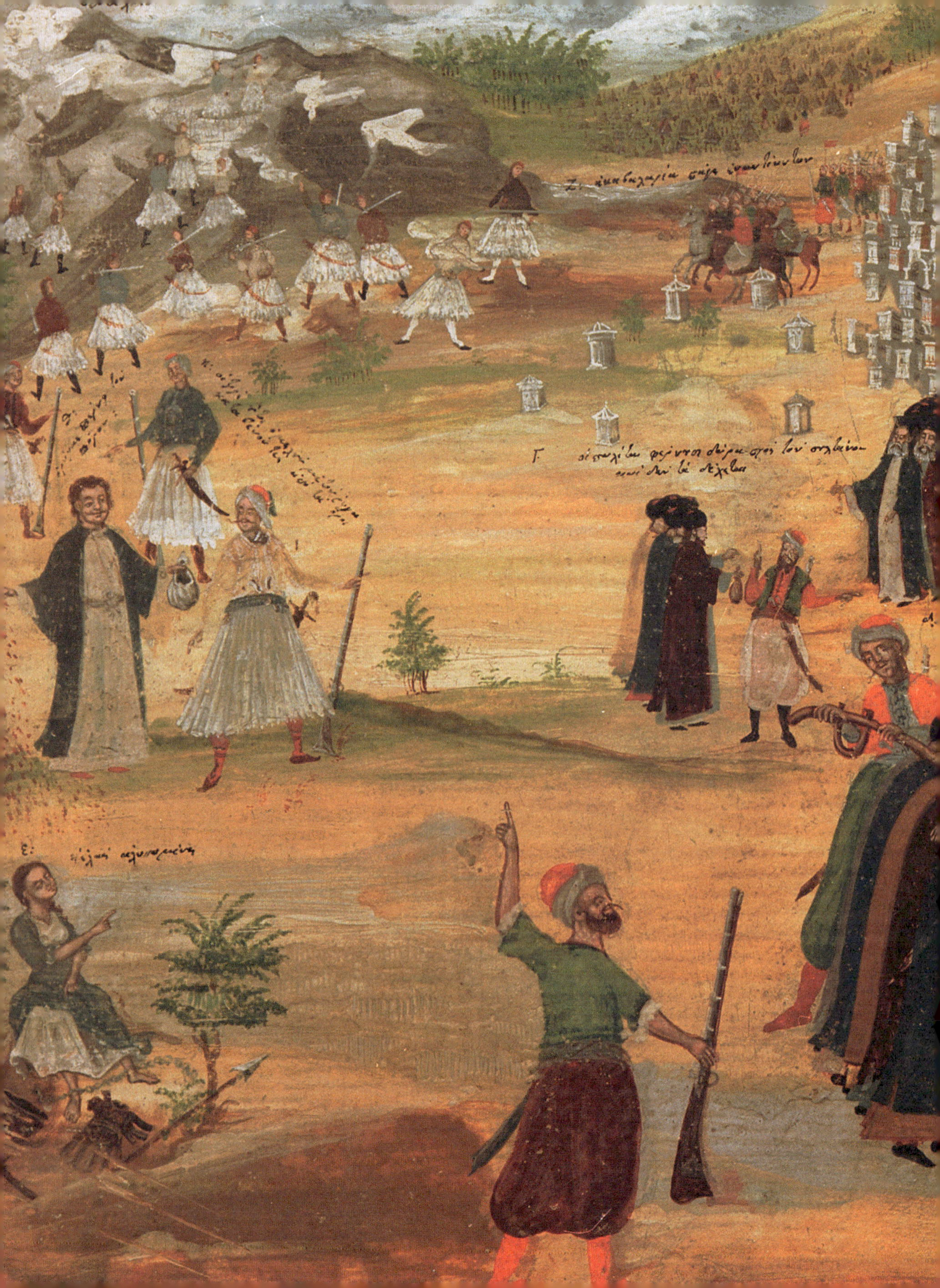
Ζ:
Γ.
Ε:

β. ὁ τζαλίκινος

THE WESTERN EMPERORS

OTTO IV

THE GUELF EMPEROR

NAME: Otto von Brunswick
BORN: Normandy, France, 1176
RULED: Emperor, 1209–1215
DIED: Accidentally beaten to death, Harzburg, Saxony, 1218

EMPEROR HENRY VI had a son, Frederick, but as there was no automatic right of succession, the death of every Western emperor led to chaos as rivals claimed the title, a process complicated by the requirement that the pope crown the emperor. In 1198 two claimants sought the German crown and thus the imperial throne—Philip Hohenstaufen, brother of Henry VI, and Otto, son of Henry the Lion, duke of Saxony.

Otto detested the Hohenstaufens, and his main backer was Pope Innocent III, who was also eager to see the Hohenstaufens brought low. For ten years Otto fought a losing battle, as Philip had the French king's backing, and so eventually even Innocent began listening to Philip's overtures. Otto was about to be driven from his final refuge in 1208 when he was saved by Philip's murder, which saw all opposition to Otto's claim wither away, and he was crowned Roman emperor in 1209.

Otto soon discovered that Innocent had not been idle. He had steadily eroded imperial control in Rome and northern Italy in favour of papal authority, as was highlighted when he threatened to withhold the crown unless Otto relinquished key prerogatives in running the church. Things came to a head with Otto's invasion of southern Italy, which Innocent held in trust for young Frederick Hohenstaufen, son of Henry VI. Innocent excommunicated Otto in 1210, declaring him deposed. Rebellions began in Germany in favour of Frederick, again forcing Otto to battle King Philip of France, who had eagerly responded to Innocent's call. Unable to defeat both Philip and Innocent, Otto abdicated the throne in 1215, retiring to his castle. He died in 1218, accidentally beaten to death by monks while confessing his sins in order to lift his excommunication.

FREDERICK II

THE WONDER OF THE WORLD

NAME: Friedrich Hohenstaufen
BORN: Iesi, Italy, 1194
RULED: Emperor, 1220–1250
DIED: Of dysentery, Lucera, Italy, 1250

FREDERICK HOHENSTAUFEN, son of the emperor Henry VI and Constance of Sicily, was more Norman than German and it showed in everything he did. Brilliant and clever, he was a scholar and a poet, soldier and statesman; speaking six languages, he was one of the most learned men of his time, named 'the wonder of the world'. His Sicilian upbringing exposed him to diverse cultures living side by side, making him the most tolerant man of his age towards members of different faiths. This put Frederick on a collision course with the church, which distrusted all forms of heterodoxy—after his death, the poet Dante consigned Frederick to the circle of hell that housed heretics.

> **I stayed overnight in Jerusalem, in order to overhear the prayer call of the Muslims and their worthy God.**
>
> FREDERICK II

Frederick was born in a public square to eliminate any doubts about his parentage, and after the deaths of his parents he was protected by Pope Innocent III, who guarded his Sicilian and German interests. Collapsing support for Otto IV in 1211 saw calls for the seventeen-year-old Frederick to come to Germany; he travelled north in secret, joined the rebel German princes and was crowned king at Aachen in 1215. He remained there until 1220, consolidating his power and keeping his Guelf enemies in check. Apart from one return visit in 1236–37, he spent the rest of his reign outside Germany.

Crowned emperor at Rome in 1220, Frederick owed the popes a great deal for their support, and one of their conditions was that he undertake a new crusade to liberate Jerusalem. Yet for the next seven years problems in Italy left him unable to fulfil his vow, and when he did try in 1227, illness and adverse weather conditions forced him to cancel the crusade. Pope Gregory IX was furious; believing Frederick's claims were just an excuse, he excommunicated the emperor.

Unrepentant, Frederick set sail the following year, infuriating Gregory to the point where he attempted to ruin Frederick by encouraging the northern Italian cities to rebel and ordering the clergy in Palestine not to cooperate with the emperor. Upon his arrival in the Holy Land, Frederick shrewdly negotiated a settlement instead of fighting a costly and uncertain war. The sultan of Egypt, eager to avoid a war, agreed to surrender Jerusalem and other important cities. In an incredible feat of

THE GREAT INTERREGNUM

With Frederick II's death, the Western Empire fell into a period of internal confusion and political disorder. The papacy and other aligned nobles elected their own candidates as King of the Romans, but none was strong enough to crush the opposition.

Conrad IV, Frederick II's son, was not acknowledged by the pope, who tried to overthrow him.

Henry Raspe was elected with papal support in opposition to Conrad IV but died after a year.

William II of Holland replaced Henry Raspe as anti-king, though his power was limited.

Richard of Cornwall was crowned by half the electors in 1256 (see page 339).

Alfonso X of Castile was elected in opposition to Richard of Cornwall but he could not manage his role as Roman king.

Rudolf I was the first of the Habsburg Roman kings, but he was unable to control or influence the German princes and died in 1291.

Adolf was the first king deposed by the electors without having been excommunicated.

Albert I was elected in opposition to Adolf, whom he killed. Albert was murdered in 1308 while trying to end the chaos.

diplomacy, Frederick managed to achieve what decades of warfare had not. However, the church declared such a victory was worse than any failure. Frederick marched to receive the crown of Jerusalem, but no bishop would agree to crown him, and so he crowned himself in the Church of the Holy Sepulchre. The conflict was now so bad that the militant religious orders considered joining forces with the Muslims to defeat the excommunicated emperor. Considering his vow completed, Frederick returned to Italy.

Although Pope Gregory soon revoked the excommunication, tensions remained, with Gregory encouraging Frederick's eldest son, Henry, King of the Romans, to rebel. Though Frederick imprisoned Henry in 1235, the turmoil continued, both in Germany and, especially, in Lombardy. As the northern Italian city-

Pope Innocent IV deposes excommunicated Emperor Frederick II

states hardened their stance as either pro-papal (Guelf) or pro-imperial (Ghibelline), years of warfare produced only ruined and burning cities, with Rome enduring repeated sieges as Frederick tried to crush papal power.

Frederick was now confronted by his most implacable enemy—Pope Innocent IV. The two heads of the Christian west were consumed by hatred for each other and were determined to fight to the bitter end. Scornfully they insulted each other, the emperor calling the pope a mad priest and the pope naming the emperor a pestilential king. Declaring Frederick deposed and excommunicated in 1245, Innocent supported a rebel in Germany, creating a descent into chaos. Frederick was defeated in Italy in 1248, in the process losing his treasury, which limited his ability to prosecute the war. Though the devastation continued, Frederick played little further part in it as he was now old and clearly ill. He died still trying to impose his will on what was now a bitterly divided empire and leaving the imperial title to his son Conrad, who could not retain it as the empire fell into anarchy.

Frederick's reign was a defining moment in European history. In order to prosecute his Italian wars, Frederick conceded much to the German princes, and the emperors became increasingly impotent. Further, the popes had broken the back of imperial power by destroying the Hohenstaufens and they now believed nothing prevented them exercising secular power throughout Christendom. They could not have been more wrong—a strong imperial presence was the only thing protecting them against the predatory kings of Europe, as they soon discovered.

HENRY VII
RESURRECTING IMPERIAL DREAMS

NAME: Heinrich von Luxemburg
BORN: Valenciennes, France, c. 1275
RULED: Emperor, 1312–1313
DIED: Of fever, Buonconvento, Italy, 1313

FOR SIXTY YEARS, DIVISION and confusion wracked the empire. The German kings, intent on preserving their throne, took their eye off Italy. In the emperor's absence, Italy had divided into factions, the rival parties still calling themselves Guelf and Ghibelline, although no one now remembered the old meanings of the terms. Meanwhile, the popes, now residing in Avignon, were trying to fend off the French kings, who were seeking to extend their influence into Germany.

> I send you the most joyful news,
> that terrible tyrant Henry,
> Count of Luxemburg, whom the rebels
> call King of the Romans and Emperor
> of Germany, is dead.
>
> GUELF PARTISAN

Into this mess stepped the French-speaking Henry of Luxembourg, King of the Romans. Brave and conciliatory, he was determined to resurrect the old imperial claims, and to do that he needed to reimpose control on the Italian states. His approach was eagerly anticipated by the Ghibellines, who were his natural supporters. Yet so great were the problems afflicting the Italians that Henry was at first welcomed by all parties. That soon changed, as the Lombard states regretted allowing a foreigner to tax them and introduce imperial agents.

Henry was marching towards Rome when Guelf and Ghibelline bitterness and animosity burst forth once again. He managed to get to Rome, but the pope's absence at Avignon forced him to accept coronation from papal legates at the Lateran church in 1312. Turning his attention towards Robert, king of Naples, who was actively supporting the Guelfs, Henry was marching to confront him when he became ill and died.

LOUIS IV

THE BAVARIAN

NAME: Ludwig von Wittelsbach
BORN: Munich, Bavaria, 1282
RULED: Emperor, 1328–1347
DIED: Of apoplexy, Fürstenfeldbruck, Bavaria, 1347

LOUIS OF BAVARIA was weak, greedy and focused upon increasing his family's influence instead of ruling the empire. Henry VII's death had again seen the electors of Germany divided over two candidates—Louis of Bavaria and Frederick of Austria. They had been friends in the past, but ambition turned them into the bitterest of enemies. Both were crowned King of the Romans, and from 1314 to 1322 Germany again endured a destructive war. Though Frederick had victory within his grasp, he was defeated and captured, while Louis emerged victorious but so damaged that he was forced to accept that Frederick would be King of the Romans, while he would be crowned Roman emperor.

Watching the chaos and hoping that the empire would exhaust itself was the pope, who was by now a creature of the French king. A zealous Frenchman, Pope John XXII was angered by Louis's triumph and plotted his destruction. Louis's intervention in Italy and his attacks on the Guelfs in 1323 allowed John to excommunicate him and nominate Charles, the French king, to be the next Roman king and emperor. Such blatant partisanship only rallied the German princes behind Louis, who by 1327 was ready to invade Italy.

He was at first welcomed and was crowned emperor at Rome by the aged senator Sciarra Colonna. Tired of Pope John's machinations, Louis declared John deposed and had an antipope, Nicholas V, elected. This caused northern Italy to erupt into war, and by 1330 Louis had abandoned the country, taking Nicholas with him. Demoralised, he was now ready to do anything to placate Pope John and thus secure his rule. His weakness was exploited by successive popes, who were only too happy to humiliate him further.

They rejected Louis's apologies. Refusing to recognise his title, they decreed that he must present himself at Avignon for judgement. Louis even proposed resigning the purple, but the German princes and clergy convinced him to stand firm, and in 1338 he declared that election by all or the majority of the electors automatically conferred the royal title and rule over the empire, without papal confirmation. With the support of the German princes, Louis might have overcome his problems, but a habit of promoting his family aggravated the princes. By 1346 they had withdrawn their support, while his continued humiliation at the papacy's hands hindered his cause. Still excommunicated, he agreed to renounce his crown and his claims to Italy, even agreeing not to act without the express permission of the pope. It was not enough. Deposed as King of the Romans in 1346, he died the following year while hunting bears.

CHARLES IV

PAPAL PUPPET

NAME: Wenceslas Karl von Luxemburg
BORN: Prague, Bohemia, 1316
RULED: Emperor, 1355–1378
DIED: Of natural causes, Prague, Bohemia, 1378

OPPOSING LOUIS IV was Charles, the son of Bohemia's King John. Elected Roman king in 1346, by Louis's two bitterest enemies, King John and Pope Clement VI, Charles's support was limited, as many bishops and nearly all the imperial cities remained loyal to Louis. Louis's death prevented a civil war, but still the electors sought other contenders to fill the vacancy. Charles eventually managed to overcome opposition by virtually buying the throne, though it was rumoured that he had poisoned one of the imperial contenders.

Charles had a good education, spoke at least four languages and was a supporter of learning and the arts. He was also cunning, selfish, vindictive and greedy. To obtain the purple he prostituted his authority by relinquishing imperial claims to southern Italy and agreeing not to act in Lombardy or Tuscany without papal approval, and to remain in Rome only for his coronation. His acquiescence earned him the mocking title of *Rex Clericorum*—the priest's king. He kept his word, travelling to Rome with few attendants, and was crowned there by the papal legate in 1355, before leaving the city immediately. Not wanting to waste time in a useless attempt to govern Italy, he sold his remaining imperial rights to the Italian cities and nobles and quit Italy as soon as possible.

> **You carry back with you both the iron and the golden crown, but the title of emperor is empty.**
>
> PETRARCH (referring to Charles IV)

During Charles's reign, there arrived the calamitous Black Death, which depopulated much of the empire, while Charles neglected the governance of Germany, concentrating on accumulating wealth and property for his family. These two factors saw the countryside thrown into confusion, ruled by robber knights and barons who fought against the cities while more and more imperial authority passed into the hands of the German princes.

Charles's major law reform was the Golden Bull of 1356, which regulated the election of the King of the Romans in detail, listing explicitly where, when and under what circumstances specific activities had to be carried out. Interestingly, the Bull made no mention of the pope or Italy, showing that imperial rule over Italy was now impracticable at best. Of course, Charles ignored the Bull in 1376 by bribing the electors to ensure his son Wenceslas's succession. He died peacefully two years later.

SIGISMUND

COUNCIL CHAMPION

NAME: Sigismund von Luxemburg
BORN: Nuremburg, Franconia, 1368
RULED: Emperor, 1433–1437
DIED: Possibly poisoned, Znaim (Znojmo), Bohemia, 1437

WENCESLAS, THOUGH CROWNED king and thus Caesar, never became Roman emperor; that privilege fell to his younger brother, Sigismund. Handsome, arrogant and devious, Sigismund was also a hard worker who took very seriously his role as Christendom's chief defender.

Dynastic connections made him king of Hungary in 1387, and he confronted the Turks, who had overrun most of the Eastern Empire and were besieging Constantinople while pressing on the Danube frontier. At the Eastern emperor's urgent request, in 1396 he led the combined armies of Christendom against the Turks in one last crusade, which ended in his army's destruction. Sigismund was a fugitive for eighteen months, throwing Hungary into confusion. So great was the defeat, he was only able to regain control after 1403.

The confused situation in Germany in 1410 allowed him to be crowned King of the Romans. A conscientious son of the church, Sigismund began the arduous task of repairing a schism, which by 1413 saw three popes claiming to be head of the Catholic Church. He forced one of the rivals to summon a church council at Constance in 1414 and the council eventually encouraged the three to resign, though John XXIII escaped and Sigismund had to hunt him down to force his abdication. Although the council failed to get papal agreement for the supremacy of church councils over the pope, it closed in 1418 having achieved the denunciation of the popular radical John Huss.

Huss gave himself up to Sigismund on assurances of his safety, but Sigismund reneged on the deal and Huss was killed after a trial in 1415. Anger about Huss's treatment simmered in his native Bohemia and the people burst into revolt when Sigismund became their king in 1419. The Hussite War saw Sigismund's armies defeated regularly, as the Hussites defied his every attempt to impose his authority. Taking the fight to Germany, they ravaged the countryside as war erupted between the bishops and the people in the imperial cities. Sigismund's only hope lay in a new church council, which met at Basel in 1431.

The pope, Eugenius IV, was not a fan of church councils, particularly one as radical as this one promised to be. He not only refused to attend, but also issued a bull on December 1431, dissolving the council. The council refused to dissolve itself, declaring itself superior to the pope, and demanded that Eugenius appear before it. Sigismund, as a supporter of the church council, was determined to resolve the empire's religious problems. He marched to Rome to become emperor in 1433 and his presence forced Eugenius to recognise the council's validity. Eugenius withdrew his 1431 bull and agreed to leave Rome and go to Basel. To the emperor's relief, the bishops agreed to some Hussite demands, giving Sigismund some much-needed breathing space, and he used the concessions to divide his enemies and reassert imperial control, ending the war in 1436. But by now he was an old man and he could only watch as the pope and council fell out, undoing his designs for church reform, while his wife plotted to undo his succession plans. He died after arresting his wife, and some claim she poisoned him.

Sigismund, Holy Roman Emperor and King of Hungary, Germany, Bohemia and Lombardy, receiving presents from delegates

THE EASTERN EMPERORS

CONSTANTINE XI

FINAL RESISTANCE

NAME: Kōnstantinos Komnēnos-Laskaris
BORN: Unknown
RULED: Emperor, 1204–1205
DIED: Died in battle, Anatolia, 1205

CONSTANTINOPLE HAD FALLEN to the crusaders and Alexius V Murtzuphlus had fled the city, preferring to fight another day. The remaining defenders gathered in Hagia Sophia and proceeded to elect a new emperor to lead the city's defence. Two possibilities presented themselves—Constantine Ducas and Constantine Lascaris—and the decision was made by lot.

> I am best suited to be the emperor.
>
> CONSTANTINE XI LASCARIS

Lascaris was from a minor noble family that presumably was aligned with the Comnenian clan and he had displayed some military skill, but on his election he refused to don the imperial regalia. Instead, he tried to rally the imperial guard and local citizens to attack the crusaders, but to no avail. His troops fled before the mail-clad knights, forcing him to abandon Constantinople. Accompanied by a stream of refugees, he set out for Nicaea, sixty kilometres (forty miles) from the capital. Making that city his base, he was soon leading troops against the Latins but was defeated in the battle of Adramytteion, where it is assumed he died.

THEODORE I

A NEW BEGINNING

NAME: Theodōros Komnēnos-Laskaris
BORN: Constantinople, c. 1174
RULED: Emperor, 1205–1221
DIED: Of illness, Nicaea (Iznik), Anatolia, 1221

THEODORE, CONSTANTINE Lascaris's younger brother, also distinguished himself in Constantinople's final stand. A small man, courageous and active, he found favour with the imperial family, becoming the son-in-law of Alexius III in 1199.

Fleeing into Anatolia in 1204, he established his base of operations in Bithynia. Soon, nearby towns began acknowledging his authority, notwithstanding some initial defeats by the crusaders. Theodore's obvious abilities and the Bulgarians' defeat of the Latins under Baldwin I at the battle of Adrianople encouraged the city of Nicaea to acclaim him as Roman emperor in 1205. Although his brother Constantine XI was dead and he was the son-in-law of Alexius III, it was not until 1208 that the patriarch-in-exile eventually crowned him at Nicaea.

> **The Greek is not a conqueror, he is ruined!**
>
> HENRY OF FLANDERS (referring to Theodore I Lascaris)

The break-up of the Eastern Empire saw Theodore fight for survival in the face of aggressive competing states. The Latin rulers of Constantinople made repeated attempts to conquer Theodore's territory, but he managed to hold on to much of it. Eventually, in 1214, the Latin emperor Henry of Flanders recognised the Nicaean state's existence, as well as Theodore's position as Roman emperor. In Epirus, to the west of Constantinople, another Greek state had been established under Michael Comnenus Ducas, first cousin to Isaac II. Meanwhile Alexius Comnenus, establishing himself at Trebizond, sought opportunities to extend his influence into Bithynia. Then there were the Turks, who tried to crush the newly established empire in 1211. Urged on by Theodore's father-in-law, the troublesome Alexius III (who had sought shelter at Theodore's court), the sultan invaded and the battle of Antioch saw much of the Roman army destroyed. Theodore was almost killed by the sultan but he managed to turn the tables, skewering the sultan with his sword.

By the time of his death in 1221, Theodore had saved the Eastern Empire from complete oblivion. Given the circumstances, the survival of any part of the empire was miraculous, let alone that it flourished. With his caution and courage, Theodore laid the foundations for Constantinople's eventual reconquest.

NICHOLAS

CONTINUING TRADITIONS

NAME: Nikolaos Komnēnos-Laskaris
BORN: Unknown
RULED: Co-emperor, 1208–1212
DIED: Of unknown causes, Nicaea (Iznik), Anatolia, 1212

NICHOLAS, ONLY SON of Theodore I and Anna Comnena Angelina, was crowned co-emperor with his father in 1208 in an effort to continue as many of the old imperial traditions as possible. As he was only a child, there were preparations for his possible succession as a minor. In the end, it was a pointless exercise; he died four years later.

ALEXIUS COMNENUS

THE FIRST CHALLENGER

NAME: Alexios Komnēnos
BORN: Constantinople, c. 1182
RULED: Usurper (Trebizond), 1204–1222
DIED: Of natural causes, Trebizond (Trabzon), Anatolia, 1222

ANDRONICUS I'S GRANDSON, Alexius was a child when his father was murdered. He remained in Constantinople with friends, forgotten by the imperial court, and grew up to be a handsome young man. When the crusaders arrived at the city gates, he took advantage of the confusion to flee to Colchis, where his royal Georgian aunt resided. With her money, he raised a mercenary army that proclaimed him emperor before he occupied Trebizond and ousted the imperial governor, who was not talented enough to stop him.

Haughty and proud, Alexius's imperial heritage saw him officially crowned emperor within Trebizond after Constantinople's fall. He soon established himself through rapid and brilliant conquests, within a year pushing both westwards and southwards. Initially he attracted support from the exiled Romans, but the rise of the Lascarid dynasty in Nicaea soon saw his territory whittled away by both Nicaea and the Turks. To preserve what remained of his empire he formed an alliance with the Latin rulers of Constantinople, but was unable to stem the defeats.

The Turks eventually surrounded Trebizond, and in 1214 they forced Alexius to recognise the sultan as his superior and to provide tribute and military service to preserve his independence. By the time he died in 1222, they had reduced the empire of Trebizond to a strip of land along the Black Sea coast.

ANDRONICUS (I) GIDUS

FIGHTER FOR INDEPENDENCE

NAME: Andronikos Gidos
BORN: Unknown
RULED: Usurper (Trebizond), 1222–1235
DIED: Of unknown causes, Trebizond (Trabzon), Anatolia, 1235

ANDRONICUS GIDUS WAS a talented general. Serving under Theodore I, he had fought against the Latins and Alexius of Trebizond. In a sign of how easily allegiances changed, he joined Alexius in exchange for marrying his daughter. On Alexius's death he became ruler of Trebizond and inherited the claim to be the legitimate Roman emperor.

Andronicus was the Turkish sultan's vassal, and in 1224 the sultan decided to end the empire's existence by laying siege to Trebizond. Andronicus emerged victorious, even capturing the sultan, who freed Trebizond from his suzerainty. Unfortunately, in 1230 a new sultan forced Andronicus to renew his vassalage to preserve the realm.

JOHN (I) AXOUCHOS

POLO LOVER

NAME: Iōannēs Megas Komnēnos Axoukhos
BORN: Unknown
RULED: Usurper (Trebizond), 1235–1238
DIED: Falling off a horse, Trebizond (Trabzon), Anatolia, 1244

JOHN, ALEXIUS COMNENUS'S son, inherited the imperial title at Trebizond after the death of Andronicus Gidus. Very little is known about him. After a brief and uneventful reign he died after falling off his horse while playing polo.

JOHN III

THE MERCIFUL

NAME: Iōannēs Doukas Vatatzēs
BORN: Didymoteichon, Thrace, c. 1192
RULED: Emperor, 1221–1254
DIED: Of natural causes, Nymphaion (Kemalpaşa), Anatolia, 1254

THEODORE I DIED without a legitimate male heir and thus his son-in-law, John Ducas Vatatzes, became emperor at a very delicate time. Though the situation at Nicaea had stabilised, it could easily have unravelled under a weak emperor. It is to John that the Eastern Empire's re-establishment really owes its existence.

Gentle and compassionate, he truly put his people's interests before his own. Giving complete attention to the state's administration, he also improved the state of agriculture in the empire. Free of avarice, frugal with money and keen to reduce the extravagance of the court, he was also a good soldier and a cautious leader, able to exploit situations as they arose. He also possessed a great deal of luck. The crusaders at Constantinople found they could not sustain themselves without new recruits from Western Europe, as the imperial usurper Theodore at Epirus and the newly resurgent Bulgarians slowly sapped what little military strength they possessed. Over the next thirty years all three haemorrhaged to death while John held back, watching as Nicaea grew stronger.

John's uncles by marriage, Alexius and Isaac Lascaris, triggered the first crisis, believing the throne should have been theirs. Fleeing to Constantinople, they urged Robert of Courtenay to attack before John could settle into the role of emperor. John quickly demonstrated his superior military skills: neutralising the Latin heavy cavalry, he inflicted a crushing defeat in 1224, capturing and blinding his uncles. Pressure from Epirus saw the Latins negotiate a peace, resulting in Nicaea gaining everything in Anatolia that was not in Turkish possession.

Resumption of hostilities in 1233 saw further Latin humiliations, as John formed an alliance with the Bulgarians. Throwing the Latin armies out of Anatolia again, he crossed the Hellespont, capturing additional territory in Thrace, but his success caused King Asen of Bulgaria to betray him and strike an alliance with the Latins. It seemed that John's European gains would be lost, but his lucky streak continued with the deaths of Asen's wife and son, which, to Asen's superstitious mind, was a punishment from God for breaking the treaty, and so he halted his attacks.

Having survived a final Latin attempt to overthrow him, John took advantage of Asen's death in 1241 to finally confront the rebel emperors of Epirus. Though they had managed to survive the attacks of the Bulgarians, they were no match for John. He invited the blind ex-emperor Theodore over for a conference to discuss a coordinated effort against their enemies; instead, he held Theodore prisoner until he agreed to abdicate the title of emperor for John and his son. From then on Epirus was in terminal decline until John put an end to its misery, conquering it in 1251.

Unfortunately, John's health was growing worse. He had always suffered from epilepsy, but his attacks grew more frequent and appeared to cloud his judgement. In 1253 he accused a young general, Michael Palaeologus, of conspiracy on the flimsiest of evidence, demanding he hold a red-hot iron to prove his innocence. The case collapsed, and within a few months John promoted Palaeologus to a higher command. Such lapses of judgement became more common, but they never destroyed the people's love and respect for their emperor. He had worked tirelessly for them, establishing orphanages and hospitals, supporting churches and monasteries and, above all, restoring a sense of pride that had been absent since Constantinople's fall. Though he did not see the ancient capital's reconquest, the people remembered him as the best of emperors and he was canonised by the Orthodox Church as St John the Merciful.

THEODORE COMNENUS DUCAS

TROUBLESOME USURPER

NAME: Theodōros Komnēnos Doukas
BORN: Constantinople, c. 1185
RULED: Usurper (Thessalonica), 1225–1230
DIED: Of natural causes, Nicaea (Iznik), Anatolia, 1253

NICAEA WAS NOT THE ONLY centre of resistance against the Latin kingdom. On the Adriatic side of the Balkans the state of Epirus was established by relatives of the Angelus emperors in 1205. In 1215 the assassination of its ruler, Michael, saw the throne pass to his half-brother, Theodore.

A first cousin of Isaac II Angelus and descended from Alexius I, Theodore was restless and relentless. Constantinople's fall saw him take refuge at Nicaea before his urgent call to Epirus and nomination as heir by his half-brother in 1210. On taking over, he began pushing towards the second most important city in the old empire, Thessalonica, now a Latin kingdom ruled by Demetrius of Montferrat under the protection of the Latin emperor, Peter of Courtenay. When Theodore captured the Latin emperor, Pope Honorius III preached a crusade to liberate Peter, but Theodore deceived Honorius by declaring he was ready to acknowledge the pope's supremacy. This allowed him to resume his advance into Thessaly. By 1224 he had conquered Thessalonica; the following year

Nicaea—seat of the Roman emperors during their period of exile

he was acclaimed Roman emperor, although he was not formally crowned until 1227, when he found a bishop—the Bishop of Orchid—willing to show disrespect for the patriarch at Nicaea.

Things went well during the following years, with Theodore steadily reclaiming territory held by the Latins, but in 1230 he overreached when he attacked King Asen of Bulgaria. Captured at the battle of Klokotnitsa, he remained a prisoner until 1237, losing his eyesight at one point as punishment for his involvement in a conspiracy. The situation changed when Asen married Theodore's daughter and released his new father-in-law. Theodore headed back to Thessalonica to find his brother Manuel ruling the city, while Epirus had broken away. He contrived to overthrow Manuel but his blindness meant he could not resume the imperial crown. Although he relinquished that to his son John, he continued to direct the affairs of state.

> **How dare you not make obeisance to an emperor!**
>
> THEODORE COMNENUS DUCAS

The threat from John Vatatzes saw Theodore commit an error, trapped at a conference in 1241 discussing joint action against the Latins and Bulgarians. To regain his freedom he acknowledged Vatatzes's imperial supremacy and, in return, his son John was given the title of Despot of Thessalonica.

When John died, Theodore replaced him with another son, whose incompetence soon caused another war with Vatatzes, which resulted in the loss of Thessalonica and Theodore's flight to Vodhena, which he ruled as a semi-independent state. Then in 1251 he convinced his nephew, the ruler of Epirus, to attack the Nicaeans. His nephew obliged, only to surrender when Vatatzes invaded. Vatatzes confined Theodore to a monastery, where he remained for the rest of his life.

JOHN COMNENUS DUCAS

UNWILLING USURPER

NAME: Iōannēs Komnēnos Doukas
BORN: Place unknown, c. 1226
RULED: Usurper (Thessalonica), 1237–1242
DIED: Unknown causes, Thessalonica, Thessaly, 1244

THEODORE DUCAS'S FAMILY were with him at the disastrous battle of Klokotnitsa and they ended up at the Bulgarian court. Eventually they were released with Theodore, and upon their return to Thessalonica Theodore's son John was crowned emperor.

John's youth meant his father became the effective ruler of Thessalonica. This suited John, who did not want to be emperor; instead, he was a pious and chaste young man who desired to enter a monastery. He was relieved when his father's capture in 1242 forced him to abandon all imperial claims. Granted the title of despot under the authority of the emperor at Nicaea, he lived only two years more.

THEODORE II

EPILEPTIC EMPEROR

NAME: Theodōros Doukas Laskaris
BORN: Nicaea (Iznik), Anatolia, 1221
RULED: Emperor, 1254–1258
DIED: Of epilepsy, Nymphaion (Kemalpaşa), Anatolia, 1258

FOR JOHN III, suffering from epilepsy was a minor inconvenience, but for his son Theodore it was a life-threatening condition, leaving him physically prostrate and incapacitated. Yet he refused to let it adversely affect his life and ambitions, although he did suffer from extreme mood swings ranging from bleak depression to uncontrollable anger.

His epilepsy and his scholarly upbringing saw Theodore underestimated as a ruler. Almost immediately, he faced an invasion by the Bulgarians, who tried to take advantage of his perceived weakness. Despite his epilepsy, he personally led his army, crushing the Bulgarians in two campaigns.

Theodore distrusted the aristocracy, and so he gave important positions to lowborn men of ability. In particular, he distrusted Michael Palaeologus, who soon became the focus of aristocratic discontent. Having grown up together at court, the two knew each other well but the bookish and sickly Theodore seemed to resent the brilliant and handsome young general. Theodore's paranoia seemed to grow with every passing year, and at one stage he accused Michael's sister of using spells to cause his ever more violent epileptic attacks. In 1258 Theodore caused Michael to flee to the Turks, where he offered his services in fighting the Mongols. The war in Epirus forced Theodore to recall him, but he ensured Michael's failure by not providing enough men. Eventually he recalled Michael in disgrace and threw him into prison, and it was during this crisis that Theodore finally lost his struggle against his illness.

JOHN IV

FORGOTTEN EMPEROR

NAME: Iōannēs Doukas Laskaris
BORN: Possibly Nymphaion (Kemalpaşa), Anatolia, 1250
RULED: Emperor, 1258–1261
DIED: Of natural causes, Bithynia, Anatolia, c. 1305

A THRONE HELD BY an eight-year-old boy tempts overly ambitious men, as John IV learnt to his cost. Placed under a regent, he became embroiled in the intrigue that saw the murder of the regent and the rise of Michael Palaeologus, who had himself crowned co-emperor by the patriarch, but ensured that John was absent.

I forgive what your father did to me.

JOHN DUCAS LASCARIS (to Andronicus Palaeologus)

After Constantinople's reconquest in 1261, John remained at Nicaea, forgotten by almost everyone—except Michael. To prevent any future threat, and in violation of his repeated oaths, he had the ten-year-old boy blinded on his birthday and sent to a fortress in Bithynia to live out his life. Becoming a monk, John lived a life of saintly prayer and solitude. He was disturbed twice, the first time when Michael trotted him out to disprove the claims of a blind pretender who was a figurehead for rebels at Nicaea. The second time was twenty-eight years later by Michael's son, Andronicus. He visited John, begging his forgiveness for his father's crime. John freely gave it and more, formally abandoning all claims to the purple. For his actions, locals revered him as a saint long after his death.

MICHAEL VIII

CONQUEROR OF CONSTANTINOPLE

NAME: Mikhaēl Doukas Angelos Komnēnos Palaiologos
BORN: Nicaea (Iznik), Anatolia, 1224
RULED: Co-emperor, 1259–1261; senior emperor, 1261–1282
DIED: Of natural causes, Pachomion, Thrace, 1282

SOME HAVE QUESTIONED whether Michael Palaeologus was guilty of the accusations the Lascarid emperors hurled at him. It is certain that after their poor treatment of him, he was definitely conspiring against them by Theodore II's final years. Repeated arrests and threats turned him against them, and John IV's minority presented him with an excellent opportunity.

Michael, related in one form or another to many of the empire's major dynasties, was not a brilliant general. He was, nonetheless, a formidable opponent, pragmatic and cunning, deceitful when the situation required it, and not averse to throwing money around to buy support. He was also untrustworthy. He took an oath to respect the legitimacy and safety of John IV but he broke it at the first opportunity, and he got away with it because he had achieved the long-held dream of the exiles—Constantinople's reconquest.

After becoming co-emperor in 1259, he spent two years preparing for an assault on the Latin kingdom. While he was still finalising his plans, word came back that his advance scouting party had managed to enter Constantinople while the principal Latin army was elsewhere and had secured the city in Michael's name. It was July 1261. Baldwin II fled at their coming, while the returning army was neutralised by the presence of their families still locked in the city. Michael took his time, entering the city in August, but though they celebrated with traditional pomp and ceremony, Constantinople was a mere shadow of its former glory.

There were consequences for dethroning and blinding John IV. The patriarch excommunicated Michael and ordered him to make reparations for his crime. Michael refused and attempted to depose the patriarch and punish anyone who had links to the former emperor. Nicaea rose up in rebellion, as Michael tried unsuccessfully to cheat his way out of his predicament. It was not until 1268 and two patriarchs later that Michael was absolved. However, this was not the end of his troubles with the church.

> **They rage terribly against us, though these renegades are Roman, just as we are.**
>
> MICHAEL VIII PALAEOLOGUS

Michael's desire to restore Constantinople and his need to purchase support for his regime saw him plunder the peoples of Anatolia, and they willingly opened their towns to the Turks, who slowly pushed the empire out of the lands that had sheltered the Lascarids. Michael's policies weakened Anatolia, exposing it to a new enemy—the Ottomans. Yet it was not only here that the empire saw its fortunes begin to decline. Constantinople's recapture again inspired estern rulers to contemplate an attack on the Eastern Empire. Chief among these was the king of Sicily and Naples, Charles of Anjou.

To fend off Charles, Michael formed alliances with the Genoese and Venetians, playing them off against Charles and each other. But in doing so, he gave these naval powers concessions that were extended with each new treaty negotiation. This eroded the revenues generated through trade, the empire's chief source of wealth. Meanwhile, to fend off the pope, Michael entered into negotiations to unify the Catholic and Orthodox churches. This strategy culminated in the Council of Lyon in 1274, which saw the formal union of the churches.

While the Greek Church rejected the union outright, the popes, initially enthusiastic for the union, dissuaded Charles from launching his long-cherished assault on Constantinople. For his trouble, the Orthodox Church excommunicated Michael in 1277, at the same time as the popes began losing patience with the Eastern Empire. In 1280 the new pope, Martin IV, was a devotee of Charles. Though Michael had risked his throne to make union a reality, Martin also excommunicated him, giving Charles free rein to attack. Charles was only stopped by the Sicilian Vespers, an uprising in 1282 incited and paid for by Michael in a last ditch effort to derail his enemies.

It was Michael's last great success. He died shortly afterwards, still condemned by the Orthodox Church, which never understood the political reality under which Michael had to operate. His attempts at union, though distasteful to his Orthodox subjects, had saved the empire from almost certain subjugation by a determined and able foe.

MANUEL COMNENUS

THE GREAT CAPTAIN

NAME: Manouēl Megas Komnenos
BORN: Place unknown, c. 1218
RULED: Usurper (Trebizond), 1238–1263
DIED: Of natural causes, Trebizond (Trabzon), Anatolia, 1263

MANUEL, THE YOUNGER, the son of Alexius Comnenus, obtained the throne at Trebizond by forcing his nephew into a monastery after his brother

John Axouchos's death. It was now that Trebizond's commercial prosperity began, but Manuel remained a vassal of the Turks and then the Mongols. This did not prevent him from trying to expand his influence, possibly by military means, which culminated in his capture of Sinope, which had been lost to the Turks in 1214. For his efforts against the Turks he was nicknamed The Great Captain.

Trebizond's small size enabled it to survive under the Mongols, who considered it a trading city rather than an empire. It also meant no one really took it seriously, as Manuel found out when he sent a delegation in 1253 to France's King Louis IX, seeking a French princess as a bride. They firmly rebuffed his request. He died in 1263 after a prosperous reign.

ANDRONICUS (II) COMNENUS

SHRINKING DOMINIONS

NAME: Andronikos Megas Komnēnos
BORN: Trebizond, Anatolia, c. 1240
RULED: Usurper (Trebizond), 1263–1266
DIED: Of unknown causes, Trebizond (Trabzon), Anatolia, 1266

ANDRONICUS WAS THE eldest son of Emperor Manuel of Trebizond. Michael VIII asked both Andronicus and his father to abandon their claims to be legitimate Roman emperors, but to no effect. During Andronicus's reign Trebizond continued to grow as a mercantile centre, receiving traders from across Europe, but the important city of Sinope, captured during his father's reign, was lost to the Pervane emirate. Andronicus died childless in 1266.

GEORGE COMNENUS

THE WANDERER

NAME: Georgiōs Megas Komnēnos
BORN: Trebizond (Trabzon), Anatolia, c. 1255
RULED: Usurper (Trebizond), 1266–1280
DIED: Cause and place unknown, some time after 1284

GEORGE, ANDRONICUS'S younger, violent half-brother, immediately pursued a more aggressive policy towards his internal and external enemies. Gaining a little independence from the Mongols, he joined an alliance with Charles of Anjou and those opposed to church union in Constantinople to topple Michael VIII. His adherants, fearing his increasing power, betrayed him to the Mongol khan and George became his prisoner in 1280.

Imprisoned for two years until the khan's death, George then invaded Trebizond to reclaim his throne from his brother John. Defeated in 1284, he escaped to the mountains, where he wandered from hiding place to hiding place. Eventually captured, he retained the title of emperor but without any responsibilities.

JOHN (II) COMNENUS

RENOUNCED THE PURPLE

NAME: Iōannēs Megas Komnēnos
BORN: Trebizond (Trabzon), Anatolia, c. 1262
RULED: Usurper (Trebizond), 1280–1282
DIED: Of unknown causes, Limnia, Anatolia, 1297

JOHN HAD THE FORTUNE of becoming emperor when Trebizond was no longer a vassal state of the Mongols, and while Michael VIII was under pressure from both Charles of Anjou and the anti-unionists within the

TURKS AND MONGOLS

For most of its existence, the Eastern empire's greatest adversaries were the Muslim states that had conquered the majority of its eastern provinces during the seventh century. By the eleventh century, the empire was coming into contact with new tribes that were putting pressure on its possessions in Anatolia. Of these, the most important in terms of the empire's future were the Turks, a conglomeration of tribes who had settled in the Black Sea steppes during the ninth century. By the tenth century, one tribe—the Seljuk Turks—had moved into Persia and they began to expand their sphere of influence. It was this tribe that smashed Roman power at the battle of Manzikert in 1071, and by 1092 the Seljuks had amassed an enormous swathe of territory. Called the Sultanate of Rūm (named after Rome), it stretched from the Bosphorus to modern-day Afghanistan. The crusades were launched against the Seljuks, who survived them only to be brought low by the Mongols in 1243.

The Mongols were a steppe people who emerged from Mongolia in the late twelfth century, and during the course of the thirteenth century they lay waste to every culture or empire they encountered, erecting an empire that dwarfed any that had preceded it and holding sway from the China Sea in the east to the gates of Vienna in the west. They conquered the Seljuks and destroyed the old Abbasid Caliphate, radically redrawing the balance of power in the Middle East. However, their empire did not survive intact; it split into four competing khanates. Although they occasionally acknowledged the authority of a Great Khan, they would mostly exist independently in their respective spheres for centuries to come.

In the power vacuum that emerged following the collapse of the Seljuks, another Turkic tribe stepped in to fill the breech—the Ottoman Turks. Named after their founder, Othman, they came to power in 1300 as a minor emirate that eagerly took advantage of the chaos. They soon came to be the dominant power in Anatolia, gradually taking territory from the Eastern Roman Empire, with the Romans seemingly unable to stop them, especially during the civil war between John V and John Cantacuzenus. By the 1350s the Ottomans were in Europe, and they slowly surrounded the crumbling Roman *imperium*. They would eventually erect an empire centred on Constantinople, ruling much the same territory as the Eastern Roman Empire did during the reign of Heraclius, before it went into a slow decline. Ottoman rule finally ended in 1923 when the Republic of Turkey was established.

---

empire. Had he possessed any ability, he would have turned these factors to his advantage.

Young, weak and stupid, John assumed the purple after his brother was betrayed by the nobility. Yet neither he nor they possessed the talents to take what was offered in 1281—Constantinople's throne. Michael VIII was deeply unpopular because of his reunion of the churches and the anti-unionists were looking for a new Orthodox imperial candidate—and John was the only other crowned emperor around. To remove this threat, Michael sent ambassadors to convince John to renounce the title his family had claimed for over seventy-five years.

John refused, but the ambassadors stirred up a rebellion in Trebizond, resulting in John's capture. Though he was released, he had had such a fright that when Michael's ambassadors returned, he agreed to form an alliance. Initially he resisted going to Constantinople, fearing that he would end up like John IV Lascaris, but he was eventually convinced of his safety. The outcome was his marriage to Michael's youngest daughter in 1282; the cost was abandoning all support for Charles of Anjou and laying aside the title of Roman emperor. Instead, he obtained a new title: Emperor of the East, Iberia and Perateia. With this in tow, he returned to Trebizond and continued to rule until his death fifteen years later. None of his successors ever tried to reclaim the title of Roman emperor, and the little empire of Trebizond managed to outlast the emperors of Constantinople, before drowning in the Ottoman tide in 1461.

and he focused his attention on this to the detriment of everything else. Burying his heretical father in a small, unmarked grave outside the capital, without a state funeral or church service, he rejected union with Rome and excommunicated its supporters. Disputes between various Orthodox factions crippled his administration, as the church's power had increased considerably after it was made responsible for civil and judicial matters, as well as religious ones.

ANDRONICUS II

THE EMPIRE IN CHAOS

NAME: Andronikos Palaiologos
BORN: Nicaea (Iznik), Anatolia, 1259
RULED: Co-emperor, 1261–1282;
senior emperor, 1282–1328
DIED: Of natural causes, Constantinople, 1332

ANDRONICUS, MICHAEL VIII'S eldest son, inherited an empire that, although nearly bankrupt, was still extensive and capable of growth. By the time of his deposition in 1328, the empire was falling apart, and responsibility for this belongs to Andronicus, a man lacking in administrative or military ability. A born intriguer, peevish, without vigour or caution, he was also an extreme micromanager, forever focusing on trivia instead of the empire's urgent needs.

Although he was made co-emperor at the age of two, he remained uncrowned until 1272. In a sign of things to come, when he was given command of the war against the resurgent Turks in 1280, his cowardice and incompetence allowed the Turks to capture many important cities. Upon Michael's death, Andronicus showed where his true passions lay. Pious and Orthodox, he felt his duty was to heal the divisions in the church

Although the Devil cannot afflict people with all the harm he intends, even still he manages to achieve a great deal.

ANDRONICUS II PALAEOLOGUS

Even worse, Andronicus's religious mania crippled the armed forces. Money urgently needed to maintain the army was diverted to the court and the church, while the numbers of soldiers steadily declined, with men avoiding military service by either becoming monks or paying a land tax. Those who remained in the military were in a constant state of sedition over arrears in pay. Consequently, the Eastern Roman armies now consisted almost wholly of mercenaries. In the case of Turkish mercenaries, this was a double-edged sword: when they went unpaid, or when their nominal imperial commander could not control them, they used this opportunity to ravage and occupy any remaining imperial territory in Anatolia. Within a generation, the Greek language all but disappeared from an area that had spoken it for almost two millennia. Andronicus watched the unfolding calamity with indifference, so moribund that he was incapable of preventing the war between the Venetians and Genoese spilling into his empire, and into Constantinople itself. When the Ottoman Turks began burning towns within sight of the capital, it seemed nothing could prevent the empire's collapse.

Then, in 1302, came salvation: a troop of Spaniards known as the Catalan Grand Company offered their services to Andronicus. The most feared mercenary group in Europe, they were—according to their leader, Roger de Flor—invincible. Andronicus agreed to their hefty asking price and by 1303 the Turks were retreating from Anatolia, but at a cost—the arrogant Catalans grew ever more unruly, alienating the empire they were meant to serve. A stronger emperor would have kept them in check, but Andronicus's weakness encouraged Roger to seek a kingdom held in fief in Anatolia, and by 1305 he was the newest Caesar. To pay the Catalans, Andronicus debased the coinage and levied onerous taxes. Yet by now, no one trusted these mercenaries, and the empire's officials were ordered not to obey Roger.

The Catalans were about to launch a new campaign against the Turks when Roger was assassinated. This unleashed their fury; crossing into Thrace, they devastated the land. Too late, Andronicus tried to repair the damage. He begged them to stop; he tried to bribe them; he sent army after army to halt their depredations—all to no avail. They massacred everyone they could lay their hands on,

Arrival of Roger de Flor in Constantinople, 1303

FALL OF THE EASTERN EMPIRE

turning Thrace, one of the empire's richest and most fertile provinces, into a wasteland. This rampage continued for six years, until they established a duchy at Athens and left what remained of the empire alone. In a decade they had inflicted such a wound that the empire never recovered. This would have been bad enough for Andronicus; unfortunately, things were going to get much worse.

The death of Andronicus's son, Michael, meant that next in line for the throne was Michael's eldest son, Andronicus the Younger. However, this debauched and unstable youth was displaced as Andronicus's heir after an incident involving the death of his brother Manuel. Yet the emperor's rule was now deeply unpopular and the opposition gravitated to his grandson, resulting in three devastating civil wars. The first, in 1321, saw the terrified emperor agree to partition the empire. The second, a year later, was instigated by the betrayal of a key rebel supporter but still ended with the elder Andronicus coming to terms: this time he and his grandson would rule the empire jointly. The peace lasted five years before the younger man's ambitions and the older man's resentment saw war resume. This time the Serbians and Bulgarians took advantage of the fighting to encroach on imperial lands. The younger Andronicus took Constantinople, forcing the emperor to resign and enter a monastery. Here Andronicus the Elder took the name of Antony and lived out the rest of his days, still fuming over his unjust treatment.

MICHAEL IX PALAEOLOGUS

UNLUCKY IN EVERYTHING

NAME: Mikhaël Palaiologos
BORN: Constantinople, 1277
RULED: Co-emperor, 1294–1320
DIED: Of depression, Thessalonica, Thessaly, 1320

MICHAEL, ANDRONICUS II'S eldest son, tried hard to succeed as a military leader, but as commander of the Alan mercenaries—by now the mainstay of the imperial armies—he never won a single major battle against any enemy, showing that good intentions and the right attitude are not enough.

Roman soldiers are prohibited from serving in the company of the Catalans.

MICHAEL IX PALAEOLOGUS

It was evident that he could not defeat the Turks or restrain the mercenaries who mutinied under his watch. In 1300 he abandoned his headquarters at Magnesia on the Hermus to the Ottomans and his retreat opened up the Asian provinces. Roger de Flor replaced the humiliated Michael as commander in 1303, thus earning Michael's undying resentment. Michael ordered the citizens at Peges not to open their gates to his replacement; when they were forced to, Michael vindictively fined them. His ill will was a key reason why Roger decided to look after his own interests even more than usual.

Michael's new posting was at Adrianople, keeping an eye on the Bulgarians, against whom he managed to win some minor skirmishes. The emperor asked Roger to join Michael, but Roger's wariness and the army's protests over the Catalans' behaviour saw the situation deteriorate. Michael compounded the situation by ordering that no imperial troops serve in conjunction with the Catalans. Attempting to defuse the situation, in 1305 Roger visited Michael's headquarters, where he was murdered, probably at Michael's instigation. Michael then killed as many Catalans as he could find in the area.

The Catalans' response was swift and deadly, and Michael bore the brunt of it. They defeated army after army, and when Michael led one attack he barely escaped with his life and was carried badly wounded from the field. Nothing he did halted their assaults. Turkish mercenaries soon joined in the destruction, and

Michael was unsuccessful in defeating even these, fleeing before them and leaving behind his crown. By 1312 he had had enough, retiring to Thessalonica to live out the remainder of his reign in abject apathy. His spirit was finally broken upon receiving news of his son Manuel's death, the result of a foolish plot instigated by his other son, Andronicus. Weighed down by failure and severely depressed, he welcomed the relief of death.

ALEXIUS PHILANTHROPENUS

THE BLIND GENERAL

NAME: Alexios Philanthropenos
BORN: Place unknown, c. 1270
RULED: Usurper, 1295
DIED: Of natural causes, Lesbos, c. 1343

THE INCOMPETENCE OF Andronicus II, frequent Turkish incursions and excessive taxation saw the Asiatic provinces search for a saviour. They selected Alexius Philanthropenus, a nobleman distantly related to the Palaeologus emperors.

A gifted general, Alexius came to prominence during Michael VIII's reign by gaining an improbable naval victory over the Latins off Thessaly. Eventually appointed *doux* of the *theme* of Thrakesion and given command of the war against the Turks by Andronicus II, he stemmed the Turkish onslaughts and from 1293 started gaining significant victories over them. His troops, placing their faith in him, proclaimed him emperor, but though he captured Andronicus's brother, his daring spirit seemed to desert him. He hesitated, and during negotiations with Andronicus II, where he was offered the title of Caesar, his own men took him prisoner. Handed over to the governor of Neokastra, the *protovestiarios* Livadarios, he was blinded.

Alexius's military reputation remained, however, and in 1324 Andronicus recalled him in a final effort to preserve Philadelphia from falling to the Turks. Though old and blind, he managed to lift the siege, becoming governor of the city until 1327. Then, in 1336, now in his sixties, he led a fleet and recaptured the island of Lesbos, which had fallen to the Genoese. As a reward, he became the island's governor, a position he held until his death. His contemporaries named him the new Belisarius; soon they would wish he were still alive.

ANDRONICUS III

BAD BOY TRANSFORMED

NAME: Andronikos Palaiologos
BORN: Constantinople, 1297
RULED: Co-emperor, 1313–1328;
sole emperor, 1328–1341
DIED: Of natural causes, Constantinople, 1341

THE YOUNGER ANDRONICUS was completely different from his grandfather Andronicus II. Though he was energetic and impulsive, his youthful indiscretions did not inspire much confidence. Indulged by his grandfather, he grew up selfish and spoilt, and he set in motion a tragedy that ripped his family apart. Discovering his mistress had a secret lover, he dispatched thugs to deal with the matter. In a stupid mix-up, they attacked and killed Andronicus's brother, Manuel, resulting in his father's rapid death and his own disinheritance by his furious grandfather.

The result was civil war, with his close friend John Cantacuzenus leading his cause. Gathering an army, they marched on Constantinople in 1321, forcing his grandfather to acknowledge him as his successor and give him Thrace to govern. However, his reckless lifestyle soon antagonised key supporters, who convinced the old emperor that his grandson had merely been lucky. War recommenced within a year, but young Andronicus was victorious, this time becoming co-emperor. Five years later saw the final act in this family dispute, as the elder Andronicus accused his grandson of stealing from the public purse. Again, young Andronicus won, though this time both sides had help from foreign nations, who took advantage of the chaos to occupy imperial territory. The old emperor was deposed, freeing Andronicus to rule the empire.

To everyone's surprise, the young tearaway had matured. He approached the throne with much vigour and enthusiasm, his only vice being an excessive love of hunting. He abandoned unnecessary court ceremonials, stopped abuses in imperial administration and expanded the long-neglected imperial fleet. Guided by the able John Cantacuzenus, his new prime minister, he tackled the problems that the civil wars had exacerbated.

Success did not match his vigour, however. The empire lost almost all of its territory in Anatolia to the Ottomans. Though he managed to repulse a number of invasions across the Hellespont into Europe, the Turks pushed deeper into Thrace as his reign progressed. A major campaign to relieve Nicaea ended in disaster, with Andronicus wounded and the army retreating in disorder. Meanwhile, Bulgaria and Serbia made

THE DESPOTS

A feature of the late imperial system in Constantinople was the development of the *despotes*, or despots. Originally an epithet applied to the emperor, 'despot' was converted into an official title in the reign of Manuel I Comnenus. It outranked the *sebastokratores* and the *kaisares*, and the holder was second only to the emperor. This title was often given to the younger sons of the emperor (the oldest having usually been crowned as co-emperor, *symbasileus*).

Although originally a courtly dignity, without specific military or administrative functions or powers, by the fourteenth century the position became associated with the administration of specific territories—the *despotates*. As the empire was cut up into increasingly non-contiguous entities, it required the presence of a governor to manage each particular region. There were three recognised despotates: Thessalonica (ceded to Venice in 1423 and conquered by the Ottomans in 1430), Epirus and the Morea. Each was administered as a semi-autonomous region by an imperial relative, who was assigned by the ruling emperor in Constantinople.

The Despotate of Epirus was located on the western coast of central Greece and arose from the independent state established by Michael Comnenus Ducas in the aftermath of the sack of Constantinople in 1204. When Theodore Comnenus Ducas was defeated by John III Vatatzes in 1242, Theodore's son John was awarded the title of despot, in exchange for recognition of the Nicaean emperors' claims to the imperial title of the Roman Empire. This title was renewed for most of the rulers of Epirus until the despotate was conquered during the 1350s by the Serbians, who continued to use the title for their own independent rulers.

The Despotate of the Morea covered the Peloponneses in southern Greece and was established in the mid-1350s by John Cantacuzenus. It was ruled by a member of that family until 1383, when it was seized by the ruling Palaeologus dynasty. The Morea was then governed by the sons of the emperor—first by the son of John V and then by Manuel II's sons—until its extinction in 1460, when it was swept away by the Ottoman tide.

significant inroads into Macedonia, though victories in Epirus and Thessaly saw some old territory restored to the empire.

Although many conspiracies plagued Andronicus's reign, none got past the planning stage. His opponents should have waited, as his health was not the best. Prematurely worn out by his youthful indulgences, Andronicus died in 1341, aged only forty-four.

JOHN V
THE SULTAN'S VASSAL

NAME: Iōannēs Palaiologos
BORN: Didymoteichon, Thrace, 1332
RULED: Emperor, 1341–1391
DIED: Of nervous shock, Constantinople, 1391

THE REIGN OF JOHN V, Andronicus III's son, was one of the most disastrous in Roman history, though admittedly it mostly was not his fault. Initially he was only a spectator in the civil war between his mother and John Cantacuzenus, a conflict that finally ended in 1347 when Cantacuzenus was acknowledged co-emperor. Eight days later, John V married Cantacuzenus's daughter against his will. Knowing he was in no position to complain, he bided his time, waiting for the right moment to strike.

It came when he was eighteen and found himself at Thessalonica free of Cantacuzenus's presence. His youth and good looks made him popular, and so he refused to return to Constantinople, causing civil war to erupt once again. Divorcing his wife, he asked the Serbians and the Bulgarians for help in reclaiming the throne. Though the war went badly, support within the capital saw John launch a sudden strike in 1354 with the help of the Genoese, forcing Cantacuzenus to resign.

John found an empire shorn of territory and surrounded by enemies, in particular the Ottomans. Despairingly, he turned to the pope, hoping that a massive crusade would save the Eastern Roman Empire. Although he held out the grand dream of union with Rome, it was not enough. Murad I's accession as Ottoman sultan and the rapid spread of his troops across Thrace and Bulgaria forced John to travel to Europe to beg for assistance, the first Eastern emperor to suffer this humiliation. His first stop was Hungary in 1366, but no help came. Worse, while returning, he was imprisoned by the Bulgarians for over six months. Undeterred, but unable to get the Orthodox Church to agree to union, in 1369 he went to Rome and converted to Catholicism. It achieved nothing, and again John became a prisoner, this time of the Venetians, who wanted repayment of outstanding debts. His son Manuel managed to gather the money and he returned home in 1371, a broken man.

By 1373 Murad's conquests had forced John to become his vassal and he was compelled to campaign alongside the sultan. Even worse, Murad ordered John to blind his son Andronicus for his part in a conspiracy against the sultan. John took a risk by removing only one eye, but his action alienated Andronicus, who overthrew his father in 1376 and imprisoned him. John escaped in 1379 and this time was forced to rely on the sultan's aid to reclaim his crown, in exchange for handing over more cities.

> **The Church of Rome is the mother church, and she alone has the authority to decide questions of faith.**
>
> JOHN V PALAEOLOGUS

By now a fearful old man, he watched as Murad continued conquering imperial territory before annihilating the Serbians at Kosovo in 1389. Meanwhile, his family constantly conspired against him, with his grandson John managing briefly to overthrow him. It took a new sultan, Bayezit, to rouse him from his lethargy and begin repairs on the Golden Gate fortress. He was quickly put in his place: the sultan ordered the demolition of the fortress or John's son Manuel would be blinded.

In misery, John agreed. This was the last straw. He retired to his room, lay on the bed and faced the wall, waiting for death, which was not long in coming.

JOHN VI CANTACUZENUS

HELPING HIS ENEMIES

NAME: Iōannēs Kantakouzēnos
BORN: Constantinople, c. 1295
RULED: Co-emperor, 1341–1354
DIED: Of natural causes, Mistra, Morea, 1383

JOHN CANTACUZENUS WAS Andronicus III's boyhood companion. A wealthy nobleman who possessed military and administrative abilities, he made himself indispensable to the young prince. Andronicus II tried to remove his influence by making him governor of Thessaly, but he used that position to launch and support the younger Andronicus's rebellion. Frequently appearing at the head of the rebel troops, he was instrumental in the young man's eventual victory. As a reward, Cantacuzenus became Andronicus's *megas domestikos*, the highest rank in the empire after the Caesar.

Cantacuzenus ran the state during Andronicus III's reign, trying unsuccessfully to repair the damage of the civil wars. On the emperor's premature death in 1341, he assumed he would govern in the name of Andronicus's nine-year-old son, John V, only to find himself opposed by John's mother and a coalition of jealous rivals who planned his overthrow. Believing only he was capable of arresting the empire's decline and learning of his partisans' arrest in Constantinople, he had himself declared emperor by the army in late 1341, while he was reclaiming parts of the Peloponnese. This, the fourth civil war, was calamitous for the empire, as both sides used foreign armies to support their cause. The Ottomans aided John Cantacuzenus and helped themselves to vast tracts of territory in Thrace, all the while carrying off anything they could. By the time the war ended in 1347, there was hardly anything left of the Eastern Empire.

Victorious, Cantacuzenus entered Constantinople without bloodshed and was recognised emperor on condition that when John V turned twenty-five they would rule jointly. Cantacuzenus soon beheld the realities of the situation. The state was broke, and he took unpopular measures to redress the dire situation, raising taxes to crushing levels. Wars against the Genoese and Serbians consumed precious resources, and he seemed unable to control his son's extravagant spending. Meanwhile, civil war again erupted in 1351 when the young John V, taking advantage of Cantacuzenus's absence, declared him dethroned. Cantacuzenus's Turkish alliance turned popular opinion against him; nonetheless, he crushed John V's Serbian and Bulgarian supporters and by 1354 was eager to end this latest civil war. Unfortunately, he discounted the Genoese, who ferried John V and his soldiers into Constantinople, forcing Cantacuzenus to resign the purple.

> **[Civil war] is like the deadly heat of an incurable fever, devouring the health of the state.**
>
> JOHN VI CANTACUZENUS

Weary of the constant struggle to rule a declining empire, he hoped to spend his last years in contemplative solitude. Becoming the monk Joasaph, he composed a history of his time as emperor. He did, however, find favour again with John V, who sought his advice on many key initiatives, and he led negotiations with the Catholics in a proposed church reunion. After Andronicus IV took power and accused him of attempting to restore John V to the throne, he retired to Mistra, where he died, convinced that his civil wars had been a necessary evil.

John VI Cantacuzenus, President of the Fifth Council of Constantinople

MATTHEW CANTACUZENUS

DETERMINED SON

NAME: Matthaios Asanēs Kantakouzēnos
BORN: Constantinople, c. 1325
RULED: Co-emperor, 1353–1357
DIED: Of natural causes, Morea, c. 1391

THE DECISION TO MAKE John V senior co-emperor pleased just about everyone—except John Cantacuzenus's son, Matthew. From a young age he had believed himself destined for great things, marrying into the Palaeologi in 1341. Therefore, during 1347 he took possession of much of Thrace, including Adrianople, which his father reluctantly allowed him to govern. In 1350, with the help of Turkish pirates, he triumphantly engineered the capture of Thessalonica, which had not acknowledged Cantacuzenus's legitimacy.

> **I will not return to the court or my church unless you swear never to proclaim your son Matthew emperor.**
>
> PATRIARCH PHILOTHEOS KOKKINOS
> (to John Cantacuzenus)

John V, convinced that Matthew was going to supplant him, attacked him at Adrianople, triggering a civil war. Appealing to his father, who went on the offensive with thousands of Turkish troops, Matthew returned to Constantinople, where his father proclaimed him co-emperor in 1353, though it was not until 1354 that the patriarch was convinced to abandon John V and crown Matthew, who returned to Adrianople.

Cantacuzenus's abdication did not initially affect Matthew, as John V agreed to rule with him, but mutual suspicion saw the civil war continue and it ended only when the Serbians captured Matthew in 1357. He was forced to abdicate but John V permitted him to stay in Constantinople with his father. In 1361, fleeing an outbreak of the plague, he travelled to the Morea where he joined his brother, the Despot Manuel. Made co-despot, he left the actual management of the region in Manuel's hands. Upon Manuel's death in 1380, he took over the reins of government for two years, before resigning in favour of his son.

ANDRONICUS IV

RESTLESS SPIRIT

NAME: Andronikos Palaiologos
BORN: Constantinople, 1348
RULED: Co-emperor, 1369–1373;
usurper, 1376–1379; co-emperor, 1381–1384
DIED: Of natural causes, Selymbria, Thrace, 1385

ANDRONICUS IV ABSOLUTELY detested his father, John V, making for a difficult relationship. Although he was not John's favourite son, as the eldest he had certain responsibilities. During John's trip to Hungary in 1366, Andronicus was regent, evidently doing a reasonable job, since his father entrusted him with the throne as co-emperor during his trip to Italy in 1369.

John's capture by the Venetians in 1370 gave Andronicus a golden opportunity. John offered Venice the island of Tenedos as part payment on outstanding debts. Andronicus, under pressure from his Genoese allies, refused to relinquish it, before pretending he could not raise any money to set his father free. His plan failed when his brother Manuel rescued the emperor, who returned to the capital. Andronicus's next attempt to rid himself of his father was an agreement with the Turkish sultan's son, whereby each would help kill the other's father. The plot failed and Sultan Murad blinded his son, demanding that John do the same to Andronicus. John, half-hearted as always, took out only one of Andronicus's eyes before imprisoning him in the Tower of Anemas for three years.

The Genoese, desperate to prevent Tenedos falling into Venetian hands, eventually freed Andronicus and, burning for revenge, he went to the sultan, who agreed to provide him with troops. Returning to Constantinople, he placed John and Manuel in the very tower that had held him. He was crowned in 1377; his reign was devoted to attacking Tenedos.

Now Venice intervened, helping rescue John and Manuel, who also went to the sultan. The constant squabbling of the Palaeologi always benefited the Ottomans, and so the sultan again agreed to help. Andronicus agreed to lay down his arms in return for his reinstatement as co-emperor and heir, but it was probably too much to expect this restless man to abide by the agreement. Rebelling once again in 1384, Andronicus was deposed and died the following year in semi-exile at Selymbria.

JOHN VII

FAMILY REUNION

NAME: Iōannēs Palaiologos
BORN: Constantinople, 1370
RULED: Co-usurper, 1377–1379;
usurper, 1390; co-emperor, 1399–1408
DIED: Of natural causes, Thessalonica,
Thessaly, 1408

JOHN, SON OF ANDRONICUS IV, inherited both his father's control of the northern coast of the Marmara and a dislike of his grandfather John V. He was only a child when Andronicus crowned him co-emperor, but his opportunity came when he was twenty. Using a dispute over a border fortress as his excuse, he asked Sultan Bayezit to help overthrow his grandfather. Entering the city, he drove the old emperor into the Golden Gate fortress, but for eight months the old man stubbornly resisted until Manuel rescued him, forcing John into exile with the sultan.

Hearing the news, Bayezit was furious and he summoned a humiliated John VII and Manuel to join his assault on the last remaining Roman town in Anatolia. It was there news came of John V's death. Young John, fearing the sultan, remained where he was, but Manuel fled to Constantinople to be crowned emperor. John turned to Bayezit for retribution, but the sultan grudgingly accepted the new situation, though in 1394 he began blockading Constantinople, saying he would relent if they elected John emperor.

> **We are in poverty and distress and there is no great power to whom we may turn to except God Himself, who gives aid to the powerless and overcomes the powerful.**
>
> JOHN VII PALAEOLOGUS (to Sultan Bayezit)

John, sulking at Selymbria, was desperate, and in 1397 he tried unsuccessfully to sell his imperial title to King Charles VI of France. Then his luck turned. After Constantinople had endured a five-year siege, Manuel decided to seek help in Europe, and the only person capable of ruling in his absence was John. The two were reconciled, with John becoming co-emperor in 1399. Brave and defiant, he continued the defence, his support including French soldiers, who were there as an act of good faith. Nevertheless, the city could not hold out forever, and Manuel's failure to gain military support forced John to begin negotiations with Bayezit in 1402. What saved him was a miracle beyond all hope. Recalled urgently to deal with a new Mongol invasion under Timur, Bayezit was captured and his army destroyed. John's determination had seen Constantinople through its gravest peril. His treaty negotiations with the shattered Ottomans saw the empire regain Thessalonica and much territory along the Black Sea coast, while the new sultan declared he was the emperor's vassal. It was a stunning reversal of fortune.

On Manuel's return in 1403, John quietly handed over power to Manuel, but they soon had another falling out, most likely over John's son Andronicus. Exiled to Lemnos, John was about to launch a new civil war when Manuel came to his senses. He allowed John to rule at Thessalonica as *basileus*, and John remained there, quite content, for the rest of his life. Before dying, he relinquished the imperial throne, becoming the monk Joasaph, just like his great-grandfather, John Cantacuzenus. With his death, the Palaeologus family squabbles that had crippled the empire for over ninety years ended. Unfortunately, no one could undo the damage, as Manuel would soon discover.

Timur the Mongol holding captive the Ottoman Sultan Bayezit in a golden cage

ANDRONICUS V
END OF THE ELDER LINE

NAME: Andronikos Palaiologos
BORN: Constantinople, 1400
RULED: Co-emperor, 1403–1407
DIED: Of unknown causes, Thessalonica, Thessaly, 1408

BORN DURING THE OTTOMAN siege of Constantinople, Andronicus's existence probably caused the dispute between his father, John VII, and Manuel after the latter's return from Europe in 1403. He was recognised as co-emperor while John VII ruled at Thessalonica, but it is possible that his crowning occurred at Constantinople during his father's regency—potentially disrupting Manuel's plans for the succession of his son, the future John VIII. In the end, the dispute was irrelevant, as Andronicus did not live to see his ninth birthday, dying a year before his father.

MANUEL II
MIRACULOUS RESCUE

NAME: Manouēl Palaiologos
BORN: Constantinople, 1350
RULED: Co-emperor, 1373–1391; senior emperor, 1391–1425
DIED: Of natural causes, Constantinople, 1425

MANUEL II, MOST ABLE and energetic of the Palaeologi, had the misfortune of leading an empire not worthy of the name. With a deep love of literature and theology, he wrote many works before and after becoming emperor. Unfortunately, for many years he seemed destined to waste his time rescuing his poor, pathetic father from one difficulty after another.

As despot of Thessalonica, Manuel had managed to retake territory from the Serbians, but in 1369 he had to gather the money to free his father from a Venetian debtor's prison, travelling in the depths of winter to secure his release. Andronicus IV's failed rebellion in 1373 saw Manuel created co-emperor, thus earning his brother's undying resentment, and after Andronicus successfully usurped the throne in 1376 he locked Manuel in prison for three years along with their father. Using his initiative, Manuel escaped with his father to Sultan Murad and negotiated for his assistance. In exchange, Manuel served in the sultan's wars, and it was there that he discovered his father had been reconciled with Andronicus. Furious, he went to Thessalonica, ruling there in his own name and fighting the Ottomans, to his father's embarrassment.

After five years, it was clear that Thessalonica was doomed. Manuel tried to rally the citizens but they refused to listen, forcing him to leave as they opened the gates to the enemy. Returning home, he was banished by his father for deserting the sultan. Incredibly, his ungrateful father then asked for his help, this time against Andronicus's son, John. Having found allies among the Venetians, Manuel returned with a small fleet to rescue his father, causing John VII to flee to the new sultan. Bayezit ordered Manuel to attend him on campaign as his vassal, alongside his rebellious nephew, whom he could barely stand, much to the sultan's amusement. His amusement faded when Manuel rushed back to Constantinople without permission for his coronation. Celebrated with all the traditional pomp and ceremony, it was meant to convey the Roman Empire's majesty; yet in a depopulated and dilapidated city, all his coronation showed was that the days of glory were truly gone.

Bayezit, a brilliant but unstable ruler, planned to murder Manuel and other Christian vassals in the Balkans in 1393. He changed his mind, but Manuel was determined to avoid such a situation again, refusing to answer Bayezit's summonses. This and the unauthorised coronation drove the sultan to attack Constantinople, which he besieged from 1394 to 1402. As the siege dragged on, Manuel decided to argue the case for Constantinople's relief by travelling to Europe. From 1399 he visited Venice, Padua, Vicenza, Pavia, Paris and London, but no substantial help came. Sad and disillusioned, he was still in Paris when news arrived of Bayezit's defeat and capture by Timur. He returned to find a changed situation.

The sons of Bayezit were fighting to inherit the Ottoman Empire, and one of them, Suleiman, ceded territory to the empire. Nevertheless, Manuel was a realist, and so he continued to push for western intervention, especially while the Turks were at their weakest. His fears were realised when Suleiman was killed in 1411 by Musa, who continued where Bayezit had left off, besieging both Thessalonica and Constantinople. Manuel turned to the only other brother left standing, Mehmet, and offered to help overthrow Musa. Mehmet agreed, and when he emerged victorious, he rewarded Manuel by recognising the newly returned territory and agreeing to a permanent peace. He kept his word, and the Eastern Empire remained at peace until his death in 1421.

Manuel used this time wisely, strengthening the defences of Constantinople and the Morea, the remaining imperial territory in southern Greece. He also began discussions with Sigismund, emperor of the west, about military intervention but these, as always, foundered on church union. However, his wisest decision was to pursue good relations with the Ottomans, notwithstanding a growing faction at court—led by his son John—that favoured a more aggressive approach. By the time Mehmet died, Manuel was old and growing weaker, allowing John a more active role, and his last great service to the state was his quick thinking in causing family trouble for the new sultan, Murad II, who was forced to abandon the latest siege of Constantinople to deal with a rebellious brother. After Manuel suffered a stroke in 1422 he retired, and though he still provided advice, John usually ignored it. Just prior to his death Manuel put on a monk's habit and, taking the name of Matthew, waited for the end, content that he had done everything possible to preserve the empire.

JOHN VIII

CHURCH UNIONIST

NAME: Iōannēs Palaiologos
BORN: Constantinople, 1392
RULED: Co-emperor, 1408–1425;
sole emperor, 1425–1448
DIED: Of natural causes, Constantinople, 1448

MANUEL BELIEVED THE empire's only hope was to seek aid from the west and not antagonise the Ottomans. His son John had a very different outlook. Groomed to be the next emperor, John was well read, intelligent and a decent soldier. Although he was made co-emperor by 1408, he was subsequently crowned as *autokrator* in 1421, during his wedding to Sophia of Montferrat, who was so plain that John kept her as far away from him as possible, never consummating the political marriage.

With his father's health declining, John took over the government, but his policies backfired disastrously. For some time Manuel had, on Mehmet's orders, kept in prison a certain Mustafa, who claimed to be Sultan Bayezit's eldest son. But after Mehmet's death, John pressured Manuel to establish Mustafa as a rival to the new sultan, Murad II. Manuel resisted, but John wore his father down. With Mustafa's release, it became obvious they had made a terrible mistake. With a rebel Ottoman army at his back, Mustafa conquered Gallipoli from Murad but refused to hand it back to John as he had promised. Worse, when Murad heard of this betrayal, he ripped up the agreements made by his father, took back the lands granted to the empire and besieged Thessalonica and Constantinople in 1422. While the siege of Constantinople failed, John lost Thessalonica, handing it to Venice in the hope they would defend it better than the Romans. Obviously, Murad was determined to wipe the last vestiges of the Eastern Roman Empire off the map.

At John's formal coronation in 1425, the Eastern Empire consisted only of Constantinople itself and a couple of scattered outposts. Now fully aware of his powerlessness, he returned to his father's policy of appeasing the sultan with tribute and by relinquishing territory, while seeking the west's aid. He also strengthened the defences of the Morea as a place of refuge should Constantinople fall. It was news of a church council that gave John renewed hope.

The Catholics had been in crisis for decades when Pope Eugenius IV established a new General Council at Ferrara. John attended, accompanied by the cream of Orthodox thinkers and clerics, to hammer out the details of church reunion, which he hoped would trigger a crusade. The council moved to Florence, where it required all of John's authority to convince his bishops to agree to the terms of union, which adopted the Catholic position on all important matters. On 6 July 1439 the decree was proclaimed at high mass in Florence, with John hoping that it was worth it.

When he returned to Constantinople in 1440, his hopes turned to ash. To a man, the Orthodox Church rejected the union as surrendering to heresy. John could not overcome the opposition, and his authority in Constantinople was damaged. The promised crusade did finally get off the ground, under the command of the brilliant general John Hunyadi, leading an army composed mainly of Hungarians and Poles. The crusaders achieved some notable victories, but they were annihilated at the battle of Varna in 1444. John, as Murad's faithful vassal, was obliged to congratulate him on his stunning victory, completing his humiliation and fuelling his despair. In 1445 Murad launched a brief assault on the Morea, reminding the emperor of his weakness. By now, the worry and stress of the past few years had broken John, who died within days of hearing of the second defeat of Hunyadi and the Hungarians at Kosovo in 1448. In revenge, the Orthodox Church refused to perform the last rites for the emperor. The contempt was undeserved: John had done his best, but his temperament and abilities were not suited to the times.

DEMETRIUS

AMBITIOUS BROTHER

NAME: Dēmētrios Palaiologos
BORN: Constantinople, 1407
RULED: Usurper, 1442 and 1448
DIED: Of natural causes, Adrianople (Edirne), Thrace, 1470

DEMETRIUS WAS THE MOST cunning of John VIII's brothers and was often in conflict with his siblings. John took him to Europe, where he signed his acceptance of church union. However, having returned to his despotate at Messembria on the Black Sea, Demetrius took advantage of the anti-Catholic hysteria sweeping the capital by declaring himself Orthodoxy's champion.

In 1442 he claimed the purple based on his being *porphyrogenitus*, and with a band of Turkish mercenaries he besieged John in the capital. He received no support within Constantinople; his army deserted him; and his capture saw him placed under house arrest at Selymbria. He was still there in 1448 when he heard that John had died and nominated his brother Constantine to succeed him. Determined to gain the throne, Demetrius appeared in Constantinople and declared himself emperor. He was rejected by the aristocracy, and his mother, Helena, supported Constantine, declaring herself regent in his absence. Constantine then made Demetrius despot of the Morea to remove him from the capital.

Constantinople's fall in 1453 was not the end of Demetrius. His surviving brother, Thomas, disputed his rule in the Morea and Demetrius requested Turkish aid. Thomas was forced out of Greece, but Demetrius lost his own position as the sultan refused to return the Morea. He lived most of the rest of his days in the Ottoman court, eventually becoming a monk and assuming the name of David.

CONSTANTINE XII

THE FINAL EASTERN EMPEROR

NAME: Kōnstantinos Dragasēs Palaiologos
BORN: Constantinople, 1405
RULED: Emperor, 1449–1453
DIED: Killed in battle, Constantinople, 1453

THE CHILDLESS JOHN VIII chose as his successor his brother Constantine. Constantine supported union with the Catholics and he was the most able and energetic of Manuel II's sons. As the despot in the Morea, he did all he could to strengthen the region, sometimes to its detriment—it was Constantine's aggression that prompted Sultan Murad II to launch a devastating raid in 1446 from which Constantine was lucky to escape with his life. With Constantine thoroughly humiliated by this chastisement, Murad had no problem approving his election as emperor in 1448 and his subsequently crowning at Mistra in January 1449.

During his first few years, Constantine tried enforcing the union of the churches, as the Orthodox Church's failure to endorse it kept Constantinople isolated from the only groups who could conceivably provide aid against the Turks. In vain, Constantine appealed to the pope about the difficulties that union had created and his own unwavering support for it; the Orthodox Church was in schism and he could do very little. How little he could do became clear when Mehmet II became Turkish Sultan in 1451. Over Constantine's protests, Mehmet began constructing a fortress on imperial territory to the north of Constantinople, with the purpose of cutting off relief ships sailing down the Bosphorus. As the fortress grew ever higher, Mehmet rebuffed the first embassy from the emperor, and killed the second. It was a warning everyone took seriously, and at the end of 1452 the union of the churches was proclaimed in Hagia Sophia. By then it was too late, even though foreign troops began arriving in the capital. By March 1453 the Ottoman forces were marching across Thrace, and by April they were before the walls of Constantinople. The final siege of Constantinople had begun.

Constantine's subsequent actions were to define his reign. He was brave, defiant and seemingly possessed of almost superhuman energy, as from 6 April to 29 May 1453 he directed Constantinople's defence. Daily he toured the walls, and he always seemed to be where the fighting was fiercest, encouraging the defenders to give their all. By the beginning of May, provisions were running out and defenders began leaving their posts, looking for food to feed their families. The few relief squadrons that tried to break through were destroyed, although on the twenty-third one ship managed get through, reporting to the emperor what he feared most of all—no relief fleet was anywhere near Constantinople. Constantine thanked the sailors for the news, unshed tears glistening in his weary eyes. On the twenty-fourth his ministers begged him to get on a boat and flee to the Morea. During their pleas he fainted from exhaustion, but on recovering he made it clear he would stay and fight.

> **Is there not one Christian who will cut off my head?**
>
> CONSTANTINE XII PALAEOLOGUS

The evening before the final attack, he made his way to Hagia Sophia, where all Christians gathered together, pro- and anti-unionist, Orthodox and Catholic, for one final mass, where all differences were forgotten. He asked forgiveness from all the bishops present of whatever creed. Afterwards he stayed in the darkened church to pray in silence before the expected trial. Taking himself to the land walls to do one final inspection, for an hour he gazed impassively at the Ottoman tents spread out before the walls. Then at half past one in the morning of the twenty-sixth, the final assault began. Standing where the fighting was thickest, he watched in horror as an arrow struck down the leader of the Genoese contingent, forcing him to retreat to his ship. Desperately, Constantine begged

Entry of the Turks of Mehmet II into Constantinople, 1453

FALL OF THE EASTERN EMPIRE

him to remain at his post, he was soon gone, taking with him most of the Genoese who had been manning the walls. With the defences now weakened, the Turks began flooding through numerous breaches. Constantine, seeing all was lost, at first begged someone to kill him so that he could avoid capture. Then, taking matters into his own hands, he discarded every article of clothing that identified him as emperor, grabbed hold of his bloodied and dented sword, and plunged into the fray, fighting until he was swept away from view. He was never seen again.

The line of Eastern Roman emperors, stretching back to Constantine the Great, was now at an end. No more would they rule in the eastern provinces, for their territory was usurped by a new entity—the Ottoman Empire. Yet it was not the end of the imperial Roman dream: the Western emperors still reigned, though in a very different empire, and it was in them that the inheritance of Augustus and his successors still shone, however imperfectly.

ANDREAS PALAEOLOGUS

With the death of Constantine XII, the claim to the throne of the Eastern Roman Empire passed to his brother Thomas, despot of the Morea. In 1460 Thomas surrendered to the Ottomans and fled from the Morea to Rome, where his claim to be the Eastern Roman emperor was accepted by the west, which thereby rejected Sultan Mehmet II's claim to be the legitimate Roman emperor in the east. However, no help was forthcoming from the pope or any European state. After Thomas's death in 1465, the claim was inherited by his eldest son, Andreas, who also travelled to Rome, where he too was recognised as emperor. However, without an actual empire, without an army and without a coronation, such imperial claims were meaningless.

Andreas was the titular Eastern Roman emperor from 1465 until his death in 1502. Yet he found himself a resident in the Papal States for the majority of his 'reign', barring the occasional trip to Russia to see his sister, wife to the Grand Duke Ivan III of Russia, to beg for money and the occasional tour of Europe to convince Europe's kings to support his proposed reconquest of the Morea. While in Rome he converted to Catholicism and styled himself *Imperator Constantinopolitanus*, or Emperor of Constantinople.

Although he received a pension from the pope, it was meagre, and his own extravagant lifestyle, as well as the maintenance of a small retinue, meant he was always short of money. By 1475 he was offering to sell his rights to the thrones of Trebizond and Constantinople, and he entered into fruitless negotiations with the king of Naples, the duke of Burgundy and perhaps the duke of Milan.

Andreas did make efforts to reclaim his inheritance, such as his attempt in 1481 to launch an expedition to reconquer the Morea. This saw him move to Brindisi in southern Italy to plan and seek funds for the mission, but it failed because he could not gather the required amounts of cash, or muster the needed level of enthusiasm from the states that were to provide supplies or troops.

A decreasing papal pension meant that by 1494 Andreas was forced to sell the rights to the imperial crown to King Charles VIII of France. Upon Charles's death in 1498 the rights reverted to Andreas, but by the time he died in 1502, he had again sold his imperial title, this time to Ferdinand II of Aragon and Isabella of Castile. Andreas left no descendants, and with his death the last claimant to the eastern throne of the Caesars was gone.

THE END OF IMPERIAL DREAMS

(1453–1806)

We may view the state and contrast of the Roman empire of Germany, which no longer held, except on the borders of the Rhine and Danube, a single province of Trajan or Constantine. Their unworthy successors were the counts of Hapsburgh, of Nassau, of Luxemburgh, and Schwartzenburgh, [who] received the gift or promise of the vacant empire from the Roman pontiffs, who affected the dominion of the earth. [They were] saluted king of the Romans, and future emperor; a title which, in the same age, was prostituted to the Caesars of Germany and Greece. The German emperor was no more than the elective and impotent magistrate of an aristocracy of princes, who had not left him a village that he might call his own.

EDWARD GIBBON
The Decline and Fall of the Roman Empire, 1880

FOLLOWING PAGE: Destruction of Magdeburg during the Thirty Years' War

7 S. Anna. 8 zum h. Geist. 9 S. Ulri
14 S. Maria Magdalena. 15 Hunen
Rathaus. 21 S. Laurentz. 22

MA

ALBIS FLUVIUS

11 das Rathaus. 12 Barfüsser. 13 S. Catharina.
17 S. Iacob. 18 S. Augustin. 19 Hohepfort.
23 Sudenburg. 24 Newstatt. 25 Zollschantz.

...URG.

Die Elbe Flu:

FREDERICK III

LAZY EMPEROR

NAME: Friedrich von Habsburg
BORN: Innsbruck, Bavaria, 1415
RULED: Emperor, 1452–1493
DIED: Of a stroke after fasting, Linz, Austria, 1493

INTOLERANT, HEARTLESS, apathetic, hypocritical, greedy, indecisive and superstitious—such were people's opinions of Frederick III. Uninterested in the needs of the empire, he had the habit of falling asleep in the Diet, the German parliament; once during an important debate he got up to check on his plants, as he was concerned about the frost. Frederick the gardener was more conscientious than Frederick the emperor.

Crowned King of the Romans in 1440, he sought confirmation from Pope Eugenius IV, which put him in the middle of the ongoing dispute between council and pope. The Council of Basel had been convened in 1431 and was dominated by reforming bishops who wanted to place the authority of a church council over that of the papacy. Eugenius convened a rival council at Ferrara in 1438 and excommunicated the prelates assembled at Basel. They, in turn, formally deposed him as a heretic in 1439 and elected a rival pope, Felix V.

Frederick took Eugenius's side, helping the papacy eventually emerge triumphant against the council supporters. Papal support was costly, forcing him to renounce some imperial prerogatives in order to receive the imperial crown. By 1452 he was ready to become Roman emperor at Pope Nicholas V's hands and made his way to Rome, where he also celebrated his marriage to the daughter of the king of Portugal. At first he refused to consummate the marriage, fearing that conceiving a child there would mean it would inherit an Italian temperament. He eventually overcame his fears by using spells and magic charms to ward off undue influences.

Crowned emperor, Frederick soon returned to Germany, where the calamitous news of Constantinople's fall in 1453 reached him. The Turks continued their advance, attacking Hungary and Poland before crossing the border of Austria and threatening both the empire and Frederick's ancestral lands. His response was underwhelming. Diet after Diet was called, yet Frederick could not be bothered to appear, happy merely to order a bell—known as 'the Turk's bell'—to be rung at midday throughout the entire kingdom. By this stage, the German princes were indulging in private feuds and devastating the country, leaving the Hungarians to defend themselves and the rest of Europe against the Turks. Frederick, in the meantime, had entered into a feud with his brother Albert, archduke of Inner Austria, and this resulted in numerous defeats for Frederick and the loss of much of Austria that fell under his control. It was only with Albert's death in 1463 that the lost territories were returned to him. Frederick then repeated his mistake by needlessly antagonising Matthias of Hungary, resulting in Hungary taking possession of much of Austria, and even the temporary loss of Vienna in 1485.

> **The highest happiness is to forget what cannot be recovered.**
>
> FREDERICK III

It says much that though he reigned as Roman emperor for forty years, Frederick was completely overshadowed by his contemporaries, who virtually ignored him, doing as they pleased. Events in Austria, Hungary, Italy, France and Burgundy all passed by in spite of his presence or, perhaps more accurately, his absence. He seemed to prefer it that way, reigning in obscurity and hoping that events would work in his favour. He spent his last years shut up in his castle of Linz, dwelling on astrology, researching heraldry, coming up with acronyms and trying to turn lead into gold. It is, therefore, ironic that such a man, who cared nothing for his imperial heritage, was not only the first Roman emperor not to have an equal since the crowning of Charlemagne 653 years before but was

Bishop of Siena presents Frederick III to his bride, Eleanor of Portugal

also the last emperor crowned in Rome. Constantine Palaeologus was a man who understood the glories of the empire; Frederick, though possessing the title, had nothing in common with him. Rumour had it that he died after breaking his fast by eating eight melons and drinking copious amounts of cold water.

MAXIMILIAN I

THE LAST KNIGHT

NAME: Maximilian von Habsburg
BORN: Wiener Neustadt, Austria, 1459
RULED: Emperor-elect, 1508–1519
DIED: Of natural causes, Wels, Austria, 1519

IT FELL TO MAXIMILIAN, son of the incompetent Frederick III, to restore the empire, and on the surface he was just the man to do it. Virtuous, talented, brave and just, and with an adventurous spirit, he was seen by his contemporaries as a throwback to the knights of old. He was also physically very strong; reportedly, when attacked by a she-bear he choked her with his bare hands. His main problem was a lack of financial resources with which to pursue his ambitions.

On the other hand, he was very well placed politically. Apart from the imperial territories and the Habsburg lands he inherited from his father, he married the heiress to the state of Burgundy, which included Flanders and the Netherlands, while his son married the eventual heiress to the Spanish thrones of Castile and Aragon. Nevertheless, it was not all smooth sailing: before his father's death, he was involved in some fierce disputes with the Flemings, who revolted against his plans to rule in the name of his young son. In 1488 they seized Maximilian from a pharmacist's shop and imprisoned him for several months. His terrified father was for once actually motivated to do something and came to his rescue at the head of an army.

Maximilian's other problems were with France, which felt increasingly threatened by the advantageous alliances he was making through marriages. It was his third marriage, this time into the Sforza family of Milan, that triggered the French invasion of Italy in 1494, though the marriage was deeply unpopular in Germany, with most believing the Sforzas were beneath the imperial dignity. As the French ravaged Italian imperial territory, the Italians looked to the King of the Romans and future emperor to come to their aid. Yet try as he might, he could not convince the German princes to raise the money or armies needed until he had dealt with matters back home.

In 1495 Maximilian convened the Diet of Worms, which issued the Proclamation of Public Peace, banning private warfare between the nobles. He also established the Imperial Chamber, which acted as a court of arbitration. As a result of both these acts, the anarchy that had permeated the empire slowly began to recede, and the empire once again began to resemble a coherent state. Maximilian was now free to turn his attention to France and Italy, and wars would occupy the remainder of his reign.

> **I may succeed to the papacy and become a priest, and afterwards a saint!**
>
> MAXIMILIAN I

His first expedition into Italy in 1496 fizzled because of a lack of resources and he followed this up with a failed attempt to reclaim Switzerland as a Habsburg dominion. By 1501 French intervention in Italy saw the loss to the empire of the vital duchy of Milan, and Maximilian was powerless to prevent it as a result of German isolationism. With Italy once again sliding into chaos, there was one other person who was equally keen to throw out the French—Pope Julius II. He offered the imperial crown to Maximilian if he would come down and fight alongside him. This he did in 1508, but he found his progress blocked by the Venetians, who refused him permission to travel through their land. His attacks against them failed, and so he retreated to Germany, but his efforts were not in vain. Julius II conferred on him the title of emperor-elect, and the ability to use the title without a papal coronation at Rome.

For the next eight years, Maximilian saw the imperial domains in Italy gradually diminish under French and Venetian encroachment. He made occasional efforts to stem the tide, while also finding time to serve under King Henry VIII of England during his invasion of France in 1513, for the meagre sum of a hundred crowns per day. His third expedition into Italy in 1516 was no more successful than the previous ones, confirming his loss of territory and reputation. Wild schemes to fight the Turks filled his final years and, as he travelled around, he always carried a coffin with him. Of greater import was his securing of the succession to the Hungarian and Bohemian thrones by marrying his granddaughter Mary to Louis, the heir to the thrones, thereby expanding the power available to his grandson and heir, Charles, after Louis's death in 1526.

CHARLES V

GLOBAL EMPEROR

NAME: Karl von Habsburg
BORN: Ghent, Flanders, 1500
RULED: Emperor-elect, 1520–1530; emperor, 1530–1556
DIED: Of natural causes, San Jerónimo de Yuste, Spain, 1558

CHARLES INHERITED AN empire that stretched from Spain to Poland and from the Netherlands to Sicily. He was also the ruler of the Spanish possessions in the Americas, making him by far the strongest emperor that had ever sat on the Western throne, and it was within his grasp to completely crush the French and curtail the power of the Ottomans, if he so chose. What prevented him from achieving his goals was the fracturing of Christendom in the Reformation, which in turn destabilised the empire to such an extent that it was never again able to achieve any sort of unity.

Graceful, handsome and elegant, Charles was a late bloomer, developing his skills over time. Though kind to those around him, he appeared cold and indifferent as he spoke very little, seldom laughed and exercised a rigid control over his emotions. Consequently, he was calculating and deliberate, and when he decided on a plan, he pursued it to the end, no matter how difficult or dangerous. His enemies, of whom there were many, considered him duplicitous and exceedingly ambitious.

Charles was already the king of Spain when he was elected King of the Romans in 1519 and the German electors were concerned about his vast dominions, and thus his priorities. Charles agreed, therefore, not to introduce foreign troops into the empire; any conquests were to be on behalf of the empire; and he was to remain within Germany the majority of the time. Yet he assumed the imperial throne mostly for prestige: his true love was for the Netherlands where he had spent his youth, while he considered Spain the core of his dominions and spent most of his reign there.

Almost immediately he was at war with France and, like most imperial conflicts, the battleground was Italy. Initially very successful, he then had victories against a French league that included England, Florence, Milan and the papacy. These culminated in 1527 with the sack of Rome, making Charles the only Roman Emperor ever to sack the old imperial capital, earning him the hatred of the Italians in the process. He also imprisoned Pope Clement VII, who ensured that he would not get on the wrong side of Charles again by crowning him emperor in Bologna in 1530. These victories freed Charles to deal with the forces that had been unleashed in Germany by the Protestant Reformation.

By 1521 the arguments between Martin Luther and the supporters of the pope had been running for four years, with Luther becoming ever more hostile to the papacy. His popularity encouraged him to write to Charles and explain his theological beliefs, including the idea of the superiority of the emperor over the pope. Though the thought tempted Charles, he was a firm Catholic and supported papal authority, while he believed that Luther's inconstancy and teachings would lead to upheavals in society. Therefore, when Pope Leo X excommunicated Luther, Charles complied wherever his authority extended, though his support for the excommunication was counterbalanced by those German princes who supported Luther's cause and sheltered him. They pushed for permission to have Luther present his case at the Diet of Worms in 1521, but his eloquence did him no good. Charles banned him from the empire, forcing him to remain in those areas that were outside the empire's jurisdiction. It was to Luther's advantage that Charles was by now distracted by wars and events in Flanders and Spain. When his gaze returned to Germany, the situation had changed markedly.

The differences between the Lutherans and the Catholics had widened considerably, and both groups were beginning to attack each other. German peasants had used Luther's teachings on Christian liberty to rebel against the nobility, reinforcing in Charles's mind the

Martin Luther before the Diet of Worms

dangerous and disruptive influences of Luther's teachings. Radical, dissident groups began emerging throughout the empire, destroying churches and killing Catholic priests, while Protestant German princes used the conflict to sell off church property in their domains to feather their own nests, as well as to bring the religious hierarchy directly under their control. This conflict between Catholic and Protestant princes finally forced Charles to summon the Diet of Augsburg in 1530 in order to bring peace to the two warring parties. Though a Lutheran statement of faith was presented for discussion, the meeting was overwhelmed by endless debates that went nowhere. Charles, therefore, decreed that both sides should reunite until there was a council of the church, and that Protestant teachings were to cease. Disobedience was not an option.

His measures failed; in 1531 the Protestant princes formed a self-defence league, whose activities soon extended to the creation of Protestant-only states that repressed all Catholics. Charles was preparing to deal with them when news arrived of a renewal of hostilities by France; at the same time, the Ottomans were marching through Hungary, attacking the empire directly. The Protestants advised Charles that unless he met their demands they would join the Turks, and in this critical situation he had to compromise, allowing the existing state of affairs to become the new status quo. Over the next ten years, with Charles distracted by foreign wars, the Protestants extended their domains, thus further entrenching their religious structures while dismantling the old Catholic ones. The Catholic princes were also fiercely holding the line, and both sides bombarded Charles with complaint after complaint about treaty violations. At the Diet of Ratisbon in 1541 Charles did all he could to achieve peace between his angry subjects, but to no avail. The German princes began to field armies in the hope of achieving an outcome through force rather than debate, but things were now about to change radically.

In 1545 the pope and emperor convened the Council of Trent to begin the renewal of the Catholic Church, though Charles's wish for it to focus firstly on church abuses was rejected. Then, in 1546, Charles began his long-awaited assault on the Protestant princes in an attempt to forge unity by force. By 1548 victory was his, and he issued an interim statement on faith that was loose enough to satisfy most of the parties; it would remain in place until the completion of the reforms of Trent. Though many agreed with Charles's solution, the most radical of the Protestant princes did not, causing war to erupt again. This time it went against Charles, forcing him to come to terms with the Protestants. After nearly three decades of warfare, he was tired. In 1552 he signed a peace that granted certain freedoms to the Protestants and these were confirmed in 1555 in the Peace of Augsburg: this legitimised Lutheranism as defined in 1530 and stated that the religion of the ruling prince would determine the official religion of each region of the empire.

> **I cannot even make two clocks keep time together, and yet I set myself to force a million souls to conform to one belief.**
>
> CHARLES V

Charles's dream of religious unity within the empire had vanished. He had always found the imperial crown a heavy burden and it grew only heavier as the years progressed. Having seen his authority gradually diminish, bitter at all the opposition the religious divisions had caused, distrusted by one side and hated by the other, he decided to abdicate the throne and spend the rest of his life in a monastery in Spain, away from the endless bickering and ceaseless conflict. It is indicative of how badly the empire had fractured that his abdication remained unratified for two years because the electors were not able to meet because of the religious divisions.

FERDINAND I

IMPARTIAL EMPEROR

NAME: Ferdinand von Habsburg
BORN: Alcala de Henares, Spain, 1503
RULED: Emperor-elect, 1558–1564
DIED: Of natural causes, Vienna, Austria, 1564

CHARLES'S ABDICATION SAW the division of his dominions into two separate spheres. Spain, the Americas, Italy and the Netherlands went to his son, Philip. The empire and the Habsburg ancestral lands in Austria went to his brother, Ferdinand.

Ferdinand was dynamic and compassionate, a very different character from his cold and calculating brother. It was to Ferdinand that Charles had entrusted the governance of the empire and Austria during his lengthy absences in Spain and Italy. Made archduke of Austria in 1521 and King of the Romans in 1531, Ferdinand was a devout Catholic, and Charles confided the defence of Catholicism in the empire to him. In the beginning Ferdinand was determined and resolute, with regular persecutions of Protestants, but like Charles he was eventually brought to the realisation that rapprochement was the only way forward, especially as his Austrian domains were constantly under threat from the Ottomans, and Protestant distractions were something he could ill-afford.

> **Let justice be done, though the world perish.**
>
> FERDINAND I

By 1537 Ferdinand was making tentative advances towards clerical reform, and it was he who convinced Charles to begin the peace process that led to the Peace of Augsburg in 1555. His pragmatic approach, combining a push for visible but minor changes in Catholic practices with recognition of Lutheranism, ensured him the support of the German electors when the time came to nominate a new emperor. There was just one problem—Pope Paul IV declared Charles's abdication in 1556 was invalid without papal permission. It was not until 1558 that Paul IV declared that he would acknowledge Ferdinand as emperor, but only if he would reject the Treaty of Augsburg. Keenly aware of the strength of the Protestants in his realm, Ferdinand refused. This debacle convinced the electors never again to request papal confirmation of an imperial nomination.

Ferdinand's reign as emperor saw him strive to keep a middle path between the two religious groups, and generally he was successful at keeping the peace. He supported the Council of Trent, which completed its deliberations in 1564, but was unable to heal the divisions that had by now so firmly taken root. His impartiality towards the Protestants, as well as his enthusiasm for the Catholic Reformation, showed he had society's best interests at heart; consequently, he was loved and respected by all his subjects and was deeply mourned when he died in 1564.

MAXIMILIAN II

COVERT LUTHERAN

NAME: Maximilian von Habsburg
BORN: Vienna, Austria, 1527
RULED: Emperor-elect, 1564–1576
DIED: Of natural causes, Regensburg, Bavaria, 1576

BY THE TIME MAXIMILIAN became Roman emperor, strains had emerged within the House of Habsburg. He was not supposed to inherit the imperial throne; originally it was to belong to his cousin King Philip of Spain, who was Charles V's son, thus reuniting the Habsburg dominions. Maximilian, Ferdinand I's son, thwarted these plans, but in doing so he poisoned relations with his Spanish kin, creating an animosity he added to with his religious policies.

The volatile mix of Catholic and Protestant German princes meant that the emperor was obliged to walk a fine line between the two religious extremes, and it is to Maximilian's credit that he managed to preserve the religious peace in his realm by being outwardly impartial to all parties. Reassuring the Catholic electors by his declaration of Catholic fidelity, he won over the Protestant electors with his promise to accept the Treaty of Augsburg. Fearful of a destructive civil war, he resisted all calls from the Catholic princes to support persecution of the Protestants, while he forbad the Lutheran princes from stripping away the rights the Catholics had retained at Augsburg. Although nominally Catholic, he was suspected by his co-religionists, probably rightly, of being a Lutheran sympathiser. Pressured to recommence attending Catholic services, he felt that remaining a Catholic would place him in the best position to effect change within the Catholic Church and pushed the popes to agree to some of the changes advanced by the Lutherans, ostensibly to weaken the Lutherans but in reality to bring about Catholic reformation through stealth. In this, he was unsuccessful, and Pope Pius V warned him not to meddle in matters of faith or church discipline, or else he would be deposed.

The Ottomans in the south threatened his realm, but in 1568 a treaty and the payment of tribute to the sultan was enough to buy peace, and it freed him to pursue his desire to obtain the Polish crown. He was

THE IMPERIAL DIET, THE IMPERIAL CHAMBER AND THE AULIC COUNCIL

The Diet of the Roman Empire, after its re-establishment by Charlemagne, was a gathering of the dukes and princes of the various states of the empire, to discuss important affairs of state and to elect the new king. By the sixteenth century, the Diet was composed of three colleges. First was the Council of Electors, those princes who could vote for the new King of the Romans (the title that the German kings possessed upon their election, and a preliminary step for their crowning as emperor). Second was the Council of Princes, consisting of all the other princes in the empire. Finally there was the Council of Imperial Cities, representing those cities not under the control of the German princes. These three acted as an advisory and collegiate body that would work in concert with the emperor, as well as agreeing to implement the emperor's edicts. The Diet gradually gained more power until, by the 1650s, the emperor could make no decision without its authorisation.

In 1495 the Diet of Worms created the Imperial Chamber, a judicial institution covering nearly all the legal proceedings of the empire. This included breaches of public peace, cases of arbitrary imprisonment, actions against the treasury, violations of the emperor's decrees or the laws passed by the Diet, and disputes between or against citizens of the empire.

The Aulic Council originally began life as another court, this one for criminal cases and for disputes over feudal obligations. It eventually became a virtual royal council and gradually usurped many of the functions of the Imperial Chamber, partly because that chamber could take years to reach a decision. During the years of religious division, it tended to support the emperor's wishes, as the majority of its members were Catholic.

beginning preparations to make good his claim when he died, refusing in his final moments to accept the Catholic last rites.

Maximilian had consistently tried to steer the middle course of conciliation and tolerance during his reign, and he was to a large degree successful. Yet the time when an emperor could maintain such a course was ending. Already in France the first signs of an impending bloody struggle between Catholics and Protestants had emerged, and both sides were rapidly reaching the point of no return. Both sides would soon abandon any hope of reunion and begin to seek the destruction of their rival, dragging the emperor down with them.

RUDOLPH II

RENAISSANCE EMPEROR

NAME: Rudolf von Habsburg
BORN: Vienna, Austria, 1552
RULED: Emperor-elect, 1576–1612
DIED: Of natural causes, Prague, Bohemia, 1612

RUDOLPH TRIED TO RULE like his esteemed father, Maximilian II, but two things stood in his way: the first was a new Protestant militancy that was no longer interested in maintaining the status quo, and the second, his own personal shortcomings.

Though his enemies liked to portray him as a Jesuit-raised, bigoted Catholic, there is much to suggest that he had no particular attachment to the old faith; indeed, that religion did not interest him at all when it did not affect his other pursuits. His demeanour did not do him any favours: dour, reserved and secretive, uncertain of himself and suspicious of others, he relied on the advice of favourites to rule the empire. State business bored him, and he was much more concerned with his personal interests, principally alchemy and astrology. He was a keen devotee of the arts and sciences and gave a great deal of his time and money to promoting them within the empire. He was the quintessential Renaissance prince.

Such a man might be keen to preserve agreed-to political settlements, but Rudolph did not have this luxury, and he did not have the skills to navigate a new and dangerous world. Almost immediately, the Lutheran princes began to test his mettle and quickly found him inflexible and uninterested in their needs—and very different from Maximilian. They began with the persecution of Catholics in Austrian cities where Protestants were numerically superior; Rudolph's response was to prohibit public displays of Protestantism. There were increasing violations of the 1555 Augsburg treaty, as Protestant extremists saw any attempt to uphold the status quo as evidence of Rudolph crushing the Protestant faith. They refused to provide Rudolph with men and arms to halt the Ottoman threat. They even recast simple, secular matters of ducal inheritance as religious issues in order to advance the claims of Protestant princes.

Such a great Prince.

NOSTRADAMUS (prophesying about the young Rudolph II)

In return, Rudolph sought to disable the agitators in any way possible. He tried to take advantage of the schism between Lutherans and Calvinists by playing off one against the other. When the Imperial Chamber came to be dominated by Protestants, he discontinued its assembly and relied instead on the Catholic dominated Aulic Council, which upheld traditional Catholic rights against Protestant aggrandisement. Such actions only served to convince the more fervent Protestants that a league for self-defence was essential, and this soon turned from defensive measures to offensive tactics. At their head they placed the French king Henry IV, who—as a former Protestant and the king who had enacted a guarantee of religious liberty for the French Protestants—seemed best positioned to support their cause. Henry, of course, was only too keen to sow dissent within the empire. Each new attempt by Rudolph to enforce control saw an enlargement of the anti-Catholic league, which swore to defend their religion to the death and refused to acknowledge the jurisdiction of the Aulic Council. The emperor's impotence convinced the Catholic German states also to band together for self-defence, and the two hostile camps began eyeing each other with mutual suspicion.

By now the emperor was slowly descending towards a permanent state of manic-depression. He shut himself in the palace, alone with his paintings and sculptures, for longer periods, refusing to see anyone and even eating his meals alone. He became obsessed with clocks, had his bedroom windows barred and would erupt into explosions of anger at the slightest noise, so much so that his servants and courtiers approached him in a

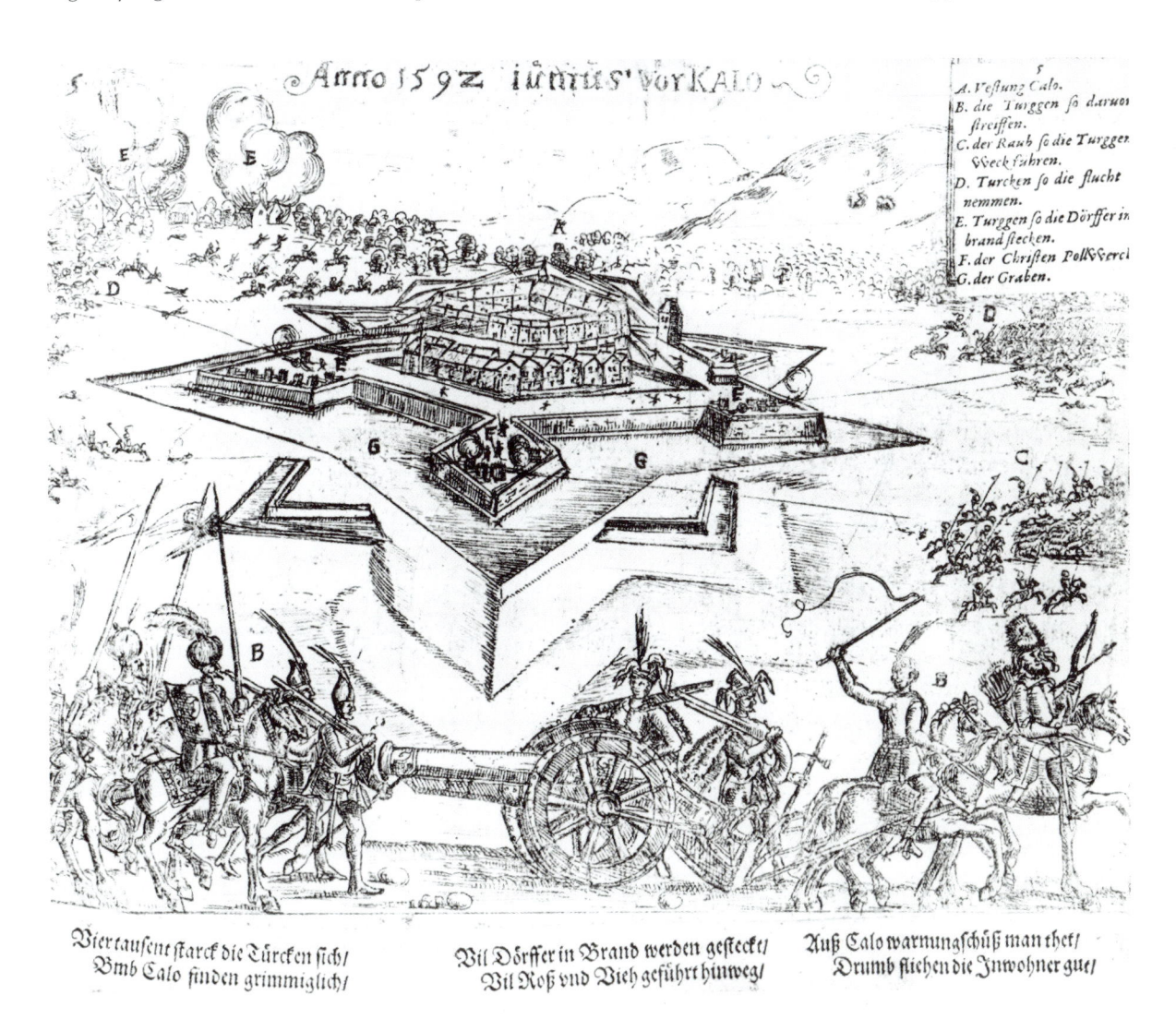

Turks, led by Rudolph II, pillage villages around Calo, 1592

THE END OF IMPERIAL DREAMS

permanent state of fear. The only thing that seemed to rouse him was his dream of a grand crusade against the Ottomans. In 1593 he launched a war against the Turks that, because of a lack of resources, dragged on until 1606. The Hungarians bore the brunt of the fighting and by 1604 they had had enough. Their revolt and the emperor's instability saw him increasingly sidelined by his ambitious brother, Matthias. Rudolph unwillingly relinquished control of the Hungarian and Ottoman wars, and peace was soon established.

Rudolph, still obsessed with a great victory over the Turks, tried to start a new war, and this was the final straw. With Protestant help, Matthias rebelled against his brother, forcing Rudolph to relinquish the crowns of Hungary, Austria, Moravia and Bohemia, so that by 1611 Rudolph had lost all his crowns except for the imperial one. Imprisoned in his castle at Prague, he hid himself in the deepest part and placed his hands over his ears to block out the sounds of rejoicing as Matthias was crowned king. When approached to sign the abdication papers, he was so furious he could not even hold the pen straight, and when he had finished he tore the pen to pieces with his teeth. Rudolph did not survive his humiliation long: nine months later he was dead, forgotten, and grieved by none.

MATTHIAS

BALANCING ACT

NAME: Matthias von Habsburg
BORN: Vienna, Austria, 1557
RULED: Emperor-elect, 1612–1619
DIED: Of natural causes, Vienna, Austria, 1619

MATTHIAS WAS AMBITIOUS and ruthless, and for years he had watched as his brother mishandled the delicate balance between Catholic and Protestant forces in the empire. Believing himself to be the more capable ruler, and aware that Rudolph had not yet named an heir, he used Protestant dissatisfaction to build up a coalition to overthrow the emperor. He had previously lifted restrictions against the Protestants in his own lands, and so they had great hopes for his reign. He soon understood the reality of the empire's problems.

> **I have not formed any resolutions inimical to your religion, or your privileges, and that my present preparations were forced upon me by your own.**
>
> MATTHIAS

Prior to his election, in a foretaste of things to come, the Catholic states had refused to obey the interim administrators of the empire because they were Protestant. Though the German states had divided themselves into Catholic, Lutheran and Calvinist, the situation was complicated as each ruler would change faith for political advantage, and all secular matters now became religious questions. The new emperor tried to be conciliatory to all parties, in the manner of Maximilian II, but both Catholics and Protestants thwarted him. Attempts to enforce the rule of law through the Aulic Council only exacerbated the conflict, while the emperor's age began to tell against him.

The spark that began the long-dreaded religious war occurred in Prague in 1618. Fear of the new pro-Catholic king of Bohemia, Matthias's nephew Ferdinand, together with a decision to close two Protestant churches built on Catholic land, saw the Bohemians rise up in revolt. They appealed to Matthias, but he rejected their application and supported the Catholic archbishop of Prague. In anger, the Bohemians threw the royal governor of Prague and his secretary from an open window and asked for aid from the Protestant league, which sent troops, while one of the Protestant German princes launched a bid for the throne of Bohemia. Matthias tried to broker a peace, but both parties wanted a war. King Ferdinand now took effective control of the empire and sidelined him. Matthias was too old and broken to resist, dying soon afterwards in despair.

FERDINAND II

CATHOLIC COUNTER-STRIKE

NAME: Ferdinand von Österreich
BORN: Graz, Austria, 1578
RULED: Emperor-elect, 1619–1637
DIED: Of natural causes,
Vienna, Austria, 1637

TO HIS ADMIRERS, Ferdinand II was a conscientious man, moral and upright, unwavering in his beliefs, determined, yet merciful and just, and a supporter of freedom. To his enemies, he was an untrustworthy bigot who closed Protestant churches, burned their Bibles and hymnbooks, and forced the people in every way he could to attend the Catholic mass. The truth, as always, lay somewhere in between.

> **Disobedience, lawlessness and insurrection went always hand in hand with Protestantism.**
>
> FERDINAND II

For some years, Ferdinand had been a member of the hard-line Catholic faction of the Habsburgs, who were convinced that conciliating the Protestants only encouraged them to go further, with their ultimate aim being the destruction of Catholicism. The Protestant princes detested him; so his elevation as king of Bohemia and King of the Romans became the trigger for all-out war in the empire. The Bohemians declared the throne vacant, and in 1619 they elected the Calvinist prince Frederick as their king. Ferdinand fled into Germany, where he claimed the imperial crown through the numerical superiority of the Catholic electors. This act enraged the Bohemians further, and they placed their trust in their fellow Protestants to come to their aid. Yet though Hungary had also rebelled and Protestant armies overran Austria, Ferdinand's armies crushed the Bohemians, forcing Frederick to flee.

Thus began the Thirty Years' War, a conflict that would devastate the empire. Ferdinand, triumphant, now began to enhance Catholic power in the empire, to the fear of the Protestant league, which in 1625 appealed to King Christian IV of Denmark to intervene on its behalf. This caused the Catholic princes to rally around the emperor as they had never done in the past, as they considered their religion in danger of being completely repressed. By 1629 Ferdinand's armies had humbled the Protestant states and the Danes were thrown out of the empire. The emperor now believed he was unstoppable: he banned Protestant services in Bohemia; by the Edict of Restitution ordered the return of Catholic property usurped by Protestants; and mandated toleration to the Lutherans only. He might have got away with his plans and eventually fully restored Catholicism had it not been for the fear the Catholic princes now had about his enhanced standing and power, and the possibility that he might turn around and attack them at some future date. They encouraged the Protestant princes to resist the emperor, and Ferdinand beheld with astonishment not only the reversal of his hopes, but Sweden's King Gustavus Adolphus leading the anti-Catholic forces.

In a ruthless and inspired campaign, Adolphus pushed Ferdinand's forces back to Austria and forced the Catholic princes to capitulate. He was on the verge of crushing the empire when he died at the battle of Lützen; victory by Ferdinand's son over the Swedes and German Protestants that same year forced the key German Protestants to come to terms with Ferdinand. The result was the 1635 Peace of Prague.

The fiercely proud Ferdinand was lucky, and it showed in the terms of the treaty. He came within a whisker of losing his throne to the genius of the Swedish king, while his plans to overthrow Protestantism in the empire were unfulfilled, as the principle of the prince determining the religion of the people was established for good. Outside of Bohemia, he agreed to a forty-year deferral of the Edict of Restitution, while his own powers were severely restricted and he was unable to make alliances, impose new taxes or declare war without the consent of the German electors. He did obtain one important concession, the creation of a unified imperial army that was not dependent on the German princes for its existence. By the time he died in 1637, the peace was holding and the Habsburgs were still the most powerful house in the empire.

Attack on the French camp in the battle of Diedenhofen during the Thirty Years' War, 1639

FERDINAND III

STRIPPED OF POWER

NAME: Ferdinand von Habsburg
BORN: Graz, Austria, 1608
RULED: Emperor-elect, 1637–1657
DIED: Of natural causes, Vienna, Austria, 1657

LIKE HIS FATHER, Ferdinand III was committed to the Catholic cause, and though nature had endowed him with military ability, as demonstrated in 1634 at the battle of Nordlingen, his desire was to establish a permanent peace. All his adult life he had witnessed the sufferings of the people and the devastation of the empire. Less influenced than his father by the Spanish Habsburgs, he was more likely to listen to the voices promoting toleration and peace. He was the leader of the peace party at court that negotiated the 1635 truce. But what for his father had begun as a war of religious conformity, for Ferdinand became a war for survival.

Ferdinand had been crowned King of the Romans in his father's lifetime and thus was recognised as the legitimate imperial successor on his father's death. Almost immediately, he beheld the entry of the Catholic French into the Thirty Years' War on the side of the Protestant rebels. Their presence motivated the Swedes and reignited the conflict, to the detriment of the empire, and for the next eleven years the war raged across Germany with no one gaining a clear advantage. Ferdinand tried his best, but the inconstancy of the Protestant princes, who changed sides at the drop of a hat, as well as the ambitions of the French and Swedes, kept the war going. In order to obtain the princes' fickle support, by 1644 Ferdinand had introduced extreme measures, including allowing the individual German states the privilege of conducting their own foreign policy, independent of the emperor.

By 1645 it was clear to all parties that if the war were to continue, there would be no empire left to speak of and the German states might well become dependencies of the French. Ferdinand used this sentiment to obtain a peace, and he needed all of his patience and skill to appease the foreign nations involved, as well as resolved the religious tensions that had begun the war in the first place. It is to his credit that he was able to achieve both in the 1648 Peace of Westphalia, but at a tremendous cost.

The Netherlands, Switzerland and the Lombard States gained formal independence, ratifying a situation that had, in effect, existed for the past century. The French gained all the provinces of the empire on the east bank of the Rhine, including Alsace and Verdun, which had been part of the empire since its re-establishment by Charlemagne, while the Swedes obtained a number of northern territories. On the religious question, the imperial dream of a Catholic empire lay in ruins, but so did the Protestant quest to bury Catholicism. The ratification of the 1555 Peace of Augsburg legislated that the faith of the prince would dictate the official religion of the territory. Calvinists were now on the same level as Lutherans, and the persecution of variant faiths in the respective territories was prohibited.

> **During my reign, no-one can reproach me with a single act which I knew to be unjust.**
>
> FERDINAND III

Internally, the empire underwent a radical change due to post-war treaties, with power stripped from Ferdinand and returned to the states. Many bishoprics were secularised and turned into duchies, further reducing the power of the Catholic Church in the empire, while the Aulic Council now had to accept Protestant members. However, the greatest change was the virtual independence given to the various Germanic territories within the empire. Their ability to act as sovereign states fatally weakened the empire from within. Though they were still part of the empire in name, the reality was that the emperor was now merely a figurehead. Power was decentralised, and the empire would never again be able to act as one unified authority. For Ferdinand, the price of this capitulation was peace, and the remainder of his reign was untroubled by religious questions. For his successors, the price was a slow and lingering death, an empire ruined by war and emperors unable to govern the realm.

LEOPOLD I

THE HOGMOUTH

NAME: Leopold Ignaz Joseph Balthazar Felician von Österreich
BORN: Vienna, Austria, 1640
RULED: Emperor-elect, 1658–1705
DIED: Of natural causes, Vienna, Austria, 1705

WITH LEOPOLD'S ACCESSION, we see the beginning of a shift in the emperors' focus from the empire to the Habsburg homelands. For years, Leopold had been destined for a career in the church until his elder brother died in 1654; fate forced this weak but good-natured young man to become the next Roman emperor. Raised by the Jesuits, he naturally gravitated to the Catholic Church for guidance but never slavishly adhered to the papacy. Of course, this background raised great suspicion in his Protestant subjects, who painted him as talentless, tight-fisted, feeble, bigoted and untrustworthy. Closer to the truth was the fact that as emperor he had to deal with the immense challenge presented by King Louis XIV of France with very few resources at his disposal.

Of course, the young emperor's physical appearance did little to inspire confidence. A small, dark and sickly man, he had an excessively protruding lower lip, causing his teeth to stick out and impairing his speech. He was devoted to Catholic ceremonies, to the consternation of his courtiers, who had to endure eighty services during Lent every year, while he displayed no love or enthusiasm for military matters, in an age when every prince and nobleman was measured by his military prowess.

Leopold inherited an empire fracturing from within, at risk of French aggression from without, and with an army that was numerically and militarily inferior to its contemporaries. To correct these defects he developed two strategies, one to rectify his standing within the empire and one to deal with his external problems. To bolster his image at home, he undertook a major propaganda exercise focused on the Habsburg dynasty and expressed through art and culture.

> **My heart breaks ... but always may Your Will be done.**
>
> LEOPOLD I (on the death of his beloved first wife)

During his reign, he mounted over four hundred major public theatrical events to emphasise the glory of the Habsburgs. In a number of these, Leopold participated himself—for example, in the climax to the opera *Il pommo d'oro*, its final scene (*The Court of Austrian Glory*) showed the emperor, in armour, hoisted atop a mound of Turkish armour and weaponry. The court pressed music and paintings into service, with Leopold himself composing over a hundred musical pieces for performances at official and church functions, while paintings of the emperor showed him surrounded by the trappings of imperial regalia, with one famous painting depicting him as Hercules dressed in ancient Roman armour while carrying an enormous club. Meanwhile, the printing presses were working overtime, printing panegyrics and histories of the Habsburgs, not to mention thousands of prints of the emperor himself. These actions solidified Leopold's hold on his ancestral lands.

On the foreign front, the emperor was soon involved in lengthy wars against the Ottomans in the south. He fought most of these battles using Austria's resources, as the German princes were, as always, reluctant to provide support to the emperor. It was not until the 1683 siege of Vienna that Leopold's political talents came to the fore. He skilfully negotiated with the German princes as well as the king of Poland; this combined force fell on the Ottoman Turks and saved Vienna. Over time, more victories by the imperial army forced the Ottomans to concede Hungarian territory to the emperor, strengthening his eastern frontiers.

To the west, Louis XIV was interfering in the affairs of the empire, using the perpetual conflict between princes and emperor to further his ambitions. A unified response by the empire was by now impossible because of the virtual independence of the German princes, and initially the conflict went in France's favour. Again, Leopold's political and diplomatic skills provided the empire with a chance of survival, as he formed various leagues with other European nations to stem the French expansion, most importantly the League of Augsburg and the Grand Alliance. This culminated in the War of the Spanish Succession, a conflict caused by the death of the childless Habsburg king of Spain. Leopold and the major powers of Western Europe fought against France and Spain, and it soon became apparent that the wars against the Turks had blooded a new generation of imperial generals who were as good, if not better, than the French. Though the war went in France's favour at first, their comprehensive defeat at Blenheim by a coalition army under the joint command of the British Duke of Marlborough and the Imperial Prince Eugene of Savoy saw the war turn against them.

Leopold lived just long enough to see the victory at Blenheim, dying later that year. Because of his moral lifestyle and attachment to the Catholic Reformation, the Jesuits called him Leopold the Great. He was not quite that, but he had demonstrated impressive political skills that compensated for his lack of military successes early in his reign, so much so that by the end of his life he had managed to regain much of the territory lost during the Thirty Years' War.

JOSEPH I

DISTRUST THE JESUITS

NAME: Joseph von Österreich
BORN: Vienna, Austria, 1678
RULED: Emperor-elect, 1705–1711
DIED: Of smallpox, Vienna, Austria, 1711

JOSEPH I WAS VERY different from his father, Leopold I, and they clashed over most issues. He was named after St Joseph, whom Leopold had asked for a son, and he grew into a restless young man, tall and fair, with piercing blue eyes. Where Leopold was prudish, Joseph was a notorious womaniser, and his prospective father-in-law was advised to avoid having any attractive young ladies-in-waiting at his court. Joseph was also charitable and humane, liberal and quite tolerant.

Given a low-level command during the early stages of the War of the Spanish Succession, Joseph carried out his duties with aplomb. His instincts were to modernise the state and his first gesture upon becoming Roman emperor was to dismiss many of the Jesuits who had taken on ministries in his father's government. His distrust of the Jesuits put him at odds with the papacy, but he was determined to adhere to an independent course for Austria and the empire. The cost was the papacy's withdrawal of support in Spain, and Joseph ordered Austrian troops to attack the Papal States.

Success continued to follow the empire, as the later stages of the War of the Spanish Succession saw the humiliation of Louis XIV, who proposed abandoning his candidate for the Spanish throne as part of his overtures for peace, though fighting still continued. Discussions were underway when Joseph came down with smallpox. His doctors insisted that he be kept in a room with no ventilation and then be wrapped in metres of red cloth. Not holding out much hope for his survival, he begged forgiveness from his wife for all his infidelities. He died soon afterwards, at the age of thirty-five.

CHARLES VI

TOO GREEDY

NAME: Karl Franz Joseph Wenceslaus Balthazar Johannes Anton Ignatius von Österreich
BORN: Vienna, Austria, 1685
RULED: Emperor-elect, 1711–1740
DIED: Of gastric flu, Vienna, Austria, 1740

NOT AS TALENTED or as educated as his brother Joseph, Charles seemed to take after his father, Leopold, in both looks and attitude. Slightly built, with skinny legs, he possessed large brown eyes and the classic Habsburg underlip. A womaniser with a love of hunting, he was cold, serious and imperious; he was also honest and conscientious, and determined to rule in the best interests of his subjects. Although a Catholic, he was not prepared to allow the church excessive influence in matters of state. He was also greedy, and that lost him many of the advantages gained by his father and brother.

Charles had been the allied contender for the Spanish throne during the War of the Spanish Succession to counter Louis XIV's nominee, Philip V. He spent most of his time fighting in Spain and was in Barcelona when news came of Joseph's unexpected death. He had just managed to expel Philip from Madrid, and most of the Spanish cities had acknowledged his authority as king. He rushed back to Vienna to claim the imperial crown, convinced that both kingdom and empire would soon be his. However, while the allies had not wanted to see a Bourbon on the Spanish throne, they were even less thrilled to see a Habsburg holding both the Spanish throne and the empire. Led by Britain, they abandoned Charles and made peace with Louis XIV, agreeing to Philip's accession to the Spanish throne. The emperor was incensed; he accused the allies of betrayal and, confident in the strength of his armies, continued the war. Although his armies had had many successes, alone and without a superior general they could never win against France.

By the time Charles had negotiated a separate peace, he had lost some of the territory gained from the war, but the greater portion of the Spanish Netherlands, northern Italy and Naples passed into Habsburg hands. It was not to last: the Dutch Republic slowly whittled away Austrian lands in the north, while Spain reconquered Naples within twenty years. Charles was also engaged in a war with the Turks that did not go nearly as well as he had hoped. By the end of his reign, he had conceded territory that his father had acquired in his wars and destroyed the reputation that the Austrian armies had achieved just a generation before.

> **England has never failed to give me promises both before and since the commencement of the war; but instead of fulfilling those promises, she has even favoured my enemies.**
>
> CHARLES VI

As emperor, Charles spent less and less time dealing with the affairs of the empire, consumed as it was by the conflict between Catholics and Protestants that the Thirty Years' War had quieted but not solved, not to mention the petty jealousies of the German princes. Though the empire's boundaries had remained unchanged since the Peace of Westphalia, Austrian territory and power had increased during the past century. It was, therefore, ironic that Charles was now heavily involved in the affairs of northern Italy, not as Roman emperor, but as archduke of Austria. It was also inevitable that Charles would focus ever more on his Austrian homeland. To improve the lot of his people he began opening roads and canals, constructing bridges and encouraging trade. He also undertook a massive building program, with churches, monasteries, palaces and libraries erected across the length and breadth of the land. It was supposed to be the next step in the glorification of the Habsburgs, yet he was well aware that the dynasty was now under threat.

Charles VI

THE END OF IMPERIAL DREAMS

He was the last male in the direct imperial line: with no sons to inherit, he placed all his hopes on his eldest daughter, Maria Theresa.

Charles spent the greater part of his final years trying to persuade the leaders of Europe to accept Maria Theresa as the legitimate successor to the state of Austria and all its dominions. He hoped the agreement, known as the Pragmatic Sanction, would preserve his kingdom intact, but his obsession with the succession saw him neglecting his army and his treasury, with the result that by 1740 the Austrian army was in clear decline and the treasury was empty. He died complaining of stomach pains, which worsened after he consumed a plate of mushroom stew.

in 1742. For their aid, he agreed that the French could retain any territory they managed to conquer in the Netherlands. He did not enjoy his title long: Maria Theresa was soon on the warpath and drove him out of his Bavarian homeland, forcing him to relocate to Frankfurt. Although the French and the Prussians supported him, it took three years before they could make any headway against the Austrians, with the recapture of Munich occurring only months before Charles's death. These years had left him a broken and disillusioned man, and so, before dying, Charles urged his son to seek reconciliation with the Habsburgs.

CHARLES VII

FRENCH PUPPET

NAME: Karl Albrecht von Bayern
BORN: Brussels, Spanish Netherlands, 1697
RULED: Emperor-elect, 1742–1745
DIED: Of gout, Munich, Bavaria, 1745

REGARDLESS OF WHAT the major powers had promised, within days of Charles VI's death all his plans for the succession lay in ruins. Rejecting Maria Theresa's right to the throne, a number of princes and kings began to lay claim to various crowns and among them was the young prince-elector of Bavaria, Charles Albert. His family's support of the French in the War of the Spanish Succession had seen them placed under house arrest for a number of years. When Charles joined in the war against the Turks, he had earned imperial favour again, so much so that he gained the hand of Emperor Joseph I's daughter in marriage.

Charles rejected the Pragmatic Sanction, bringing about the War of the Austrian Succession. He claimed the crown of Bohemia in 1741 and, with French help, he was crowned king and then elected Roman emperor

FRANCIS I

SECOND FIDDLE

NAME: Francis Stefan de Lorraine
BORN: Nancy, France, 1708
RULED: Emperor-elect, 1745–1765
DIED: Of a stroke, Innsbruck, Austria, 1765

THE REIGN OF THE FIRST Francis was one of perpetual warfare against either France or Prussia, but the burden of these wars was not borne by him. For Francis was a minor noble, and the real power lay with his wife, Maria Theresa, who ensured that he was elected Roman emperor after she drove her enemies out of Austria, a process in which he participated by commanding the armies that kept the French in check on the banks of the Rhine.

Apathetic and unambitious, Francis was quite content to leave the actual exercise of power to his determined wife, limiting his actions to assisting her to govern the many Austrian domains, for by this time the emperor was merely a figurehead in Germany. Francis spoke only French and never bothered to learn German, so that French ended up the de facto language of the court. He was also a notorious womaniser, with the unfortunate habit of being very indiscreet about it. He was generally uneasy bearing the imperial title, conscious of the fact that his wife asked for his opinion for the sake of appearances only.

Throughout these years, Maria Theresa endeavoured to humiliate all those who tried to steal her birthright, in particular King Frederick of Prussia. Her desire for vengeance saw her join forces with Austria's traditional enemy, France, in order to wage war against the Prussians. This was one of the few times that Francis tried to exert his will, as he vehemently objected to any alliance with the French, and Maria Theresa had to use her powers of persuasion to gain his agreement. The Seven Years' War was the result of the alliance, but though France, Austria and Russia tried to cripple Prussia, Frederick was able to hold them off long enough for peace to look desirable, especially as Britain took Prussia's side. By 1763 the war was over, with no clear winner. Francis lived long enough to see the peace, but a sedentary lifestyle had seen him grow quite fat and his health was starting to deteriorate. He went to Innsbruck to attend the marriage of his son Leopold but collapsed after returning from the opera. The doctors could do nothing for him, as he was dead by the time they got to him. Despite his infidelities, Maria Theresa mourned him deeply.

JOSEPH II

ENLIGHTENED DESPOT

NAME: Joseph Benedict August Johannes Anton Michel Adam von Österreich
BORN: Vienna, Austria, 1741
RULED: Emperor-elect, 1765–1790
DIED: Of natural causes, Vienna, Austria, 1790

JOSEPH II BECAME ROMAN emperor under highly unusual circumstances. On the death of his father, Francis I, he became the emperor; yet that title was by now well and truly devoid of any authority. His mother was sovereign of virtually all the Habsburg lands, the only exception being the duchy of Tuscany, which he had relinquished to his brother in order to obtain the imperial title. Consequently, he watched impotently as his mother ruled in his name, and yearned for the day when he could take control of his destiny and be the driving force, even though the only guarantee of his imperial title against the designs of King Frederick of Prussia was the Austrian army, which was under his mother's control.

> **Were I to mix only with my equals, I should be obliged to go down into my family vault and spend my days beside the bones of my forefathers.**
>
> JOSEPH II

It did not stop him from trying to usurp his mother's authority, but she was too wily an opponent for her obviously ambitious son to outwit. It was inevitable that mother and son would clash frequently during these years, in particular over policy and future directions for Austria and the empire. In 1777 Joseph's plan to usurp the electorate of Bavaria saw Austria once again embroiled in a war against Prussia. Maria Theresa, fearful that Joseph would lose his throne, agreed to peace in 1779, much against Joseph's wishes, as he did not fully comprehend just how strong the Prussian army was. Yet he would not have long to wait for his chance, as his mother eventually died the following year.

Growing up, Joseph had drunk deeply from the well of the Enlightenment philosophers, particularly Voltaire. That, combined with the example of Frederick of Prussia, turned him into what could only be termed an enlightened despot. Therefore, when he finally became effective ruler in 1780, he introduced a raft of radical reforms to overhaul all his Austrian territories, but he could make no changes to the German imperial

THE END OF IMPERIAL DREAMS

territories without approval from the Diet. Though his intentions were good, his top-down approach to change meant that all his reforms ended badly. His decision to make German the official language of all his kingdoms caused an outcry. He standardised the structures and mechanisms of government and abolished the separate jurisdictions of each state. Vienna controlled all departments, causing each subject people to fear that they would be subsumed under an Austrian homogeny. A decree that the will of the emperor was to be the basis of all administration only made things worse.

Joseph's Edict of Taxation, though meant to relieve peasants of their feudal obligations, alienated the landholders, who took out their grievances on the peasants. His religious reforms, which included closing nunneries, banning papal bulls that did not have government approval, making marriage and divorce civil matters, and banning pilgrimages, processions and the veneration of religious icons, completely alienated the infuriated clergy. Even his Edict of Toleration, which allowed all persons the freedom of religion in his realm, caused conflict. High trade duties hit tradesmen and merchants, causing prices to skyrocket. By the end of his reign far-reaching changes had alienated almost everyone, especially the foreign subject nations, to the point of revolution.

Joseph was equally unsuccessful in his foreign policy dealings. France or Prussia blocked every attempt to increase Austrian power in the region, forcing him to back down repeatedly, whether it was in the Austrian Netherlands, against the Turks in the Crimean War, or about the annexation of Bavaria. Even the German princes united against him to prevent any increase in his power. It was only with the death of Frederick of Prussia in 1786 that he felt he could move more freely, and he turned his attention to the Ottomans. He personally led an army against them in 1788, but it was a pathetic campaign that culminated in the debacle at Karánsebes. Here, he and his troops ran away from an imaginary Ottoman army, firing on each other in the ensuing confusion, leaving ten thousand Austrians dead in the field. The 1789 campaign, which Joseph left to his generals, was a greater success, and they were on the verge of driving the Ottomans back to the city of Constantinople when news reached Joseph of a revolt in the Austrian Netherlands.

It was the Netherlands that most despised Joseph's widespread reforms and he introduced violent methods of coercion, which only made things worse. In 1790 French republicans, who encouraged the Netherlanders to aim for independence, inflamed the situation. As Joseph recalled his armies from the south, news came through of a rebellion in Hungary. The emperor's health began to deteriorate rapidly. Broken by years of failure, abandoned by his ministers, who refused to implement any more of his policies, he soon passed away, a sad and demoralised man.

LEOPOLD II

REPAIRING THE DAMAGE

NAME: Peter Leopold Joseph Anton Joachim Pius Gotthard von Österreich
BORN: Vienna, Austria, 1747
RULED: Emperor-elect, 1790–1792
DIED: Of a stroke, Vienna, Austria, 1792

WHERE JOSEPH WAS IMPATIENT and filled with flights of wild fancy, his brother Leopold was sensible, cautious and, most importantly, well loved and respected. He was originally destined for the priesthood, but a death in the family saw him become Grand Duke of Tuscany in 1765.

Ruling Italians for twenty-five years taught Leopold the virtues of moderation, patience and the art of managing a troubled and argumentative people. He, too, was a reformer, but he was far more restrained in the way he introduced his reforms, and though the Italians never grew to love him, they respected his steady, consistent and intelligent administration. He was the first ruler to abolish the death penalty and legislate for the hospitalisation of the mentally ill. Tuscany proved to have been a good training ground when he inherited the imperial throne from his childless brother.

Leopold found imperial authority on the verge of total collapse and quickly sought to rectify the situation. He immediately abolished his brother's most objectionable reforms, normalised the strained relations with Prussia and Britain, and obtained an advantageous peace with the Ottomans. Pacifying Hungary, he turned his attention to the Austrian Netherlands; though he offered to restore their system of government, they refused to make terms. He invaded, therefore, and by 1791 had recovered the provinces, though this continued to be a trouble spot because of the interference of the French revolutionaries.

> **Announce this message; that your sovereign is desirous to rule by the laws, yet still more anxious to rule by love.**
>
> LEOPOLD II

The chaos emanating from France consumed the rest of his reign. The collapse of royal authority in France, the radicalism of the French Parliament and, in particular, the rhetoric of the Jacobins greatly disturbed Leopold. Even so, he went to great lengths to ensure he was not entangled in the deteriorating situation. Against his better judgement, the insults heaped upon his sister Marie-Antoinette and the threats against her life forced him to act: he forged an alliance with Prussia against the revolutionaries, setting Austria and the empire against the fury of the republicans. Soon, the rights of German princes on the west of the Rhine were under attack, and war was brewing when he died suddenly, leaving his son to face the coming storm.

FRANCIS II
END OF THE LINE

NAME: Franz Joseph Karl von Österreich
BORN: Florence, Tuscany, 1768
RULED: Emperor-elect, 1792–1806
DIED: Of fever, Vienna, Austria, 1835

GROWING UP IN THE courts of his father and uncle, young Francis absorbed the Enlightenment philosophies that directed these reforming emperors. His formative years were a case study in extremes. Until 1784 he was at Leopold II's court in Florence, where the atmosphere was carefree and jovial, and the young man had free rein to do as he chose. Then, given his status as future emperor because his uncle lacked a son, he was sent to the stuffy court at Vienna, where he came under the control of the severe and authoritarian Joseph. Believing the young man to be spoilt, Joseph isolated Francis and forced him to endure a Spartan lifestyle in order to make him more resilient.

Neither his father nor his uncle believed Francis to have any real talents, and they considered he possessed only mediocre intelligence. Yet to him fell the task of dealing with the upheavals sparked by the French Revolution; believing that it was unrestrained Enlightenment thought that had brought about this crisis, he turned his back on his father's and uncle's agenda of reform and became a reactionary despot determined to preserve what remained of the old order from the forces of chaos. To do this he set up an extensive network of police spies to monitor any subversive activities. There was no toleration of dissent and censors ensured that there were no publications or performances of anti-government or pro-democracy material. This brought about a state of oppression that Francis's attempts at openness and approachability did not alleviate, regardless of his regular meetings with petitioners of all classes and nationalities to hear their grievances.

Into this volatile mix was added the aggressive designs of the French revolutionaries. Convinced that the old order (including Austria and the Roman Empire) was planning to eliminate their movement, they struck first, attacking Austria within two months of Francis's accession. These wars would continue throughout his reign as emperor, as the French were determined to spread the revolution to all countries in Europe so as to preserve the new regime in France. Though the emperor managed to hold his own for the first few years, the arrival of Napoleon Bonaparte changed the balance of power across Europe. His elevation saw the French motivation change from a desire to spread the ideals of the revolution to an outright war of conquest. Repeatedly defeated by

Meeting between Napoleon and Francis II after the battle of Austerlitz, 1805

the French, Francis was forced to make concession after concession. In 1797, he gave up imperial territory to preserve Habsburg lands, without the permission of the Imperial Diet and the German princes. Though this was an illegal act by Francis, the empire was so divided that no coherent response was possible, further weakening the imperial efforts against Napoleon. Defeats in 1800 saw the loss of more territory and the division of the empire into yet smaller units, weakening it further.

> **That we, considering ourselves thus acquitted of all our duties towards the Germanic empire, do resign the imperial crown, and the imperial government.**
>
> FRANCIS II

Peace was established, but not for long. The coronation of Napoleon as emperor in 1804 was an insult Francis could not ignore. Seeing that there was no Roman Empire left to speak of, he had himself crowned emperor of Austria that same year and entered into an alliance with the Russians to crush Napoleon. The result was their humiliating defeat at Austerlitz in December 1805. Napoleon forced Francis to agree to the break-up of the Roman Empire and reorganised the many German states into what he termed the Confederation of the Rhine, which was to be under the protection of the French emperor, not the Roman emperor. Thus was modern Germany born, making this the death sentence of the Western Roman Empire as re-established by Charlemagne just over 1000 years earlier. This act made it clear to Francis that the title Roman Emperor was now truly an empty one. In November 1806 he declared the dissolution of the Roman Empire under his authority as emperor and abdicated his title, while retaining the title of emperor of Austria. Though this was unconstitutional, by this stage no one was in a position to do anything about it.

Thus ended the reign of the last Roman emperor, 1833 years after Augustus first erected the imperial edifice upon the crumbling remains of the Roman Republic. It was somehow fitting that the event that would see the final collapse of the empire was the French Revolution, which in so many ways gave birth to the modern world. Although Francis continued to rule in Vienna and would see out the threat of Napoleon and the temporary return of the old order, his devotion to the old imperial principles died the moment he abdicated that ancient title. The days and dreams of Imperial Rome were well and truly over; the era of the democratic nation state had dawned and, with it, the rise of new powers that would change the world forever.

BIBLIOGRAPHY

THE UNIFIED EMPIRE
(27 BC–AD 480)

Ambrose. 'Select Works and Letters', trans. H. De Romestinin, in *Nicene and Post-Nicene Fathers*, ed. Philip Schaff, 2nd series, vol. 10. Buffalo: Christian Literature Publishing Co., 1890.

Ammianus Marcellinus. *Roman History*, vols II and III. Cambridge: Loeb Classical Library, 1940 and 1939.

Bédoyère, Guy de la. *The Golden Age: Roman Britain in the 4th Century*. Stroud: Tempus, 1999.

Birley, Anthony Richard. *The Roman Government of Britain*. Oxford: Oxford University Press, 2005.

Bowman, Alan K., Garnsey, Peter & Cameron, Averil. *The Cambridge Ancient History: The Crisis of Empire AD 193–337*. Cambridge: Cambridge University Press, 2005.

Bowman, Alan K., Garnsey, Peter & Rathbone, Dominic (eds). *The Cambridge Ancient History: The High Empire, AD 70–192*. Cambridge: Cambridge University Press, 2000.

Brennan, Peter, Turner, Michael & Wright, Nicholas L. *Faces of Power: Imperial Portraiture on Roman Coins*. Sydney: The Nicholson Museum, 2007.

Cameron, Averil, Garnsey, Peter & Boardman, John. *The Cambridge Ancient History: The Late Empire AD 337–425*. Cambridge: Cambridge University Press, 1998.

Chadwick, Henry. *The Early Church*, rev. edn. London: Penguin, 1993.

Davis, William Stearns. *Readings in Ancient History: Illustrative Extracts from the Sources*, vol. II, *Rome and the West*. Boston: Allyn and Bacon, 1913.

De Imperatoribus Romanis: An Online Encyclopedia of Roman Rulers <http://www.roman-emperors.org/>

Dio, Cassius. *Roman History*, vols IV–IX. Cambridge: Loeb Classical Library, 1916–1927.

Downey, Glanville. 'Libanius' Oration in Praise of Antioch (Oration XI)', *Proceedings of the American Philosophical Society*, vol. 103, no. 5, 1959, pp. 652–86.

Eusebius of Caesarea. 'The Life of the Blessed Emperor Constantine', trans. Arthur Cushman McGiffert, in *Nicene and Post-Nicene Fathers*, ed. Philip Schaff, 2nd series, vol. 1. Buffalo: Christian Literature Publishing Co., 1890.

Fagan, Garret G. *History of Ancient Rome*. Chantilly: The Teaching Company, 1999.

Gibbon, Edward. *The Decline and Fall of the Roman Empire*, 6 vols. Philadelphia: J.B. Lippincott & Co, 1880.

Grierson, Philip & Mays, Melinda. *Catalogue of Late Roman Coins in the Dumbarton Oaks Collection and in the Whittemore Collection: from Arcadius and Honorius to the accession of Anastasius*. Washington: Dumbarton Oaks, 1992.

Holland, Richard. *Augustus: Godfather of Europe*. Stroud: Sutton Publishing, 2005.

Keppie, Lawrence J. F. *Understanding Roman Inscriptions*. Baltimore: CRC Press, 1991.

Lenski, Noel Emmanuel. *Failure of Empire: Valens and the Roman State in the Fourth Century A.D.* Berkeley: University of California Press, 2002.

Magie, David (trans.). *The Historia Augusta*, 3 vols. Cambridge: Loeb Classical Library, 1932.

Martindale, John Robert, Jones, Arnold Hugh Martin & Morris, J. *The Prosopography of the Later Roman Empire*, vol. 1. Cambridge: Cambridge University Press, 1980.

Smith, William & Anthon, Charles. *A New Classical Dictionary of Greek and Roman Biography, Mythology and Geography*. New York: Harper and Brothers, 1862.

Suetonius Tranquillus. *The Lives of the Twelve Caesars*, trans. J.C. Rolfe. Cambridge: Loeb Classical Library, 1913.

Syme, Ronald. *Ammianus and the Historia Augusta*. Oxford: Clarendon Press, 1968.

Syme, Ronald. *Emperors and Biography: Studies in the 'Historia Augusta'*. Oxford: Clarendon Press, 1971.

Syme, Ronald. 'Antonius Saturninus', *Journal of Roman Studies*, vol. 68, 1978, pp. 12–21.

Tacitus, Publius Cornelius. *The History of Tacitus*, trans. A.J. Church & W.J. Brodribb. London: Macmillan, 1864.

Tacitus, Publius Cornelius. *Annals of Tacitus*, trans. A.J. Church & W.J. Brodribb. London: Macmillan, 1895.

Victor, Sextus Aurelius. *A Booklet about the Style of Life and the Manners of the Imperatores, Abbreviated from the Books of Sextus Aurelius Victor*, trans. Thomas M. Banchich, Canisius College Translated Texts, no. 1. Buffalo, New York: Canisius College, 2000.

Zonaras, Joannes, Banchich, Thomas & Lane, Eugene. *The History of Zonaras: From Alexander Severus to the Death of Theodosius the Great*. New York: Routledge, 2009.

THE EASTERN EMPIRE
(c. 480–1453)

Bury, J. B. *A History of the Later Roman Empire from Arcadius to Irene*, vols 1 and 2. London: Macmillan & Co., 1889.

Bury, J. B. *A History of the Eastern Roman Empire from the Fall of Irene to the Accession of Basil I*. London: Macmillan and Co., 1912.

Cameron, Averil, Ward-Perkins, Bryan & Whitby, Michael. *The Cambridge Ancient History: Late Antiquity: Empire and Successors, AD 425–600*. Cambridge: Cambridge University Press, 2000.

Choniates, Nicetas. *O City of Byzantium: Annals of Niketas Choniatēs*, trans. Harry J. Magoulias. Detroit: Wayne State University Press, 1984.

Comnena, Anna. *The Alexiad*, trans. Elizabeth A. Dawes. London: Routledge, Kegan, Paul, 1928.

Constantine, Emperor of the East. *De Administrando Imperio*, ed. & trans. Gyula Moravcsik, Romilly James Heald Jenkins & F. Dornik. Washington: Dumbarton Oaks, 1985.

De Imperatoribus Romanis: An Online Encyclopedia of Roman Rulers <http://www.roman-emperors.org/>

Dumbarton Oaks. *Catalogue of the Byzantine Coins in the Dumbarton Oaks Collection and in the Whittemore Collection*, 5 vols. Washington: Dumbarton Oaks, 1999.

Echols, Edward C. *Herodian of Antioch's History of the Roman Empire*. Berkeley: University of California Press, 1961.

Ehler, Sidney Z. & Morrall, John B. *Church and State Through the Centuries: A Collection of Historic Documents with Commentaries*. New York: Biblo & Tannen Publishers, 1988.

Evagrius Scholasticus. *Ecclesiastical History, Book 3*, trans. E. Walford. London: H. G. Bohn, 1846.

Finlay, George. *The History of Greece from its Conquest by the Crusaders to its Conquest by the Turks and of the Empire of Trebizond 1204–1461*. London: William Blackwood and Sons, 1851.

Finlay, George. *History of the Byzantine Empire from 716 to 1057*. London: William Blackwood and Sons, 1853.

Finlay, George. *History of the Byzantine and Greek Empires from 1057 to 1453*. London: William Blackwood & Sons, 1854.

Garland, Lynda. *Byzantine Empresses: Women and Power in Byzantium, AD 527–1204*. London: Routledge, 1999.

Goodwin, Jason. *Lords of the Horizon: A History of the Ottoman Empire*. London: Vintage, 1999.

Harris, Jonathan. *A worthless prince? Andreas Palaeologus in Rome 1464–1502* <http://digirep.rhul.ac.uk/items/8d5e5f50-eb89-df4b-2cb9-e031304df8a1/1/A_worthless_prince_Andreas_Palaeologus_in_Rome_by_Jonathan_Harris.pdf>

Herodian. *History of the Empire*, vol. I, *Books 1–4*, trans. C. R. Whittaker. London: Loeb Classical Library, 1970.

Kazhdan, Alexander P. (ed.). *The Oxford Dictionary of Byzantium*, 3 vols. Oxford: Oxford University Press, 1991.

Kinross, Lord, *The Ottoman Centuries: The Rise and Fall of the Turkish Empire*. London: Perennial, 2002.

Macrides, R. J. *George Akropolites: The History*. Oxford: Oxford University Press, 2007.

Madden, Thomas F. *Empire of Gold: A History of the Byzantine Empire*. Prince Frederick: Modern Scholar, 2006.

Mann, Horace K. *Lives of the Popes in the Early Middle Ages*, vol. 1, *The Popes under the Lombard Rule*. London: Kegan Paul, Trench, Trubner, & Co., 1902.

Martindale, John Robert, Jones, Arnold Hugh Martin & Morris, J. *The Prosopography of the Later Roman Empire*, vols 2 & 3. Cambridge: Cambridge University Press, 1992.

McClanan, Anne L. *Representations of Early Byzantine Empresses: Image and Empire*. New York: Palgrave Macmillan, 2002.

Miller, William. *Trebizond: The Last Greek Empire*. London: Macmillan, 1926.

Nicol, Donald M. *The Last Centuries of Byzantium, 1261–1453*. Cambridge: Cambridge University Press, 1993.

Nicol, Donald M. *The Immortal Emperor: The Life and Legend of Constantine Palaiologos, Last Emperor of the Romans*. Cambridge: Cambridge University Press, 2002.

Nixon, C. E. V., Mynors, R. A. B. & Rodgers, Barbara Saylor. *In Praise of Later Roman Emperors: The Panegyrici Latini: Introduction, Translation, and Historical Commentary, with the Latin Text of R.A.B. Mynors*. Berkeley: University of California Press, 1995.

Norwich, John Julius. *Byzantium: The Early Centuries*. London: Penguin, 1990.

Norwich, John Julius. *The Normans in Sicily*. London: Penguin, 1992.

Norwich, John Julius. *Byzantium: The Apogee*. London: Penguin, 1993.

Norwich, John Julius. *Byzantium: The Decline and Fall*. London: Penguin, 1996.

Payne, Robert. *The Crusades*. Ware: Wordsworth Editions, 1998.

Procopius. *History of the Wars*, 7 vols, trans. H. B. Dewing. Cambridge, Mass.: Harvard University Press, 1914.

Procopius. *Secret History*, trans. Richard Atwater. New York: Covici Friede, 1927.

Psellus, Michael. *Chronographia*, trans. E. R. A. Sewter. New Haven: Yale University Press, 1953.

Runciman, Steven. *The Emperor Romanus Lecapenus and His Reign: A Study of Tenth-Century Byzantium*. Cambridge: Cambridge University Press, 1988.

Runciman, Steven. *The Sicilian Vespers*. Melbourne: Cambridge University Press, 2000.

Sinogowitz, B. 'Uber das byzantinische Kaisertum nach dem vierten Kreuzzuge (1204–1205)', *Byzantinische Zeitschrift* 45, 1952, pp. 345–51.

Southern, R. W. *Western Society and the Church in the Middle Ages*. London: Penguin, 1990.

Stephenson, Paul, *Theophanes Continuatus*, <http://homepage.mac.com/paulstephenson/trans/theocont.html> October 1998, rev. November 2006.

Treadgold, Warren T. *A History of the Byzantine State and Society*. Stanford: Stanford University Press, 1997.

Vasiliev, A. A. *History of the Byzantine Empire 324–1453*, 2 vols. London: The University of Wisconsin Press, 1952.

Villehardouin, Geoffrey de. *Memoirs or Chronicle of The Fourth Crusade and The Conquest of Constantinople*, trans. Frank T. Marzials. London: J.M. Dent, 1908.

Zosimus. *New History*. London: Green and Chaplin, 1814.

THE RESTORED WESTERN EMPIRE
(800–1806)

Barker, J. Ellis (trans.). *The Foundations of Germany*. New York: E. P. Dutton, 1916.

Bryce, James. *The Holy Roman Empire*. New York: The MacMillan Company, 1913.

Chadwick, Owen. *The Reformation*. London: Penguin, 1990.

Cobbett's political register, vol. 10, *July to December 1806*. London: R. Bagshaw, 1806.

Coxe, William. *History of the House of Austria, from the Foundation of the Monarchy by Rhodolph of Hapsburgh to the Death of Leopold II: 1218 to 1792*, 3 vols. London: G. Bohn, 1847.

Dunham, S. A. *History of the Germanic Empire*, 3 vols. London: Longman, Rees, Orme, Brown, Green, & Longman, 1835.

Ekkehard. *History of the Vicissitudes of St. Gallen in a Medieval Garner*, ed. G. G. Coulton. London: Constable, 1910.

Grant, A. J. (ed. & trans.). *Early Lives of Charlemagne by Eginhard and the Monk of St. Gall*. London: Chatto & Windus, 1926.

Henderson, Ernest F. *Select Historical Documents of the Middle Ages*. London: George Bell, 1910.

MacCulloch, Diarmaid. *Reformation: Europe's House Divided 1490–1700*. London: Penguin, 2005.

Mann, Horace K. *Lives of the Popes in the Early Middle Ages*, vols. 2–18. London: Kegan Paul, Trench, Trubner, & Co., 1925, 1932.

Marshall, H. E. *A History of Germany*. London: Henry Frowde and Hodder & Stroughton, 1913.

Pastor, Ludwig. *The History of the Popes from the Close of the Middle Ages*, vols 1–37. London: Routledge & Kegan Paul Ltd, 1952.

Riché, Pierre. *The Carolingians: A Family Who Forged Europe*, trans. Michael Idomir Allen. Philadelphia: University of Pennsylvania Press, 1993.

Robertson, William. *The History of the Emperor Charles V*, 4 vols. London: Cadell & Davies, 1817.

Robinson, J. H. *Readings in European History*. Boston: Ginn, 1905.

Schiller, Johann Christoph Friedrich von. *History of the Thirty Years War*, trans. Alexander James W. Morrison. London: Henry G. Bohn, 1846.

Stubbs, William D.D. *Germany in the Later Middle Ages, 1200–1500*. London: Longmans, Green and Co., 1908.

Turner, Samuel Epes, *Einhard: The Life of Charlemagne*. New York: Harper & Brothers, 1880.

Wheatcroft, Andrew. *The Hapsburgs: Embodying Empire*. London: Penguin, 1996.

ACKNOWLEDGEMENTS

IN MANY WAYS, this book has been a cathartic experience for me, a way to channel a thirty-year obsession about Rome and its emperors that first fired the imagination of a ten-year-old boy, watching endless repeats of those 1950s sword and sandals movies on lazy Saturday afternoons, eyes glued to my parents' TV screen. Much has passed since then, but my passion for that period of history endured, as my long-suffering friends, acquaintances and family can attest to, having sat through interminable conversations (well, soliloquies really) about the glories of Rome and Byzantium. So as this journey reaches its end (for now), it is only fitting that I pause for a moment to thank all those who made this work possible.

A big thank you goes to my editors, Sophia Oravecz and Christine Eslick, who edited a long and at times complex manuscript with welcome rigour. Their critical eye and attention to detail saved me from making any number of embarrassing and careless mistakes, while anyone who can keep up with the minute changes of the break-up of the Tetrachy without losing the plot has my undying admiration. My deepest gratitude goes to my publisher, Diana Hill, whose unwavering support, encouragement and belief in me has allowed me to fulfil my lifelong ambition to write works of history, and so share my passion with the world. My thanks also go to everyone else at Murdoch Books, for bringing my vision to life.

Not having an army of willing (or unwilling as the case may be) researchers meant that all the research for this book was done by myself in my own time—usually at weekends or at night into the wee small hours of the morning. However, I do wish to thank the staff at the Macquarie University Library for their help in tracking down the various texts I needed to consult to bring order to the chaos. Consequently, while any mistakes remaining are my own, they are now far fewer due to all your efforts.

To my parents, Alfredo and Maria, who encouraged me to study and so set me on this road—this would not have been possible without you. Above all, to my beloved family, Teresa, Claudia, Daniel and Gianluca, for supporting me and putting up with my lengthy and, at times, infuriating periods of seclusion. It is your love that sustains. Last, but not least, to God, who grants all things to those who but ask.

IMAGE CREDITS

AKG images: pages 10–11, 25, 28, 32–33, 36, 46–47, 53, 68, 75, 81, 84, 88, 90, 102, 121, 137, 142–143, 145, 148, 154, 159, 162, 164, 171, 194, 197, 200, 219, 225, 233, 259, 262, 278, 285, 292–293, 305, 322, 330–331, 333, 341, 344, 349

Australpress: page 246

Bildarchiv Römisch-Germanisches Zentralmuseum, Mainz: page 130

Corbis: pages 2, 48, 60, 112, 127, 191, 204, 215, 220

Getty images: pages 20, 174, 209, 238, 327

Photolibrary.com: cover, pages 4, 16–17, 65, 78–79, 94–95, 99, 108–109, 111, 124, 150–151, 178–179, 183, 184, 212–213, 254–255, 273, 289, 296, 313, 319, 336, 354

Picture desk / The Art Archive: pages 268, 300

Shutterstock / Bill Perry: page 41

Captions for images on: page 2, Augustus, the first emperor of Rome; page 4, Otto II with symbols of the four parts of his empire: Germany, France, Italy and Alemannia; pages 10–11, Chariot racing in the Circus Maximus

INDEX

In this index, rulers are listed in accordance with their regnal or most familiar name. Where the same name is shared by many individuals (such as 'John'), they are listed alphabetically and then in this hierarchical order—popes; emperors; kings; other members of the nobility; usurpers—and in their numbered order (such as 'John I, John II'). Descriptions (such as 'usurper') have been included in brackets only where necessary to distinguish between individuals who have the same name but no regnal number. Non-reigning people are listed under family name.

A

Abrittus, battle of, 70, 71
Achilleus, 118
Acts of Pilate, 123
Adolf, 295
Adrian IV, Pope, 214, 263
Adrianople, battle of, 136, 302
Aelia Eudoxia, 147
Aemilianus, 73–4
Aetius, Flavius, 158, 159–60, 161, 163
Agrippa, Marcus, 21
Agrippina the Younger, 26, 27
Alamanni, 80, 82, 85, 93–4, 101, 103; fifth century, 129, 138

Alans, 138, 149, 155, 314
Alaric I, 146, 147, 149, 150, 152, 154–5, 164
Albert I, 295
Alexander, 241
Alexander III, Pope, 262
Alexander of Alexandria, Bishop, 128
Alexius I Comnenus, 272, 274, 276, 277–9, 280, 281, 284
Alexius I, 277, 279, 305
Alexius II, 282, 283, 284
Alexius III, 264, 284, 286–7, 288, 290, 301, 302
Alexius IV Angelus, 284, 287, 288, 289, 290
Alexius V Ducas Murtzuphlus, 287, 288, 289, 290, 301
Alexius Branas, 285–6
Alexius Comnenus, 280, 281
Alexius Comnenus, 302–3, 309
Alexius Contostephanus, 287
Alexius Philanthropenus, 315
Alfonso X of Castile, 295
Allectus, 115
Amandus, 114
Ambrose, Saint *see* Ambrose, Bishop
Ambrose, Bishop, 138, 139, 140, 144, 145
Anacletus (antipope), 261
Anastasius I, 180–1, 182, 185, 188

Anastasius II, 202, 203
Andreas Palaeologus, 328
Andronicus I, 282–3, 284, 285, 287
Andronicus II Palaeologus, 307, 312–14, 315, 318
Andronicus III Palaeologus, 314, 315–17, 318
Andronicus IV Palaeologus, 317, 318, 320–1
Andronicus V Palaeologus, 322, 323
Andronicus (I) Gidus, 303
Andronicus (II) Comnenus, 310
Andronicus Ducas, 241, 242, 274
Anthemius, 147, 165, 166–7, 168, 175
Anthimus of Rome, Saint, 122
Antoninus Caracalla *see* Caracalla
Antoninus Pius, 39–40, 43
Antonius, 39
Antony, Marc, 18, 33
Apsimarus (Tiberius III), 199, 200
Arabs, 192, 195, 198, 199, 200, 202, 203, 205, 236; *see also* Islam; Saracens
Arbogast, 139, 140
Arcadius, 146–7
Arch of Titus, 42
Arduin, 227
Areobindus, 181
Ariadne, 180

Arianism, 128, 129, 130–1, 133, 138, 139, 182
Arnulf, 221, 222, 223
Arsabar, 230
Artabasdus, 206–8
Arvandus, 167–8
Asen of Bulgaria, 304, 306
Aspar, 164
Athanasius, Bishop, 133
Athaulf, 155, 156
Attalus, 154–5, 156
Attila the Hun, 148, 160, 161, 163
Augsburg, League of, 347
Augsburg, Treaty of, 337, 338, 339, 340, 345
Augustus, 18, 19, 20–1, 23, 24, 355
Aurelian, 90, 92–6, 98, 100, 101, 119, 192
Aurelius Theodotus, 87
Aureolus, 86, 88, 89, 90, 96
Austerlitz, battle of, 355
Avars, 186, 187, 190, 193, 215
Avidius Cassius, 42, 43, 44
Avitus, 163

B

Bagaudae, 114, 115
Balbinus, 64–5, 66
Baldwin I, 302
Baldwin II, 308
Ballista, 85, 86
barbarians: third century AD, 44

barbarians *see* Franks; Goths; Huns; Ostrogoths; Vandals; Visigoths
Bardanes (emperor) *see* Philippicus
Bardanes (usurper), 230, 231, 235
Bardas, 237, 239
Bardas Phocas, 247, 248, 250, 251
Bardas Sclerus, 248, 251
Basel, Council of, 300, 332
Basil I, 238, 239, 240, 241
Basil II, 247, 248, 250–1, 252
Basil II, 265, 268, 270, 271
Basil (usurper), 244
Basil Vatatzes, 286
Basiliscus, 165, 170, 173, 175, 176
Bayezit, 317, 321, 323, 324
Belisarius, 93, 182, 184–5, 186, 315
Berengar, 221, 222, 223, 224
Berenice, 31, 33
Bernard (son of Charlemagne), 217
Blenheim, battle of, 347
Blues political faction (Chalcedonians), 180–1, 182, 187, 188, 189, 199
Bohemund, 279
Boniface, Count, 160
Boniface of Montferrat, 288
Boniface III, Pope, 193
Bonosus, 103–4
bride show, imperial, 237
Bulgar incursions, 197, 198, 199, 200, 201, 202, 203, 205, 207, 209, 217, 230–1, 235, 237, 239, 240, 241, 243, 244, 247, 246, 247, 248, 251

Burgundian incursions, 103, 155, 168, 169
Byzantium, 127

C

Caesar, Julius, 18, 19, 21, 24, 35, 37, 44, 96
Caesar (title), 110
Caligula, Gaius, 23, 24, 26
Calixtus II, Pope, 260
Calocaerus, 129
Caracalla, Antoninus, 52, 54–5, 59, 64
Carausius, 115
Carinus, 82, 105, 106, 110
Carloman, 219, 222
Carnuntum imperial conference, 120, 122, 123, 124
Carus, 103, 104, 106, 110, 119
Catalan Grand Company, 312–14
Catherine of Alexandria, Saint, 111, 122
Catholic–Protestant conflict, 335–7, 338, 339, 340–1, 342, 343, 345
cavalry, development of heavy 83, 89, 90, 93, 112
Celestine III, Pope, 264
censor, 69
Censorinus, 91
Cerularius, Michael, 216
Chalcedon, Council of, 161, 175, 181, 201
Chalcedonians (Blues), 172–3, 175, 180–1, 182, 185, 192
Charlemagne, 210, 214–17, 218, 219, 221, 223, 227, 230, 232, 257, 260, 332, 339, 355

Charles I *see* Charlemagne
Charles II, 218, 219
Charles III, 220–1, 222, 223
Charles V, 335–7, 338
Charles VI, 348–50
Charles VII, 350
Charles (son of Charlemagne), 217
Christian IV of Denmark, 343
Christians and Christianity, 67, 72, 96; conversion of empire, 112, 144, 145, 146, 164, 203; doctrinal disputes, 126, 133, 139, 144, 161, 195, 201, 203–4, 206, 216; imperial intervention in doctrinal disputes, 127, 129, 161, 172–3, 180, 181, 185, 188, 192, 197–8, 203–4; martyrs, 111, 122; persecution, 29, 69, 76, 112, 119, 120, 123; persecution of heretics, 164–5; separation church and state, 127; toleration, 125, 126–7, 134; *see also* Arianism; Catholic–Protestant conflict; Chalcedonians; iconoclasm; Monophysites; Monothelites; Nicene creed; Nicene orthodoxy; Reformation
Christopher, 244
citizens, Roman, 19
Claudius I, 24, 26, 27, 42
Claudius II Gothicus, 89, 90, 91, 92–3, 97
Charles of Anjou, 309, 310, 312
Charles of France, 298
Charles IV, 298–9

Charles VI of France, 321
Charles VIII of France, 328
Clement II, Pope, 257
Clement III, Pope, 258
Clement VI, Pope, 298
Clement VII, Pope, 335
Clodius Albinus, 51–2, 53
Clovis, 181
coinage, 72
Colosseum, 31, 37, 42
Column of Trajan, 42
Commodus, 42–3, 48–9, 50
Comnenus, Anna, 277, 279, 280
Comnenus, John, 279
Comnenus Dukas, Michael, 302
Conrad II, 256–7
Conrad III, 264, 281
Conrad IV, 295
Conrad of Hohenstaufen, 261
Conrad of Montferrat, 285–6
Constans I, 129, 130–1
Constans II Pogonatus, 153, 193, 194–5, 196, 197, 198
Constantine I, the Great, 114, 119, 120, 121, 122, 124, 125, 126–9, 130, 131, 133, 187, 328
Constantine II, 129
Constantine III, 193
Constantine IV, 196–8, 199
Constantine V, 205–6, 207, 208, 234
Constantine VI, 208–9, 235
Constantine VII Porphyrogenitus, 241–2, 243–4, 245
Constantine VIII, 247, 252, 265
Constantine IX Monomachus, 267–8, 269, 270, 273

Constantine X Ducas, 271, 272, 275, 276
Constantine XI Lascaris, 301, 302
Constantine XII Palaeologus, 326, 328, 334
Constantine (III) (usurper), 152–3, 155
Constantine Angelus Ducas, 286
Constantine Ducas, 242, 277, 301
Constantine Lecapenus, 244–5
Constantine (son of Basil I), 239, 240
Constantine (son of Theophilus), 237
Constantinople: foundation, 127–8; First Council, 201; Second Council, 201; Third Council, 201
Constantius I Chlorus, 113, 114, 115, 119, 120, 122, 129, 131
Constantius II, 129, 130, 131, 132–3, 134
Constantius III, 150, 152–3, 155, 156, 158
Constantius Ducas, 274
corpus iuris civilis, 185
Cosmas, 205
Councils, Imperial, 339
Crispus, 127
crusades, 279, 288, 295, 299, 305, 325; First, 279; Second, 281; Third, 263, 284; Fourth, 284, 287, 288
Curcuas, John, 243

D

Daniel the Stylite, 168, 175
Decebalus, 37
Decius, 67, 69–70, 71
Demetrius, 325
Demetrius of Montferrat, 305
despot (title), 316
Diadumenianus, 58
Didius Julianus, 50–1
Diocles *see* Diocletian
Diocletian (Valerius Diocles), 96, 105, 106, 110–13, 114, 115, 120, 122, 126, 129, 187, 192, 207
Domitia, 34
Domitian, 33–4, 35, 36, 37
Domitian Pius, 96
Domitius Alexander, 123
Domitius Domitianus, 118
Drusus, 21, 22, 24

E

Ecloga, 203
Ecumenical Councils: Sixth, 197–8, 201; Seventh, 209
Edict of Milan, 125
Edict of Prices (AD 301), 112–13
Edict of Restitution, 343, 344
Elagabalus, 58–60, 73, 96
Eleutherius, 192–3
El-Gabal *see* Sol Invictus
Ephesus, Council of, 201
equestrians, 19
Ernest of Swabia, 256
Eudocia (wife of Basil I), 240
Eudocia (wife of Constantine X Ducas), 271, 272, 276
Eugenius, 118
Eugenius IV, Pope, 300, 324, 332
Euphemius, 236
Eusebius of Caesarea, 125, 126

F

Faustinus, 100
Ferdinand I, 338
Ferdinand II, 342, 343–4
Ferdinand III, 245–6
Ferdinand II of Aragon, 328
filioque clause, 218, 239, 268
Firmus, 135
Flavius Eugenius, 140
Florian, 101, 103
Formosus, Pope, 221
Francis I, 350–1
Francis II, 353–5
Franks, incursions by, 80, 88, 101, 103, 114, 115, 138, 139, 149, 163, 165, 181, 195, 203, 206, 210
Franks, kingdom of, 214–17, 221
Frederick I Barbarossa, 261–3, 264, 281, 284, 286
Frederick II, 294–7
Frederick III, 332–4
Frederick of Prussia, 351

G

Gabras, Theodore, 279
Gaeseric, 161, 164, 168, 173
Galba, 27, 29, 30, 31
Galla Placidia, 158, 159, 160
Galerius, 112, 113, 114, 119–20, 121, 122, 123, 124, 125
Gallienus, 54, 74–5, 80–3; usurpers, 85, 86, 87, 88, 89, 90, 92, 97
Gallus *see* Trebonianus Gallus
Gallus (Caesar), 133
Gellius Maximus, 59
George, Saint 122
George Comnenus, 310
George Maniakes, 266, 268
Germanicus, 22, 23, 24, 27

Germanus, 189
Gerontius, 153, 156
Geta, 54, 55
Ghassanids, 186
Ghibellines, 261, 264, 297
Glycerius, 169, 170
Golden Bull of 1356, 299
Gordian I, 62, 63, 64, 66, 74
Gordian II, 63, 64
Gordian III, 65–6, 67
Goths, incursions by, 42; third century, 69, 70, 71, 72, 73, 74, 75, 80, 83, 89, 90, 91, 95, 97, 103; fourth century, 129, 136, 138, 144; fifth century, 147, 153, 155, 156, 165, 166; sixth century, 182, 184, 185; *see also* Ostrogoths; Visigoths
Gratian (Flavius Gratianus), 138, 139, 144
Gratian (The Briton), 152
Great Fire of Rome, 28
Great Schism, 216
Greens political faction (Monophysites), 180–1, 182, 187, 188, 189
Gregory I, Pope, 37, 188
Gregory VII, Pope, 258, 260
Gregory IX, Pope, 295
Gregory (usurper), 195–6
Gundoblad, 169
Guelfs, 261, 264, 295, 297
Guimar IV of Salerno, 257
Gustavus Adolphus of Sweden, 343, 344
Guy, 221, 222, 223

H

Habsburgs, 295, 332–42, 345, 346, 348, 350, 355
Hadrian, 38–9, 40, 52, 82
Henry II, 226, 227

Henry III, 257–8, 259, 264
Henry IV, 257, 258, 277
Henry V, 260
Henry VI, 263–4, 287, 294, 295
Henry VII, 297, 298
Henry IV of France, 340–1
Henry VIII of England, 335
Henry of Flanders, 286, 302
Henry the Lion of Saxony, 261, 294
Heraclian, 156
Heraclius (emperor), 190–2, 193, 196, 247
Heraclius (co-emperor), 198
Heraclonas, 193, 194
Herennius Etruscus, 70
Historia Augusta, 82–3, 87, 90
Hohenstaufen, Philip, 294
Hoenstaufens, 261–3, 264, 294–5, 297
Honorius III, Pope, 305
Honorius, 146, 147, 149–50, 152, 153, 155, 156, 158, 159
Hostilian, 71, 73
Humbert, Cardinal, 216
Humbertopolis, Constantine (rebel), 279
Huns, incursions by, 147, 148, 158, 160, 161, 165, 215
Huss, John, 299–300
Hussite War, 300
Hypatius, 185–6

I

iconoclasm, 203–4, 206, 207, 208, 209, 216, 234, 235, 236
Illus, 172, 175, 176
Ingenuus, 80, 83, 84, 89
Innocent II, Pope, 261
Innocent III, Pope, 294, 295
Innocent IV, Pope, 296, 297
Iotapianus, 67–8
Irene, 208, 209–10, 217, 230
Isaac I Comnenus, 270–1, 283
Isaac II Angelus, 283, 284, 285, 286, 287, 289, 290, 302, 305
Isaac Comnenus (usurper), 283–4, 286
Isabella of Castile, 328
Isaurians, 164, 172, 175, 176, 180
Islam, expansion of, 192, 195, 196, 203, 243; see also Arabs; Saracens

J

Januarius, Saint, 122
Jews, persecution of, 160, 189–90
Joannes, 158
John VIII, Pope, 219
John X, Pope, 223
John XII, Pope, 224
John XIII, Pope, 224
John XV, Pope, 226
John XXII, Pope, 298
John XXIII, Pope, 299
John I Tzimisces, 226, 246, 247–8, 250, 251, 265
John II Comnenus, 277, 279, 280, 288
John III Vatatzes, 303–4, 306, 316
John IV Lascaris, 307, 308, 311
John V, 311, 317–18, 320, 321, 323
John VI Cantacuzenus, 311, 315, 316, 317
John VII Palaeologus, 321–2, 323
John VIII, 323, 324–5
John Comnenus (co-emperor, son of Andronicus I), 283
John (I) Axouchos, 303, 310, 318, 319, 320, 322
John (II) Megas Comnenus, 310–12
John Comnenus Axuch (the Obese), 288, 290
John Comnenus Ducas (usurper), 306
John Ducas (usurper), 272, 275, 276, 277
John of Bohemia, 298
John Chrysostom, Bishop, 147
John the *orphanotrophus*, 266, 269
Joseph I, 347, 348
Joseph II, 351–2, 353
Jovian, 134
Jovinus, 155, 156
Judaean War, 31, 33, 42
Julia (daughter of Augustus), 21
Julia Domna, 55
Julia Maesa, 59, 60
Julia Mamaea, 59, 60–1
Julian the Apostate, 133–4, 138
Julianus, 114–15
Julius II, Pope, 334–5
Julius Nepos, 146, 169–70, 214, 264
Justin I, 181–2, 185
Justin II, 186–7
Justinian I, 181, 182–5, 186
Justinian II, 198–9, 200, 201, 203, 207

K

Karykas, 279
Khazars, 199, 200, 201
Khosrow II, 188, 189, 190, 191, 192
Krum, 230–1, 235

L

Laelianus, 91
Lambert, 221, 222, 223
Lecapenus, Basil, 248, 250
Leo I, Pope, 160, 161
Leo III, Pope, 215
Leo VIII, Pope, 224
Leo IX, Pope, 257, 268
Leo X, Pope, 336
Leo I (Flavius Valerius), 163, 164–5, 166, 168, 169, 173, 175
Leo II, 172
Leo III, 203–4, 205, 207
Leo IV, 208, 209
Leo V, 231, 232–4, 235
Leo VI, 239, 240–1, 242
Leo Diogenes (co-emperor), 272
Leo Tornicius (usurper), 269
Leontius (emperor), 199–200
Leontius (usurper), 176
Leopold I, 346–7, 348
Leopold II, 351, 352–3
Lepidus, Marcus Aemilius, 18
Lex Romana Visigothorum, 149
Libius Severus, 166
Licinianus, 71
Licinius, 123, 124, 125, 126
Livia, 21
Lombards, incursions by, 186, 187, 192–3, 195, 206, 214
Longinus, 180
Lothair I, 217–18, 219, 223
Lothair III, 261, 280
Louis I, 217–18, 220, 223, 235, 236

Louis II, 218–19, 240
Louis III, 222
Louis IV, 298
Louis VII of France, 281
Louis XI of France, 310
Louis XIV of France, 346, 347, 348
Lucilla, 48
Lucius Ceionius Commodus, 39, 43
Lucius Verus, 39, 40, 43–4
Luther, Martin, 335–7
Lyon, Council of, 309

M

Macedo, 62
Macer, Lucius Clodius, 27
Macrianus, 85–6, 87, 89, 96
Macrianus Junior, 85
Macrinus, 58, 59
Magnentius, 131, 132
Magnus Maximus, 138, 139–40, 144, 150
Marcus Aurelius, 39, 40–3, 44, 48, 52, 74
Magyars, incursions by, 222, 224
Mamun, Caliph, 235
Manuel I Comnenus, 263, 280–2, 283, 284, 316
Manuel II Palaeologus, 317, 320, 321, 322, 323–4, 326
Manzikert, battle of, 272, 273, 275, 276, 279, 311
Marcellinus, 167, 169
Marcellus, 138
Marcian, 160–1, 166
Marcus (co-emperor), 175
Marcus (usurper), 150, 152
Maria of Antioch, 282, 283
Maria Theresa, 350–1
Marie-Antoinette, 353
Marius, 91
Marjorian, 163–4, 165, 168
Martin I, Pope, 195, 196, 309
Martina, 193–4
Martinianus, 126
Matthew Cantacuzenus, 320
Matthias, 342–3
Maurice, 187–8, 189
Mausoleum of Augustus, 42
Mausoleum of Hadrian, 42
Maximinus, 61–2, 63, 64, 65
Maxentius, 114, 120, 121–3, 124, 125, 126
Maximianus, 110, 112, 113–14, 115, 119, 120, 121, 123
Maximilian I, 334–5
Maximilian II, 338–40, 342
Maximinus Daia, 120, 123–4
Maximus, 153
Mehmet, 324
Mehmet II, 326, 327, 328
Messalina, Valeria, 24
Mezezius, 196
Michael I, 231, 232, 235
Michael II (Michael the Amorian), 231, 234–5, 236
Michael III, 237, 239, 240
Michael IV, 265, 266, 267, 268, 269
Michael V Calaphates, 266–7, 270
Michael VI, 270
Michael VII, 273–4, 275, 276
Michael VIII Palaeologus, 304, 307–9, 310, 311, 312, 315
Michael IX Palaeologus, 314–15
Milvian Bridge, battle of, 123, 126
monarchy, creation of, 112
Mongols, incursions by, 307, 310, 311, 321
Monophysites (Greens), 172–3, 175, 180–1, 185, 187, 192, 197–8, 203–4, 216
Monothelites, 192, 195, 196, 197–8, 201, 202, 216
Mons Seleucus, battle of 131
Moors, 215
Muawiyah I, Caliph, 197
Murad I, 317, 320, 323
Murad II, 324, 326
Mursa Major, battle of 131
Musa, 324
Muslims, 279, 281, 288, 295, 296; see also Arabs; Islam; Saracens
Mussius Armilianus, 87
Mustafa, 324

N

names, Roman, 19; see also titles, imperial
Napoleon, 354, 355
Narses, 189
Nepotian, 131–2
Nero, 26–9, 30, 31, 35, 42
Nerva, 35, 36
Nicaea: First Council, 126, 128, 201; Second Council, 201
Nicene Creed, 128, 131, 216, 217, 239
Nicene orthodoxy, 138, 144, 164–5
Nicephorus I, 210, 230–1, 232, 235
Nicephorus II, 245, 247, 248
Nicephorus III, 277
Nicephorus III Botaniates, 271, 274, 275–6, 277
Nicephorus Diogenes (co-emperor), 272
Nicephorus (usurper), 206–8, 209
Nicephorus Basilakes (usurper), 276–7
Nicephorus Bryennius (usurper), 276–7
Nicephorus Phocas (usurper), 247, 251–2
Nicephorus Melissinus (usurper), 276–7
Nicetas, 207
Nicholas Cannavus, 289
Nicholas V, Pope, 332
Nicholas V (antipope), 298
Nicholas I, Pope, 218–19
Nicholas (co-emperor), 302
Niger see Pescennius Niger
Normans, incursions by, 257, 261, 268, 274, 275, 277, 279, 280, 283, 285, 295
Numerian, 105, 106, 110
Nymphidius, 29

O

Octavian see Augustus
Odaenathus, Septimius, 86, 95, 97
Odoacer, 170, 171, 173, 181
Olybrius, 167, 168
Olympius, 195, 196
Opsikion rebels, 201, 202
Orestes, 170
Orghuz Turks, 276
Ostrogoths, incursions by, 149, 165, 169, 182
Otho, 29, 30, 31
Otto I, the Great, 223–6, 245, 247, 257, 258
Otto II, 226, 247
Otto III, 226–7
Otto IV, 294, 295
Ottoman Turks, incursions by, 309, 311, 312, 316, 317, 318, 321, 324, 326, 328, 335, 338, 342, 347, 352
ovation, celebration of, 93

P

Pacatianus, 68–9
paganism, bans, 180
Palaeologus, Manuel, 314, 315
Papal States, creation of, 206
Paschal II, Pope, 260
patricians, 19
Paul IV, Pope, 338
Paul the Patrician, 204–5
Peace of Prague, 343, 345
Pechenegs, 268, 271, 277
Pepin, 206
Pepin (son of Charlemagne), 217
Pepin III, 214
Pertinax, 50, 51
Pescennius Niger, 51, 52
Peter the Hermit, 279
Petronius, 136, 137
Petronius Maximus, 160, 161, 163
Philaretus, 275
Philip I, 66–7, 68
Philip II, 67
Philip II of France, 263
Philip IV of France, 294
Philip II of Spain, 338
Philip V of Spain, 348
Philip of Germany, 288
Philippicus (Bardanes), 199, 200, 201–2
Phocas, 188, 189–90, 192
Phocas, Leo (rebel), 247
Photios, Patriarch, 237, 239
Picts, 119, 135, 139
Piso, 86, 87
plebeians, 19
Poppaea Sabina, 27, 29, 30
Postumus, 80, 88–9, 90, 91, 92
porphyrogenitus, 274
Pragmatic Sanction, 350
principate, creation of, 18, 20, 21, 23
Priscus, 68, 70, 71
Probus, 101, 103, 104, 105, 119
Procopius, 136–7
Procopius Marcianus, 175–6
Proculus, 104
Pulcheria, 147, 160
Pupienus, 64–5, 66

Q

Quadi, 105, 106, 135
Quartinus, 62
Quietus, 85, 86
Quintillus, 92, 93

R

Rapsomates, 279
Raspe, Henry, 295
Ratisbon, Diet of, 337
Reformation, 335–7, 338, 339, 347
Regalianus, 85
Richard I of England, 263, 284
Richard of Cornwall, 295
Ricimer, 163, 164, 166, 167, 168, 169
Robert Guiscard, Duke, 276, 277, 279
Robert of Naples, 297
Roger de Flor, 313, 314
Roger of Sicily, 261
Romanos Skleros, 268, 269
Romanus I, 241, 242–4, 245
Romanus II, 245, 250
Romanus III Argyros, 265, 266, 267, 268, 269
Romanus IV Diogenes, 271–2, 272, 274, 275, 279
Romanus (usurper), 168
Romulus, 170, 171, 173
Rudolf I, 295
Rudolf of Germany, 260
Rudolph II, 340–2
Rudolph of Burgundy, 256
Rufinus, 146, 147
Rufus, Lucius Verginius, 27, 29
Russians, incursions by, 247

S

Sabinianus, 66
Sabinus Julianus, 106
Saladin, 263, 284, 286
Sallustius, 59
Salomon, 279
Saloninus, 88, 89
Saracens, 197, 201, 203, 209, 210, 219, 222, 231, 235, 236, 237, 239, 240, 242, 243, 245, 246, 250, 263, 265, 268; *see also* Islam; Arabs
Sarmatians, 83, 85, 105, 135, 138
Saturninus (usurper, first century), 34–5, 36
Saturninus (usurper, third century), 104
Saxons, 135, 215
Scribonianus, 26
Scots, 135, 139
Sebastianus, 155, 156
Sejanus, 22, 23
Seleucus, 59
Seljuk Turks, 268, 272, 275, 276, 311
Senate, 19
Septimius, 97
Septimius Severus, 51–2, 52–4, 61
Sergius, Pope, 198
Sergius, 204, 205
Seven Years' War, 351
Severus, 120–1, 122, 125
Severus Alexander, 59, 60–1, 62, 62, 73
Shapur I, 75, 76
Shapur II, 133, 134
Sigismund, 299–300
Silbannacus, 72
Silvanus, 132
slaves, 19
Slavs, incursions by, 188, 190, 198
Sol Invictus (El-Gabal), 59, 60, 96, 127
Sophia, 186, 187
Sponsianus, 72
Stephen VI, Pope, 221
Stephen (co-emperor), 244–5
Stilicho, Flavius, 146, 149, 150, 152, 156, 164
Strauracius, 231
Sueves, 149
Suleiman, 275, 324
Symbatios Constantine, 234

T

Tacitus, 100–1
Tancred, 263–4
Taronites, Michael, 279
Tatikios, Constantine, 284
Taurinus, 59
Tervel, 207
tetrarchy, 110, 112–13, 119, 120, 126, 129, 135, 146, 207
Tetricus, 95, 98, 100
Tetricus II, 100
Theodora (wife of Justinian), 182, 183, 184, 186
Theodora (mother of Michael III), 237
Theodora (empress), 265, 267, 269–70
Theodore Comnenus Ducas, 304–6, 316

Theodore I, 301–2, 303
Theodore II, 306–7, 308
Theodore Lascaris, 287
Theodore Mankaphas, 286
Theodoric, 163, 173, 181, 182
Theodosian Code, 148–9
Theodosius I the Great, 135, 139, 140, 144–6, 158
Theodosius II, 147–9, 158, 166
Theodosius III, 202–3
Theodosius (co-emperor), 188–9
Theophano, 245, 247
Theophilus, 236, 237
Theophylactus, 234
Thirty Years' War, 343, 345, 348
Thomas Palaeologus, 325, 328
Thomas (usurper), 235
Tiberius I, 21, 22–3, 24, 26, 31
Tiberius II, 186, 187, 188
Tiberius III (Apsimarus), 198, 200
Tiberius (co-emperor, son of Constans II), 198
Tiberius (co-emperor, son of Heraclius), 193, 194
Tiberius (co-emperor, son of Justinian), 200
Tiberius (usurper), 204–5
Tironites, Gregory, 279
titles, imperial, 49, 192, 207, 249, 316
Titus, 31, 33, 34
Trajan, 35–7, 38, 42, 52, 74, 105
Trebonianus Gallus, 70, 71–3, 74
Trent, Council of, 337, 338
triumph, celebration of, 33, 67, 93, 95–6, 98, 100, 103, 155
Truce of God, 257, 264
Turks, incursions by, 129, 268, 271, 272, 273, 276, 277, 279, 280, 281, 284, 285, 286, 287, 303, 307, 308, 310, 311, 312, 313, 314–15, 320, 325, 326, 328, 332, 335, 337, 339–40, 341, 352
Tzachas, 279

U

Ummayads, 205
Uranius, 59
Uranius Antoninus, 73
Urban, Pope, 279
Urbanus, 96
usurpers: first century AD, 26, 29, 34; second century AD, 44, 51–2; Severan, 59; third century AD, 44, 62, 66, 67–9, 70–1, 73, 80, 81, 83–92, 96–100, 103–4, 106; third century, 113, 114–15, 118; in Britain, 113, 114, 115; fourth century, 121–3, 129, 130–2, 135, 138, 139–40; fifth century, 150, 152–6, 158, 160, 166–9, 170, 175–6; sixth century, 185–6, 192–3, 195–6; eighth century 204–5, 206–8; ninth century, 231, 235; tenth century, 244, 248, 250, 251–2; twelfth century, 263–4, 268, 269, 273–4, 275, 283, 285–6, 287, 288, 289, 290; thirteenth century, 302–6, 309–12; fourteenth century, 315
Uzes, 271

V

Vaballathus, 95, 97–8
Valens, 136, 137, 138, 144, 146
Valens Thessalonicus, 86–7
Valentinian I, 134–5, 144, 146, 158
Valentinian II, 139, 140, 144
Valentinian III, 149, 158–60, 161, 163, 168
Valerian, 69, 71, 73, 74–6, 80, 81, 83, 85, 86, 87, 101, 110
Valerianus, Cornelius Licinius, 83
Valerius Diocles *see* Diocletian
Valerius Valens, 125
Vandals, incursions by, 95, 103, 148, 149, 160, 161, 162, 163, 164, 165, 166, 168, 169, 172, 173
Verina, 172, 175, 176
Verus, 59
Vespasian, 30–1, 34
Vetranio, 131
Victor, 140
Victorinus, 91, 92, 96, 98
Vikings, incursions by, 217, 219, 221, 222, 250
Villa Jovis, Capri, 22, 23, 42
Vindex, Gaius, 27, 29
Visigoths, incursions by, 146, 147, 149, 150, 152, 154, 156, 163, 165, 167, 168, 169
Vitalian, 181, 185
Vitellius, 30, 31
Volusianus, 73

W

War of the Spanish Succession, 347, 348, 350
Wenceslas, 299
Westphalia, Peace of, 345, 348
William II of Holland, 295
William of Sicily, 263
Worms, council at, 260
Worms, Diet of, 334, 336, 339

X

Xiphias, Nicephorus, 252

Z

Zeno, 164, 165, 170, 172–3, 175, 176, 180, 181
Zenobia, 95, 97–8, 99, 100
Zoe, 241, 242
Zoe (daughter of Constantine VIII, empress), 265, 266, 267, 269, 270

Published in 2010 by Pier 9, an imprint of Murdoch Books Pty Limited

Murdoch Books Australia
Pier 8/9
23 Hickson Road
Millers Point NSW 2000
Phone: +61 (0) 2 8220 2000
Fax: +61 (0) 2 8220 2558
www.murdochbooks.com.au

Murdoch Books UK Limited
Erico House, 6th Floor
93–99 Upper Richmond Road
Putney, London SW15 2TG
Phone: +44 (0) 20 8785 5995
Fax: +44 (0) 20 8785 5985
www.murdochbooks.co.uk

Publisher: Diana Hill
Illustrator: Ian Faulkner
Project Editor: Sophia Oravecz
Designer: Susanne Geppert

Text copyright © Alexander Canduci 2010
The moral right of the author has been asserted.
Design copyright © Murdoch Books Pty Limited 2010

All rights reserved. No part of this publication may be reproduced, stored in a retrieval system or transmitted in any form or by any means, electronic, mechanical, photocopying, recording or otherwise, without the prior written permission of the publisher.

Maps are for illustrative purposes only.

National Library of Australia Cataloguing-in-Publication Data

Author:	Canduci, Alexander.
Title:	Triumph and Tragedy : the rise and fall of Rome's immortal emperors/ Alexander Canduci.
ISBN:	978-1-74196-598-8 (pbk.)
Notes:	Includes bibliographical references and index.
Subjects:	Emperors–Rome.
	Holy Roman Empire–History.
	Holy Roman Empire–Kings and rulers.
	Rome–Kings and rulers.
	Rome–History.

Dewey Number: 937.06

A catalogue record for this book is available from the British Library.

Printed on FSC certified paper in China by 1010 Printing International Limited.